UNQUIET UNDERSTANDING

SUNY series in Contemporary Continental Philosophy

Dennis J. Schmidt, editor

Unquiet Understanding

Gadamer's Philosophical Hermeneutics

Nicholas Davey

State University of New York Press

Published by
State University of New York Press, Albany

© 2006 State University of New York

For information, address State University of New York Press,
194 Washington Avenue, Suite 305, Albany, NY 12210-2384

Production by Kelli Williams
Marketing by Michael Campochiaro

Library of Congress Cataloging-in-Publication Data
Davey, Nicholas, 1950–
    Unquiet understanding : Gadamer's philosophical hermeneutics / Nicholas Davey.
        p. cm. — (SUNY series in contemporary continental philosophy)
    Includes bibliographical references and index.
    ISBN-13: 978-0-7914-6841-8 (hardcover : alk. paper)
    ISBN-10: 0-7914-6841-0 (hardcover)
    ISBN-13: 978-0-7914-6842-5 (pbk.)
    ISBN-10: 0-7914-6842-9 (pbk.)
    1. Gadamar, Hans Georg, 1900– 2. Hermeneutics. I. Title. II. Series.
B3248.G34D38   2006
121'.686092—dc22

                                                                2005033879

10 9 8 7 6 5 4 3 2 1

Experience as a whole is not something that anyone can be spared.

—Hans-Georg Gadamer

For Angelica,

d. 9 September 1990

Death is "voice robbing" (Hesiod)

Contents

CONTENTS

Preface

Bless thee, Bottom! Bless thee! Thou art translated!
—Shakespeare, A Midsummer Night's Dream

If there can be no last word in philosophical hermeneutics, there can be no first. The question is how and where to join a continuing "conversation." Gadamer's hermeneutics has evolved in large part as a response to provocative questions concerning the finitude and subjectivity of understanding in the work of Dilthey and Heidegger. The character of that response is far from settled. The Wirkungsgeschichte of Gadamer's Werke continues to unfold. This essay seeks to answer some of the key questions prompted by Gadamer's hermeneutics and to contribute to its discussion of the relationship between language and understanding. This is not an essay on Gadamer per se. Though he may have coined the term philosophical hermeneutics, what is at play within the movement of thought it represents far exceeds his authorship. This essay endeavors to critically engage with and draw out the practical and ethical implications of philosophical hermeneutics. It concentrates on the question of what happens to us when we "understand." The concern with the "event" of understanding is reflected in two of the essay's principal themes, translation and transcendence. How does the act of translating the strange and the foreign into a more familiar idiom effect a moment of transcendence in which we come to understand ourselves differently? How does the work of hermeneutics work?

Philosophical hermeneutics is not always its own best advocate. Gadamer's written style may reflect the twists and turns of conversation but it obscures a philosophical articulation of what underpins its dynamics. His defense of intuitive insight (speculative understanding) could not be more laudable within the humanities but his philosophical articulation of its nature is in some respects not as strong as it might be. Gadamer's re-accommodation of "tradition" within philosophical debate is of great consequence but its poignancy has been lost in the debates about Gadamer's alleged conservatism. Central to a dialogical notion of tradition is the idea of a continuity of intellectual conflict. This implies that tradition is not opposed to modernity but is one of its principal drivers. The evidence for a more radicalized conception of tradition within philosophical hermeneutics is plain, yet rarely is it discussed. Likewise, the critical thrust of Gadamer's approach to the finitude of linguistic meaning has been obscured by deconstructive critiques of hermeneutics. Far from being opposed to deconstruction, philosophical hermeneutics requires it. Without difference and without language's endless deferral of meaning, the achievement of new understanding would not be possible. Philosophical hermeneutics contends that the vitality of understanding actually depends on difference. This essay will argue that philosophical hermeneutics has a provocative character more radical than is often supposed.

To elicit the subversive character of philosophical hermeneutics, the essay adopts an "Anglo-Saxon" style. Eleven theses about the nature of philosophical hermeneutics are proposed. The strategem may seem insensitive to Gadamer's critique of reducing philosophy to "statements." Yet his work needlessly assumes a ready opposition between the meaning of an assertion residing in what is actually stated as opposed to lying in what it invokes or brings to mind. Gadamer is, of course, overwhelmingly concerned with the latter and has, accordingly, expressed an understandable hostility toward the analytic tradition of philosophy.[1] Nevertheless, such "prejudice" blinds Gadamer to what for the purposes of this essay is the key purpose of precise philosophical statement. The quest for linguistic exactitude is not indicative of having succumbed to the illusion that the complexities of experience or the intricacies of a philosophical commitment can be definitively "stated." To the contrary, the quest for precision can express a sensitivity to the "poetic charge" of the statement. The precise philosophical statement can share the same strategic purpose as Nietzsche's aphoristic "arrows" (*Pfeile*): to transport the reader as speedily, as efficiently, and with as much clarity of mind as possible to what is at issue, namely, the unspoken subject-matter. Precision of statement can correctly align the reader with such subject matter, not appropriate it.

Chapter 1 forwards eleven theses concerning the substantive nature and character of philosophical hermeneutics: philosophical hermeneutics (1) requires difference, (2) promotes a philosophy of experience, (3) entails a commitment to hermeneutic realism, (4) seeks otherness within the historical, (5) reinterprets transcendence, (6) entails an ethical disposition, (7) redeems the negativity of its constituting differential, (8) affirms an ontology of the in-between, (9) is a philosophical practice rather than a philosophical method, (10) constitutes a negative hermeneutics, and (11) recognizes the *mysterium* of linguistic being. Each thesis charts the different philosophical commitments of philosophical hermeneutics to better triangulate its nature. Chapters 2, 3, and 4 explore the different aspects of these theses in order to draw closer to what the experience of understanding entails.

The pivotal thesis embedded in all the others is thesis five: philosophical hermeneutics reinterprets transcendence. Philosophical hermeneutics is an antimetaphysical philosophy. Gadamer contends that "there's no such thing anymore as a metaphysics that believes it has a truth that withstands everything."[2] For Gadamer, postmetaphysical philosophy becomes "a knowing that is . . . restricted and circumscribed by limits. This . . . is why we have [philosophical] hermeneutics."[3] Gadamer follows Heidegger in thinking that the renunciation of metaphysical philosophy initiates a "return to being" but, "[W]e never know what being is . . . it always seems to be a *topos*, an unattainable place that never becomes (fully) accessible." Being only presents itself to us as *Ereignis* (event), as an appearing, relative to us, through time. The argument retrieves the notion of transcendence: "Every *Ereignis* is basically ungraspable. . . . *Ereignis* remains incomprehensible because being is precisely transcendence."[4] Being is transcendence because as *Ereignis* being is the process of appearing within time so that every appearance points beyond itself in the double sense of pointing to what has already appeared and to what has yet to appear. As Gadamer grasps understanding as an event of being, transcendence is integral to understanding. The reappropriation of transcendence as the process of understanding is the philosophical move that initiates the central reflections of this essay. If understanding is a process, what are its formal ontological features? Chapter 2 uses the theme of *Bildung* to explore the ontological drivers of transcendence within understanding. If understanding involves transcendence, how do the dynamics of transcendence manifest themselves within hermeneutic consciousness? Chapter 3 considers the nature of speculative insight in order to examine the dynamics of transcendence within the subjective dimensions of understanding. If understanding involves transcendence and if transcendence involves an awareness of the limits of understanding, how does a consciousness of such limits affect the nature of hermeneutic practice? Chapter 4 focuses on Gadamer's philosophy of language and will reveal the disruptive consequences of transcendence within hermeneutic understanding.

Further elucidating the theses laid out in chapter 1, chapter 2 examines the principal ontological actualities that form and sustain hermeneutic consciousness. Tradition is identified as a continuity of conflicts and understanding is examined as transformative and formative *Bildungs*-process. Gadamer's approach to *Bildung* is not an apologetics for bourgeois education but an outline of a hermeneutic ontology. Because it grasps understanding as an event, it proposes that understanding does not merely interpret the world but changes it. The ontological actualities underwriting understanding deprive hermeneutic consciousness of any certainty of interpretation. What they reveal is the ever-present difficulty of residing within "the quietness of a single interpretation."[5] Hermeneutic practice is indeed difficult but therein lies its vitality.

Whereas chapter 2 addresses the ontological objectivities that shape the possibility of understanding, chapter 3 considers how hermeneutic consciousness grasps those objectivities. If understanding is an event, how is it experienced by hermeneutic consciousness? Chapter 3 occasions a detailed discussion of "speculative understanding" and of how understanding entails a moment of transcendence. Philosophical hermeneutics makes important claims about the specific nature of literary and aesthetic understanding and its role in the formation of an interpreting subject's sense of self. Though philosophical hermeneutics possesses the conceptual means to discuss the matter, Gadamer does not explicitly address the experiential dynamics of what happens to a subject when addressed by an artwork. Chapter 3 demonstrates that reflection on the nature of speculative understanding can successfully address this question. However, the discussion of speculative understanding reveals that Gadamer overplays its integrative aspect. Speculative understanding also sets hermeneutic consciousness at a distance from itself and disrupts what it thought it understood. The themes of difficulty, distance, and difference appropriately dominate chapter 4 of the essay, where the unease and disquiet of understanding will be explored.

Chapter 3 substantiates a major claim of this essay: philosophical hermeneutics embodies a significant critique of both Nietzsche's philosophy of language and nihilism. Philosophical hermeneutics offers a sustained defense of "speculative" insight. This entails the view that the world (is) *world* only insofar as it comes into language. This does not reduce the world to words or assume that the world can be put into words. To the contrary, it supposes that the power of the well-chosen word lies in its ability to sound out and to resonate the unspoken world of meaning it is woven into. For Gadamer intense experience is not beyond words. It sets us the task of finding the right words. This places him at odds with Nietzsche who is wary of how the common framework of language sullies and contaminates profound experience. Gadamer's case for speculative understanding stands on his conviction that experience itself seeks and finds words that endeavor to express its content. In other words, for its case to stand, philosophical hermeneutics must demonstrate that Nietzsche's skepticism about language is ill founded. Chapter 3 contends that philosophical hermeneutics reveals Nietzsche's attempt to isolate intense experience from the contamination of the linguistic market place to be a pretentious sham and to be in conflict with his advocacy of a wilfully individualistic philosophy of becoming. Philosophical hermeneutics demonstrates that the ability to "become more" does indeed depend upon a willingness to enter the marketplace of language.

Dialogical engagement is not necessarily easy or comfortable. It requires a willingness to be subject to the address of the other and to place one's self-understanding before the other's claims. Chapter 4 proposes that the difficulty of understanding and of becoming-difficult-to-oneself is a primary concern of philosophical hermeneutics. Deconstructive critics of philosophical hermeneutics regard it as being in serious philosophical difficulty. This essay will argue that such critics are right but for the wrong reasons. What are perceived as the weaknesses of philosophical hermeneutics—its inability to arrive at a final interpretation and to achieve a *Letztbegründung* for its operation—are indeed its strengths. Chapter 4 offers a critical meditation upon Hamacher's claim that "understanding is in want of understanding" and claims that his fundamental confusion between *logos* as word and *logos* as reason not only brings forth central points about the formal character of philosophical hermeneutics but establishes in a clear and decisive manner the nature of its case against nihilism. Linguistic difference, deferral, and temporal postponement do not disrupt the possibility of philosophical hermeneutics. To the contrary, they maintain the vitality of the "word," animate its dialectic, and preserve the possibility of renewed hermeneutic insight and transcendence. This essay argues that the importance of philosophical hermeneutics resides in a formidable double claim that strikes at the heart of both traditional philosophy and deconstruction. To seek control over the fluid nature of linguistic meaning with rigid conceptual regimes or to despair of such fluidity because it frustrates hope for stable meaning, is to succumb to nihilism. Both are indicative of a failure to see that understanding and the hermeneutic translation and transcendence it affords depend upon the vital instability of the "word."

In addition to Gadamer's work, the essay discusses Wolfgang Iser's interpretation theory. Iser offers valuable insights into the nature of interpretative practice. Whereas Gadamer reflects for the most part upon how the ontological foundations of understanding impose finitude upon its claims, Iser extends Gadamer's position by showing how the practice of interpretation both generates and is driven by the conditions of its own incompleteness. This essay contends that distance, and difference are not detrimental to hermeneutic endeavor as deconstruction supposes but are constitutive of hermeneutic consciousness itself. The essay also refers to the work of such contemporary theologians as Oliver Davies and Daphne Hampson. The pertinence of their arguments lies not in their religious but in their ethical content. Theology and philosophical hermeneutics share a common concern with *application* and the issues of *practice*. This essay argues that philosophical hermeneutics does not constitute a "philosophical position" but a philosophical dis-position. It is a practice of disposing or orientating oneself toward the other and the different with the consequence of experiencing a dis-positioning of one's initial expectancies. The theme of difficulty is once more invoked. If philosophical hermeneutics is a practice of attentiveness, then like all reflective and spiritual disciplines it inhabits and articulates a tense space, the space of being in between. Openness to the other requires a particular refinement: the skill of being critically distant while remaining involved, attentive, and caring. Hermeneutic practice is indeed difficult. It involves the testing discipline of not residing in the quietness of a single interpretation. Maintaining an outward openness to the multiple voices of the other upholds an inward openness to the possibility of translation and transcendence upon which the furtherance of understanding depends.

Acknowledgments

My thanks to the University of Dundee for the period of research leave (2002-2003) that enabled me to write the initial draft of this book. A great intellectual debt is owed to all those who took part in the Heidelberg Hermeneutics Seminar (1989-2002). For tutoring me in the ways of the unspoken, I owe so much to Barbara, Cecily, and Felix. I am grateful to Dorothea Franck and Karin Hiscock for the openings their conversations enabled. I offer heartfelt thanks to my teachers, especially to Prof. Gordon Leff of the University of York.

CHAPTER ONE

Philosophical Hermeneutics
Navigating the Approaches

INTRODUCTION

Philosophical hermeneutics is not a traditional theory of interpretation. It does not seek to establish a generally acceptable method for the reading of obscure and difficult texts. Philosophical hermeneutics is, much rather, an interpretation of interpretation, a prolonged meditation upon what "happens" to us within "hermeneutic experience" when we are challenged by texts and artworks, ancient and modern. Though it eschews formal methodologies of reading, it does not privilege subjective responses to a text. Philosophical hermeneutics is *philosophical* in that it strives to discern objectivities within the subjective voice. It reflects on the historical and cultural preconditions of individual hermeneutic experience and seeks to discern in it something of the predicament, character, and mode of being of those who "undergo" such experience. And yet the philosophical within philosophical hermeneutics remains *hermeneutical* for it is not concerned with the abstract nature of such objectivities but with how they manifest themselves and are encountered within the particularities of experience and their ramifications.

Nietzsche observed that one is never finished with profound experience.[1] Similarly, good conversations have no end. Their insights open unexpected avenues of experience and can initiate a review of what has been previously understood. Their sense is slow to unfold. Not everything said may be meant and not everything meant need be said. With patient reflection and comparison, their insights alter and accrue an unexpected critical efficacy. Over time, a telling conversation reveals more of itself. Its

1

specific manner of handling a subject matter is gradually disclosed, its guiding presuppositions emerge and the applicability of its insights to other areas of concern becomes clearer. It is in the nature of conversation that its self-understanding changes. Conversation shows how an experience of change is part of understanding and demonstrates that, like itself, understanding has no end. The achievement of understanding is and will always remain difficult. It is a task, the object of a practice.

Philosophical hermeneutics is not just *about* conversation. In its operation it exhibits something of the disclosive, summative, and anticipatory *dynamics* of conversation. These dynamics are clearly displayed in Gadamer's approach to the nature of interpretation. Reflection upon what Gadamer explicitly states about interpretation and its preconditions *discloses* that his implicit and understated ambition is to find a response to the challenge nihilism makes to the possibility of meaning. This disclosure prompts, in turn, a *summative* reappraisal of philosophical hermeneutics as a subtle and sanguine reply to Nietzsche's *Interpretationsphilosophie*. The reply, in its turn, duly *anticipates* a critical response to poststructuralist critiques of hermeneutics inspired by Nietzsche. Furthermore, that response proceeds to intimate how hermeneutics might transcend Gadamer's own conception of the discipline. From the perspective of the dynamics of conversation, philosophical hermeneutics is true to itself as a philosophical disposition. Its dialogical stance exposes it to processes of change in self-understanding which are characteristic of conversation itself. For philosophical hermeneutics it is more important to remain loyal to an *experience* of language as opposed to the formal claims of philosophical method. This gently re-poses an ancient question that we shall reflect on in this essay. Is the proper stress of philosophical reflection to fall upon matters academic or upon finding an appropriate response to the complexities of human experience?

Philosophical hermeneutics has been the subject of much misunderstanding. For some readers Gadamer's interest in ancient philosophy, historiography, and intellectual tradition lends a conservative profile to his thought. His attempt to rethink tradition and *Bildung* (cultural and educative formation) has brought the inevitable accusation of reactionary purpose.[2] In the opinion of some critics, his preoccupation with the nature of interpretation points to a fixation with meaning, with its sameness, and with its decoding.[3] His critique of objectivist methodologies suggests to other commentators that his thought is a scant apology for both relativism and romantic irrationalism. Such accusations are misleading misunderstandings and they detract from the radical character of philosophical hermeneutics.[4] Our strategic purpose is to reevaluate these cardinal elements of Gadamer's thought and to uncover the poignancy of an underrated and undervalued philosophical disposition.

The integrity of any hermeneutical essay would be compromised were it to claim to be *the* interpretation of Gadamer's thought. For this essay, it is more a question of where the proper stress of interpretation should fall. We shall contend that just as Gadamer's thinking has the ability to force a radical change in our understanding of experience, so it also has important implications for appreciating both the *philosophical* elements in hermeneutics and the *hermeneutic* aspects of philosophy. An important qualification is necessary.

Nietzsche implied that philosophers should submit themselves to the laws they postulate.[5] Gadamer should not be exempted from this maxim. Since Gadamer insisted that the meaning and significance of a body of thought extend beyond what its author may have intended, it is not inconsistent for an essay devoted to philosophical hermeneutics to strive to go beyond what Gadamer actually states about philosophical hermeneutics. What is articulated in this essay as philosophical hermeneutics is not restricted to Gadamer's explicit definition. The eleven theses presented below derive from what Gadamer has written but they have a philosophical reach that stretches beyond what he initially envisaged.[6]

ELEVEN THESES ON PHILOSOPHICAL HERMENEUTICS

Philosophical hermeneutics betokens a reflective practice. While it addresses hermeneutic questions of aesthetic, historical, and philosophical understanding, it reflects philosophically on the ethical dimensions of interpretative practice: how to orientate oneself toward and how to interact with the claims of the other be it a text, a person, or a remote historical horizon? Practises are, however, informed by the received historical labyrinths of working traditions. They cannot in consequence be definitively articulated. Though the practice of philosophical hermeneutics cannot be conceptually captured, its nature can be discerned among the spectrum of philosophical refractions that a variety of interpretative perspectives bring to light. This essay argues that as a practice, philosophical hermeneutics is more a constellation of philosophical outlooks than a specific philosophical system or method. The character of these outlooks becomes more apparent when juxtaposed against one another. We shall, accordingly, present eleven theses concerning philosophical hermeneutics with the purpose of bringing more of its implicit nature to light.

It is entirely appropriate that "the approaches" to philosophical hermeneutics be *navigated* in this way. A reflective practice that is linguistic in nature always knows, in Gadamer's phrase, more than it thinks it knows. The words and concepts deployed in communicative practices are invariably shaped by complexities of historically formed meaning and insight. It is a key axiom of Gadamer's thought that words have a *speculative* nature that reflects something of the etymological horizons that transcend their particular usage. In many practices acquaintance with such networks of meaning is more *tacit* than reflective. The strategic aim of philosophical hermeneutics is to promote hermeneutic encounters that prompt our interpretative horizons to disclose their *speculative* nature. To this end, the practice of philosophical hermeneutics pursues dialogue and dialectical encounter with the other. It seeks a disciplined openness to the strange and foreign. It encourages a creative tension between the assumptions and expectancies of our own horizon and those that are different. In the fine-tuning of such differences, our interpretative horizons can be induced to reveal more of their speculative nature. Philosophical hermeneutics is, therefore, not a practice of analyzing texts per se but a means of bringing something *unexpected* about, a way of inducing interpretative interactions that not only expose us to the unusual and unanticipated but which also place the assumptions of our customary horizons at risk. The following eleven theses attempt to bring forth something of the speculative nature of philosophical hermeneutics itself.

The following theses are not in a form characteristic of philosophical hermeneutics. Gadamer does not engage his readers in prolonged philosophical argument or analysis but prefers instead to approach his subject matter discursively. He is intent on exploring what happens to us in our dialogical engagement with a text. It is, however, a grotesque underestimation of Gadamer's texts to suppose that because of the absence of such analysis they lack serious philosophical foundation. To the contrary, the philosophical insights that drive Gadamer's thought are embedded within and to some extent derive from the practice of hermeneutic engagement. In order to draw out and clarify the insights that guide the practice of philosophical hermeneutics, it is necessary to translate that practice into a more formal language. Translation can distort an original text but precisely because it renders a text differently, it can clarify what is in an original. The formulation of these theses offers an overview of the conceptual territory that philosophical hermeneutics occupies and reveals the broad conceptual commitments that inform the way philosophical hermeneutics discusses specific issues. Philosophical hermeneutics has not always been its own best advocate. For all its conviviality, Gadamer's discursive style can seem rambling and indecisive. There is good reason, therefore, to articulate the specific philosophical commitments that underlie its operation. The intention is not to abuse the intricacies of hermeneutic practice, nor to force the complexities of hermeneutic experience into words and concepts. It is not even to translate such experience into a linguistic medium. To the contrary, the aim of such articulation is to use words in a way *appropriate* to deepening our sense of what underwrites and is implied by such experience. In this context, philosophical reflection is indeed the proper handmaid of experience. The theses to be presented are as follows.

Thesis One: Hermeneutical Understanding Requires Difference

Philosophical hermeneutics does not suppose that understanding occurs when a reader's grasp of a text is the *same* as its author's. To the contrary, understanding requires and perpetuates a mode of differentiation (the hermeneutic differential), which sustains understanding as an enduring *task*. A misleading emphasis has too often been placed upon the role of *sameness* in philosophical hermeneutics.[7] Within the broad spectrum of what the term *understanding* can mean, it cannot be denied that understanding the *same* as another is vital in the operation of mathematical or navigational skills. However, the specific stress which philosophical hermeneutics gives to understanding concerns those revelatory moments of realization when it becomes apparent that the other *does not* think the *same* as me or that I can no longer think the *same* as I did about a person or a text. Acknowledging difference in the other permits me to become different to myself. Were philosophical hermeneutics to stress but *sameness*, neither could it concern itself with understanding as a transformative experiential processes, which it clearly does, nor could it be the philosophy of learning and becoming (*Bildungsphilosophie*) which it manifestly is.

Thesis Two: Philosophical Hermeneutics Promotes a Philosophy of Experience

Gadamer's rejection of methodology challenges received, regulatory frameworks of institutional knowledge. He reinvokes the value of experientially acquired wisdom (*paideia*). Philosophical hermeneutics endeavors to show that what is learned from experience extends beyond the strictures of formalized method. It offers a gentle (but pointed) reminder that philosophy is more than a love of formalized knowledge. Philosophy participates in a dialectic of shared experience and refines a *sense* of the communal, of belonging to something larger than oneself.

Dwelling on the experience of interpretation, philosophical hermeneutics concerns itself with an interpretation of experience. As encounters with texts (and others) are *lived*, learning from experience derives not just from that which is encountered but from the character of the encounter itself. Acquiring a sense for the weakness of hasty judgments or for the vulnerability of initial interpretations requires long exposure to the experience of interpretation. No one method teaches such skill, tact, or wisdom. The value of both receptiveness and attentiveness is not learned as an item of information. Rather, their value is made manifest in the practice of such virtues. Understanding their value exhibits the fact that within interpretative practice, one has become *skilled* in their application.

Though the insights of a practitioner—"knowing" how to find one's way about within an endeavor—are a consequence of "experience," they nevertheless fall outside the strictures of "method." In cultural horizons where objectivist scientific paradigms tend to monopolize evaluations of what counts as knowledge, two outcomes are apparent. First: no heed need be given to the lessons of experience. Those who are preoccupied with method and with the credentials of truth claims incline to the judgment that such lessons are both relative and subjective. Devaluing the insights of practice unfortunately encourages those who defend method to be forgetful of the practical insights guiding and locating their own interests. Philosophical hermeneutics openly exposes the nihilism within the shrewish methodological preoccupations of much modern philosophy but, more important, it strives to articulate what method neglects, that is, the wider, more complex, dimensions of human encounter, experience, and learning.

Thesis Three: Philosophical Hermeneutics Entails a Commitment to Hermeneutic Realism

What is learned from experience derives not just from the object encountered but from the character of the encounter itself. This permits philosophical hermeneutics to concern itself with a great deal more than an individual's (subjective) assimilation of a text. It is not what an individual imposes on a text that interests philosophical hermeneutics but the nature of that which imposes itself on the reader by virtue of her encounter with the text.

Engaging with a text can check or frustrate a reader's presuppositions and reveal the inadequacy of previous understandings. Being so thwarted can expose a reader to the extent of his or her previous oversights. These experiences are not sought out but a reader *risks* them in the encounter with a text. Such experiences acquire an important status within philosophical hermeneutics. They become individual experiences of *finitude* in which the *real* limits of human understanding are encountered. Philosophical hermeneutics attempts to discern in what we do (interpretation) the real character of our being. It seeks an encounter with the real and is, therefore, plainly committed to a form of hermeneutic realism. As we shall see, this commitment underwrites Gadamer's response to the challenge of Nietzsche's nihilism. Furthermore, the realistic quest in philosophy and literature acknowledges the actuality of human suffering. Philosophical hermeneutics is no exception: the inescapable negativity of experience—*pathei mathos*—is truly educative.

Thesis Four: Philosophical Hermeneutics Seeks Otherness within the Historical

Philosophical hermeneutics and the historical stance that informs it, strive to do justice to the integrity of the world lying beyond the self.[8] It does not seek to assimilate the historical other within its own horizon, nor to become fully immersed in the other's "form of life." To translate (subsume) the other into one's own voice renders the strange familiar and converts what ought to be a *dia*-logue into a monologue. To suspend one's own horizons and be translated into the other's "form of life" renounces (albeit temporarily) one's own way of "knowing how to go on." Neither assimilation nor immersion constitutes what philosophical hermeneutics conceives of as understanding. Assimilation of the other within one's own horizon preserves rather than challenges the presuppositions of one's initial perspective. Immersion within the monologue of the other also makes dialogue impossible. The renunciation of one's own horizon for that of the other surrenders the ground upon which other can be encountered as *other*. By neutralizing the provocation of the other, assimilation and immersion diminish the likelihood of those disruptive experiences of limit which are integral to the possibility of understanding as philosophical hermeneutics conceives of it. Recognizing the integrity of the other is therefore fundamental to philosophical hermeneutics. *It is not sameness—neither rendering the other the same as ourselves nor becoming the same as the other—but difference that is vital for philosophical hermeneutics.* It is difference that preserves the reality of alternative possibilities that are not our own.

Hermeneutic realism entails a commitment and a willingness to surrender to the undeniable reality of finitude, to limit-experiences, and to the possibility of horizons of meaning that are presently not our own. Philosophical hermeneutics is not, in other words, an antiquarian body of thought. To restore and, indeed, to strengthen the "living voice" of an ancient text so that it becomes less obscure and "more itself," is not to become prone to a false historical objectivism that pursues the past in and for its own sake. Nor is it to succumb to a romantic flight from the present. It is, to the contrary, to uphold and sharpen the difference between present and past horizons. It is, indeed, to preserve the possibility of an encounter with those ways of thinking and seeing that offer answers that *question* those we give to the problems which preoccupy us.

Thesis Five: Philosophical Hermeneutics Reinterprets Transcendence

Transcendence is intregral to what philosophical hermeneutics grasps as the "experience" of understanding. Hermeneutic encounters with the different, with finitude, and with limit, suggest that understanding involves an experience of transcendence. Understanding is the process of coming to understand that when we understand, we understand differently.[9] Understanding is not only dependent upon but makes a difference. The difference between what we once understood and now understand is itself understood. As a result, our understanding of ourselves, of our past, and of the world we find ourselves in, acquires new coordinates and reconfigures itself accordingly. When we understand ourselves differently, we have "moved on." Transcendence does not betoken surpassing the range or grasp of human experience. It does not concern what lies beyond experience but what lies within it or, much rather, it has to do with experiencing those fundamental shifts within passages of experience that can quite transform how such passages are understood.[10] Hermeneutic transcendence involves the transforming experience of coming knowingly to see, to think, and to feel differently. Philosophical hermeneutics recognizes that movement and transcendence is the life of understanding or of what Gadamer sometimes *pace* Hegel calls *Geist*.[11]

Thesis Six: Philosophical Hermeneutics Entails an Ethical Disposition

For philosophical hermeneutics, hermeneutic experience is inseparable from an ethical recognition of the other and otherness. The other's *assertive* demand for recognition (Hegel) is not the issue. The recognition that philosophical hermeneutics demands is that a subject acknowledge that its *self-consciousness* is profoundly dependent upon what lies outside it, that is, upon the *otherness* of different language horizons, of different cultures and persons.

With its roots in the philosophy of consciousness, philosophical hermeneutics seems at first sight to lack an ethical orientation. Its stress upon the individual nature of hermeneutic experience suggests a romantic subject-centered thought preoccupied with the inwardness of experience but not with the joys and pains of ethical involvement. On closer inspection, a rich vein of ethical thinking becomes discernible. Philosophical hermeneutics de-centers subjective experience and brings the subject to an awareness of its profound dependence upon cultural realities that are not of its own making. The argument is that it is not strictly speaking *I* who understand. Whatever I understand, I come to understand through the mediation of another. It is the other who (in the form of a person, text, or painting) brings me to understand something. The event of understanding is not an individual achievement but presupposes an ethical encounter with an other. The event of understanding also depends upon that which transcends the understanding subject, namely, the hermeneutic community in which the subject participates and through which the subject is socialized. Yet socialization within an interpretive horizon is not merely a condition of hermeneutic experience: the event of hermeneutic experience also *socializes*. That understanding is something more than an individual achievement is sustained by the following points.

All understanding is dependent upon a prior acquisition of linguistic practices. All understanding is dependent upon a prior acquisition of linguistic practices and horizons of meaning, which guide our initial conceptions of self and world. The extent of our initial dependence upon such fore-understandings (*Vorverständnisse*) is for the most part overlooked. Such "forgetfulness" is not inappropriate. Most human practices are orientated initially toward the achievement of practical ends rather than historical or reflective awareness. It is often only when an individual or community encounters otherness in the form of practices different from its own that the nature of its background assumptions becomes apparent.

Hermeneutic understanding requires an encounter with the other. The reflective reappropriation of our guiding and defining fore-understandings needs engagement with the other. The contrast between our perspective and that of the other allows the other to be *other* while the relation between the perspective of the other and that of our own, reveals our perspective to be distinctively our own. Understanding is, then, not to be appraised as an individual achievement. It is facilitated by what is not of the individual's making (the background assumptions of a cultural practice) and any conscious repossession of those assumptions is dependent upon an encounter with the other which in large part remains in the other's gift.

Understanding involves negotiation and agreeing to differ knowingly. Understanding does not fall exclusively within the provenance of the subjective since it is a *social* achievement. Philosophical hermeneutics labors not only against the subjectivism of its romantic heritage but also against those theories which regard the attainment of understanding as the achievement of a *consensus* (Habermas) that, having overcome disturbances within a dialogue, permits one to "go on" (Wittgenstein) within its framework of assumptions. Yet achieving an *entente* or "*arriving* at an understanding" by no means implies an unqualified agreeing with the other. It can involve an *agreeing to differ* based upon a mutual, sympathetic dialogical awareness and tolerance of difference. Within philosophical hermeneutics, the *relation* of difference preserves a crucial "dialecticity"[12] of encounter. For those involved, the encounter with difference opens the possibility of a mutual transformation of the initial understanding each party brings to the encounter. On the one hand, strengthening the integrity of the other preserves the reality of alternative possibilities that are not *my* own. On the other hand, developing my own understanding offers the other alternative possibilities that are not immediately hers.[13] It is the dialecticity of the hermeneutic encounter, rather than the wills of the participants, that achieves a fundamental shift in how different parties understand themselves and each other.

Understanding is not, then, a purely individual achievement. It emerges from that unpredictable dialecticity of encounter between the linguistic and cultural horizons of individuals. Indeed, the event of understanding opens us to, manifests our dependence and reveals the extent of participation within "supra-individual ontological realities" that are not of our making.[14] By virtue of this and contrary to its conservative reputation, philosophical hermeneutics attributes a socializing influence to acknowledgments of difference.

Now, the conservative dimension of philosophical hermeneutics' ethical comportment falls discernibly within Heideggerian orthodoxy. When an encounter with the other exposes the dependence of an individual or community upon its overlooked fore-understandings, a reflective *reappropriation* of those enabling assumptions (tradition) becomes possible. In revealing the understandings upon which the individual or community rests, the other enables that individual or community to return to itself, that is, to knowingly "bind itself" to the mode of existence that such exposure has brought to light.[15] Heidegger remarks,

> It is the temple (art) work that first fits together and at the same time gathers around itself the unity of those paths and relations in which birth, disaster and blessing, victory and disgrace, endurance and decline acquire the shape of destiny for human being. . . . Only from and in this expanse does the nation first *return* to itself for the fulfillment of its vocation.[16]

As Vattimo points out, it is difficult to separate Heidegger's aesthetics of disclosure from a Hegelian notion of *Geborgenheit* (founding).[17] However, the particular emphasis which philosophical hermeneutics gives to difference enables its ethical orientation to pass beyond the conservatism of Heidegger's account of cultural consolidation and belonging.

The *socializing* aspect of hermeneutic experience is twofold. First, the encounter with the other sharpens loyalty to the exposed assumptions within one's tradition. Second, because that exposure reveals my dependence on the other for opening me to the reality of alternative possibilities that are not my own, it also binds me to that which is different and which does not immediately spring from within my horizon. I am indebted to the other for revealing to me what is strange in me. The other holds the key to me becoming other to myself. In effect, the other demonstrates to me that "*Je est un autre monde*" and that it is in such otherness that I can glimpse a hitherto unseen self. Hermeneutic experience involves an ethical revelation of the extent to which I can become bound to that which is both different from and stands at the limit of my horizon.

If communities are bound by the shared needs and the occupation of a common space, hermeneutic encounters (especially those which are stressful) plainly have the capacity to bind together those who undergo them more closely. It is beyond question that our capacity to understand "more," to become different to ourselves, depends upon an encounter with the other. In short, the ability to understand "more" rests not just upon a recognition of what initially lies within a native horizon but also upon an acknowledgment of that which stands at the limit of that horizon. Here philosophical hermeneutics ceases to be conservative and moves toward the constructive. *The hermeneutic encounter grounds a civility among those who have come to know what it is to become different to themselves and who realize, as a consequence, that they are indeed mutually dependent upon each other for expanding the possibilities within their understanding.* Such individuals know that their ability to understand and become "more" does not depend exclusively upon a recognition of what is entailed *within* their horizon but also upon a recognition of that otherness which challenges their horizons from outside. The locus of such a civility is not to be found within the landscape of a common history or language but in the border terrains of shared hermeneutical encounters. Philosophical hermeneutics indicates, then, how participation in the hermeneutical experience of becoming different to oneself can engender a hermeneutic civility that *transcends* the initial horizons of birth and custom. Philosophical hermeneutics clearly surpasses the conservatism of Heidegger's cultural orthodoxy. As we shall see, acknowledgment of an ethical dependence upon the other and the different enables philosophical hermeneutics to give a far from trite sense to the notion that understanding *civilizes.* That hermeneutic experience has the potential to draw one into a civility of difference strengthens the ethical insight that *understanding is far from being an individual achievement.*

Thesis Seven: Hermeneutic Understanding Redeems the Negativity of Its Constituting Differential

While avoiding the pitfalls of a systematized Hegelian dialectic, philosophical hermeneutics claims that understanding is driven by "the power of the negative." The negative perimeters of hermeneutic understanding are fourfold.

1. Hermeneutic encounters reveal the "negativity of experience": a hermeneutic experience worthy of the name *disrupts* the expectancies one has of an artwork or text so that one is forced to think again.[18]

2. Hermeneutic understanding is finite. It is limited by both its time and its horizon. The determinate historical location of any understanding prevents it from being able to claim completeness.

3. Understanding is perspectival. It presents but one of several other logically possible points of view of its subject matter.

4. No act of understanding is complete. No hermeneutic encounter can exhaust its subject matter.

Two views of negativity can be discerned within these perimeters. First, negation is portrayed as the due punishment for that hermeneutic hubris which forgets that all understanding is dependent upon unstated horizons of meaning. Any claim to be the definitive interpretation, to be "whole" and complete, is subject to negation, that is, to the risk of being exposed as a particular expression of a more complex "whole" or nexus of other understandings. Second, the "power of the negative" is associated with an ineliminable space or with a hermeneutical differential, which, though it drives understanding toward completion, continually defers the possibility of its attainment.

That the "power of the negative" is inherent within hermeneutic operations is established by the following. Philosophical hermeneutics perceives that such inherited subject matters as truth, beauty, justice, etc. would lie dormant were they not kept "functional."[19] Understanding must translate a subject matter from the register in which it has been historically received into one that enables it to operate in a contemporary manner. Wolfgang Iser argues that this "fashioning" of a subject matter exposes a difference between "what is to be interpreted and the register into which it is to be translated."[20] Interpretation opens an ineliminable space between registers. While this space or hermeneutic differential incites and drives further interpretation, it also prevents understanding from ever completing its task. In short, the negativity that inspires and brings understanding to its task—the recognition of the difference between the received register of a subject matter and the one it must be translated into—is also that negativity which prevents understanding from fulfilling its task. Yet the negative aspects of hermeneutic understanding are redeemed by the positivity residing within them. That which prevents understanding from completing its task also lures it into further efforts, thereby keeping its task open. It is not openness per se which matters. In sustaining that openness, understanding's vulnerability to the serendipitous challenge of the other and the unexpected is preserved. Keeping understanding exposed to the risk of such interventions allows understanding to "become more," for by being prompted to disclose more of its overlooked presuppositions, understanding grasps more of itself. The positivity of the negative aspects in hermeneutic understanding shows itself in another light too.

The charge that a given understanding is *particular* in relation to a "whole" body of other interpretations is simultaneously negative and affirmative. The invocation of what an interpretation *is not* (i.e., not the whole of the matter) also reveals what the interpretation *is* (i.e., one element of a larger nexus of mutually related understandings). Such a "dialectical" shift in perception does not negate the negative aspects of hermeneutic understanding but refigures them positively. Five points are salient.

1. The "negativity of experience" may disrupt one's expectancies of a text but it also opens unexpected alternatives. An awareness of the finitude of understanding exposes one to different interpretative possibilities.

2. The very limitedness of one's understanding provides a position from which one can negotiate with other forms of interpretation. Such limitedness does not so much indicate the incomplete or distorted nature of one's understanding as provide the foundation for one to understand "more."

3. Gaining an awareness of that which limits one's understanding (other horizons), strengthens a sense of belonging to an expanding whole. Becoming conscious of the limitedness of understanding is a precondition of hermeneutical transcendence.

4. A grasp of what makes one's understanding perspectival (i.e., being in a relation to other perspectives) allows one's understanding of a subject matter to become more complete (multiperspectival).

5. The hermeneutic differential that formally blocks understanding from completing itself, perpetuates the motion necessary to keep understanding open to the possibility of further responses to a subject matter.

Philosophical hermeneutics recognizes the "power of negativity." It strives to remain open to the different and to learn from the teachings of such suffering. Philosophical hermeneutics displays the *eclat* of a life-affirming mode of thought that recognizes that the (tragic) endurance of its own negativity contains the promise of its redemption. It *understands* that the possibility of hermeneutic transcendence follows on the affirmative embrace of its own negativity.

Thesis Eight: Philosophical Hermeneutics Affirms an Ontology of the In-between

Philosophical hermeneutics indisputably aligns itself with the Heideggerian argument that understanding is a mode of being. Gadamer articulates this mode as a *"being in-between"*: "Hermeneutics is based upon a polarity of familiarity and strangeness . . . the true locus of hermeneutics is this in-between" (TM, 295).[21] Philosophical hermeneutics proposes an ontology of the in-between that attempts to articulate what *occurs* within the *process* of understanding. This ontology displays what is within philosophical hermeneutics a characteristic dialectical reversal, a reversal that stresses the transformative processes of encounter which negotiating parties are subject to. Philosophical hermeneutics does not seek to analyze the perspectives of two negotiating subjects in order to discern the de facto differences between them. To the contrary, the process of encounter itself is regarded as an ontological power capable of generating differences in and between subjects. Within the differences generated by such encounters, subjects are opened to the transformative possibilities for further understanding. As a process of encounter, the *being* of understanding resides in the continuous generation of the in-between. This is no "no man's land" between isolated subjects. It is, rather, the disclosive space of the hermeneutic encounter itself. It is this space which subjectivizes the participating individuals.

Hermeneutical encounter requires engagement. Engagement involves more than an acknowledgment of the proximity of perspectives and horizons other than my own. Such *factic* acknowledgment changes and risks nothing. Hermeneutical understanding entails a great deal more than tabling theoretical statements of the obvious, such as, between opposing traditions there are different points of view. It is, above all, concerned with the transformative potential of that differential space that *emerges* when two parties engage one another. Hermeneutical understanding is ontologically generative: it brings a differential space into being. It is the generative space of the in-between that discloses the contrast between our perspective and that of the other. It shows the other to be *other* while revealing our outlook to be distinctively our own. It is the generative space of the in-between, the space of the hermeneutical encounter, which discloses the reality of alternative possibilities not presently my own but which might yet become *my* own.

The process of subjectivization does not just take place between two selves but also places us between ourselves. It opens a differential space between unquestioned past self-understandings and future potentialities for understanding. The event of hermeneutical understanding is the emergence of such a being-in-between. The gift of the other is not merely their otherness per se. It is much rather that such otherness discloses possibilities that are not presently my own. This places us between ourselves, so to speak, between what is disclosed of how we have in the past understood ourselves as being and what is intimated of how we might be transformed by future understanding. However, the gift is reciprocal. While the other invites me to become open to alternative possibilities that are not *my* own and to develop and enhance my own understanding, in so doing I become more other to the other. Yet it is precisely because of this transformation that I can offer to the other alternative possibilities that are not immediately her own. Philosophical hermeneutics evidently assigns a dignity to difference and contends that the differential space of the in-between has its genesis in the processes of hermeneutical encounter, which invites us to allow those who see things differently to enlarge our world.

It is with good reason that the locus of hermeneutics is identified as the in-between. The locus of our understanding invariably involves being in between what, on the one hand, we have understood and what, on the other hand, we intuit we have yet to understand. Understanding entails the process of becoming different to ourselves. We do not merely encounter the different but become different to ourselves because of that encounter. The hermeneutical experience of difference is not just a confrontation with the unfamiliar. It involves the recognition of the familiar having been rendered strange by the unfamiliar. We reside, it would appear, somewhere between our once and future selves. This suggests that understanding is a mode of relatedness or, to put it another way, it expresses the *coming into being* of a mode of relatedness. What emerges within me as a singular *subjective* awareness, philosophical hermeneutics regards as an *objective* expression of a relationship. Self-awareness is, it is argued, not a precondition of being-with-others. Rather, its emergence demonstrates the fact of already having entered into such a relationship. There is no preexistent "inwardness" in which the self is found. Reflexive inwardness emerges from the world of exchange, of converse and interaction.[22] The self that emerges is far from transparent. Its emergence denotes that it has become a problem to itself. It is problematized by the very relationship whose being it expresses. Philosophical hermeneutics recognizes that the linguisticality of our being always renders us vulnerable to different narratives of ourselves. The encounter with the other opens a differential space between what I have come to grasp as myself and how others come to see me. Understanding, in other words, entails a great deal more than recovering what is implicitly understood "between ourselves." It also grasps that self-awareness entails a being placed in between our past and future selves. To be hermeneutically aware is to understand that the self resides in the differential space between what we understand ourselves to be and what others think us to be. In the eyes of philosophical hermeneutics to be a subject is always to be in between. A being who resides in the in-between is a being whose being is always open, vulnerable, and in question.

Thesis Nine: Philosophical Hermeneutics Is a Philosophical Practice Rather Than a Philosophical Method

The sound practice of a discipline requires that appropriate training and experience regulate attitude and behavior. The notion of a practice demands that its disciples be *methodical* and *disciplined* in their chosen approach. Being an experienced practitioner does not strictly speaking impose limits on deployable methical devices or tactics. To the contrary, becoming an experienced practitioner entails sharpening if not acquiring a guiding *sense* for judging which approach to a task is more plausible or appropriate than another. *Knowing* when a decisive judgment is demanded is the mark of a skilled practitioner. Yet such judgment is not a matter of deploying methods or rules. Philosophical hermeneutics offers a valuable reminder of what philosophical and hermeneutical *practice* should entail. What philosophical hermeneutics understands as its practice will be the subject of discussion below. Chapter 4 of this essay will discuss the implications of Gadamer's notion of hermeneutic practice at length. That philosophical hermeneutics is indeed orientated toward a form of philosophical *practice* rather than to philosophical theory is obscured by the shortcomings of Gadamer's approach to the question of method.

The "integrity of interpretation" no longer distinguishes the humanities from the natural sciences, as is amply demonstrated by Paul Feyerabend and Mary Hesse, for whom contemporary science has become thoroughly "hermeneuticized."[23] Gadamer's hasty slighting of the objective and universal pretensions of scientific method has needlessly drawn to philosophical hermeneutics the hostile charges of subjectivity and methodological arbitrariness. As a result, philosophical hermeneutics often stands accused of exactly the same shortcomings it perceives in

Nietzsche's nihilism. Yet a twist in this irony serves philosophical hermeneutics unexpectedly well.

Integral to philosophical hermeneutics' critique of Nietzsche's nihilism are arguments that attempt to discern objectivities within the subjective voice and to show that interpretation is far from groundless, but is rooted in specific ontological structures. Both sets of argument are central to Gadamer's attempt to articulate the ontological foundations of practice. Discerning them enables Gadamer to turn the tables on Nietzsche: any practice that does not recognize how it is enabled by the conceptual perimeters of its historical and cultural inheritance or, indeed, which tries to break with that inheritance, is nihilistic. By default, the argument provides philosophical hermeneutics with a riposte to the accusations of subjectivism and of methodological arbitrariness. The objectivity and methodological rigor frequently demanded of philosophical hermeneutics also reflects a nihilistic outlook, that is, the supposition that there are or ought to be ways of thinking and seeing purged of every element of historical and cultural determination. Such methods of reasoning are far from being independent of historical determination. The demand to make them so would deprive them of the cultural foundations upon which their drive and focus depends.

The implicit charge that (positivistic) models of scientific reasoning are nihilistic makes two points about how philosophical hermeneutics operates. First: many of its methodical insights (and specifically those to do with the philosophical foundations of practice) are unduly understated. A principal aim of this essay is to correct this and formulate some of the key methodical insights that underwrite philosophical hermeneutics. Second: though philosophical hermeneutics does not constitute a system or method, its critical procedures have a clear style and a discernible signature. With regard to the latter, consider the following.

The *riposte* that scientific reasoning betrays a nihilistic trait, does not refute the accusation that philosophical hermeneutics is governed by subjective prejudices and methodological arbitrariness. Rather, it indicates an intellectual maneuver characteristic of Gadamer's style of thought which invites us to think *differently* about the concepts in the accusation. Does not the charge against philosophical hermeneutics betray a very particular and somewhat limited epistemological understanding of the concepts *subjectivity* and *objectivity*? Yet if these concepts were to be rethought so as to include their ontological dimension, it becomes possible to think differently about them. Philosophical hermeneutics can suggest that subjectivity is not a block to greater objectivity but rather a gateway to it. Subjectivity (in the sense of having a distinct but negotiable point of view) can be regarded as enabling. The observation in support of this derives from another question: "Is it not precisely when our expectancies and 'prejudices' are challenged that we begin to learn?" If the concept of subjectivity is accorded the positive value of an enabling ontological prejudice, philosophical hermeneutics is indeed guilty of subjectivism. But (and this is the point) it is no more guilty of such subjectivism than scientific reasoning itself, which also rests upon a series of enabling fore-understandings. The tactic in such reasoning is plain: it endeavors to expose the objection to philosophical hermeneutics as embracing only one of a much more complex nexus of meanings that cluster around the term *subjectivity*. Such a move mirrors a classic figure within hermeneutic criticism: an allegedly universal claim is *particularized* against an implicit background (*whole*) of hidden or forgotten assumptions (*Vorverständnisse*) and comes to be understood differently when reread against the reappropriated background.[24] Furthermore, such a rereading initiates other changes in understanding. To grasp conscious subjectivity as entailing a positive commitment to deepening and exploring its enabling assumptions, suggests that objectivity can no longer be understood as the absence of subjectivity. Objectivity can be rethought phenomenologically as a critical recovery, as a widening and, perhaps, as a deepening of the enabling assumptions that guide the subject's perspective in the first place.[25] A subjectivity blind to its formative assumptions is a danger to philosophical hermeneutics *and* scientific reasoning in that it runs the risk of becoming nonobjective, that is, of becoming inconsistent with its enabling presuppositions.

Now, the invitation to think differently about core concepts within a criticism demands that philosophical hermeneutics opens itself to renegotiating its own understanding. This is indeed precisely what the *practice* of philosophical hermeneutics aspires to. The result of dialogical encounter should be that *both* parties retire thinking in different and unexpected ways about criticisms made and received. The formal employment of part/whole figures of thought clearly contributes to the transformation of understanding yet such transformations *happen* to us in an unpredictable fashion. They are not achieved by the application of method alone.[26] Philosophical hermeneutics is not a philosophical method but there is a clear style in the manner of its reasoning.

A discernible assemblage of intelligent intuitions informs the hostility of philosophical hermeneutics to the formalities of method. They are as follows.

The Finitude of All Thought and Experience. A leitmotif that virtually defines philosophical hermeneutics is the conviction that all human experience is particular and finite. Faithful to Heidegger's ontological axiom of thrownness (*Geworfenheit*), it maintains that all thought and expression are articulated within historically and culturally specific frameworks.[27] Though the interconnectedness of language patterns may link them, no one framework speaks for all or can claim universal completeness. That understanding remains a perpetually unfinished task renders suspect the certainty claimed by the adherents of method.

The Hermeneutic Differential. Given the huge variety of intellectual and artistic traditions, one of understanding's tasks involves the translation of one framework of expression into another. However, the hermeneutic differential that drives such translation also puts the task beyond completion. By definition, no translation or interpretation can claim completeness. In this respect, philosophical hermeneutics seems rather partisan in its opposition to method. It trumps an epistemological claim (a methodological claim to universality or completeness) with an ontological claim concerning either the finitude of understanding or the inability of propositional language to capture the full nature of a subject matter. Philosophical hermeneutics is indeed committed to an ontology of becoming but that commitment is used somewhat bluntly in its quarrel with method. The point against method is surely subtler.

If the claims of methodology are rethought as expressions of a "will to method," that is, as a specific mode of interpretation, the will to method appears as self-defeating. The methodological aspiration to translate the complexities of human experience into a comprehensively intelligible framework is doomed by the very differential that makes its task appear plausible in the first place. If the methodological aspiration is an act of translation, fashioning the complexities of experience for methodological assimilation only serves to generate an ineluctable difference between what it is to be translated and the register into which it is to be transposed.[28] This suggests that as a mode of interpretation, the "will to method" produces a residual untranslatability which simultaneously drives and yet frustrates its endeavor.[29] From the point of view of the "will to method," such untranslatable excess spells failure, but from the perspective of philosophical hermeneutics it opens the possibility of new forms of understanding.

Ethical Resistance. Philosophical hermeneutics expresses a modest but discernible ethical distaste for the ambitions of strict philosophical method.

This discomfort indicates a clear clash of philosophical dispositions. Three aspects of the "will to method" disconcert philosophical hermeneutics.

As an "alienated" form of consciousness, the will to method is Nihilistic. Philosophical hermeneutics regards conscious understanding as always being more than it knows itself to be: it is underwritten by complex *Vorverständnisse* which influence its orientations. With regard to the ontology of Bewusstsein (consciousness), the actuality of its underlying *Sein* (being) is always more than what it can consciously grasp (bewusst).[30] The intricacies of our individual and collective being are beyond full capture, which is to say that consciousness is sustained by what is beyond its cognitive grasp, namely, the "living certainties" of received historical and cultural practice. The will to method is blind to such dependence. It lacks sensitivity for the "thrownness" of its being and encourages the belief that we are epistemological subjects to whom the world is given as a manipulable object. In Schopenhauer's formulation, the phenomenal world is represented to the subject as if it were its object (or resource).[31] *Sein* is subordinated to *bewusst*. The will to method, furthermore, prioritizes its *own* frameworks of certainty and validity. These are of a different order from those attached to the inherited "prejudices" or "immediate living certainties" of tradition. Without knowing it, the will to method devalues the *Vorverständnisse* that enable it to operate in the first place.[32] Such nihilistic disregard for the actualities that sustain consciousness alienates the knowing subject from the very world that upholds its being. The will to method blinds the subject to the throwness of its being and prevents it from appreciating that it does not simply stand over and against the subject matters it studies but is part of their being. The will to method promotes an alienated form of knowing that not only distances the subject from the subject matters that shape its sensibility but which also renders it increasingly deaf to their address.[33] Philosophical hermeneutics senses something worrisomely nihilistic in the will to method.

The "will to method" exhibits a colonizing tendency. On one level, the focus and drive that attaches to the organizing power of the will to method is philosophically attractive. However, the energetic impetus toward orderliness and closure betrays an imperviousness toward alterity. The will to method has an imperious insensitivity to other voices and reduces the complex variety of human experience to its own terms. This reductive impetus is not an expression of invincibility but of an inability to face the risks of dialogical exposure.

The "will to method" promotes a dehumanizing mode of consciousness. Because it attacks the strictures of scientific and philosophical method, philosophical hermeneutics has been characterized as an irrational and unmethodical mode of thought. Philosophical hermeneutics is, however, opposed neither to the values of academic rigor, nor to the virtues of methodical research. What it is implacably opposed to is the attempt to privilege or monopolize reductive approaches to truth and actuality. The ethical danger implicit in the quest for methodological invincibility is that it masks a failure (or a fear) to confront the risks of what it is to be merely human. Hermeneutic understanding is born of an ethical encounter with an other, an encounter that leads to the participating subjects coming to think in different and unexpected ways of their positions. Learning and the possibility of hermeneutic transcendence depend upon a subject's preparedness to risk its self-understanding while encountering the other. In this respect, the tendency of the will to method to regard its particular approach to truth as the only legitimate approach has two negative consequences. As the need to remain open to otherness is by definition marginalized, the will to method blinds itself to the possibility of sensing the limits of its understanding. It renders itself immune to the risks and challenges of alterity upon which the furtherance of hermeneutic learning and insight depend. The ontological shortsightedness of the will to method renders it, potentially, a dehumanizing form of consciousness.

If the will to method tends to closure, philosophical hermeneutics inclines toward an open and attentive philosophical disposition. Philosophical hermeneutics is shaped by the belief that while any particular interpretation cannot embrace the whole of the story concerning a given subject matter, as one among others its very particularity contributes toward making that story more whole. The contrast between the will to method and philosophical hermeneutics is clear. The will to method seeks endorsement (or a corrective amendment) of its guiding presuppositions whereas the hermeneutic disposition expects (even wishes) it assumptions to be challenged by the unexpected. In other words, the tendency of the will to method to remain circumscribed by its own presuppositions is at odds with the dialogical conviction of philosophical hermeneutics that the particularity and value of a given perspective only becomes apparent when it is both challenged and brought into community with others. Philosophical hermeneutics believes that no single philosophical or scientific method can faithfully render the intricacies of human experience. The ethical preparedness to face the risks and challenges of dialogical encounter offers a better chance of sensing what those intricacies entail.

The Notion of Subject Matter. Philosophical hermeneutics fuses a phenomenological concept of intentionality with a quasi-platonic conception of universals. Dialogue intends and turns upon discernible issues and subject matters of enormous range (love, fairness, truth, beauty, etc). These subject matters are not merely what partners in dialogue conceive of their conversation as being about.[34] Participants bring to their debate numerous preconceptions about a subject matter. Many of these are assimilated from cultural practices that have implicitly shaped a given intellectual perspective. Such practices are influenced, in turn, by practices from other historical horizons. The skeptical disposition of philosophical hermeneutics toward the universal claims of method is underwritten by the conviction that a subject matter is always more than what can be said about it. The historical openness of a subject matter implies that no interpretation can be exhaustive. Its meaning cannot be finalized. For philosophical hermeneutics, then, the restricted ambitions of closed methods are at odds with the possibility of understanding more and understanding differently.

The Speculative Character of Language. Philosophical hermeneutics is committed to a speculative theory of language that prompts further doubts about the scope of philosophical and scientific method. These doubts concern the adequacy of the propositional form characteristic of many such methods for conveying what we actually "know" of language and what it discloses of the world. The speculative theory opposes the view that the nature of actuality can be captured in propositional language and that linguistic communication is best understood as the exchange of propositions or assertions (*Aussagen*). A clear caveat to these points is necessary.

Gadamer mistakenly allies issues appertaining to apodictic (statemental or propositional) language with the question of scientific method. The substantive question, however, is not to do with scientific method per se but with the elevation of propositional language to being the only legitimate form of expressing knowledge about the world. The question has both a philosophical and a cultural aspect. First: there is the philosophical question as to whether apodictic language can express the nature of humanity's linguistic being. Philosophical hermeneutics is burnished by its belief that there is more to understanding our linguistic being than understanding the nature of propositions. Second, there is the cultural question concerning the consequences of being encouraged to believe that the language of assertions is the only legitimate form of expressing knowledge of actuality. Philosophical hermeneutics has a deep cultural foreboding about how the elevation of *apodictic* language[35] might encourage the atrophying of speculative sensitivities.

The speculative theory of language involves a language ontology wedded to the conviction that "with a word, one is never alone."[36] As individual language speakers, we derive our linguistic being from a collective language world that does not exist over and against us but expresses its being in and through how we speak.[37] A word or concept is never solitary but resides within a web of associated meanings and uses. Philosophical hermeneutics opposes the instrumentalist (nominalist) view of language which maintains that a knowing subject (individually or collectively) determines the meaning of words. The language ontology of philosophical hermeneutics insists to the contrary, that whatever our chosen usage of terms, it will always convey or mean more than we imagine or intend. The etymological provenance of words is not under our control. The weight of a term's received meaning can sometimes take command of what we intend by it. Whatever we say will be inflected by the incalculable nuances and associations of inherited meaning lodged within our linguistic horizons. It is not always we who speak but it is we who are spoken through. To the discerning ear, the "speculative *turn*" in language occurs when the presence of inherited frameworks of meaning start to resonate in someone's words.

The axiom of semantic excess—that as linguistic beings we can always convey or mean more than we intend—is allied to the argument that the meaning of what we say is not always limited to what is actually spoken. If the meaning of a proposition is not exhausted by the relation of terms within it, then the unspoken and unwritten aspects of language are key determinants of what is communicated. What propositions and assertions communicate needs not be explicitly stated or spoken. This does not place the unsaid meaning beyond all utterance. Someone who fails to see the "point" or relevance of an argument or who fails to catch an allusion can have such meaning spelled out to them retrospectively. The argument is, then, that any theory of language neglectful of the domain of the unspoken will simply fail to convey the significance of the speculative dimension of linguistic meaning.

The case that philosophical hermeneutics makes against apophantic and apodictic language is not merely formal. It is also part empirical. The cultural status attached to the apodictic view of language encourages us to suppress our experience of language operating speculatively as well as apodictically. The experience of good conversation or good poetry bringing to mind (sometimes inexplicably) unexpected dimensions of meaning over and above what was actually stated, demonstrates that the speculative functioning of language is fundamental to our understanding. Philosophical hermeneutics contends that if language were solely the exchange and analysis of propositions, we would be limited to talking only of those sets of assertions that were logically connected or deductively derivable from their primary subject. But when language works, when it brings things to mind, it works speculatively and when it does so, it also operates synchronistically. Metaphor, simile, and other modes of imaginative juxtaposition demonstrate how language can by means of nuance and indirect association link subject matters that are not logically or causally connected.[38] Conversation for Gadamer is paradigmatic of language's speculative capacity. When in full flow, conversation discloses of itself subtleties of association that logical analysis cannot foresee. Conversation's unpredictable twists and turns reveal how in our linguistic being, we are prone to being "carried away by words." Our connectedness to unspoken realms of meaning can spontaneously manifest itself through the words of our immediate horizon. The disclosive capacity of language has a wildness about it that is not subject to propositional enclosure.

Philosophical hermeneutics regards these speculative manifestations as "events," as ontic disclosures. They expose our connection with a linguistic community that transcends our subjective being. Insofar as it is a language event that brings us to this insight, language reveals that disclosure is the essence of its own mode of being. Furthermore, although propositional idioms may themselves be used to summon a sense of our connectedness with linguistic being, inasmuch as they are already linguistic and therefore grounded in linguistic being, they can only speculatively "magnify" such being but never capture it. Philosophical hermeneutics contends that apophantic language will never capture being. Such language is itself already captured by linguistic being. It is held within established frameworks of linguistic meaning and practice upon which the intelligible operation of all apodictic language depends.[39] Indeed, were apodictic language not already captured by linguistic being, it would lose its (overlooked and undervalued) speculative capacity.

The resistance of philosophical hermeneutics to apodictic language does not express hostility toward scientific discourse or method per se. What it opposes is a cultural tendency that, because of its awe of science, elevates propositional language to the status of being the only legitimate framework within which what we know of the world can be communicated.[40] Such an elevation augurs a dangerous impoverishment of our appreciation of how language operates. This impoverishment diminishes how we *experience* the world. The primary status given to the statement or assertion desensitizes our "inner ear" for the unspoken speculative dimension of language. Because propositional language gravitates toward the public and the confirmable, it is distrustful of subjectivity and tends to demean the individual nature of speculative disclosure. The insights into the connectedness of meaning afforded by speculative insight are *not* reducible to arbitrary *subjective* association.[41] Conscious thought invariably articulates (recovers) connections that are already laid down in language. This sustains a primary leitmotif of philosophical hermeneutics: subjective experience makes manifest a significant range of linguistic and phenomenological objectivities. A worry gnawing at philosophical hermeneutics is that the cultural prejudices that encourage insensitivity both to the speculative intricacies of our linguistic being and to the subjective dimensions of experience, not only diminish access to the objectivities that subjectivity makes discernible but also reduce the scope of understanding for transformation. Philosophical hermeneutics does not celebrate novelty or the unexpected for their own sake. It values them for the speculative insight they enable into unforeseen aspects of received subject matters and their meaning. Philosophical hermeneutics is not about acquiring entertaining cultural divertimenti. The practice of remaining open to the possibility of speculative disclosure is nurtured precisely because it reveals the different. In so doing, it prompts us to think differently about ourselves. Sustaining speculative sensitivities ensures that the opportunities for hermeneutic transcendence remain open. To this end, philosophical hermeneutics makes a rigorous case for educating our speculative sensitivities for it is in the speculative functioning of language that the hardwiring of hermeneutical transcendence may be found.

In conclusion, philosophical hermeneutics is not a philosophical method but a philosophical practice with a discernible grammar to its reasoning. Its intelligent intuitions concerning the finitude of thought and experience, the unfinished nature of meaning, the function of the hermeneutic differential, the incomplete nature of subject matters and the speculative character of language, all operate with a characteristic dialecticity. Their negative dimension deconstructs (or particularizes) the universal claims of method by revealing their historical and cultural limitedness. Such a tactical stricture has a positive dimension. It is a means to undertaking a larger strategic maneuver which aims to strengthen an orientation toward hermeneutic openness as opposed to the temptations of methodological closure. The affirmative function of these tactical arguments is to reinvoke the numerous opportunities for hermeneutic transcendence contained within the inexhaustible nature of understanding. *These possibilities, however, are discerned, not demonstrated.* Philosophical hermeneutics is less a method of interpretation but more a disciplined practice of speculative sensibility.

Thesis Ten: Philosophical Hermeneutics Is a Negative Hermeneutics

The tactical arguments underpinning the skepticism with which philosophical hermeneutics regards the ambitions of method, reveal philosophical hermeneutics as a *negative* hermeneutics. Like the arguments of negative theology, the skeptical contentions of philosophical hermeneutics cause the formal languages of philosophical methodology to ring hollow.[42] In its negative mode, philosophical hermeneutics demystifies the universal claims of method by particularizing them as expressions of a specific historical *Weltanschauung*. Yet a discernible signature of philosophical hermeneutics is that its *via negativa* effects a shift from a perspective of doubt regarding universal claims to meaning toward an ecstatic, almost untheorizable, awareness of the inexhaustible possibilities for understanding. The tactical criticism that a given understanding is particular in relation to a "whole" body of other interpretations has negative consequences when viewed epistemologically, but when interpreted ontologically the consequences are affirmative. The invocation of what an interpretation *is not* (i.e., not the whole of the matter) stands on the skeptical intuition that neither being nor the complexities of its subject matters can be encompassed by (or made subject to) the methodological will of a cognitive subject. When considered ontologically, however, the invocation of what an interpretation is not (i.e., not the whole of a subject matter), affirms and magnifies what it is, that is, one element of a larger nexus of mutually related understandings. The affirmation speculatively illumines the presence of horizons of meaning which inform but nevertheless transcend that interpretation. The negative disclosure of what a particular interpretation is not (not the whole of the matter) allows our understanding of it to become more but never fully what it is. The interpretation is grasped as a component within a larger nexus of related understandings. The negation of an interpretation's claim to being the whole of a given matter is the *via negativa* by means of which that which cannot itself be stated (the infinite horizon of understanding underwriting each and every particular interpretation) is speculatively invoked. As a negative hermeneutics, philosophical hermeneutics esteems understanding as a *mysterium*.

Thesis Eleven: Philosophical Hermeneutics Looks upon Linguistic Being as a "Mysterium"

Philosophical hermeneutics is persuaded that linguistic being is a *mysterium*, an ineffable and irreducible source of understanding. In this respect, two points

are immediately worth making. First: when philosophical hermeneutics returns to older ways of thinking and their idioms, a more radical intellectual
thrust within its character becomes apparent. Following the example of Heidegger's reappropriation of *theoria* as the proper contemplative mode for philosophy, Gadamer's speculative theory of language (and its associated language
ontology) looks back to Bultmann's demythologization of religious language.[43]
Philosophical hermeneutics contends that some features attributed to religious experience are not specifically religious but are, as the instance of
hermeneutic transcendence exemplifies, integral elements within the dynamics of profound experience itself. The example of hermeneutical transcendence suggests that what has been appropriated as religious experience
properly belongs to an experience of *linguistic being.* In its approach to the *mysterium* as a thought limit, philosophical hermeneutics anticipates the recent
poststructuralist rapprochement with religious thought.[44] If, however, an experience of linguisitic being as a *mysterium* does not belong to another of level
experience, how is it present in our ordinary experience of language? An answer to this lies in the second point. The invocation of the *mysterium* of linguistic being attempts to clarify rather than mystify the ontological dimensions
of understanding. In its debate with scientific method, philosophical
hermeneutics would have been on stronger ground had it invoked more
clearly the distinction between mysteries and problems. The mysterium of linguistic being is of importance to philosophical hermeneutics for the following
reasons. Philosophical hermeneutics is *philosophical* in that it attempts to for-
malize the preconditions that enable but are not directly objectified in
hermeneutical experience. Formalizing them as the *Vorverständnisse* that underwrite interpretative activity invokes something of even larger status. What
we allude to here is that which, although beyond us, opens us toward a speculative experience of language. Although the source of interpretation and speculative insight, linguistic being cannot itself be directly experienced in the
modes of understanding it makes possible. Though it cannot be brought
under the control of method, it nevertheless abides within every thought and
word. Thus, the philosophical dimension of philosophical hermeneutics remains resolutely *hermeneutical.* What is philosophically invoked as the source
of understanding (linguistic being) can only be approached through the speculative *experience* of language. The philosophical impetus within philosophical
hermeneutics seeks to elucidate a subjectively experienced intimation of that
linguistic objectivity that abides within and has been present within us all
along. In so doing it guides us toward a sense of that which though beyond
conceptualization remains within and is revealed by every speculative
experience of language.

The mystery of linguistic being plays three discernible roles within philosophical hermeneutics. First, there is its ontological role. As that which informs our particular language horizons and yet transcends them, linguisitic being is a *mysterium*. As such, it is the ontological *source* of understanding. Nevertheless, as that which enables and is manifest in individual acts of understanding, linguistic being "surpasses all understanding" and thereby sets a limit to all claims to understanding. Second, there is its ethical role. Philosophical hermeneutics has an evident regard for the mystery of persons. The hermeneutical experience of difference opens a differential space between what I have come to grasp as myself and how others come to see me. The experience of difference reveals that we are always vulnerable to different narratives of ourselves and, hence, to becoming different to ourselves. Understanding is an endless task precisely because we are, in this respect, mysteries to ourselves. Furthermore, the mystery of the other's irreducible difference must always be defended as a challenge to the complacency of our self-understanding. Third, there is its tactical role. The incompleteness of meaning and the finitude of understanding suggest that the subject matters (*die Sache*) of understanding are mysteries rather than problems. Mysteries are not subject to the methodological solutions that problems are. A problem denotes a difficulty demanding a solution. Mysteries, however, can only be understood more deeply. They are not to be explained away but are to be discerned as an ever-present limit to our understanding. They invoke an apprehension of a radical limitlessness. This does not appeal to a mystical conception of understanding as being unbounded by any limitation. It invokes the hermeneutical insight which quietly insists on the point that the extent to which there is always more to be said or more to be understood is itself without limit. Four: there is its strategic role. The notion of linguistic being as a *mysterium* is of strategic importance to philosophical hermeneutics because it grounds a speculative experience of language in something beyond subjectivity and establishes a principled otherness which ethically moderates hermeneutic practice. As D. E. Cooper remarks, "Mystery affords measure."[45] The notion of linguistic being as a *mysterium* gives substance to the belief that there will always be something more to be understood. The ever-present possibility that the world and the other person can *always* reveal something other than what is presently understood of them, limits the adequacy or completeness of our present understanding. And yet, precisely because it preserves such limits, philosophical hermeneutics inevitably invokes a radical limitlessness to understanding. The notion of linguistic being as a *mysterium* formally underwrites the hermeneutic axiom that there is always more to be said and that our understanding can always be more complete.

As a limiting concept, the notion of linguistic being as a *mysterium* silhouettes several other important aspects of philosophical hermeneutics. It reveals that the concerns that philosophical hermeneutics has about philosophies of an apodictic form are well grounded. That linguistic being cannot be captured in a propositional framework does not render the notion of such a being meaningless. To argue that it is meaningless assumes that only the apodictic form of language is appropriate for communicating what we know of the world. Philosophical hermeneutics insists that it is not the apodictic form of philosophy that is wrong but the claim that only what can be restricted to its forms of representation counts as legitimate knowledge. What this claim refuses to recognize is what philosophical hermeneutics doggedly defends, namely, that as the speculative experience of language reveals, language, and the knowledge it conveys, operates disclosively. The notion of linguistic being as an ever-present but inexpressible *mysterium* underwrites the case which philosophical hermeneutics tirelessly defends, namely, that unspoken meaning is indeed communicated through the said. As we shall see in chapter 4, this conviction is fundamental to both Gadamer's critique of nihilism and his defense of the dialogical.

The notion of linguistic being as a *mysterium* lends additional support to the claim that philosophical hermeneutics is a life-affirming mode of thought. If linguistic being cannot be objectified in language, there might seem little point in talking about it. However, given the reality of language's speculative capacity, philosophical hermeneutics is inclined to the opposite conclusion. It is, indeed, precisely because linguistic being surpasses linguistic objectification that we *must* struggle to talk about it. Philosophical hermeneutics endeavors to educate a lot more than just our powers of reason. It is persuaded that the mysteries which demand an ever-deeper understanding solicit *all* our sentient responsiveness. What we cannot bring into words explicitly does not preclude the possibility of being spoken about indirectly. Such a mode of speaking can bring a subject matter to mind speculatively without claiming to state exclusively what it is. Philosophical hermeneutics believes that precisely because our experiences of truthfulness, of beauty, or of love cannot be fully objectified in language, it is necessary to struggle toward and to seek out the appropriate words for such experiences. When such words *work*, they open speculative pathways into a deeper understanding of what the subject matters of intense experiences both entail and can, indeed, command of us. To turn one's back on the difficulty of finding such words or to refuse the attempt on the grounds that only apodictic speech is legitimate, demeans and impoverishes the complexities of human experience. It also spurns in nihilistic fashion what human life and learning depend on, namely, the ceaseless endeavor to extend and deepen experience. In the words of Andrew Louth, "The desire to make all reasoning explicit manifests a dislike of evidence, varied, minute, complicated and a desire for something producible, striking, decisive; such a desire is really irrational, as it fails to understand the realities of human behaviour and action."[46]

CONCLUSION:
PHILOSOPHICAL HERMENEUTICS AND THE QUESTION OF OPENNESS

Having outlined the eleven theses that characterize the nature and concerns of philosophical hermeneutics, several summative observations about philosophical hermeneutics and the question of openness can be made. The eleven theses make specific individual assertions about the nature of philosophical hermeneutics. They also operate collectively. When read alongside each other, additional aspects of philosophical hermeneutics disclose themselves. Although philosophical hermeneutics is not a systems philosophy, these theses have a discernible systemic connection. That hermeneutical understanding requires difference, connects with the claim that philosophical hermeneutics has an ethical disposition. That philosophical hermeneutics involves a theory of transcendence, links with its assertion of an ontology of the in-between. Yet none of these connections imply that philosophical hermeneutics embraces a philosophically closed position. If philosophical hermeneutics did aspire to such closure, any description of hermeneutic practice as seeking an encounter with difference would be self-contradictory. These eleven theses point to sound additional reasons as to why philosophical hermeneutics can be defended as being philosophically open. Three points are at issue.

First: *philosophical hermeneutics has no fixed character as a philosophical stance.* The eleven theses collectively imply that although philosophical hermeneutics has discernible commitments to a language ontology, to an ontology of becoming, and to the historical shaping of understanding, as a *practice* of encounter and engagement it cannot be explicitly defined as a closed theory. What philosophical hermeneutics is, is essentially generated from its practice. This can be elucidated as follows. To maintain itself as a *practice* of understanding, philosophical hermeneutics can only draw on what it has *already* encountered in the other and the different. To deepen its responses, it must test what it has learned in previous engagements against what arises in new encounters. If philosophical hermeneutics were governed by a strictly demarcated theoretical core or essence (thereby restricting its response as a practice), any educative transformation would become subject to limitations. Flexibility (openness) of response would be restrained.[47] It might be objected that the pursuit of unbiased openness is vacuous. The possibility of hermeneutic transcendence depends upon a degree of closure, upon having, in the first place, attachments and commitments capable of being transformed. New encounters can only probe existent preconceptions. If past experience determines what we are vulnerable to, it also can restrict the forms of encounter we are open to. Is the claim that philosophical hermeneutics advocates a genuine openness of encounter sustainable? It is unsustainable only if the notion of complete openness is itself sustainable but, arguably, it is not. A complete openness of outlook—a contradiction in terms—would render us hermeneutically blind. It would dispossess us of those preferences and prejudices that open us toward the possibility of hermeneutical transcendence precisely because they guide our existential interests. As Gadamer insists, it is experience itself that opens us to the possibility of further experience. The commitment of philosophical hermeneutics to openness is not, therefore, to a formal (vacuous) principle but to a concrete disposition. The disposition in question is to remain receptive to the possibilities for hermeneutic transcendence that the contingencies of our historical and cultural thrownness continually *open* us toward.

Second: *philosophical hermeneutics is not a theory but a practice, which is philosophically informed by a cluster of philosophical insights concerning the nature of history and language ontology.* The open nature of philosophical hermeneutics reveals an affinity with both Adorno's constellar thinking and Nietzsche's perspectivism. Neither of these modes of thought are, strictly speaking, "theories." Each of them strives to bring a cluster of intelligent intuitions into play. As a consequence, these modes of intellectual disposition exhibit a deep skepticism about the ability of systematic philosophical reasoning to capture its object. Adorno, for example, insists that as an object is always in excess of its concept, a constellation of conceptual coordinates is required to gain a fix on its characteristics. Nietzsche, on the other hand, suggests that an object is the objectification of several perspectival relationships. Gadamer asserts in a similar vein that the objects of understanding (*Sachen*) are beyond interpretative capture yet each interpretation has the potential of bringing a different *aspect* of its intended object into view. Philosophical hermeneutics displays an evident sympathy for Nietzsche's conviction that the more interpretations we gather concerning an object, the greater our objectivity will be. Yet by promoting a catholicity of interpretation, philosophical hermeneutics seeks to achieve more than adding to the stock of available perspectives. Bringing contrasting interpretations into dialogical juxtaposition is intended to provoke an "event." Promoting the emergence of new and unexpected interpretations has the purpose of not just extending but also of *changing* how we think about a subject matter. The aim is, in other words, to effect a moment of hermeneutic transcendence.

Third: *philosophical hermeneutics offers an intimation of linguistic being as a mysterium.* There is a perfectly legitimate sense in which philosophical hermeneutics places understanding *beyond* understanding. As a mode of practical wisdom, it knows that neither the roots of its understanding (*Vorverständnisse*) nor its objects (*die Sachen*) can be fully understood. If so, it might appear, as Hamacher contends, that understanding cannot fully comprehend itself.[48] Nevertheless, philosophical hermeneutics has a strategic motive for defending this position. The motive reveals the reason why philosophical hermeneutics emphasizes the *event* of understanding. Stress is laid on the *event* of understanding because its random but autonomous occurrence breaks the subject's control over understanding. It subjects the knowing subject to the disclosures of understanding. Understanding is no longer subject to the will of the subject. That understanding *occurs*, that it happens to us contrary to our willing and doing, is something about which Gadamer is emphatic. Indeed, it is precisely because the event of understanding severs understanding from the control of a subject's will to power that philosophical hermeneutics opposes any defense of a perspectivism that merely extends a subject's *repertoire* of interpretations. Philosophical hermeneutics does, however, defend those forms of perspectivism which stretch and challenge a subject's expectations, prompting it to reorientate its understanding. However, though such an aim is laudable, should it rest upon what appears to be philosophical mystification of understanding?

There is no getting away from the fact that the underlying conditions (*Vorverständnisse*) of understanding and, hence, of philosophical hermeneutics itself can never be made fully explicit. Does the case in favor of the *mysterium* of understanding amount to nothing more than a subjective assertion? There are several points to be made here. That which is incomprehensible *in totum*, is not unintelligible *in pares*. The preconditions of understanding can always be rendered more explicable, though never fully so. Furthermore, inasmuch as philosophical hermeneutics pursues the *event* of understanding, it cannot spare its own presuppositions from challenge. Nevertheless, it can still be asked whether the reluctance of philosophical hermeneutics to theoretically specify (albeit provisionally) the ground and nature of its understanding, actually frustrates the quest for what it seeks. By failing to specify its methodological grounds, does not philosophical hermeneutics isolate itself from the very critical debate that might expose it to presuppositions other than its own? In response, philosophical hermeneutics might ask how the pursuit of methodological transparency can avoid subordinating understanding to the will of the subject. Is such a pursuit a confession of tiredness and of a yearning for the intrinsically open and uncertain horizon of understanding to be closed? Does not the demand for methodological transparency tacitly require that the hermeneutic principle of the "always more" be understood be abandoned? Philosophical hermeneutics can argue that its very vagueness about method keeps the question open while the *demand* for methodological legitimacy seeks to close it and to diminish the possibility of hermeneutical transcendence. Nevertheless, the question remains: Is the strategic commitment to the *mysterium* of understanding a matter of subjective conviction? Insofar as philosophical hermeneutics remains loyal to a distinct experience of linguistic being rather than to the conventions of formal philosophical demonstration, its strategic commitment to the *mysterium* of understanding does express a subjective conviction. However, we must be careful not to miss the absolutely critical point. Philosophical hermeneutics is not indicative of a subjectivism but of a philosophy of subjectivity which strives to discern phenomenological and ontological objectivities that manifest themselves *within* subjective experience. Consequently, the strongest defense that philosophical hermeneutics can muster concerning the enigmatic nature of understanding is itself of a speculative nature. The issue is a subtle one and is inflected with the ancient antagonism between poetry and philosophy. The point is not that it is a contradiction in terms to demand that the nature of a *mysterium* should be rationally articulated. The point is rather that if one *understands* what it is about language that makes it a *mysterium*, one knows that any demand for its elucidation is misplaced. Here, philosophical hermeneutics is plainly consistent with its nature as a philosophy of subjectivity, that is, as a philosophy of *experience*. The *mysterium* of understanding is not subject to proof of demonstration, but it is demonstrated by our experience of the speculative nature of language. To have had an *experience* of the speculative depths of language is to know that the grounds of understanding can never be rendered fully transparent. The demand for such transparency betrays the fact that something vital about language being has not been understood. Even though they are not subject to formal demonstration, philosophical hermeneutics insists that our *experience* of being within language teaches certain truths. Philosophical hermeneutics is a mode of thinking that dwells on and, indeed, suffers what is given in linguistically mediated experience. Accordingly, it reinvokes the value of experientially acquired wisdom (*paideia*) and endeavors to show that what is learned from experience extends beyond the strictures of formalized method. It attempts to interpret and elucidate what linguistic experience itself *discloses*, namely, that we are grounded in and belong to something larger than ourselves. In this respect, philosophical hermeneutics clearly strives to discern the objectivities within subjective experience. Accordingly, it sides with the Sophists against Plato on the question of whether poetry teaches wisdom.[49]

Strictly speaking, it is not the explicit teachings or viewpoints of specific poetic texts per se nor the skills of rhetoric that concern philosophical hermeneutics, but what our immersion in the poetic (speculative) dimensions of language itself implicitly reveals. What philosophical hermeneutics actually defends is not the language of poetry but the *poetics of language*. By this we mean those movements of words, those language events, that confront us with the finitude of our understanding and reveal the extent to which we are always prone to being ambushed by unexpected insights. They disclose the dependence of understanding upon a linguistic being that transcends our immediate horizon and reveals our hermeneutic shortsightedness. These truths are not subject to formal demonstration but they can be shown, that is, they reveal themselves within the experience of being practically engaged in the language world. The inseparability of such truths from our ontic immersion in language is precisely the "poetic" wisdom that philosophical hermeneutics passionately defends.

Such wisdom is not, strictly speaking, the preserve of poets per se. All language speakers are in principle acquainted with the speculative dynamics of words. The importance of poetry for philosophical hermeneutics lies in the fact that, firstly, it takes seriously the inward revelations the speculative dynamics of language afford. Secondly, the public deployment of the written word can reveal that private experiences of shifts in meaning have less to do with individual subjectivity and more to do with the collective mode of linguistic being that we participate in. In this respect, the wisdom of poetry teaches the frailty of human understanding and shows that within that frailty, "no man is an island." Neither is philosophical hermeneutics making a claim about the superiority of the poetic voice over philosophical or scientific method. What it opposes is the ideologization of science and method as the *sole* criterion of truth. Philosophical hermeneutics fears the consequences that follow from the ideological privileging of method: the chastising of poetry's silent wisdom as arcane and the pillorying of inward experience as arbitrary and subjective. The privileging of method threatens to desensitize the claims of inward experience and to erode the objectivities they acquaint us with. It devalues the sensibilities of subjectivity and weakens our grasp upon those experiential truths appertaining to the finitude of our understanding. Yet it is these truths that appertain to the nature of our linguistic being. Though they cannot be the subject of outward demonstration, they are nevertheless made manifest in our *experience* of language. It is appropriate, then, that philosophical hermeneutics should passionately defend the inward wisdom of poetry (and what it opens us to) against those such as Plato who would displace it. Defending the enigmatic nature of understanding is, therefore, not an apologetics for mysticism. To the contrary, to acknowledge the *mysterium* of understanding is to acknowledge the linguistic *reality* that sustains and yet transcends our subjective being. It is to acknowledge that *language* teaches.

To conclude the first part of this essay, we suggest that philosophical hermeneutics is not a method but a philosophical practice, a mode of reflective philosophical orientation underpinned by a discernible cluster of philosophically methodical insights and intuitions concerning language, ontology, becoming, and history. With regard to the elucidation of these insights, philosophical hermeneutics has not been its own best advocate. However, these insights should and can be articulated and this essay will endeavor to do so without contravening the claim that understanding is essentially a *mysterium*. The eleven theses put forward serve as an initial clarification of the nature of philosophical hermeneutics. They map out the philosophical commitments of philosophical hermeneutics so as to better triangulate its nature. Though the character of understanding and the intense complexity of hermeneutic engagement cannot be captured in words and concepts, their *careful* use can nevertheless deepen and extend our experience of understanding, drawing us closer to what it entails. The sensitive use of language to deepen experience is an integral part of what philosophical hermeneutics understands as *Bildung* (education) and it is to this notion that we now turn.

CHAPTER TWO

Philosophical Hermeneutics and *Bildung*

Ich Hab Mein Sach auf Nichts gestellt (I have founded by
affair on Nothing).
                              —Goethe, *Vanitas, Vanitatum Vanitas*

"This floating world . . ."
                                                        —Basho

INTRODUCTION

No term in Gadamer's philosophy is more worthy of undergoing a form
of Heideggerian *Destruktion* than the concept of *Bildung*.[1] The term has a
variety of plain and obscure meanings, which respectively imply formation, cultivation, and education. These lend the term its traditional grav-
itas though some of the more conservative resonances have notably
detracted from the *philosophical* intentions of philosophical hermeneutics.
The concept plays a central role in philosophical hermeneutics. It emphasizes that hermeneutic understanding is formative in that the deepening of hermeneutic experience prepares for further, more demanding
experience. Hermeneutic understanding involves the process of comprehending what a text or dialogue imparts and in addition the development
of a practice, of a preparedness or skill in changing mental perspectives.
The nurturing of such preparedness is an integral element within the refinement of a hermeneutic discipline. The formation of these virtues is
what is meant in part by *Bildung*. Acquiring a mental openness and a flexibility of response toward the strange and unexpected is to have become
experienced in the discipline. This process of formation, of acquiring
experience by acquaintance, is what is rendered in German as having

become *gebildet*. Given the strategic and tactical importance of the concept, it is important to seek a degree of clarity about the meaning of the term in its various shadings.

Strictly speaking, *Bildung* is not a distinct concept but an indistinct idea, something that might be described in Baumgarten's terms as a *campos confusionis*.[2] Far from being negative, such a description positively affirms the conceptual field or cluster of ideas which the notion of *Bildung* denotes. *Con* + *fusion* implies an intertwining and mutual determination of elements which is appropriately paralleled by Gadamer's notion of a fusion of horizons (*Horizontverschmelzung*). As will become evident, *Bildung* involves an intricate blending of most of the theses proposed above concerning the nature of philosophical hermeneutics. *Bildung* entails a sense of the other and different, of history and tradition, of ethical dependence, of the transcendent within both language and cultural formation as well as an acute experiential awareness of the finitude of one's hermeneutic horizons. The constellation of ideas that constitute *Bildung* is complex and for the purposes of this essay it is important that they be carefully charted. Before we enter this constellation of ideas, one theme in particular should be emphasized. It concerns the tendency in German philosophy to convert nouns into verbs so that, for example, history becomes not merely the grammatical subject of a sentence, that is, something inherited, but also that which historicizes, that which actively influences our attitudes toward the past and future. We see a similar stress in the use of the word *understanding*. The noun *Verständnis* implies *that* which we understand (or have an understanding of) whereas the verb *verstehen* refers to the *process* of understanding itself and/or that which the process of understanding brings about. To have achieved an understanding of a certain subject matter implies that a certain body of knowledge has been acquired. To have an understanding of driving implies the acquisition of a goodly number of technical facts and legal information. Philosophical hermeneutics is not interested in the acquisition of facts and information (knowing *that*) but in what happens as a consequence of embarking upon such a quest for knowledge. It is interested in how in the pursuit of learning to drive, one learns of oneself, of the impetuous nature of one's reactions to others, of one's arrogance about controlling fast machines and about one's confidence in dealing with awkward or dangerous situations. Acquiring facts and information about a practice does not per se make a good practitioner. Yet one cannot become a good practitioner without acquiring such information. What is important here is the transformative capacity of the process of engaging with a subject matter. Only by exposing oneself to the *experiences* that the practical acquisition of the facts and skills pertinent to a given discipline expose one to, is it possible to become a good or, rather, a *more understanding* practitioner. Philosophical hermeneutics includes, then, as part of the *event* of understanding, the transformation of awareness and attitude that can occur as a result of *engaging* with a given subject matter. It is vital to grasping the way *Bildung* operates within philosophical hermeneutics that it too should be understood as functioning as a substantive entity *and* as a formative process.

One meaning of *Bildung* is culture. *Bildung haben* can mean to be or to become cultured. To be cultured supposes an acquaintance with the various stocks of knowledge and attitudes that constitute a given culture. Yet acquaintance with such knowledge does not of itself enable one to become cultured. Once again, it is the *process* of becoming intellectually and spiritually tempered by the experiences one undergoes during the acquisition of such knowledge that matters. In that it attests to the transformative educative process of formation through engagement and involvement, philosophical hermeneutics embodies a defiant defense of the humanist tradition. That which makes the process of becoming *gebildet* difficult to grasp is that although it may require a sound training in the language and history of a culture, such formation is not reducible to a matter of training alone. A good technical training acquaints one with a predictable set of responses to problems, the skill often being in the discovery of the problem rather than its solution, which is normally well prescribed. However, there is no manual that prescribes the proper response to difficulties posed by literature or philosophy though immersion in a given cultural tradition might enable one to *discern* more clearly what *appropriate* responses might be available. Whereas it is in the nature of technical training to offer known and, therefore, predictable responses to problems, immersion in a cultural discourse does not teach predictable answers. This is because within such discourses there are not "problems" to be solved but difficulties that can only be understood more deeply. The process of "becoming cultured" does not involve the acquisition of predictable responses to known problems but the accumulation of sufficient practical experience within a discipline so as to offer a spontaneous and yet informed response to a question permitting it to be grasped in a new and unanticipated way. Indeed, it is precisely the ability to risk informed but spontaneous judgments which the humanities aim to foster. Becoming acquainted with predictable solutions to known technical difficulties does not transform the technology within which such learning takes place. However, it is precisely because they can transform our understanding of a discourse, that the unpreictable and spontaneous judgments nurtured by a cultural discipline are so valued. Becoming cultured (*Bildung haben*) is enabled by being rooted in a given culture (*Bildung*). It is exhibited by the successful acquisition of a practice understood as the ability to make appropriate, insightful, and indeed unpredictable judgments capable of transforming our understanding of the cultural process out of which they emerge. There is, in other words, a complex ontological interdependence between *Bildung haben* and *Bildung*. *Bildung haben* requires the prior existence of a specfic *Bildung*. However, no *Bildung* or culture can sustain its being without being renewed by the various processes of *Bildung haben* which constitute it. *Bildung* is therefore also ontologically dependent on *Bildung haben*. The being that is *Bildung* is transformed by the understanding it facilitates. As we shall see, being open to the risks and challenges posed by the transformative powers of "understanding" and, what is more, knowing how to navigate that openness is regarded by philosophical hermeneutics as a qualitative mark of having become *gebildet*. Having made these initial observations about the nature of *Bildung*, let us turn to the broader characteristics of Gadamer's deployment of the term.

Gadamer invokes the term *Bildung* for a strategic purpose: to demonstrate that alongside scientific and technical knowledge there exists another body of knowledge that is not the result of proof and demonstration but is laid down by tradition, received wisdom, and practical experience. Despite this laudable purpose, the invocation of *Bildung* is problematic on various counts. Contrary to Gadamer's belief, the term does not decisively distinguish between the *Geisteswissenschaften* and the *Naturwissenschaften*. As recent debates have indicated, judgments deriving from tradition and received practice operate as effectively in the sciences as they do within the humanities.[3] Furthermore, the term has a number of troublesome associations. If Gadamer wishes to stress what is (supposedly) at the term's core—the invocation of an unending educative (experiential) process—the term's association with a *specific* bourgeois educational ideal needs to be decisively broken. Despite these obstacles, the term and the body of ideas associated with it are *more* fundamental to the cause of philosophical hermeneutics than philosophical hermeneutics itself recognizes. This part of our essay will argue accordingly that as a body of thought philosophical hermeneutics points toward a radical extension of the meaning of *Bildung*. Its primary characteristics are as follows.

1. *Bildung* is both a formative and transformative (dialogical) *process* implicit within the dynamics of hermeneutic encounter. Insofar as the parties involved in a hermeneutic encounter emerge from it thinking differently about themselves, *Bildung* is transformative. *Bildung* is, in part, the process of coming to understand what we have understood differently. *Bildung* is formative in that it brings something into being from *within* the encounter. It forms a hermeneutic civility between those who are obliged to each other for becoming different to themselves, and who know that they are dependent upon the other for opening potentialities for understanding that are not presently theirs.

2. *Bildung* plays a foundational role within philosophical hermeneutics. Its pursuit requires engagement with the ontological basis of understanding (linguistic being, history, and tradition) and involves recognizing the metaphysical *contingency* of received traditions and stocks of knowledge which establish understanding's initial orientation. Philosophical hermeneutics conceives of such stocks as being built up, consolidated, and perpetuated by the communicative interactions that constitute a cultural community. When thought of as specific cultural tradition, *Bildung* constitutes the historically formed but metaphysically contingent ground upon which the possibility of understanding rests.

3. *Bildung* offers a conceptual defense against the charge that philosophical hermeneutics is both relativistic and inclined toward a romantic privileging of subjectivity. The notion suggests how such an accusation can be reversed. Philosophical hermeneutics argues that to spurn the claims of historical and aesthetic understanding in the name of an abstract mode of knowing stripped of the influence of tradition and subjectivity, is to act (perhaps unwittingly) in the name of nihilism. As we have argued, philosophical hermeneutics does not seek to remove subjectivity from understanding but to become aware of the received objectivities within it. As cultural formations and patterns of interpretation constitute such objectivities, it is appropriate that *Bildung* should have such a prominent place in the reflections of philosophical hermeneutics. In addition, it is important to remember that *Bildung* and becoming *gebildet* is a practice, the formation of a capacity,

the ability to keep oneself *open* to what is other in order to gain a sense of oneself (TM, 15; TM, 17). *Bildung* therefore has a clear ethical dimension. However, let us consider the nature of *Bildung* and its place in philosophical hermeneutics in greater detail.

BILDUNG AS A TRANSFORMATIVE AND FORMATIVE PROCESS

There is a clear philosophical connection between the terms *Bildung* and culture (*Kultur*). It is explored by Ernst Cassirer in his neglected essay *The Logic of the Humanities*, where he distinguishes between nature and culture concepts.[4] Two forms of process are differentiated, the transformative and the formative. The transformative involves new realignments and reconfigurations of what is already in process. The formative signifies the emergence of something new, distinct from any reconfiguration of what already exists. Cassirer's distinction attempts to establish a formal differentiation between the *Geisteswissenshaften*, which involve concepts of the formative, and the *Naturwissenschaften*, which depend upon concepts of the transformative. Our concern is not with Cassirer's attempt to differentiate modes of knowing but with the initial distinction between the transformative and the formative. Gadamer's employment of *Bildung* alludes to *both* processes. It does so not because he is implying that *Bildung* has a natural science dimension but because he conceives of it as a process of social formation that maintains its being by means of constant transformation and renewal. In so doing, it also gives rise to formative elements. *Bildung* embraces the transformative: it alludes to those processes of cultural formation that maintain and renew themselves by means of their continuous becoming. *Bildung* also invokes the formative: it implies the processes of *Bildung haben*. Indeed, Gadamer's argument presses farther than Cassirer's insofar as he implies that the transformative elements of culture (*Bildung*) and the formative elements of becoming cultured (*Bildung haben*) are mutually dependent. Just as the educative process of becoming cultured (*Bildung haben*) is enabled by being rooted in a given culture (*Bildung*), no culture can maintain its being unless its participants seek to engage with and transform its principal concerns. Whereas for Cassirer the importance of the transformation-formation differentiation is to articulate a *distinction* between disciplines, for philosophical hermeneutics its importance lies in differentiating the elements that enter into *productive relation* within the event of understanding. This suggests that what philosophical hermeneutics grasps as understanding involves an active relation between the transformative and the formative. On the one hand, the possibility of individual understanding is preconditioned by a set of transformative relations that constitute the given cultural horizon within which that understanding takes place. On the other hand, the horizons that facilitate understanding cannot remain in being unless engaged with and transformed by individual acts of understanding. Gadamer's enquiry into *Bildung* is an enquiry into the nature of understanding.

Insofar as philosophical hermeneutics grasps understanding as coming to understand differently, both *Bildung* and understanding can be described as transformative processes. As such, both can entail the process of coming to recognize the difference between what was once understood and what is now understood. As a consequence, both *Bildung* and understanding can be *transformed,* acquiring new coordinates and points of reference and reconfiguring themselves accordingly. However, as we have suggested, *Bildung* and understanding are also *formative.* As dialogical processes, they can generate new (social) formations of understanding, formations that are not entailments of or, indeed, variations on what was previously understood. Gadamer follows Hegel in asserting that *Bildung* suggests processes of formation. The meaning of *bilden* embraces notions of forming, fashioning, and structuring. But as Hegel recognizes, the point is that unknown to itself, the hermeneutic subject in the processes of engaging with and fashioning cultural objects finds itself transformed and refashioned by the very processes it engages with. Philosophical hermeneutics grasps that being subject to both the transformative and formative aspects of understanding is indeed part of what becoming *gebildet* means. This is plainly part of the enquiry philosophical hermeneutics undertakes into the question of what happens to us in the processes of understanding. Becoming *gebildet* is part of what the process of understanding entails.

As we have suggested, whereas Cassirer uses the differentiation between the transformative and the formative for the purposes of an epistemological distinction, philosophical hermeneutics is interested in their mutual ontological interdependence. What facilitates this interdependence and allows hermeneutic experience to be both transformative and formative is the fact that *Bildung, Bildung haben,* and understanding are all grounded in *linguistic being.* However, before we elaborate this point, a further brief comment on the distinction between *Bildung* and becoming *gebildet* is relevant.

The failure of such commentators as John Caputo to draw the distinction between *Bildung* (a specific cultural form) and becoming *gebildet* (a process of educative formation) promotes the misunderstanding that Gadamer's invocation of *Bildung* is no more than a reactionary apologetics for a bourgeois ideal of education and culture.[5] However, once the above distinction is firmly drawn, the more radical nature of Gadamer's approach to *Bildung* becomes apparent. For Gadamer to advocate a bourgeois conception of *Bildung* would deprive the term of its *formative* spontaneity. Now, given the link between hermeneutic experience and becoming *gebildet*, limiting the spontaneity of the latter by restricting it to a *specific* educational program weakens the central ethical claim of philosophical hermeneutics regarding keeping oneself open to the other and to the different. Critics of philosophical hermeneutics might reply that such a defense of openness is rather vacuous. Philosophical hermeneutics may not be guilty of perpetrating a bourgeois conception of *Bildung*, but it surely does defend modes of intellectual and sensible refinement. Philosophical hemeneutics undoubtedly upholds performative norms. It demands that hermeneutic practices maintain a receptive orientation toward the unexpected. Such practices can be carried out well, with due sensitivity and care for the other, or executed badly.[6] However, *in riposte* to both this and Caputo's objection, to say that an educational practice can be executed according to virtues the practice itself generates, is *not* to say that the practice is determined by (or advocates) an externally imposed institutional ideal or program. That *Bildung* is linked to a notion of formative spontaneity undermines the charge that Gadamer's defense of the term is an apology of a bourgeois mode of education. The notion of spontaneity is also central to *Bildung's* ontological status as the groundless ground (the metaphysically contingent precondition) of hermeneutic understanding.

Chapter 1 of our discussion claimed that although philosophical hermeneutics is not a philosophical system, the different elements within its reasoning are systemically connected. The transformative and formative character of *Bildung* and hermeneutic experience relates to metaphysical issues that underpin philosophical hermeneutics and its ontology. To claim that *Bildung* and the process of becoming *gebildet* are genuinely *formative* is to claim that they are, metaphysically speaking, *without* intrinsic essence. Neither mode of becoming is governed by a predetermined essence. In this respect philosophical hermeneutics follows both Nietzsche and certain postmodern idioms of thought in denying a necessary ground to understanding and interpretation. Philosophical hermeneutics differs from Nietzsche's defenders in that it does not conclude that the

absence of a metaphysical ground for understanding condemns all interpretation to being arbitrary and subjective. Indeed, the invocation of *Bildung* is central to the claim of philosophical hermeneutics that the
absence of a metaphysical ground for understanding does not render its
claims arbitrary. However, before we explore how *Bildung* gives a compelling weight to the claims of understanding we should return to the
issue at hand. The claim that both *Bildung* and becoming *gebildet* have no
intrinsic essence has a curious consequence. If becoming *gebildet* entails
the ability to enter a dialogical relationship with the unfamiliar and unusual, the claim implies that the outcome of such an engagement is neither certain nor predictable. If so, Gadamer's conception of becoming
gebildet as the practised pursuit of a dialogical openness toward the unpredictable is, philosophically speaking, distinguishable from the bourgeois conception of *Bildung*. Philosophical hermeneutics *does not* posit an
"ideal" humanity that education should anticipate and be disciplined by.[7]
If anything, philosophical hermeneutics implies that humanity is a
species whose very essence is always in question. Philosophical hermeneutics is not prescriptive in this respect. It does not state what ought to take
place within in the process of becoming *gebildet*. To the contrary, it attempts to discern *what* takes place. It views the formative aspects of *Bildung* not as the acquisition of a given theory but as the consolidation of a
practical process, a process of becoming open to interaction and exchange. Inasmuch as philosophical hermeneutics conceives of the shaping of experience as *dialogical*, the process of becoming *gebildet* is
essentially interactive and not an individualistic pursuit. Unlike Nietzsche, philosophical hermeneutics does not propagate the romantic individualism associated with the bourgeois interpretation of *Bildung*. To
accuse philosophical hermeneutics of reinvoking a bourgeois conception
of *Bildung* is to fail to see the truly formative and dialogical nature of the
term. We can now return to a question raised above. If hermeneutical experience is an instance of becoming *gebildet* and if *Bildung* entails a
process of hermeneutical transformation, what links the two? The ontological concept of linguistic being provides the connection.

    The intractable question of the relation between the origins of lan-
guage and the development of human culture need not presently concern
us. It is clear that the development of both language and culture are intimately connected. Wolfgang Iser argues that language and culture involve
processes of constant translation, processes that facilitate interchange between the foreign and the familiar.[8] Philosophical hermeneutics contests
that language and the hermeneutical transformations it affords are not

merely linked to the process of *Bildung* but actually generate it. How, then, do language, *Bildung*, and *Bildung haben* interact?

Philosophical hermeneutics presents language, culture and community as being tightly interwoven. Their mutual interaction is made possible by the formative and transformative capacities of language. The following points are pertinent.

1. To be a language speaker is to be a member of a *Sprach-welt* and to find that one's words are both guided by and give expression to the values and dispositions of that world. To be a competent language speaker is to be shaped and formed (*bilden*) by that world.

2. Gadamer's conception of a linguistic horizon is not merely passive. Our linguistic being betrays the fact that we have already become communalized by a speech world. The question for Gadamer is how participation in language brings a speech-created world (a cultural community) into being that transcends the limitations of our natal linguistic horizon(s)? How does participation in language bring a hermeneutic civility into being and how does involvement in language effect a genuinely *formative* moment of *Bildung*?

3. The term *Bildung* is connected with the English words *building* and *construction*. When Richard Rorty describes involvement in hermeneutics as *edifying* he misses the poignancy of his description. With its link to the term *ed-ifice*, edification refers to that which *builds up*.[9] Language enables the building of a cultural world over and above the natural environment. As Gadamer recognizes, written language in particular has the capacity to transcend the limitations of both the physical—the location and duration of the spoken voice—and the restrictions of a given historical horizon.[10] As Marino notes, the emergence of a *civitas litterarum* has a liberating *formative* potential not merely in the sense that a *disciplinae liberales* frees writing from the needs of religious consecration[11] but because it surpasses the linguistic constraints prescribed by birth and geography. A *civitas litterarum* crosses (transgresses) the frontiers of local history and culture.[12] In this sense, the formative capacity of language effects a genuinely creative moment of becoming, the emergence of something that did not previously exist.

4. The liberating capacity of a *civitas litterarum* attests to
    Seneca's dictum *vita sine litteris mors est*. It also attests to
    the *transformative* and indeed speculative functions of
    language. The speculative power of language reveals that
    because of their etymological connection to other
    language worlds, countless words within my particular
    horizon are charged with unexpected resonances. This
    underwrites one of the key propositions of philosophi-
    cal hermeneutics: *the possibility of hermeneutic transcen-
    dence rests on the fact that being a citizen of a particular
    "Sprachwelt" does not exhaust my linguistic being*. Terms that
    have a reach beyond my immediate linguistic horizon
    can seem formal and remote. Yet they can also achieve
    an immediate particularization within my present hori-
    zon. The Latin word *histrionicus* (behaving for the benefit
    of others) no longer seems so remote when we hear its
    traces in the English word histrionic. Ordinary everyday
    words gain weight and majesty when they site what is
    seemingly beyond our horizon within our horizon.
    Thus, the speculative function of language attests to the
    fact that because of our linguistic being we not only be-
    long to the *Sprachwelt* of our birth but also to the larger
    community of speech worlds that influence our own.

5. A *civitas litterarum* extends the possibilities for her-
    merneutic translation and transcendence. Like my im-
    mediate horizon, a *civitas* is formed out of or involves
    the merging of speech worlds and is, as such, related to
    other modes of linguistic being. Membership of a *Sprach-
    welt* is a condition of entering a *civitas litterarum*. The in-
    terests, themes, and expressions of that *civitas* can
    accordingly be brought into and potentially *transform*
    those of my initial *Sprachwelt*.

6. By no means should such a *civitas* be thought of merely as
    a community of *literati*. It also forms around the subject
    matters (*Sachen*) a given language brings into being. A *civi-
    tas* is a communion of ideas, a social affiliation, which
    exchanges and gives access to ideas. More specifically,
    it is communion formed by those who are open to the
    possibility of hermeneutic transcendence. Philosophical
    hermeneutics demonstrates, then, how a linguistic *Bil-
    dungsprozess*—submission to the hermeneutical experience
    of becoming different to oneself—is genuinely formative

in that it can promote a hermeneutic civility that transcends the initial horizons of birth and custom.

7. A *civitas litterarum* does not emerge as a community merely because of an insight into how diverse language worlds are commonly rooted in linguistic being. Its emergence is a reflection of the genuinely formative dimensions of language. The latter bring something into being that was not present before: a *civitas hermeneuticum* forms from out of the dialogical space hermeneutic exchange facilitates.

8. In addition to the formative capacity of linguistic being, there is also the transformative capacity. The transformative capacity relates to both the speculative and epiphanic functions of language in that it reveals what was there before, that is, the hidden, forgotten, or unseen connections between language worlds. The transformative capacity of language opens us to both our own horizons and to those of others. The capacity to understand more requires a collision of horizons and is dependent upon ongoing encounters with the other and otherness.

9. In answer to the question, "How do language, *Bildung*, and *Bildung haben* interact?" philosophical hermeneutics contends that it is linguistic being that grounds the interactions. First: linguistic being facilitates the formative dialogical space out of which a *civitas* can emerge. A *civitas* presupposes the prior existence of *Sprachwelten* but is not reducible to any one of them. In this sense, the formative capacities of linguistic being are genuinely creative. Linguistic interaction enables the formative emergence of *Bildung* and, hence, of that hermeneutical *civitas* which stands on the recognition that we are reliant upon the other in order to become different to ourselves. Because of linguistic being we are also able to become transformatively different to ourselves. We can leave our initial horizon and become located in between what we have understood ourselves as being and what the other now shows us we are capable of becoming. Seeing this difference is part of the process of becoming *gebildet* and it is language that grounds this formative possibility. Citizenship of a hermeneutic *civitas* is made possible by the formative capacity of language to generate "speech

worlds" that transcend the indigenous horizon of any speaker. The transformative capacity of language effects changes in our self-understanding, and changes in our comportment toward a subject matter can change the form of how that subject matter is communicated. In other words, *Bildung* (the formative) and *Bildung haben* (the transformative) are different but mutually dependent modes of linguistic being.

10. To move outside our native language horizon and to engage with another—"to walk on the wild side" as Hans Peter Duerr puts it—does not leave us adrift between communities, as some believe.[13] It is, rather, to find oneself in a new hermeneutic *civitas*: it is to lose or alter aspects of one's former self by being among those who (in relation to each other in their otherness) have become open to becoming other themselves. From an ontological perspective, linguistic being opens the possibility of a linguistically enabled *ex-change* (becoming different to oneself) and, in this respect, linguistic cum hermeneutic interaction can also be genuinely formative. Such *ex-changes* may transform the understanding of those who undergo such experience but they also form a community of "border crossers," a community of those who recognize that they are indeed dependent upon the other for becoming other to themselves. This has the clear implication that "becoming *gebildet*" is not a matter of attaining a *level* of culture but of attaining the ability to be responsive to, to adapt to, and to pass between different cultural borders.

The interconnectedness of language, culture, and community indicates that whereas the process of becoming "experienced" (*gebildet*) involves the assimilation of a body of ideas, it does not entail the acquisition or the imposition of a *determinate* set of ideas. This strengthens the claim that philosophical hermeneutics articulates a philosophical *practice*, a *way* of responding to the challenges and transformative possibilities inherent within our linguistic being. Becoming *gebildet* is, in effect, the venture of living within, hazarding, and responding to the cross currents of ideas (subject matters) that flow across linguistic and cultural borders. Its transformative and formative aspects are made possible by linguistic being.

BILDUNG AND TRADITION

The notion of *Bildung* as a culturally transmitted stock of knowledge links it with the concept of tradition. Conservative interpretations of *Bildung* associate it with the handing-on or with the inculcation of (so called) *traditional* values. As the foregoing remarks about the *formative* and essentially interpretative nature of the *Bildung* and *Bildung haben* suggest, philosophical hermeneutics is not just, as Habermas and Caputo have argued, a thinly disguised apologetics for an anti-Enlightenment view of tradition. The seminal point overlooked by such critics is that the German term *Überlieferung* emphasizes a process of *transmission* rather than the maintenance of long established customs. That which is "given over" (*tradere*) in the form of practices or outlooks is not merely received as an unmediated given but assessed and assimilated according to the contemporary concerns of the world into which it is received. Apart from the additional question of how *selective* the past is in transmitting its own character, what a given horizon understands as its past, is not the past simply transposed into the present but a presently interpreted and partially constructed past. What is transmitted as tradition is not necessarily received as transmitted: reception is interpretative. Here philosophical hermeneutics betrays an Hegelian inflection. What is of importance is neither that which is transmitted per se nor that which is received but the transformative space which the processes of transmission and reception enable. This repeats the connection between tradition and becoming *gebildet*, for the tradition philosophical hermeneutics seeks to uphold concerns the *practice* of remaining open to the strange and the unfamiliar.

The connection between tradition and practice stands on the argument that what tradition transmits is not so much a body of work but more a manner or style of becoming engaged with those sets of questions or subject matters that are communicated by a body of received work. A *canon* is conceived by philosophical hermeneutics not as a body of set received works but as a cluster of issues, questions, and practices that over time have come to define a certain cultural practice. A key intellectual signature of philosophical hermeneutics is once more discernible. A received body of material work is not important in itself. Its importance is *expressive*: how it expresses a distinct practice of engaging with or comporting oneself toward questions and subject matters and how, in so doing, it clears new dialogical approaches to those subject matters. As sites of dialogical engagement, the works of a canon open and reopen the hermeneutical space of the in-between in which the possibility of becoming different to ourselves is preserved.[14] Tradition conserves difficulty for it is only in the strenuous difficulties of hermeneutic negotiation with the past and the other that the possibilities for hermeneutic translation and transcendence can be preserved.

The interpretative nature of historical transmission and reception drives philosophical hermeneutics toward an *engagement* with tradition that is both critical and dialogical. The philosophical character of this engagement can be outlined as follows.

1. The Heideggerian orientation of philosophical hermeneutics toward the thrownness and placedness of human existence places it at odds with any *tabula rasa* psychology. It argues that as hermeneutic subjects we do not respond to the world with an untuned sensibility or with a mind without any sense of focus or direction.

2. As linguistic beings, we negotiate the world with an outlook already sensitized by our historical and cultural horizon. Our very sense of being placed within a given horizon is indicative of having becoming receptive to the claims of the subject matters that shape that horizon's intellectual terrain. The process of becoming so sensitized is part of what it means to have become *gebildet*.

3. When we meet with the past, we meet with similar, varied, and different responses to such subject matters. We know that belonging to a certain intellectual or moral tradition disposes us toward questions concerning (say) the relationship between the demands of the state and the rights of conscience. Yet the particular demands of our contemporary world may reveal our inherited understanding of this relationship to be inadequate. Hermeneutical consciousness emerges as the play between hermeneutical differentials: past conceptions of a subject matter differentiate present conceptions of that subject matter and vice versa. The hermeneutical differential keeps the question of the nature of that subject matter open. It guarantees that the task of understanding is difficult.

4. Philosophical hermeneutics is intensely interested in such experiences of difficulty. They form part of what philosophcial hermeneutics refers to as the "negativity of experience." By disclosing the anomalous relationship between our experience of actuality and how a received body of thought

configures that reality, such experiences betray a moment of
difference. These moments are of considerable importance
for philosophical hermeneutics. They confront us with a
moment of difficulty. They probe us with the question,
"Given that previous interpretations of a subject matter can
be found wanting, how are we to respond to the claims that
that subject matter nevertheless makes upon us?" Difficulty
is one of the drivers of tradition.

The importance of seeking a response to such a question indicates
that philosophical hermeneutics does not celebrate the past in and for its
own sake. Nor, like Dilthey, does it seek out tradition in order to escape the
intellectual demands of the present. The opposite is the case. Philosophical
hermeneutics seeks out tradition precisely because of the need to respond
to the intellectual ruptures within our contemporary horizon. The relation
between philosophical hermeneutics and tradition is acutely dialogical. The
nature of this relationship can be brought out by two questions. First: if
philosophical hermeneutics advocates a contemporary response to received
subject matters and if the need for such renewal arises from the disjuncture
between past interpretations of a subject matter and how it shows itself in
the contemporary world, why concern oneself with tradition let alone endeavor to strengthen its voice? Second: isn't the endeavor to engage with
subject matters in a fresh and innovative way condemned to an inescapable
circularity? Since such subject matters give shape to our *Vorverständnisse* and
determine the range of our hermeneutic sensitivities, would they not also
mediate how we consciously reconfigure them?

In response to these two questions, it must be argued that traditions
are not monological monoliths.[15] They are plural in voice, embracing varied, sometimes conflicting approaches to a subject matter. It does not follow (as Nietzsche and other modernists seem to have believed) that
because *some* of the formative historical presuppositions that guide contemporary perspectives fall into question, one should have nothing further to do with *all* historical tradition. The fact that we cannot ever fully
escape our *Vorverständnisse* makes the modernist yearning for radically different semantic frameworks illusory.[16] Yet because we cannot escape them
does not mean that we cannot amend aspects of their nature. Seeking out
and responding to *other* historical voices and *other* ways of handling a subject matter is a means of outflanking some of those specific presuppositions that shape our particular response to a subject matter. Developing
receptivity toward the voices of the historical other is fundamental to

philosophical hermeneutics' dialogical engagement with tradition. By employing the forces of disjunction, it endeavors to expose the presuppositions that pilot our contemporary perspectives. The dialectical use of tradition to expose the limitations of our contemporary modes of thought has more than a critical purpose. It is in fact a tactic in the service of a greater end. It seeks a creative *reengagement* with the discourse around a given subject matter. *In other words, the critical-dialectical engagement with tradition aims to reopen, to renew and, to return us to those differential spaces that make hermeneutic transcendence difficult but possible.*

Tradition as conceived by philosophical hermeneutics is not just a stock of inert ideas or values but a manner or style of becoming critically engaged with (and thus continuing if not extending) the influence of a set of questions or subject matters. The ontological importance of such engagement is that it perpetuates the being of that tradition. Tradition is not static: engagement with its critical tensions sustains it. Like Heraclitus's "world order," a live and healthy tradition maintains itself by being at war with itself. MacIntyre describes traditions as being continuities of conflict.[17] In this respect, the case philosophical hermeneutics makes for engagement with the subject matters of a tradition is nothing less than a case for onto-ethical commitment. Just as the being of a hermeneutic subject is made possible by the subject matters, which both inform and open his or her intellectual horizon, so the continued being of those subject matters depends upon a subject actively engaging with them. The being of a hermeneutic subject and the being of a tradition's subject matter are mutually dependent.

In conclusion, far from offering a conservative apologetics for tradition, philosophical hermeneutics conceives of tradition as a transformative *Bildungsprozess* which enhances the being of both the hermeneutic subject and of the subject matters that shape its horizon. Such a conception of tradition *does* indeed seek to conserve stocks of inherited knowledge but, here, two important qualifications are necessary. First: what drives philosophical hermeneutics toward a defense of tradition has nothing to do with an allegiance to conservativism but to an anti-essentialism. Precisely because human beings have no behavior determining essence, the conservation of experience and its lessons is vital. Human beings have nothing to maintain their effective being other than acquired experience. Tradition embodies a stock of such experience (ways of knowing how to go about things) and is therefore of vital existential significance for philosophical experience. Second: it is not the conservation of experiential knowledge alone that is important. Conserving acquired stocks of experience is of course important, but more important is the fact that without them, the disjunction between past and present could not be kept open. Without such differences not only would the possibilities for hermeneutic transcendence be undermined but the opportunities for a tradition to maintain its being through renewal would be also be diminished. The absence of essence makes the question of inherited experience and tradition a crucial one.

BILDUNG AND THE QUESTION OF ESSENCE

To shed the reputation of propagating a conservative conception of *Bildung*, it is important that philosophical hermeneutics should articulate *Bildung* as a process without *an* intrinsic determining essence. This is precisely what philosophical hermeneutics undertakes to argue. Philosophical hermeneutics does not deny that a *Bildungsprozess* can exhibit and retain emergent characteristics but it does deny that such a process is driven teleologically. In order to sustain this claim, philosophical hermeneutics must distinguish the process of becoming *gebildet* from the values history has attached to it. Before we explore this distinction, the following can be noted.

In committing itself to a form of anti-essentialism, philosophical hermeneutics follows Nietzsche and Heidegger in their rejection of the metaphysics of presence (essence). This entails a rejection of the Aristotelean tradition of teleological thinking that infuses the historical purposefulness of the Hegelian and Marxist tradition of historic-political thought. What philosophical hermeneutics retains from the Aristotlean tradition is not the notion of history as "unfolding" but the idea of practice. Philosophical hermeneutics deploys the notion of practice in a historical manner but the deployment is free of any reference to teleology and essence. As we shall see, combining the notion of practice with an anti-essentialist stance lends an urgency to the debate about tradition.

According to Dilthey, we are only able to understand ourselves by means of what we do. What we do is express ourselves in and through political, historical, and social action. No single action can betray who and what we are. Only from a historical awareness of what we have done can we glean a more general picture of human nature and its possibilities. Dilthey is often read as if he were a Hegelian. A particular expression must be understood as if it were part of a greater whole that reveals itself historically. Dilthey does not, however, have to be read as an essentialist.

If we are *indeed* what we do, history does reveal what we are but not in the way that the essentialist thinks. A continuity of historical actions need not be taken as the external expression of an internal nature but rather as indicative of a series of practices that acquire and stabilize a set of characteristics over time. Our nature is formed from emergent sets of practical responses to the demands of the natural and social environment. For a creature without essence, the wisdom and insights of inherited practice are vital. It has nothing else to rely on. What such a creature is (or rather becomes) is formed by its communicative interactions both with its circumstances and with others. In other words, such a creature is formed by what is historically revealed as its practices. As we shall see in subsequent sections, the notion of practice is central to how we understand ourselves as hermeneutic subjects. That philosophical hermeneutics is not committed to a form of humanistic essentialism can be supported by a number of other observations.

In affirming that understanding is a mode of being, philosophical hermeneutics asserts that understanding happens. As an expression of understanding, *Bildung* also happens. As such, *Bildung* entails immersion within processes of understanding, which facilitate interchange between the foreign and familiar.[18] As linguistic beings, it is almost impossible to avoid the transformations of understanding that our linguistic involvements draw us into. Gadamer comments that experience is not something that anyone can be spared.[19] Experience and the transformation of outlook that it brings occurs to us whether we wish it or not. Now, to note this is not to attribute a value or end to such a process. It is merely to acknowledge that it takes place. Yet, the fate of the term *Bildung*, which is so barnacled by distinct cultural values, is such that the *evaluation* of the process is more often than not confused with its actual nature. The confusion is not new. The ancient world both humanized and moralized the transformative capacities of language and claimed, as Marino observed, that literature "prepares youth for humanity" by undertaking the formative role of defining, revealing, and perfecting the "human essence."[20] The nineteenth-century German understanding of *Bildung* also subordinates the process of transformation to the end of achieving a given human ideal of sensibility and delicacy. With regard to one of *Bildung*'s German synonyms, *Kultur*, Heiddeger called for its deconstruction (*Abbau*) precisely because it imposed an "ideal of humanity," which mistook merely secondary matters for fundamental ones.[21] Removing the concept of *Bildung* from a teleological framework has, then, the advantage both of reemphasizing its nature as a transformative process and of restating the intractable link between language processes and cultural formation. To argue that the process lacks an essence, aim, or purpose says nothing against its actuality but a good deal against its misappropriation by humanistic metaphysics. The nadir of such metaphysics enables philosophical hermeneutics to place the relationship between humanity, language, and culture on another more practical footing.

For philosophical hermeneutics, the historical question of what philosophical humanisms are must be separated from the ontological question of what it means *to be human*. Philosophical hermeneutics follows Nietzsche in his belief that that the only essential feature of humanity is precisely its lack of essence: *to be human is to be that being for whom the question of what it means to be human is always itself in question*. It is to be a being whose only privilege is to be a being whose nature is always at issue.[22] Such ontological openness returns us to the formative capacities of language and understanding (*Bildung*) and gives particular prominence to the notion of practice.

Human beings do not live in a cultural vacuum but in a speech-created world of their own making. Such a world provides human beings with their preunderstanding and initial points of existential orientation. The status of such preunderstanding increases for beings without an essence. Being without essence implies that humans have nothing but acquired knowledge and experience to rely on. The worth of such knowledge does not lie in the fact that it is inherited per se but in whether it can be proven as reliable when tested against the strange and the unfamiliar. Iser suggests that hermeneutic encounters appear to involve "feedback" systems: acquired experience regulates the character of responses to the unfamiliar while the success of those responses assesses the adequacy of acquired experience.[23] The ontological commitments of philosophical hermeneutics are consistent with the view that, like other living systems, human beings are *autopoietic* in nature, that is, they continually produce and reproduce themselves in processes of communicative interaction. Varela suggests that an essence would be extraneous to the workings of such interactions and indeed would limit the range of possible responses.[24] These arguments suggest that precisely because as human beings we have no intrinsic essence, we are able to constitute and transform ourselves continually throughout our hermeneutical encounters. It is clear then that the notion of linguistic engagement as formative and the notion of "hermeneutic encounters" putting our being in to question are intertwined and that both are interlocked within the concept of *Bildungsprozess*.

A lack of essence does not deprive humans of potentiality or possibility. The contingent fact of being shaped by a certain language horizon and of acquiring its *Weltanschauung* creates initial possibilities for becoming different to ourselves. Having a historical past means that there are always past potentials that have yet to be fulfilled. The capacity to become "more"—to realize potentialities for being that are not presently ours—depends upon hermeneutic encounters with the other and the different. Maintaining an openness toward such encounters facilitates two transformative functions, one retrospective and the other revelatory. The retrospective aspect of encountering the strange and unfamiliar challenges expectancies. It prompts a hermeneutic subject to summon up and review what it implicitly presumes (*Vorverständnisse*). This might initiate a review of such presuppositions or lead to a deeper commitment to them. The revelatory aspect of an encounter with the strange and unfamiliar concerns the opening of hitherto unexpected avenues of thought, which can change the coordinates of how a hermeneutic subject understands itself. Both the retrospective and revelatory aspects of hermeneutic encounter are transformative. They allow us to understand ourselves differently, either more deeply or in a way not thought of before. In either case, we, in Gadamer's phrase, "move on," and it is indeed precisely because we have no essence that we must endeavor to move on. To fail to move on and to atrophy within a limited and restricting repertoire of responses dictated by an essential nature would be to initiate a form of sclerosis within the hermeneutic subject. Gadamer never renounces his Hegelian conviction that movement is the very life of spirit.[25] In this respect philosophical hermeneutics aligns itself with an aspect of Hobbesian philosophy. Learning, insight, self-awareness and the transcendence it affords, are possible so long as the negativity of experience and its challenges keeps the hermeneutic subject in motion. By remaining open to new "experience," by being willing to test and to extend what we know, we place what we have learned under review. Only then are we able to reevaluate and perhaps transform what we know and become "more." Such transformations betray that we are without essence. According to philosophical hermeneutics, it is precisely because we are without essence that our being remains in question, and it remains in question only insofar as we remain responsively open and endeavor to "move on." It is plain, then, that philosophical hermeneutics cannot promote a *specific* type of *Bildung* (education). If, as Gadamer proclaims, movement is the life of spirit, what is important is attuning hermeneutic subjects to that movement, to initiating subjects into the life of questioning and its insatiable movement. The hermeneutic encounter conceived as a transformative process is an ever completing but never completed form of *Bildungsprozess*. The greater emphasis is placed on its ontological rather than its pedagogical nature. Articulated as a mode of being, the *Bildungsprozess* enunciates a form of philosophical practice. The nurturing of a disciplined openness and the purifying of our receptiveness to the strange and different is what makes the hermeneutic encounter a *Bildungsprozess*. Acquiring such a practice is not a matter of bookish learning but more a matter of experience, of acquiring from experience's bruises the navigational skills to voyage into the unknown and the unusual. Developing such a practice requires, as Heideigger recognizes, a deliberate choosing of what we already are, an affirmation of our transitory mode of being, an articulation of the way (*bio*) of life that is specifically ours, a conscious enhancement of (what is for us as essenceless beings) "the right form of life (*bios*)."[26] In Gadamer's words *bios* refers to a life form that precisely because it is essenceless has to interpret itself.[27]

BILDUNG AND THE IN-BETWEEN

This section will discuss what is entailed in the notion of becoming *gebildet* and will connect it with remarks in chapter 1 about the role of the in-between within philosophical hermeneutics and how the in-between connects with an experience of self.[28] As a prelude to this discussion, we need to establish the broad relationship between *Bildung* and becoming *gebildet* and show that this relationship reveals something of the intellectual style of philosophical hermeneutics.

Philosophical hermeneutics, as we have argued, is fundamentally a philosophy of subjectivity. This does not mean that it is a romantic philosophy privileging individual subjectivism. To the contrary, philosophical hermeneutics consistently betrays a Hegelian disposition to seek out that that is objective or substantive within the subjective. In the distinct language of nineteenth-century hermeneutics, Gadamer is disposed to interpret a subject's point of view as a *particular* expression of a more general *universal*, to appraise the subjective perspective as a particular moment in the historical unfolding of a *Sache*. The tactic is one of subsumption: the character and, indeed, individuality of a particular can be discerned more fully once set against the framework of the universal. The device reflects the ontological disposition of philosophical hermeneutics always to see in the subjective the presence of the wider linguistic and cultural horizons. It also echoes the conviction of philosophical hermeneutics that as hermeneutic subjects, whether we are aware of it or not, we are always "beyond" and "more" than ourselves. However, the tactic can be reversed. That which is "beyond" us might seem alien, other, and abstract until its presence in subjective consciousness can be demonstrated. The ability of hermeneutic understanding to oscillate between transcendence and epiphany reveals the nature of the connection between the notion of *Bildung* and the process of becoming *gebildet.*

One of the difficulties of getting to grips with what philosophical hermeneutics means by *Bildung* is clearly linguistic. Once an entity is named, there is tendency to believe that it stands for something specific. The named takes on the character of the name. However, it is clear that philosophical hermeneutics does not mean by *Bildung* a historically determinate form of culture or technical training. The word refers to a fundamentally experiential formative process, to the development of a mode of consciousness. In this respect, philosophical hermeneutics insists that *Bildung* is an instance of a universal that only becomes intelligible in relation to subjective consciousness, to the process of becoming *gebildet. Bildung*, it turns out, has little to do with subjecting the individual to the form of a supposed universal but with drawing out and refining that which is phenomenologically universal within the intense subjectivity of interpretative practices. The development of a consciousness of the in-between—the process of becoming *gebildet*—is an integral part of what philosophical hermeneutics regards as *Bildung*.

We have argued that the hermeneutical character of the *Bildungs prozess* implies that the latter is not a vehicle for the imposition of a specific intellectual regime or ideology. Becoming *gebildet* is concerned to open the space of what has been described above as the *in-between*. For Iser, the differential space of the in-between is generated by the process of interpretation itself. It is interpretative understanding which differentiates between the form of a culturally received subject matter and the form it assumes when translated into another horizon. Iser contends that the opening of this differential space incites the interpretative process into even greater activity. The more a process of interpretation seeks to transpose a subject matter into a new register or horizon, the more strongly the differences between the transmitting and receiving registers assert themselves. It is, however, in and between such differences that possibilities for hermeneutic transcendence arise.

The creation of such spaces is of strategic importance for philosophical hermeneutics. Voyaging into them permits us to learn, to see differently, and, thereby, to extend our horizons. It would appear, then, that the process of becoming *gebildet* or, to say the same thing differently, the process of becoming hermeneutically practised (accomplished) involves the following.

1. the ability to discern and to reside within the space *between* different horizons of hermeneutic orientation;

2. the ability to become sufficiently experienced to know that whatever past, present, or future experience presents, no experience is definitive: there is always more to be said and more to be understood;

3. the ability to be conscious of remaining in between past and future, neither ceasing to listen to the past nor becoming closed to the future;

4. the ability to approach the future as a space in which the unfulfilled potentials of past understanding can be realised.

These features allude to a philosophical point of some importance.

It may seem from the above that the process of becoming hermeneutically accomplished is one of refining subjective sensibilities. This indeed it is, but what must not be missed is that it is also a refinement of awareness of one's indisputable dependence upon what is objectively larger and other to oneself. This is what makes the process of becoming *gebildet* deeply humanistic. It demonstrates once more how the notions of the in-between and of a foundation without essence are interlinked.

The phenomenology of becoming *gebildet* which philosophical hermeneutics articulates is linked to a perception concerning the ontological interconnection between concepts of nothingness and fellowship (community). Given Gadamer's acquaintance with Heidegger and Nishitani, it is not unsurprising that philosophical hermeneutics should intimate such connections. The salient argument is as follows.

If as living organisms we are nothing, that is, have no predetermined essence or nature, everything we have become is a consequence of our interactions with like creatures within our environment. What we are (or have become) reflects our nothingness. Such nothingness neither determines nor precludes us from developing the responses to our environment that we have. Indeed, what we have yet to become is held within the encounters with the other and the different that we have not as yet gone through. Such nothingness emphasizes the ineliminable importance of our fellowship with the other. *Nothingness expresses the fact that what we have become and we have yet to become is inextricably linked to our interactions with the other.* Such nothingness establishes why being in-between is our proper mode of being. We are invariably in between what our interactions have and have yet to reveal of our potentialities. Nothingness articulates the transient nature of our "becoming": it is because we are essentially nothing that we can continually fold and unfold into fellowship with others.

This concept of nothingness is, in effect, a concept of absence. The absence of an essence that determines the character of our responses implies that the formative and transformative nature of our responses are themselves of the essence. Our nothingness emphasizes that what we have been, what we are, and what we may yet become is a consequence of our fellowship with others. The process of becoming *gebildet* not only reflects involvement in a hermeneutic *civitas*, it but extends and deepens it. Yet, is there not a paradox here?

If the process of becoming *gebildet* involves becoming "more," shouldn't we seek to pluralize and multiply the voice of the other rather then strengthening it as philosophical hermeneutics recommends? Is there not, in effect, a tension in philosophical hermeneutics between what is a deconstructive or Dionysian impetus to change and an Apollanian tendency to repetition and mimesis? There is, indeed, a tension between these two positions and, what is more, philosophical hermeneutics attempts to sharpen it.

Philosophical hermeneutics places primary emphasis not upon changing or altering the voice of the other but upon strengthening it to such an extent that it can induce significant alterations in our individual outlook. Thus, the Apollanian tendency within philosophical hermeneutics toward sameness has a Dionysian inflection. Strengthening the voice of the other can place the presuppositions of the hermeneutic subject under pressure. Philosophical hermeneutics does not aim to deconstruct the voice of the other but to strengthen it in order to deconstruct and open its own presuppositions.

That philosophical hermeneutics should emphasize achieving a change of outlook in the interpreting subject rather than in the other interpreted, is characteristic of its principal philosophical concerns. First, multiplying the voice of the other as an analytic or deconstructive exercise per se, does little to deepen a hermeneutic encounter. Increasing theoretically available options for reading or thinking differently does not in itself facilitate a change of orientation within a hermeneutic subject. Unless a hermeneutic subject is prepared to *engage* with the voice(s) of the other, no dialogue and hence no hermeneutic exchange can take place. Without a willingness to have one's horizons opened, seeking to deconstruct the voice of the other remains a subject-centered exercise. The absence of such a willingness makes it difficult to defend philosophical hermeneutics from the charge of being no more than an exercise in analytic or deconstructive imperiousness which employs the voice of the other merely as an occasion for the exhibition of its own will to power. Second, that a *Bildungsprozess* must risk its own presuppositions when it engages with an other, underlines the concerns philosophical hermeneutics entertains about the inappropriate use of method. The application of method whether philological or deconstructive remains subject centered. Method *dictates* the terms upon which the other is to be engaged. It can therefore straitjacket or sanitize the hermeneutic encounter by limiting the responsiveness of the interpreter to the interpreted. As a means of diminishing any hermeneutical risk on the part of the interpreter, method betrays a nihilistic reluctance to be open to the unpredictable and uncertain. Third, the outright advocacy of hermeneutical engagement, indicates that philosophical hermeneutics is committed to a clear *good*, namely, the maximization of hermeneutic exchange. Any limitation on the scope and extent of such exchange diminishes the hermeneutic *civitas*, impoverishes opportunities for hermeneutic transcendence, and slows the ability to "move on." Such limitation exposes our thinking to the danger of becoming stagnant for want of exposure to the strange and the other. While the *Bildungsprozess* of hermeneutical exchange should indeed be methodical in its rigor, it should not be limited to methodological restriction. Insofar as the *Bildungsprozess* is both unpredicatable and uncertain in its outcome, philosophical hermeneutics expresses a positive willingness to embrace the opportunities for understanding that are inherent in the ordinary and everyday uncertainties of our ontological condition.

It follows from the above that becoming *gebildet* involves the achievement of a qualitative level of hermeneutic engagement rather than the acquisition of formal knowledge per se. This suggests, once again, that philosophical hermeneutics and its defense of *Bildung* does not amount to an apologetics for a given form of education. The philosophical commitment philosophical hermeneutics makes to the historical finitude of understanding makes it questionable that philosophical hermeneutics could ever universally privilege what would always be a particular set of norms and prejudices. Philosophical hermeneutics is insistent upon the fact that what is received as the canon does not entail endorsing a specific

body of works that are supposedly superior to others. The canon philosophical hermeneutics defends celebrates not a specific body of works but
a body of questions, namely, those subject matters around which human
understanding locates its possibilities. This is not to say that philosophical hermeneutics does not esteem particular bodies of work. It clearly
does so, for, like all forms of practice, philosophical hermeneutics has a
criterion of best practice. This criterion concerns how far and how well
our understanding of a given subject can be transformed by an individual
work. What is esteemed is not a given *Weltanschauung* or tradition, not a
particular concept of genius or genre, but an exemplary response to a subject matter, a response to which we cannot remain indifferent because it
promises to transform our understanding of an issue and of ourselves.[29]
In conclusion, philosophical hermeneutics regards a work as canonical
when it opens a reflective space between a subject matter addressed and
how it is addressed in an exemplary fashion. In other words, the canonical work opens and preserves the space of the in-between. No wonder,
then, that philosophical hermeneutics celebrates the dialogical idiom in
philosophy and literature.

The ineliminable gap between meaning (the intended subject
matter) and its utterance (the specific way it is expressed) permits
philosophical hermeneutics to articulate a very specific sense of
"work," which relies directly upon the concept of the in-between. The
work a literary or visual art work undertakes opens the space between
meaning and utterance.[30] In this respect, an artwork is interpretative
in three respects: (1) it understands (receives) its subject matter in a
certain way, (2) it offers its own interpretation of that subject matter,
and (3) it displays its particular way of handling and contributing to its
subject matter. Such a work *works* the space between meaning and utterance. Insofar as a work discloses a subject matter, it points to something that is larger than is shown, namely, that dimension of a subject
matter which has yet to be seen or shown. By bringing to mind what is
in effect a transcendent "totality of meaning," the artwork reveals, by
contrast, the particularity of its rendition of its subject matter and reveals accordingly that its response is one of many other possible responses. The successful work commands the space that it opens,
carefully refining the space between reference and rendition. It is in its
ability to disclose and maintain this tension that the dialogical capacity of a work resides. This gives an important clue to why Gadamer
maintains that the voice of art expresses itself most effectively in the
interrogative mood.

Insofar as it opens the space that differentiates between meaning and utterance, the work *asks* the spectator how he or she might also respond to that space. Philosophical hermeneutics therefore invokes neither a psychological nor an emotional empathy with a work but invites a dialogical empathy. If I understand the work as a dialogical phenomenon (that it opens the space between the said and the meant), then, as a dialogical agent I must be able to understand that selfsame space in myself. If I understand what it is for an artwork to address a subject matter, I also understand what it is to address that subject matter myself. If I understand the question a work asks of a subject matter, I also understand what it would be for me to ask a question of a subject matter. Four important points arise from this.

1. The value of art lies not just in the fact that it can be interpreted as a response to a given subject matter. It is, much rather, that as such a response it can question the adequacy of our thinking about such a subject matter.

2. Part of the *work* of an effective artwork is to disclose the space between meaning and utterance. The task of an artwork is to *work* that space and, in effect, to reside within it. In so doing, it returns us to that selfsame space within ourselves.

3. If I am aware of the gap between presentation and subject matter in a work, I am brought to the awareness that self-awareness is not self-presence but a sense of becoming difficult to oneself, of realizing that there is an irremovable tension between how one interprets oneself and how one expresses such self-understanding.

4. The mantle that tradition therefore passes down is not so much a body of works but a becoming sensitized to a series of open but fundamental questions. What tradition passes on and what becoming *gebildet* awakens me to is the interrogative space of the in-between and the different ways of keeping that uncertain space open. It is another way of putting oneself into question.

This brings us back to a further aspect of becoming *gebildet* and its relationship to the in-between.

Though becoming *gebildet* cannot be universally characterized as involving a particular specific set of cultural values, it does involve acquiring a universally recognizable trait: becoming *distanced* from one's initial cultural horizon. However, such distanciation should not be understood as a formal estrangement or alienation. Becoming *gebildet* involves a loss of philosophical innocence, namely, the partially disorientating but exhilarating realization that how the world presents itself within one's initial language horizon is not necessarily how the world is. The distinction here is not Heidegger's division between *Welt* and *Erde*.[31] Philosophical hermeneutics insists that the "world" is not a noumenal *substratum* that exists apart from language. Rather, "world" is the totality of what can be said of it within all language worlds. Thus, no language world has a monopoly upon what the world is. Furthermore, when we acquire a different language, it is not a question of leaving our initial language world behind but of acquiring a new set of hermeneutic coordinates whereby we begin to see our initial world differently. Engaging with the interconnectedness of different *Sprachwelten* reveals the world of one's original horizon to be only one aspect of a greater complexity. Embarking from one's initial *Sprachwelt* permits one to place it among and between other such worlds, to discern its differences and thereby to allow it to become more itself. In this instance, a hermeneutic distanciation can engender a greater hermeneutic intimacy. Though becoming *gebildet* necessitates a prodigal departure, philosophical hermeneutics does not romanticize the moment of return (*heimgehen*). Learning to see the nature of one's language world relative to others means that one can never, phenomenologically speaking, return to that world as one once knew it. The process of becoming *gebildet* is more dialectical.

Entering a new *Sprachwelt* is not a matter of leaving one's native *Sprachwelt* behind. That native *Sprachwelt* operates as an initial directory for achieving a semantic coordination with a new cultural horizon: it is the basis from which one translates *into* the new horizon. Without such initial coordinates, all sense of learning to think and feel differently would be lost. There would be no sense of experiencing "more" or of having "moved on." Having acquired new linguistic and cultural perspectives, one cannot simply eliminate them or return to one's initial horizon as if one had never left. As has been previously argued, the hermeneutical experience of difference is not just a confrontation with the unfamiliar. It also entails a recognition of the familiar as having become strange precisely because of one's experience with the unfamiliar. Thus, the central point is reiterated: the process of becoming *gebildet* involves becoming attuned to the condition of being in-between.

The conceptual link between becoming *gebildet* and the condition of being-in-between emphasizes, once again, that philosophical hermeneutics does not privilege a particular set of cultural or educational commitments. If anything, it aspires to the hermeneutical transcendence of such fixity. The hermeneutic *civitas* which philosophical hermeneutics promotes concerns those who cross the boundaries of their native horizons and who acknowledge the foreign and the different as that which enables them to become different to themselves. Such a *civitas* is not a rootless cultural cosmopolitanism that feigns a bourgeois independence from any local horizon. The being-in-between of such a *civitas* is not negative but the fertile ground from which new fusions of understanding can spring. Thus, philosophical hermeneutics celebrates the places of the in-between, those places of transition, gathering, and ideational exchange. It defends a culture of public places and private transformations. In so many words, the connection between the process of becoming *gebildet* and the notion of a being in-between points to a phenomenology of hermeneutic consciousness. Such a mode of consciousness presupposes and expresses our metaphysical nothingness, which is another way of saying that, ontologically speaking, what we have become, and what we have yet to become, is inextricably linked to our interactions with the other. Becoming *gebildet* entails the refinement of a hermeneutical mode of being that maintains itself as a practice.

BILDUNG AND HERMENEUTICAL PRACTICE

If becoming *gebildet* entails the refinement of a hermeneutical being that is upheld as a practice, what is the nature of this practice? The process of becoming *gebildet* entails the acquisition of a practised receptiveness and courtesy toward what is strange, unexpected, and that which lies beyond our most immediate cultural horizon. It is a practice that seeks "eyes to see otherwise." The characteristics of such practice outline what is in effect the formation of hermeneutical consciousness.

Philosophical hermeneutics is indisputably phenomenological. Hermeneutical consciousness is presented as *intentional* in that it tends toward (or is drawn to) a subject matter (*Sache*). The relationship between hermeneutical consciousness and its intended object reveals why the formation of such consciousness develops a practical orientation toward the other. Hermeneutical awareness springs from a consciousness of differentials: the difference between what a text addresses (its subject matter) and how it addresses it, and the difference between the finitude of a given rendition of a subject matter and the endless ways it might be interpreted. The acquisition of hermeneutical awareness involves therefore a practised tolerance of the limits of the other and what is other.

The phrase "a practised tolerance of the limits of the other" conveys a duality of meaning, which once again emphasizes the importance of the in-between in hermeneutical thinking. The phrase suggests that instead of dismissing a claim or viewpoint outright, one is prepared to tolerate its mistakes, to tolerate that which *limits* it. In the eyes of philosophical hermeneutics most claims to truth are marked by the negative, by the limitation of their time and horizon. Such limitations deprive a claim of completeness and point to other ways of articulating it. The obvious question that arises is that if such claims to "definitive" truth are limited, why should such limits be tolerated? The historicist epistemology that underwrites philosophical hermeneutics not only negates definitive claims to truth but, at the same time, affirms the truth that such claims in their limitedness overlook or cover up. A hermeneutical analysis of what a claim or interpretation is not (i.e., not the whole of a given subject matter) reveals what that claim or interpretation nevertheless is (i.e., one element of a much larger nexus of responses to a subject matter). Thus, though a text is always limited in its claim to truth , it is those very limitations that open out onto the wider truths or subject matters that inform it. Hermeneutic consciousness is a practised tolerance of the limits of the other. Hermeneutical consciousness has learned that it is precisely because of such limits that the subject matters that reach beyond a text can be speculatively disclosed. Hermeneutical consciousness not only demands an ear for the voice of the other but an ear for the otherness that speaks through the other's claims. It is not only responsive to what the other has to say but also strains to hear what speaks through the other's voice. The practice of becoming *gebildet* therefore entails an ethical disposition.

Hermeneutic consciousness requires courteousness toward the other in order for that which speaks through the other to be heard. Indeed, it is precisely that which speaks through the other that allows us to enter into a dialogue with the other. The dialogue is not merely a trading of opinion. Derrida has criticized philosophical hermeneutics on the ground that "the hermeneutic good will"—the willingness to be open to the opinion of others—is a manipulative framework expressing a hermeneutic subject's will to power.[32] Letting the other have their say, Derrida suggests, is certainly polite but only a prelude to subjecting their opinion to critique. If hermeneutic dialogue consisted solely of the agonistic language of claim and counterclaim, this criticism would have some merit. Achieving the best or most persuasive argument or gaining the last word would, indeed, become the sole aim of an engagement. Mastery of argument and not the pursuit of hermeneutic transformation becomes the sole object of the exchange. Furthermore, technical superiority of reasoning can leave the presuppositions of the dominant interlocutor quite untouched while those of the less competent speaker can be needlessly displaced or left unrecognized. The aim of hermeneutical engagement is not, however, to achieve a mastery of adversarial argument but to use shared intellectual converse and intuition as a means to transcending and transforming one's initial presuppositions and outlooks.[33] Courtesy toward the other is not just an act of good will but a recognition of indebtedness. It is to recognize that our present self-understanding and its future possibilities are inseparably bound up with the other.

Such receptiveness is *dialogical*. It is self-evidently dialectical in that being open to the other risks having one's assumptions and outlooks "negated." However, hermeneutical engagement requires something more: a willingness to pass through the risks and suffering of an initial encounter in order to achieve a profounder level of *dialogical* exchange. Philosophical hermeneutics contends that the true subjects of dialogue are the subject-matters of given discourse, work, or text. What hermeneutical consciousness aspires to do is to listen to the subject matters that speak through the other's voice for it is a shared concern or a shared subject matter that enables that consciousness to approach the other dialogically rather than dialectically. If I approach the other dialectically, I adopt a more combative attitude toward him, listening not so much for what is being said but for the flaws in his argument. Dialectical engagement tends to remain subject centered. However, if I approach the other dialogically my approach is not combative: sharing a concern with the other over certain subject matters allows, potentially, the other's viewpoint to question the adequacy of my own perspective, to illumine its limits, to expose its blind points, or to reveal its advantages. The process is mutual, for the perspective of the other is also exposed to my own. In either case, different perspectives can be enriched or become "more" by mutual dialogical exposure. The encounter can promote a mutual transformation of orientation toward a given subject matter. The practice of philosophical hermeneutics does not seek agonistic, dialectical engagement with the other, for such engagements tend to promote the assertion and defense of the subject-centered. Philosophical hermeneutics is more concerned with the dialogical encounter with the other and with that which speaks through the other. The ethical orientation of hermeneutic practice entails a quiet modesty. It marks the acquisition of that knowledge which knows that whatever perspective we adopt with regard to a subject matter, it is as a limited *perspective* and that we will be reliant on the other for placing it in a new light. Hermeneutic practice recognizes its indebtedness to the other. It knows that our present understanding is dependent upon other and distant hermeneutical horizons. Such practice involves the ability to *listen* for the subject matters that speak through the other's voice.[34] It is, above all, the latter that constitute for philosophical hermeneutics the proper focus of *dialogical* exchange and which, thereby, establish the ground for (mutual) hermeneutic translation and transcendence.

BILDUNG AND SUBJECT MATTER (*DIE SACHE SELBST*)

Insofar as it regards *Bildung* (culture and tradition) as a vital formative process, philosophical hermeneutics belongs to that German philosophical tradition which gives great emphasis to the category of *becoming* (*Werden*), a term that invariably invokes a sense of "a moving away from and a moving toward something." In the cases of *Bildung* and understanding, such movement is measured not in terms of time and space but in terms of the shifts and alterations of orientation concerning the central questions and concerns around which cultural groupings gather. Indeed, the continuities and breaks in such orientations tend to form the historical narrative out of which the identity of given community emerges. These questions and concerns are named by philosophical hermeneutics as *die Sachen selbst* (subject or question matters). Becoming *gebildet* requires becoming literate with regard to the *Sachen* that form a given culture. It would, however, be a mistake to think of a culture as being structured by a determinate set of such forms. Like a vital tradition, a culture (*Bildung*) is upheld not just by a set of forms but by the transitions and transformations among them.

The rich suggestiveness of the term *Sache* stems in part from its ambiguous meaning. On the one hand, *die Sache* is treated as an *objective* entity that transcends the horizon of an individual's understanding. A *Sache* will have a scope of cultural and historical reference larger than any individual can grasp. For Iser, the meanings of words and the subject matters they address traverse different contexts in their history. Their denotation and connotation of meaning can never be within the orbit of a single language user.[35] On the other hand, *die Sachen* do not appear to be fully independent of individuals and their understanding. Subject matters would lie forever dormant if they were not made to function.[36] Their cultural effectiveness depends upon whether they are engaged with. This raises a question we shall consider below. How can that which is onto-logically autonomous be acted on or added to by individuals unable to master it?[37] Becoming *gebildet* is not just a question of the formation of an individual practice. The acquisition of that practice also entails engaging with and, hence, changing the cultural forms (*Sachen*) that enable that practice. *Bildung* as an ontological process of becoming sustains itself by means of mutual interaction. The *Sachen* that underwrite preunder-standing operate as the precondition of individual hermeneutic practices, but it is only by means of the effective operation of the latter that the *Sachen* underwriting such practices can function and be renewed. Once again, two of the major leitmotifs within philosophical hermeneutics be-come apparent. A subjective process assumes an importance because of the objectivities it makes discernible, which, at the same time, reveals to the hermeneutic subject its ethical obligation toward that which ontolog-ically sustains and yet transcends it.

Broadly speaking, Gadamer's term *die Sache* functions on a number of interrelated levels. An initial way of grasping a *Sache* is to conceive of it as the intentional object or thing that a statement or work refers to or is concerned with. As such, a *Sache* denotes the subject matter of an ex-pression, the substance of what is being addressed. It is important, how-ever, not to confuse a *Sache* with a physical object. For example, that the subject matter "landscape" can be rendered in many ways by artists nei-ther relativizes the motif, nor suggests that it exists apart from the ways it is interpreted. According to Gadamer, such a *Sache* is equivalent to what Husserl presents as the "thing-itself" (as opposed to the Kantian thing-in-itself). Over a period of time, Husserl contends that a *Sache* shows itself as a continuity of perceptions in which various perspectives on similar ob-jects shade into one another (TM, 447). For example, although Altdor-fer's and Turner's approaches to landscape are very different, each perspective helps co-constitute (with other related perspectives) the *Sache* that becomes historically effective as the genre "landscape."

A *Sache* must not be thought of as a Kantian noumenal thing-in-itself which stands outside the world of interpretation. The *Sache* "land-scape" is not the empirical ground of an interpretation. It is that conti-nuity of interpretations which in coalescing over time forms a common cultural theme or reference point that then effectively guides our percep-tions of the countryside. The *Sache selbst* is an ideal construct formed from a cluster of evolving perspectives. It is not their noumenal ground. In short, the constructed (emergent) nature of a *Sache* allies it to a theory of concept of formation.

Gadamer's thinking suggests that *Sachen* have a distinctly experiential origin. His comment that Aristotle believed that all perception (*aisthesis*) tends toward a universal (TM, 92) complies with Husserl's remarks about how a continuity of perceptions merge into one another to form a *Sache*. Gadamer takes this as supporting the view that the generalizing power of language is capable of grouping a variety of similar perceptions under the same name or concept. He is also aware, however, of Nietzsche's arguments concerning the formation of concepts and categories. Nietzsche adds a developmental twist to Hume's theory of the imagination. "After much groping and fumbling," Nietzsche contends, "there comes a point when in the formation of concepts and categories, different perceptions are collected together and given the status of a concept or category: from then on they count as something essential, as irrefutable, as a truth."[38] The contrast between Nietzsche and Gadamer here is instructive. Nietzsche regards conceptual and linguistic generalizations as falsifying the particularity of the perceptions from which they emerge. For Gadamer, however, the *Sache* permits the true distinctiveness of each perception to shine forth. Seen against the whole perceptual continuum to which they belong, the distinctiveness of each perceived aspect and how it adds to or detracts from that continuum becomes apparent.

Once a *Sache* has been formed and has entered the general vocabulary, it acquires an intellectual efficacy that transcends the circumstances of its provenance. Thus, the notion of ideology as originally articulated by Marx has come to mean a good deal more than its original definition (i.e., a way of thinking blind to a universal truth). Similarly, what is now covered by the term *aesthetics* would be beyond Baumgarten's grasp. Such examples do not imply that an original meaning has been corrupted or contravened. As we have seen in the case of tradition, in defending a continuity of meanings for a term, philosophical hermeneutics does not suppose that a *Sache* has one identical meaning. Subject matters, it can be argued, share the rope-like characteristics of Wittgenstein's description of general terms, that is, discontinuous strands are bound together so as to form an apparent identity. Discontinuous strands of meaning still inform how a semantic "whole" can be perceived. An identity of meaning would not permit a *Sache* to become more. Discontinuous strands of meaning offer a different perspective on the whole. They suggest openings or loose ends enabling other strands of meaning to be woven in, thereby adding to how a *Sache* might be perceived. It is, furthermore, precisely the moments of difference and discontinuity within a *Sache* that challenge our understanding (expectancies) of it. The discontinuities and differences of meaning within a *Sache* therefore contribute to the possibility of hermeneutic transcendence.

In time a *Sache* will come to mean incalculably more than its original creator(s) could have envisaged. Indeed, for a *Sache* to function, that is, for it to become historically effective, it must shade into meanings different to those associated with its first appearance. It is not the fact of such differences that interests Gadamer but the hermeneutic productivity of such differences. The realization that a *Sache* has come to mean something different than it once meant, can quite alter a hermeneutic subject's contemporary understanding of a term. The point here is that although the meaning of a *Sache* can, in part, be determined by the activities of a hermeneutic subject, that subject is also subject to the autonomous meanings of a *Sache*. In this sense, *Sachen* have an effectiveness of their own, for once they escape the particularity of their origin and enter general usage, they start to shape the preunderstanding of a given linguistic horizon.

How a hermeneutic subject deploys a given subject matter is never arbitrary. An articulation of a *Sache* will always be subject to how that *Sache* has shaped the historical horizon in which it is articulated. *Sachen* shape and orientate preunderstandings. As such they are key formative elements in what Husserl describes as the life world (*Lebenswelt*), that is, that anonymous world of presuppositions that grounds our subjectivity, which functions in all experiencing and thinking.[39] As an element within our life world, *Sachen* and their aspects evidently operate independently of the circumstances that produce them and are capable of generating unexpected circuits of meaning.

Sachen, it seems, have a double nature: First: they are the intentional objects of subjective consciousness, and second: they denote objective structures of meaning that influence how the world is assimilated. In the latter case, they form part of that reality beyond every individual consciousness that language makes visible (TM, 449). This duality of nature is central to what Gadamer describes as their factualness (*Sachlichkeit*). We do not experience a *Sache* in a vacuum but against a historical backdrop of received expectations not all of which are fully articulated. Both past and forgotten determinations of meaning as well as unrealized future potentialities of meaning are held within a *Sache*. Following Heidegger, Gadamer describes these aspects of meaning as "the withheld." It is, in part, the withheld dimension of a *Sache's* meaning that lend it its weight and depth. Furthermore, it is because we experience the nature of a *Sache* against the backdrop of previously experienced or expected aspects of a subject matter that "permits (us) to recognize its independent otherness" (TM, 445). A discernible distance between what we see of that subject matter and what that subject matter is in itself begins to manifest itself. A *Sache* can foreground itself "and become the content of an assertion" only because of an inherited backdrop of expectancies against which it can be experienced as such. Gadamer argues accordingly that a sense of the weight, of the depth, of the sheer givenness or factualness (*Sachlichkeit*) of a subject matter is dependent upon a consciousness of being in the presence of something that is in part hidden and undisclosed. Gaining a sense of the full magnitude of a *Sache* entails becoming sensitive to its negative dimension, that is, to the presence of those dimensions of its meaning that are withheld. For this reason Gadamer argues that whatever arises as an expressible matter of fact can do so only in relation "to the surrounding (but inexpressible) whole that constitutes the world horizon of language" (TM, 446). This explains why philosophical hermeneutics insists that *Sachen* and our understanding of them can never be fully objectified or theorized in statements but can only be made manifest or evident by the speculative dynamics of language.

The untheorizable aspects of *Sachen* are apprehendable through language's *speculative* ability to bring the *withheld* dimensions of their meaning to mind. For philosophical hermeneutics, the speculative capacity of language has nothing to do with the use of propositions to reduce a Sache's nature to a series of assertions. It concerns that careful and sensitive use of statements that bring their intended object into the listener's mind. The speculative movement of language has the power to invoke and to summon such objects. Gadamer remarks that "the finite possibilities of the word are orientated towards the sense intended as towards the infinite." A person who has something to say seeks and finds the words to make himself intelligible to the other person.

> This does not mean that he makes "statements" [for] . . . in a statement the horizon of meaning of what is to be said is concealed by methodical exactness. . . . To say what one means . . . to make oneself understood—means to hold what is said together with an infinity of what is not said in one unified meaning and to ensure that it is understood in this way. Someone who speaks in this way may well use the most ordinary and common words and still be able to express what is unsaid and is to be said. (TM, 469)

In another seminal paragraph, Gadamer argues,

> Every word breaks forth as if from a center and is related to a *whole*, through which alone it is a word. Every word causes the whole of the language to which it belongs to resonate and the whole world view that underlies it to appear. Thus, every word, as the event of a moment, carries with it the unsaid, to which it is related by responding and summoning. The occasionality of human speech is not a causal imperfection of its expressive power; it is, rather the logical expression of the living virtuality of speech that brings a totality of meaning into play without being able to express it totally. All human speaking is finite in such a way that there is laid up within it an infinity of meaning to be explicated and laid out. That is why the hermeneutical phenomenon also can be illuminated only in light of the fundamental finitude of being, which is wholly verbal in character. (TM, 458, emphases added)

These passages make several things clear. First: the nexus of meaning that constitutes a *Sache* serves as the historically received enabling condition of statements about such a thematic, that is, "*every word breaks forth as if from a center and is related to whole*" and "*carries with it the unsaid.*" Second: the full being of meaning-nexus is in effect a "withheld." As a semantic field, although a *Sache* may sustain the practice of everyday judgments, the full extent of its nature remains hidden: it is that "infinity" of the unsaid, that "totality of meaning" that cannot be expressed. Third: that such a totality of meaning cannot be fully articulated is self-evident. However, insofar as the resonance of a statement about a *Sache* depends upon being "backed up by the ground" of the *withheld*, the dark and sustaining presence of the withheld is, as such, brought to light. This does not mean that it is objectified in language but it is brought to mind by language as an intentional object of our understanding. As Gadamer remarks, "every word *causes* the world view underlying it to appear": words "summons" a totality of meaning which nevertheless they cannot bring to complete expression. Fourth: as the nexus of meaning which constitutes the *withheld* dimension of *Sache* is essentially a linguistic phenomenon, it is not in principle unknowable, that is, it is not an entity that is alien to language. What makes it unknowable is the finitude of linguistic understanding. It is the finitude of understanding rather than the intrinsic nature of the object to be known that prevents such a nexus of meaning from being grasped as a whole. Though *withheld* from us, the *withheld* is not incommensurable with our mode of understanding. The *withheld* is, ontologically speaking, the other of us. Held within it are possibilities for understanding that have yet to be grasped as our own, possibilities that would enable us to become other to our present selves. This argument establishes *die Sachen* as the effective ontological ground for hermeneutic translation and transcendence.

Before we pass to other signficant aspects of the relation between *die Sachen, Bildung,* and tradition, certain problems need addressing. What is meant by Gadamer's reference to *die Sache* and a totality of meaning? What does Gadamer mean when he speaks of the "action of the thing itself"? Both questions highlight a certain imprecision of thought which is in need of clarification. With regard to the first question, we suggest that Adorno's notion of a conceptual constellation avoids some of the difficulties that attend Gadamer's use of a term which has clear Hegelian and Husserlian overtones.

Sachen as a Totality of Meaning

In a philosophy that emphasizes both the historicity and the finitude of understanding, Gadamer's references to semantic wholes and totalities of meaning seem out of place. If philosophical hermeneutics is wedded to a concept of *becoming*, two possible interpretations arise. *Sachen* are determinate fields of meaning that like Hegelian universals unfold according to their inner teleology or, alternatively, *Sachen* are loose clusters of meaning which although they transcend individuals remain historically malleable.

Concerning the first possibility, it is noticeable that Gadamer is indeed influenced by the philosophical language of Hegel and Husserl. However, the consequences of presenting his argument in either philosopher's language are problematic. If we read *die Sache* in a Hegelian fashion, the following difficulties arise. Gadamer invokes the tradition of post-Cartesian philosophies of substance when he refers explicitly to Hegel's endeavor to "discover in all that is subjective the *substantiality* that determines it" (TM, 302). As such substances, however, *Sachen* would "prescribe and limit every possibility for understanding any tradition whatsoever" (TM, 302). The substance or *Sache* would be a totality from which only those specific characteristics that are deducible from it as a continuous essence will emerge.[40] Note that Gadamer's formulation does not explicitly intend a *fixed* totality of meaning, which would circumscribe all the possibilities within a subject's past and future understanding, but then, neither does it openly repudiate it. Now, part of Gadamer's invocation of *Sachen* is to demonstrate that meaning and interpretation are *not* reducible to the subject alone. The hermeneutic subject is immersed in fields of meaning that extend beyond the scope of its conscious willing and doing. It is clear that Gadamer is committed to asserting the ontological autonomy of *Sachen*, but does this entail a commitment to the view that they are *fixed* totalities of meaning in that they unfold toward a predetermined end? Given the commitment of philosophical hermeneutics to a fundamentally historical approach to meaning, any suggestion of a closure of meaning would seem out of place. Nevertheless, one can sense what Gadamer wants to convey: the scope and extent of our immersion within linguistic being is all-enveloping. However, to pass from an intelligible intuition concerning the nature of our existence as wholly enveloped in language to making assertions about wholes or totalities of meaning is misleading. Furthermore, it is also unhelpful to one of the primary aims of philosophical hermeneutics. To *state* that there are such wholes or totalities of meaning is to imply that such wholes can be conceptualized. Yet to imply that they can be conceptualized suggests that as concepts *die Sachen* are not independent of the will of the hermeneutic subject. But philosophical hermeneutics insists that the meaning of such *Sachen* is not reducible to the subject. Gadamer's difficulty is plain. On the one hand, he wants to say how our being is not only enveloped by language but also dispersed into networks of meaning and nuance of limitless extent beyond our control. And yet, on the other hand, to say that requires precisely what language facilitates, namely, conceptualization. But of his own admission, the boundless extent of that which makes conceptualization possible prevents him from conceptualizing it. Strictly speaking, then, Gadamer cannot *say* what he means. He cannot conceptualize the totality of that which he wants to convey about the nature of linguistic being. Gadamer might *mean* what he wants to say but he cannot *say* what he wants to mean. This is a fundamental difficulty for philosophical hermeneutics. What it wishes to convey about language and its ontological foundations cannot be articulated in conceptual terms.

Given this difficulty, philosophical hermeneutics might profitably adapt a Nietzschean argument. If our language world were to be understood not so much as an in-itself but as a world of relationships, then, "under certain conditions it has a differing aspect from every point: its being is essentially different from every point; it presses upon every point, every point resists it—and the sum of these is in every case quite incongruent" (WP, 568).[41] If Gadamer's invocation of a totality of meaning were articulated as an all-enveloping but nevertheless variable sum of actual and potential meanings, he would be able to postulate (as he clearly wants to) an objective horizon of meaning that was not reducible to conceptualization. If, however, *Sachen* are to be *conceived* as totalities of meaning that both appertain to, constitute, and define the limits of intelligible objects, Gadamer's position becomes contradictory. So what has gone wrong? When Gadamer speaks of the *activity* of the *Sache selbst* he wants to oppose an instrumentalist conception of language. Language has an ontological priority over its individual user. Hermeneutic subjects are subject to the linguistic possibilities and limitations of their linguistic horizons. However, by attributing autonomous powers to a *Sache*, powers that are normally given over to the interpreting subject, Gadamer's formulation threatens to hypostasise the subject matter as a meta-subject. The direct parallel he draws with Hegel's concept of substance seems to locate the notion of *Sache* within a philosophy of substantiality that is fundamentally at odds with the historicity of understanding, which philosophical hermeneutics normally defends.

If we read *die Sachen* in a Husserlian manner certain other difficulties arise. Husserl sometimes speaks of the intended things themselves of mental perception as ideal states of affairs that have an instrinsic being.[42] The essence of a *Sache* somehow implicates itself in our empirical perception of an object that belongs to the class or species indicated by that *Sache*. As such, *Sachen* constitute the a priori noematic meaning of empirically perceived entities. The problem with this argument is that it places *Sachen* beyond the temporal flow of ordinary historical existence. If Gadamer's *Sachen* are grasped as Husserlian entities, it would suggest that the subject matters of understanding are ahistorical entities independent of their empirical exemplars. The invocation of such (metaphysical) entities is seemingly quite inconsistent with the deep historical orientation of philosophical hermeneutics.

The awkwardness of the several philosophical implications attached to Gadamer's use of *die Sachen* serves (somewhat paradoxically in Gadamer's own case) to illustrate that a thinker is, indeed, not always in control of what he or she wants to communicate. The gravity of some of the inherited meanings attached to *die Sachen* pulls Gadamer's argument into their distorting orbit. When *Sachen* are presented as some controlling essence or idea underwriting a field of meaning and when such a "totality" is described as something autonomous, *Sachen* appear as transcendent self-contained entities *an sich* (in themselves). But, then, how can such entities emerge within language and not also be a *für uns* (for us), that is, be entities that we are in relationship with? Here the Hegelian and Husserlian overtones in Gadamer's mode of expression are at their most misleading.

To argue that subject matters are totalities of meaning (i.e., are independent of the hermeneutic subjects who invoke them) does not mean that they belong to a different order of being from those subjects. Both are encompassed by a unitary language ontology. Gadamer hints at this when he argues that someone who has a speculative turn of mind—someone who has a sensitivity for what comes into language (*Sachen*), that is, for that which can be invoked by language rather than be objectified in language—is someone who senses that the *in-itself* of a subject matter is *also* a *for-me*. If so, then, we can argue that that which is inexpressible (the totality of past and future meanings attached to a *Sache*) is not something that is in principle unknowable. To say that something cannot be known in full is not to say that it cannot be known in part. To become involved with a historically revealed subject matter is to engage with networks of meaning that extend far beyond what we are immediately conscious of. But this does not mean that what we are immediately unaware of is *an sich* in the strict sense of the term. The elements of meaning that we are not conscious of are still present as etymological elements in the language we consciously operate with. Although out of sight, they remain there to be seen once the appropriate change of linguistic sensitivity has been accomplished. The "withheld" elements of meaning are, ontologically speaking, continuous with and, indeed, cohere in the elements of meaning we are aware of. The inexplicit strands of meaning within a *Sache* are not therefore in principle unknowable, they are simply not seen, not registered or attended to. Such strands reflect the finitude of our understanding: we cannot grasp the totality of being let alone of one *Sache* even if they were spread before us.[43] What Hirsch says about the visual experience of a physical object fits remarkably well with what Gadamer could and, for the sake of avoiding ambiguity, should have said about our experience of subject matters.

Hirsch observes how some traits of a thing lie outside our explicit awareness, either because we have not experienced them or because we are not attending to them. These "unattended to" or unknown traits constitute a penumbra that may be called a unifying background, which is always present in and gives our experience the quality of being of a specific object or subject matter.[44] Although the withheld aspects of a *Sache* are from the point of view of subjective consciousness *other* to what it presently knows, and although such aspects may extend into remote and obscure language horizons which subjective consciousness can hardly envisage, the withheld nevertheless remains with and sustains subjective consciousness as what might be described as "the already there of what lies in shadow."[45] The *withheld* does not therefore denote another order of being. It denotes the level of being that we already *are*. Subjective being is grounded within it. Yet the linguistic being in which we are grounded also transcends us, extending infinitely beyond us. Nevertheless, the being of that which extends beyond is of the same order of being that we presently are. We might say that the *withheld* is the *dark matter* of hermeneutical being. Thus, with regard to the hidden, unstated aspects of a *Sache* and the way they nourish our preunderstanding, it is, hermeneutically speaking, not so much a case of *sub umbra floreo* (beneath the shade I flourish) but of *inter umbras floreo* (among the shade I flourish). The ontological nature of what Gadamer is trying to address can be clearly conveyed without having to be directly conceptualized. It is a matter of regret that he used such a philosophically misleading term as "totality" to convey that which encompasses, sustains, and yet transcends us.

Die Sachen and Negative Dialectics

The nature of what philosophical hermeneutics alludes to as *die Sachen* can be more sharply outlined when contrasted to what Adorno describes as "constellar thinking." In *Negative Dialectics* Adorno insists that "we are not to philosophise about concrete things; we are to philosophise, rather, out of those things."[46] He suggests, "[T]here is no step by step progression to a *more general cover concept*. Instead, the concepts enter into a constellation."[47] The constellation is explained as follows.

> The constellation illuminates the specific side of the [its] object. . . . The model for this is the conduct of language. Language offers no mere system of signs for cognitive functions. Where it appears essentially as a language, where it becomes a form of representation, it will not define its concepts. It lends objectivity to them by the relation into which it puts its concepts, centered about a thing. Language thus serves the intention of the concept to express completely what it means. By themselves, constellations represent from without what the concept has cut away from within: the "more" which the concept is equally desirous and incapable of being. . . . Becoming aware of the constellation in which a thing stands is tantamount to deciphering the constellation which, having come to be, it bears within it. . . . Cognition of the object in its constellation is cognition of the process stored in the object.[48]

Such thinking suggests a clear analogy between Adorno's description of the relationship between concepts and the objects they represent and Gadamer's distinction between concepts and their subject matter. What makes the analogy worth exploring is that Gadamer and Adorno share certain other philosophical traits.

Gadamer's resistance to any reduction of meaning to subjectivity and its will to power finds a parallel in Adorno's concern with the instrumentalism hidden within Enlightenment notions of emancipatory reason. Gadamer is openly insistent that a *Sache* cannot be conceptualized by a hermeneutic subject: the *Sache* will always be more than and will always question the adequacy of how its conceptualized. Adorno discerns a tyrannical dimension in the operations of a rational subject. The supposition that there is an intelligible adequation between a thing and its concept leads to the illusion that when conceptualized, the thing becomes subject to our rational will. Whereas Gadamer seeks to challenge the subjective narrowness of our understanding, Adorno attempts to expose the instrumentalism operative within reason. Furthermore, where Gadamer deploys the "negativity of experience" to expose and challenge any closure of understanding, Adorno endeavors to frustrate the hegemonic ambitions of reason by exposing its adequation of things and concepts to the play of difference. The latter involves a negative dialectics which centers upon the tension between concepts and their objects: "Living in the rebuke that the thing is not identical with the concept, is the concept's longing to become identical with the thing."[49] The more the nonidentity of a thing with its concept is exposed, the more the inadequacy of its concept is revealed and, yet, the more that difference is uncovered, the greater become the possibilities for extending the range and meaning of that concept. Eagleton observes that "we must grasp the truth that the individual is both more and less than its general definition, and that the principle of identity is always self-contradictory, perpetuating non-identity in a damaged, suppressed form as a condition of its being."[50] Despite the manifest difference between the philosophical projects of both Gadamer and Adorno, the pattern of Adorno's reasoning suggests a constructive approach to how a *Sache* might be thought of. Consider the following.

Adorno and Gadamer are equally skeptical about the possibility of defining a *Sache* or thing. A *Sache* or the thing addressed cannot be defined because it cannot be made (in its entirety) an object of conceptual thought. They cannot be conceptually contained because both *are* more than their conceptual rendition. Furthermore, they influence the nature of their conceptual rendition in the first place. Yet though they cannot be conceptually objectivized, they can be brought to mind speculatively. Contrasting and conflicting interpretations of subject matters can expand our sense of what they entail. This for philosophical hermeneutics is the particular utility of Adorno's notion of constellar thinking. No one conceptualization of a thing will exhaust what that thing is, and so a variety of conceptual approaches will allow that thing to be seen as being, in Gadamer's phrase, "more what it is." In Adorno's terminology the nonidentity of the conceptualizations of a thing intimate a greater sense of what the identity of that thing might or could be. In neither case is the *Sache* contained within or captured by a statement or conceptualization. Much rather, what it is becomes apparent (or shows itself) from within the constellar field of concepts or interpretations that orbit it. That a subject matter can show itself from within the cluster of interpretations that attempt to chart it, offers an insight into a question raised above, that is, what does Gadamer mean when he speaks of the activity of the *Sache selbst?*

That a *Sache* can be articulated as the shifting (ideal) center of a conceptual constellation allows philosophical hermeneutics to move away from the transcendentalism of Husserl's grasp of the thing itself. Gadamer's and Adorno's reasoning suggests that as the focal point of a variety of nonidentical interpretations, a *Sache* does indeed have a unitary function. Yet neither thinker argues *pace* Husserl that a *Sache* is the transcendental ground or *Wesen* that serves to identify all possible perceptions of it. Gadamer and Adorno are discernibly closer to Iser's contention that though a *Sache* can be described as constituting a given interpretative field of conceptual constellation, it is the tensions of nonidentity and difference that are to be found at its center. Both Adorno and Gadamer argue that one of the reasons *Sachen* cannot be conceptualized is because they influence the intellectual horizon within which the conceptualization takes place. Any attempt to conceptualize the nature of a subject matter will be deeply affected by the inherited *Vorverständnisse* appertaining to it. Though they may enable attempts at conceptualization, such preunderstandings cannot be comprehensibly conceptualized. Gadamer seems at times to think of the enabling powers of these preunderstandings as also being an activity of the requisite *Sachen*. If we bring Iser's argument back into play we can gain a further insight into Adorno's claim that nonidentity constitutes the dark center of a *Sache* and Gadamer's conviction that such an irreducible entity is a shifting field of interpretations whose tensions have a generative power.

Iser's analysis of *Sachen* suggests that the center of Adorno's conceptual constellation can be conceived as an ineliminable space of autopoietic differences. He presents the interpretation of a subject matter as being marked by an ineluctable duality. His vital contribution to our debate lies in the suggestion that the critical space between a subject matter and its understanding is created by interpretation itself. As a subject matter is always in excess of its interpretation, the activity of interpreting it opens a residual untranslatablity between what it is and how it is understood. This, according to Iser, serves to stimulate and drive further interpretation.

> The space . . . created by interpretation contains a residual un-translatability that, however, powers the drive to overcome it, without ever being able to do so. Such a space—which can be qualified in terms neither of subject matter to be interpreted nor of the register into which the subject matter is to be trans-posed—turns out to be auto-poetic in nature. The space is au-topoietic in nature because it produces its own shifting forms of organisation . . . [which] . . . may explode into unforeseeable iterations of the features that have adumbrated it. . . .[51]

If the preunderstandings attached to a *Sache* influence how that *Sache* is consciously interpreted, and, if what shows itself in the process of inter-pretation is also an activity of a *Sache*, then the hermeneutic field that embraces interpreting, interpreted, and interpreter can be grasped as an autopoietic space the nucleus of which is not a Husserlian *Wesen* or archetype but a play of differences generated and sustained by the hermeneutic field that constitutes the *Sache* itself. Adorno's phrase for such a space is the "togetherness of diversity."[52] Indeed, Adorno is not averse to describing this field as an *Idee*, that is, not as a concept but as an entity that like a *Sache* lives "in the cavities *between* what things claim to be and what they are."[53] The gap at issue is between what the concept of a thing asserts about that thing and the nonconceptualized "withheld" or "negative" dimension of that thing upon which the concept depends for its articulation but can never capture. Insofar as there is a conceptual link between Iser's notion of an autopoietic space, Adorno's reference to a live diversity within an *Idee*, and Gadamer's allusions to the activity of the *Sache selbst*, it is possible to suggest that what the Gadamerian usage of *Sache* evokes is the objective life of a hermeneutic field itself. It sustains and unfolds itself in and through the tensions and differences it generates from within itself. As a hermeneutic field or autopoietic space, a *Sache* might be thought of as an onto-hermeneutic process driven by the mutu-ally self-sustaining interaction of the interpreter and the interpreted. The merit of this characterization is its consistency with Gadamer's attempt to reveal how subjective interpretive processes are both made possible by and driven by objective onto-hermeneutic processes, which a subject can influence but never control.

Before we consider the how the above points illuminate Gadamer's wider philosophical concerns, other dimensions of *die Sachen* require discussion. If a *Sache* is an intelligible object that cannot be conceptualized but only discerned as the central nucleus of a constellation of perspectives, our sense of this object can be strengthened if we alter the perspectives from which we approach it. The notion of a *Sache* as being the object of interpretation and yet beyond all interpretation is certainly problematic. How Gadamer treats this issue is best approached via a short discussion of Plato's universals.

Die Sachen and Plato's Forms

In *The Republic* Plato is understood to have presented a theory of knowledge in which the true objects of knowledge are ideas or universals, the archetypes of forms which enable us to recognize variously perceived objects as being of the same class or type. As objects of knowledge, such ideas are regarded as unmade, changeless, and perfect. They transcend all sensuous exemplification, exist independently of their appearances and are unaffected by their interpretation. These objects of pure intellection are the universal forms to which contemplation always endeavors to return. It is logically consistent for any adherent of this view to regard the duplication of such objects in nature and art as a devaluation if not a counterfeit of the original. Neoplatonist thinkers attempted to ameliorate this view with the argument that the artist's image had its place within the cosmic order. Abbreviating the argument of John of Damascus, Hans Belting notes that as

> every image, no matter of what kind, originated in a prototype in which it was contained in essence (by *dynamis*), . . . so a likeness belonged to a model. The image was . . . related to its archetype, was more or less the property—indeed the product—of its model. Without the model, the image could not have come into being.[54]

However, although Gadamer tends toward the neoplatonist conception of a likeness increasing the being of its subject matter, the strict Platonic view is that while physical likenesses are at one remove from the original, artistically manufactured likenesses are at two removes from the real and can corrupt our sense of the archetype.

In certain respects Gadamer's account of Sachen shares several formal characteristics with Plato's approach to universals. Sachen and universals are always greater than their perceived instances. They are transcendent entities with an objective existence that reaches beyond the grasp of any one historical epoch. Equally, no historical epoch can monopolize the meaning of a Sache or universal. Though Sachen and universals are "more" than their particular renditions, they nevertheless ground such renditions and allow them to point beyond themselves. In these respects Sachen and universals are comparable to each other as "third world objects" (Popper). Though such objects are given to our subjective understanding they cannot be reduced to that level of understanding.[55] However, Sachen are unlike Plato's universals in the following respects.

Although Sachen transcend historical epochs, they are not atemporal ideas. Unlike Plato's timeless universals, die Sachen can, as our previous argument has suggested, have both a beginning and end in time. In contrast to universals, Sachen are perfectible and can be made more complete. Whereas Plato regards the artistic interpretation of a universal as a diminishment of its being, Gadamer values creative manufacture as a means whereby the subject matter becomes "more." Insofar as Gadamer insists that a Sache is the enabling ground of interpretation, he argues that the intepretation enriches the Sache as though it were a new event of being (TM, 140). The interpretation is not remote from what the Sache essentially is but is a presentation of the essence of the subject matter itself. The way in which a Sache presents itself is, indeed, part its own being (TM, 432). What is represented in the interpretation of a Sache facilitates an increase in its being. Gadamer follows the neoplatonic precedent: when an artist produces a likeness of his sitter, he is adding to rather than distorting the being of the sitter, allowing the sitter to understand something of herself not understood before.[56]

The contrasts and parallels between the arguments of Plato and Gadamer permit the following clarifications. Insofar as every interpretation is enabled by being rooted in an objectively existent Sachen, it is dependent upon what can be described as a third world object. As third world objects that transcend subjective consciousness, Sachen nevertheless display themselves in and through consciousness. In Gadamer's language, the objectivities that underwrite subjectivity also manifest themselves in subjective consciousness. This is congruent with Popper's remark that "all the important things we can say about a (subjective) act of understanding consist in pointing out its relation to other third world objects."[57] As far as Gadamer is concerned it is precisely the relationship between *Sachen* and subjective consciousness that enables the possibility for hermeneutic translation. The fact that subjective consciousness is grounded in the being of *Sachen*, permits subjective consciousness to become *ecstatic*, to move beyond its initial limitations. It is this "feedback" relation between *die Sachen* and subjective consciousness, which decisively distinguishes Gadamer's from Plato's approach to "third world objects."

For Plato, universals are self-contained ontic entities that can neither be generated nor corrupted. Gadamer, however, clearly regards *Sachen* as having an empirical, that is, a linguistic provenance. This is not to say that all *Sachen* are man-made in that their first appearance might be traceable to a given artist or thinker. Some clearly are. The distinct theme "animal life" first entered Western Art as a legitimate subject matter as a consequence of Dürer's animal drawings. Because of Freud, the subject matter of "unconsciousness" assumed its proper proportion. Of other *Sachen*, however, it would be more appropriate to say that they emerge from human activity rather than are made by an individual. The theme of a conversation serves as a case in point. Conversation takes place between given individuals and yet no one need necessarily know in advance what will emerge from that conversation. Conversation allows "something to emerge" which henceforth exists (TM, 383) and might do so contrary to the expectations of those who take part in that conversation. The processes of linguistic engagement can therefore generate a *Sache* irrespective of the intentions of the speakers. Gadamer remarks that the *Sache* that emerges in a conversation "is contained in neither of the partners" of that conversation solely "by himself" (TM, 462). A *Sache* can therefore originate in human activity and not be regarded as being the creation of any one individual. In arguing against the Platonic rejection of provenances for universals, Gadamer finds an ally in Popper.

Popper's "third world objects" resemble Gadamer's *Sachen* in several respects. Popper writes,

> I suggest that it is possible to accept the reality or (as it may be called) the autonomy of the third world, and at the same time to admit that the third world originates as a product of human activity. One can even admit that the third world is man made and, in a very clear sense, super-human at the same time. It transcends its makers.[58]

Whereas Popper argues that larger parts of the third world are unplanned products of human action,[59] Gadamer argues that most *Sachen* are the unplanned products of linguistic engagement. Both Gadamer and Popper agree that although ontologically speaking, third world entities are autonomous, we can nevertheless interact with that world, add to it, and alter it.

> The third world which in its origin, is our product, is autonomous in what may be called its ontological status. It explains why we act upon it and add to it or help its growth, even though there is no man [person] who can master even a small corner of this world. All of us contribute to its growth but almost all of our individual contributions are vanishingly small. All of us try to grasp it, and none of us could live without being in contact with it, for all of us make use of speech without which we would be hardly human. Yet the third world has grown beyond the grasp not only of any man, but even of all men (as shown by the existence of insoluble problems). Its action upon us has become more important for our growth and even for its growth, than our creative action upon it. For almost all its growth is due to a feed-back effect . . . there will always be the challenging task of discovering new problems, for an infinity of problems will always remain undiscovered. In spite and almost because of the autonomy of the third world, there will always be scope for original and creative work.[60]

The parallels with Gadamer are notable. The third world is beyond our grasp and yet acts upon us. Every interpretation is anchored in and is influenced by the theories such a third world can contain. This suggests that the third world is in Gadamer's terms a "withheld," a "truth-in-itself" (TM, 442). It facilitates what is known but cannot be known in its totality. Popper acknowledges that the third world cannot be known in its entirety and cannot be theorized as such. Furthermore, the contention that the autonomous world of *Sachen* and our subjective everyday world are connected by a feedback device is reminiscent of Iser's argument that *Sachen* are indeed affected by our interpretive interventions.

Despite these similarities, the positions of Gadamer and Popper differ in one profound respect. Whereas Popper wishes to diminish the subjective components of understanding by translating them into statements about third world objects, Gadamer seeks to sharpen the subjective dimensions of experience in order to prompt a speculative sense of the autonomy of *die Sachen*. Gadamer is persuaded that the in-itself becomes discernible as a speculative object within the realm of the for-us. The *Sachen* we encounter are "totalities" of meaning which have their truth-in-themselves. Yet, these *Sachen* are also linguistic phenomena. They have a truth-for-us. As a withheld, a *Sache* is an inarticulable totality of meaning but—and this is the point—although the withheld is unknowable in itself, as a linguistic phenomenon it does not stand opposed to what is knowable for us. Because the knowable for us is rooted in the unknowable-in-itself, we are also in ourselves (ultimately) unknowable for we too are upheld by the withheld. This is why for philosophical hermeneutics we fundamentally remain mysteries to ourselves and continue to find ourselves difficult. The relation between what is knowable-for-us and what is unknowable-in-itself is speculative. That which as a linguistically formed *Sache* transcends us, nevertheless manifests itself within subjective consciousness. The speculative relation, which allows the subjective world to be illumined by what is beyond it (the revelatory or centrifugal moment of understanding) and which, at the same time, allows the transcendent to manifest itself within the subjective (the epiphanic or centripedal moment of understanding) is absent from Popper's arguments.

The similarities and differences between Plato, Adorno, Popper, and Gadamer place the philosophical characteristics of *die Sachen* in better relief. We can now look more closely at how Gadamer's approach to *die Sachen* informs our discussion of *Bildung*.

Sachen, Cultural Communities, and *Cortesia*

Sachen are the subject matters of a culture. They are intentional objects attracting and reflecting the concerns of a community. The link between them and communicative activity is insoluble. As we have argued, *Sachen* are transcendent rather than metaphysical entities. Though the product of human communication, they are not reducible to the activity of individuals alone.[60] Even in the case of subject matters that do emerge as a consequence of the creative interventions of individuals, the full potential of such interventions does not become apparent until they are assimilated by a cultural community.[61] Philosophical hermeneutics is persuaded that *Sachen* emerge as a consequence of communicative engagement. That they can always mean "more," implies that no community has a monopoly upon how a subject matter is to be understood. *Sachen* may also be understood as a mode of hermeneutic relation. They are at the core of how a community comes to understand and to question itself. As preunderstood attitudes and responses to existential, political, and moral questions,

Sachen clearly *influence* how a community initially perceives itself. When such perceptions are challenged, a community is brought to confront its understanding of received *Sachen*. The point is not just that an understanding of a *Sache* is placed under review but, as a consequence, a community brings its own self-understanding into question. *Sachen* not only facilitate a community's preunderstanding but also when hypostatized as objects to which a community hermeneutically relates, provide the points around which a community can transform and measure its own self-understanding. The link between *die Sachen*, communication, and community is clearly interactive. This gives rise to an important point about the relationship between *Bildung* and *die Sachen*.

Philosophical hermeneutics makes no normative claim about what constitutes a cultural community. Its arguments suggest that what differentiates one form of culture from another are differences of degree rather than of kind: each cultural community is characterized by different perspectival responses to constituting *Sachen*. This has clear implications for Gadamer as to why cultural understanding cannot be methodized and why becoming *gebildet* is more to do with experience than with "knowledge" in the strict sense of the term. Becoming *gebildet* has much more to do with a practice, with the ability to enter into and engage with modes of relation rather than acquiring information about different lifestyles.

Becoming *gebildet* is not a matter of acquiring theoretical knowledge, because the *Sachen* that underwrite a cultural community cannot be theorized. The reasons for this are threefold. First, in underwriting a community's self-understanding *die Sachen* are partly *withheld* from that understanding. Second, because, ontologically speaking, *die Sachen* are always capable of becoming "more," they resist definitive theoretical articulation. Third, both what is theorized as a *Sache* and the theorization itself will only ever be perspectival. That *Sachen* cannot be methodized reflects the fact that they cannot be adequately objectivized in the forms that conventional knowledge requires. *Sachen* are not, therefore, *objects* of knowledge given over to a knowing subject but a *mode of relation* in which a *Sache* and a knowing *subject* moderate and (potentially) transform one another. To become engaged with a *Sache* and the otherness of its withheld is, then, to orientate oneself toward it in an appropriate way. Knowing how to orientate in such a way toward a *Sachen* involves the acquisition of "tact."

Gadamer describes "tact" as that "special sensitivity and sensitiveness to situations and how to behave in them, for which knowledge from general principles does not suffice" (TM, 16).

> The tact which functions in the human sciences is not simply
> a feeling and unconscious, but is at the same time a mode of
> knowing and a mode of being. (TM, 16)

Tact is achieved through considerable practise, through being immersed in and engaged with a variety of hermeneutic encounters through which one acquires a "sense" or a "feel" for what is being alluded to within a work or debate. Tact might be described as a speculative skill. It presupposes a willingness and an ability to be drawn into dialogue with the strange and foreign. Furthermore, tact demands a sensitive ear for what shapes a dialogue and its direction. Tact can discern what is appropriate within a dialogue without needing all its implicit terms to be made explicit. In Wittgenstein's terms, it is knowing "how to go on" within a dialogue or practice. Tact is a speculative skill insofar as it can grasp the meaning of what is immediately said or disclosed in terms of what lies beyond the self-evident. It has learned that the meaning of what is actually said depends upon the unsaid. Tact, then, involves an ability to sense the flow and direction of a given dialogue, to "read" it in the full hermeneutical sense of the term. Such "tact"—to know what is appropriate—is, of course, a matter of practice rather than method.

Becoming *gebildtet* involves the acquisition of such "tact." However, becoming tactful is not a matter of acquiring a prevailing norm or mode of behavior. It also involves an inner apprehension of one's ethical dependency upon the other for insights into one's own possibilities. George Steiner's invocation of *cortesia* carries this greater ethical weight. Rooted in the ancient etiquettes of welcome, *cortesia* negotiates the places where in text or in conversation we acknowledge and receive the approaching other. The ethics of *cortesia*, as Steiner perceives them,

> bear closely on our recognitions, on our *entente* (our hearing) of
> what the poem, the painting, the sonata would with us. We are
> the other ones whom the living significations of the aesthetic
> seek out. It is on our capacities for welcome or refusal, for re-
> sponse or imperception, that their own necessities of echoe and
> of presence largely depend. To think about *cortesia* is to think
> about the kinds of entrance which we allow them or which they
> exact into the narrows of our individual existence.[62]

> The informing agency is that of *tact*, of the ways in which we
> allow ourselves to touch or not to touch, to be touched or not
> to be touched by the presence of the other. . . . The issue is
> that of civility . . . towards the inward savour of things.[63]

Karlheinz Stierle notes how Dante's conception of *cortesia* leaves the space of understanding open: "It is always the beginning of a possible dialogue. It means an acknowledgment of difference."[64] Iser suggests that *cortesia* promotes an experience of difference between the self and the other per se. However, *cortesia* also entails an act of recognition. It is not just the other who is recognized but the fact that without the other, the self is groundless, that there is no self without the other. In short, in making ready for the other, *cortesia* bids welcome to the other of ourselves.[65] The withheldness of the other is also the withheldness of ourselves. Just as a sitter awaits from the hand of the portrait artist that which is presently withheld from them—their likeness—so, cultivating *cortesia* toward the many voices in our culture involves the recognition that any understanding of the *withheld* that is ourselves is dependent upon the *advent* of the other. The rites of *cortesia* articulate a recognition of that dependence. It is not just a matter of trusting that the other has something to say but recognising that the other in the withheldness that is either his or hers, holds *in trust* possibilities for our understanding that are not presently ours. Philosophical hermeneutics offers no formal proof that such trust can be redeemed. It points instead to our actual experience as linguistic beings, experiences that show that we are invariably dependent upon the other for any experience of self. There is a clear ethical dimension to one's preparedness to welcome the strange and alien aspects of a *Sache*.

Iser notes that subject matters "would lie for ever dormant if they were not made functional" or engaged with.[66] Gadamer, of course, intimates that *Sachen* have a certain life of their own. They form our preunderstandings and incline us toward one view of a question rather than another. The question of ethical dependency arises, then, not merely because we are dependent upon tradition and its inherited *Sachen* for our worldview but because the ontologically withheld aspects of meaning within a *Sache* are the "already there" of our own withheld. The *withheldness* of a Sache does not denote another order of being but the fact that our subjective being extends into what is presently beyond us. Now, just as we are dependent upon the activity of *Sachen* for orientating us toward what we grasp within our world and within ourselves, so too would such *Sachen* cease to function and as a consequence wither were we not to engage with them.[67] Their ability to disclose other determinations of meaning is relation-dependent. It depends upon our engagement with them. Like the traditions that form around them, *Sachen* do not perpetuate themselves by remaining the same but by being continually transformed within dialogical relationships. If that which enables us to orientate ourselves toward our world and our selves begins to atrophy, the *withheld* that is our future understanding is also harmed. Responding to and seeking to be answerable to the claims tradition and *Sachen* place upon us not only renews and sustains their being but also opens us toward engaging the withheld within ourselves. The substance of a consciousness that has become *gebildet* is therefore ethical. Its tact and courtesy expresses the profound awareness that the mystery of *withheldness* in a *Sache* and indeed within the other is inseparably bound up with the mystery of our own withheldness. It is the ontological immanence of the withheld that, as we shall now see, sustains Gadamer's powerful objections to philosophical and methodological nihilism.

"BILDUNG" AND THE QUESTION OF NIHILISM

Gadamer's philosophical rearticulation of *Bildung* does not stand alone. It is intimately connected with the attempt of philosophical hermeneutics to displace the influence of nihilism. Philosophical hermeneutics displays a deep disquiet about the nature of philosophical and methodological nihilism. By philosophical nihilism we mean that disbelief in an intelligible metaphysical world of Being and by methodological nihilism we refer to those demands for an unattainable form of methodological certainty. The differences between both these two forms of nihilism and the response philosophical hermeneutics musters are quite subtle. Gadamer's defense of *Bildung* assumes its proper magnitude in his resistance to nihilism.

Nihilism is a philosophical thematic always tracking Gadamer's thinking, but, submarine-like, it rarely breaks surface. That Gadamer keeps its questions in mind, though only occasionally addressing them directly, is the probable result of Heidgger's influence. Like his predecessor, Gadamer senses that to talk about nihilism explicitly necessarily invokes the language of the discredited metaphysics it is associated with. Gadamer is tactful in his "regard" for the question of nihilism: "To pass over something does not mean to avert one's gaze from it, but to keep an eye on it in such a way that rather than knock into it, one slips by it. . . . Tact helps one to preserve distance" (TM, 16). Be this as it may, we need to be more forthright in our discussion of philosophical nihilism.

There is a certain philosophical irony in Goethe's statement that *Ich Hab Mein Sach auf Nichts gestellt.* It turns upon the question of whether *das Nichts* is understood negatively or positively. Congruent with its humanist tendencies, philosophical hermeneutics embraces a positive approach to *das Nichts*. We have contended that though *die Sachen* are objective hermeneutic fields, they are not Platonic universals or timeless essences. Neither do they reflect, nor do they constitute an intelligible world, which, compared to the finitude of our own existence, belongs to another mode of Being. In the language of Europe's metaphysical tradition, *die Sachen* are indeed *nothing*, neither real nor stable. In this respect and this respect alone, philosophical hermeneutics does embrace and indeed assumes a form of philosophical or metaphysical nihilism. Like the latter, it is premised on a clear dismissal of the metaphysics of Being. *Die Sachen* and the insights they afford do, indeed, stand on nothing (*auf Nichts gestellt*). The world we actually inhabit is enveloped within metaphysical contingency. When viewed from the perspective of metaphysical nihilism, our traditions of knowledge appear quite groundless. In pursuing more traditional concepts of truth, reality, and meaning, we have, it would appear, based our concerns on "nothing."

In its antifoundationalist stance, philosophical hermeneutics clearly embraces Nietzsche's critique of metaphysics, but there are two aspects of his metaphysical nihilism that trouble it. Philosophical hermeneutics challenges two of the consequences that supposedly derive from the acceptance of metaphysical nihilism. The first is the belief that if the *Sachen* that sustain our horizons have an uncertain ontological ground, then we are condemned to an uncertain and *Angst*-ridden existence. The second is the supposition that disbelief in metaphysics demands disbelief in the transcendent.

Concerning the first point: does it follow that if the *Sachen* that form our horizons are without formal foundation, we are thereby condemned to an uncertain and fearful existence? This query raises several issues. What Heidegger and Gadamer regard (perhaps rather loosely) as metaphysical tradition poses fundamental questions concerning the relationships between objects of knowledge and objects in the world, between truth and Being and between word and thing. The legitimacy of our claims to know the truth of an object, our understanding of what is represented in such claims, and our belief that we can speak truthfully of a world that is independent of us, depend upon how adequately they can be correlated to the real world. When the legitimacy of truth and meaning depends upon the belief that the latter are grounded in such a world, discerning the nature of the correlation becomes a pressing matter. Whenever such a world is hypostasized as an intelligible world with ontological characteriztics different from those of subjectively tainted appearance, skepticism emerges. Doubts about whether there can be an intelligible relationship between "the real world" and our understanding of it, question the nature of what we claim to understand. In Nietzsche's mind, Kant's *Critique of Pure Reason* brings such doubts to a point of crisis: "The real world, unattainable, undemonstrable, cannot (even) be promised."[68] Once the ground of supposed meaning and truth is regarded as unknowable, it appears from within metaphysical tradition as if we are cut off from everything we had hitherto regarded as the source of meaning and truth. Indeed, what was esteemed as the ground of meaning and truth appears to recede from us, to become a form of the withheld. A sense of being abandoned in a meaningless realm of appearances is the consequence of a (false) belief in an intelligible real world of being. Nietzsche astutely remarks:

> One interpretation has collapsed; but because it was considered *the* interpretation it now seems as if there were no meaning at all existence, as if everything were in vain.[69]

However, the supposition that there is no meaning to existence is premised on the assumption that for there to be such a meaning, that meaning must be intelligibly connected to its ground in Being. Once faith in such a connection collapses, it is as if we lose our right to posit a "beyond." Heidegger perceives that from the point of view of one who holds to the old metaphysics, the disappearance of the "beyond" appears to leave an absolute and annihilating nothing. Beyond the world of mortal beings there is nothing but death. Within the metaphysical perspective, such nothingness is terrifying because it marks a point of betrayal, namely, the disappearance of the guarantor of one's belief in meaning and truth. As consequence, from within this perspective the *actual* world appears as a "threatening" and "unsafe place."[70] Heidegger and Gadamer, of course, displace the nihilistic consequences of the metaphysical perspective but before we reflect on their arguments, let us consider briefly how such nihilism affects Gadamer's approach to *Bildung* and its subject matters.

Philosophical hermeneutics is fearful that unless we are able to take leave of the metaphysical prejudices that distort our thinking about meaning and truth, then *Bildung* and tradition will fall into disrepute and their vital transforming insights be lost. Should they be forgotten, our capacity to achieve hermeneutic transcendence will also be compromised. This is because the relations that facilitate the movement of the understanding constituting our humanity will be seriously impaired. Philosophical hermeneutics locates both *Bildung* and tradition within a broad linguistic ontology. *Bildung,* tradition, and *Sachen* are not to be grasped as states of affairs but as modes of (dialogical) relation. We enter into communicative relationship with them and they with us. Their effective being can be sustained if and only if those relations are sustained. The anxiety philosophical hermeneutics grapples with is that with the advent of philosophical nihilism, the loss of faith in the supposed metaphysical grounds of truth makes the claims and values of *Bildung* and tradition *seem* unjustifiably arbitrary. Lacking any objective correlative and a universally compelling rational justification, the claims of tradition appear as if they are mere prejudice, the arbitrarily established preferences of a dominant community. In short, the claims of tradition and *Bildung* become pilloried as expressions of a given will to power. What concerns philosophical hermeneutics is that so long as philosophical nihilism holds sway (which is to say, so long as metaphysical tradition holds us in its grasp), *Bildung* and tradition will suffer the chastisement of those who are subject to metaphysical longings, that is, be regarded as the expressions of groundless subjective preference. The issue here is not critical chastisement as such but what such chastisement encourages, namely, that the claims of *Bildung* and tradition have no worth and are not worthy of any response. This, for Gadamer, is the pernicious threat of philosophical nihilism: it encourages negativity toward the very received horizons that enable us both to have a world in the first place and to take an interest in it. The nihilist believes (erroneously) that the repudiation of meaning-in-itself refutes all local meaning.[71] Worse, nihilism seeks to persuade us that received horizons of meaning are irrational and that, therefore, we should disengage from any interest or involvement with them. The concern of philosophical hermeneutics is not so much with the nihilist case per se, poor and revealing though it is, but with its implicit denigration of the subjective. On the ground that local horizons of meaning are not universally well founded, the nihilist emerges as a character who refuses the challenge to change that emanates from the absence of such horizons. The nihilist refuses to open toward the possibilities for being within localized meaning: the philosophical nihilist does not trust the call of his subjective responses to meaning and insists, instead, upon what he knows cannot be given, to wit, a philosophical warrant to change issued from the bureau of universal foundations. Philosophical hermeneutics is disturbed by the persuasive impact of the nihilist's rationalist rhetoric. That rhetoric persuades us not to listen to and not to respond to the intelligent intuitions of our subjectivity. It persuades us to devalue the disclosures of meaning from within our local horizons of meaning. Insofar as it tempts us to the latter, it persuades us—and this is its real danger—to give up on the living foundations of human transcendence and learning.[72] The need for tact concerning this issue is now clear.

To make nihilism an explicit object of criticism would necessitate defining it fully and thereby risk reinvoking the very metaphysical perspective philosophical hermeneutics must endeavor to break a way from. The question of nihilism is one that philosophical hermeneutics must keep a tactful distance from while at the same time seeking to displace it. How then does philosophical hermeneutics endeavor to negotiate the challenge of nihilism? An insight into this can be gained from looking at the arguments that surround its other concern about nihilism; that a disbelief in metaphysics leads to a disbelief in the transcendent.

The "metaphysical perspective" hijacks the notion of transcendence. Consequently, the disappearance of the "beyond" leaves for the nihilist an absolute and annihilating nothing. The belief in the possibility of transcendence—gaining either access or insight into a supposed intelligible world—is exposed as "in vain." However, it is only "in vain" if the "beyond" one wishes to access is conceived of as an ontic realm with properties other than those of the world we live in. Philosophical hermeneutics stands on the supposition that transcendence within this world is indeed possible. It believes that it is possible to "get beyond" our current perspectives and to engage with something *other* than them. Philosophical hermeneneutics insists, however, that this transcendence is possible because of and not in spite of our being in this world. It is made possible by the fact of our being grounded in a language ontology. What troubles philosophical hermeneutics is that the rhetoric of nihilism appears to proscribe the possibility of transcendence. However, all that nihilism can deny, and with good reason, is belief in the possibility of metaphysical transcendence. Yet this has no bearing upon the actuality of transcendence, which can take place in and between hermeneutical horizons. Such transcendence is fundamental to our experience of linguisticality. Because of language we live within what transcends our individual finitude. Being grounded in language enables that which is "beyond" us to actually live within us. Such arguments have a bearing on Heidegger's critique of the nihilistic presentation of the world as *unsafe*.

Heidegger argues that from the perspective of traditional metaphysics, the disappearance of the "beyond," which grounds meaning and truth, makes the world appear a "threatening" and "unsafe place," a place shrouded by the emptiness of absent Being. According to Young, Heidegger turns the experience of emptiness into an experience of plenitude by arguing for an ontological difference between "ego" and "self." One comes to understand that the individual self is rooted within the *with-heldness* of Being. There is a part of one's individual being that transcends the everyday referents of the "I."[73] Understanding one's "membership" of the mystical realm of "plenitude" abolishes anxiety and establishes one as ultimately secure in one's world. One comes to understand that that which surrounds one is no longer abysmal but contains the richness of those presently concealed possibilities for future disclosure which in addition to one's present self one also is. Such a feeling of safety enables one to dwell in mortality, for to dwell in mortality is also to dwell in immortality. One can, in Rilke's words, "face . . . death without negation."[74]

Heidegger's concept of "dwelling" has a double nature: one can dwell as an ordinary mortal in the actual world because one simultaneously dwells beyond one's immediate horizon. As Young observes, "Understanding one's transcendence transforms one's world into an unconditionally 'safe' place because one knows that nothing that happens in it can annihilate one's essential self."[75] From the perspective of traditional metaphysics, the world one dwells in is, indeed, *nothing*, groundless and utterly contingent and yet "this floating world" is *all.* As the plenitude of emptiness, it emerges as the mystery of groundless actual being. The significance of Heidegger's argument is that it establishes a clear precedent for Gadamer's case that transcendence is an intergral part of our experience of language.

If Gadamer is tactful about nihilism insofar as naming it explicitly invokes by default the tradition of metaphysical thought he wishes to escape, he is also reticent about openly discussing Heidegger's ontological difference, and perhaps for the same reason. Any open discussion of the ontological difference will inevitably invoke the traditional metaphysics of Being against which Heidegger defines his thinking. In the same manner as Heidegger's notion of dwelling, Gadamer's linguistic ontology inverts ontological insecurity, but without invoking the metaphysics of Being by default. Gadamer's declaration that the "Being that can be understood is language" (TM, 474), should be read in the context of his remark that "in language the reality beyond every individual consciousness becomes visible" (TM, 449). Gadamer is not saying that what cannot be put into language cannot be understood. The unstated and the unsaid arise in language and can be understood even though they are not put into words. He remarks, "That language and world are related in a fundamental way does not mean, then, that the world becomes the object of language. Rather, the object of knowledge and statements is already enclosed *within* the world horizon of knowledge . . . for our verbal experience of the world is prior to everything that is recognized and addressed as existing" (TM, 450).

> Language is not just one of man's possessions in the world, rather on it depends the fact that man has a world at all. . . . Language has no independent life apart from the world that comes to language in it. Not only is the world world only insofar as it comes into language, but language, too has its real being only in the fact that the world is presented in it. (TM, 443)

> What is thus conceived of as existing is not really the object of statements but comes to language in statements. (TM, 446)

Insofar as the understanding of language entails a consciousness of that which silently arises in language, the "Being that can be understood" includes the speculative. It is indeed the speculative capacity of language that reveals "the reality beyond every individual consciousness" (TM, 449). The reality revealed is not an extralinguistic reality. If something figures itself as a matter of concern within our immediate horizon, it does so because it has already been brought into language. The revealed reality that Gadamer speaks of is the world of linguisticality in which our being is rooted. Nevertheless, although that world is the ground of our experience, it "can never be given in experience as the comprehensive whole that it is" (TM, 452). In relationship to every individual consciousness (*Bewusstsein*), such a revealed reality is that transcendent totality of meaning (*Sein*) which, though it underwrites and sustains every expression, "cannot (itself) be totally expressed." Because our (collective) being in the world is linguistic, our being in the world and the being of language (TM, 443) are essentially one and the same. For linguistically constituted beings, there is no "beyond" or "behind" the world of language. This does not mean that the reality of our linguistic being in the world is reducible to what an individual consciousness is aware of. The nexus of meanings and world-horizons that an individual's being is grounded in, extends far beyond whatever that individual consciousness can grasp or express. In this context Gadamer remarks,

> All human speaking is finite in such a way that there is laid up within it an infinity of meaning to be explicated and laid out. That is why the hermeneutical phenomenon also can be illuminated only in the light of the fundamental finitude of being, which is wholly verbal in character. (TM, 458)

Yet the finitude of subjective consciousness neither bars it from the infinite, nor denies it the possibility of transcendence and insight into what is beyond. The etymological interconnectedness of language, and the dynamic capacity of language for speculative disclosure, enables language to disclose relations of meaning that such an individual might never have imagined he or she was connected to. *Linguistic being grounds all hermeneutic translation, transformation, and transcendence.*

The claim that "whoever has language 'gains' the world" encapsulates the attempt of philosophical hermeneutics to displace the anxiety and skepticism attending the demise of the metaphysical tradition. Whereas for Heidegger disclosure and holding-back are properties of Being, for Gadamer they are fundamental features of linguistic being. It is our rootedness in the transcendent elements of language that renders our dwelling in *this* world safe. Though he does not directly address Gadamer's thought, George Steiner's remarks admirably convey the direction of Gadamer's thought.

> A sentence always means more. Even a single word within the weave of incommensurable connotation, can, and usually does. The informing matrix or context of even a rudimentary literal proposition . . . moves outward from specific utterance or notation in ever widening concentric and overlapping circles. These comprise the individual, subconsciously quickened language habits and associative field mappings of the particular speaker or writer. They incorporate, in densities inaccessible to systematic inventory, the history of the given and of neighbouring tongues. Social, regional, temporal, professional specificities are of the utmost relevance. As the ripples and shot silk interference effects expand outward, they become of incommensurable inclusiveness and complexity. No formalisation of an order adequate to the semantic mass and motion of a culture, to the wealth of denotation, connation, implicit reference, elision and tonal register which envelop what one means, meaning what one says or neither. There is a palpable sense in which one can see that the total explicative context, the total horizon of relevant values which surround the meaning of any verbal or written utterance is that of the universe as human beings, who as beings of speech inhabit. Thus the equation . . . between the limits of our language and the limits of our worlds, is almost a banality.[76]

Linguistic ontology embodies the attempt of philosophical hermeneutics to displace rather than refute philosophical nihilism. With the word, one never dwells alone. Each word opens on to the "beyond" while permitting that which is "beyond" to manifest and sustain itself in us. Nihilistic rejection of the metaphysically transcendent does not disrupt the possibility of hermeneutic translation and transcendence. Let us now turn to a related issue: Why does philosophical hermeneutics regard the will to method as nihilistic?

Philosophical hermeneutics charges that the threat of nihilism does not lie in the methodical per se but in the *universalization of method*. It contends that the belief that there is but one form of rational thought and that any genuine thinking must obey that norm has serious nihilistic consequences.

> Abstracted from the fundamental relation to the world that is given in the linguistic nature of our experience of it, science attempts to become certain about entities by methodically organizing its knowledge of the world. Consequently, it condemns as heresy all knowledge that does not allow of this kind of certainty and that therefore cannot serve the growing domination of being. (TM, 476)

Such overt iconoclasm should not pass unremarked. There are serious objections to Gadamer's critique of scientific methodology, but what is of immediate concern is the nihilistic implication of the quest for this "kind of certainty." The will to method is charged with perpetrating an ideological deception: that "despite the ultimate incomprehensibility of life" and its "frightful countenance," it will impart "protection and certainty" (TM, 239). For philosophical hermeneutics, two issues arise here: first, the plausibility of the primary claim concerning certainty and, second, the broader consequences of adopting such a methodology. Concerning the first issue, Gadamer argues that "scientific certainty always has something Cartesian about it." It spawns a critical method that admits only of the validity of what cannot be doubted . . . in order to guarantee the certainty of its results" (TM, 239). If this means that everything appertaining to a scientific question must be rendered clear and must be ratified as rationally legitimate in order for it to be accepted as a legitimate "scientific issue," then such clarity is plainly impossible to achieve. The understanding of what it is for something to be a problem depends upon the hidden inheritance of not only our scientific but also our linguistic horizons. The belief that methodological consciousness can operate ex nihilo, detached from its enabling ontological premises, places that form of methodological consciousness on the same footing as aesthetic consciousness. Rooted in an ontology of the withheld, methodological consciousness is like aesthetic consciousness: it is always more than it knows itself to be (cf. TM, 116). From a hermeneutic perspective, the requirement that methodological consciousness should be transparent and acquire a grasp of all its operations is bogus. It follows, then, that as methodological consciousness cannot fully thematize its operations, its guarantee of certainty cannot be redeemed. It is the consequences of this failure that concern Gadamer. These constitute the second issue mentioned above.

In its opposition to philosophical nihilism, philosophical hermeneutics contends that, ontologically speaking, the fact of our being securely held within the withheld of language renders our dwelling within *this* world safe. The security of our being upheld by language has another kind of certainty about it, the "immediate living certainty" (TM, 238–39) of life itself. From the "living certainty" of our linguistic and cultural horizons spring the attitudes and values that prereflectively orientate us toward our everyday tasks. Dwelling within the ontological securities of language does not alleviate one from the uncertainties of choice or the instabilities of history. As we have seen, the very life of *die Sachen* is change and the essence of *Bildung* is, in effect, a becoming shaped by the "negativities of experience." In essence, then, having faith in linguistic being is being persuaded that even though all existence may, metaphysically speaking, be encircled by nothingness, such encirclement is in itself irrelevant. It is our rootedness in the transcendent elements of language that renders our dwelling within *this* world fundamentally safe and potentially meaningful. Though we will never lose our ontological buoyancy within this "floating world," life within it remains constantly challenged by epistemological and moral uncertainty. Yet, as we have seen, it is precisely upon the negativity of such provocations that hermeneneutic transcendence depends. The well-being of hermeneutic understanding and the openness of spirit it engenders depend upon *instability*. They require the challenges of having to think again, of having to confront the emergence of difference and of allowing oneself to be questioned by the disclosures of change. Without such instability, hermeneutic growth and responsiveness atrophy. Understanding is always restless, unquiet understanding.

The primary critical thrust of philosophical hermeneutics against method aims not at method per se but at the universalization of its assumptions *at the cost of other kinds of certainty*. Apart from the very real cultural danger of offering certainty where none can be given, philosophical hermeneutics points out that it is vacuous to demand that the prereflective assumptions that govern our deliberate reflections be rendered totally explicit. Such assumptions can be clarified but, stemming from within the withheldness of language, they cannot by definition be rendered transparent. That we cannot fully objectify and theorize the intuitions that inform our beliefs does not mean that they are illegitimate and should be abandoned. To abandon them would be indicative of the severest nihilism, which refuses to respond to the aquifers of meaning within language out of which our initial values grow. In effect, the universalization of method is guilty of a grotesque hermeneutic hubris. Whereas for hermeneutics that which is *bewusst* is subordinate to the *Sein* in which it is rooted, in methodological consciousness, *Sein* is made accountable to that which is *bewusst*. The danger here is twofold. First, such universalization bolsters the will to method's imperious illusion that only its norms of thought are valid. Second (and more important), the constant slandering of life's horizons as uncertain and unpredictable persuades us that they are, indeed, irrational and that we should not heed their claims. It is as if Gadamer senses that the promise of an unrealizable certainty persuades us that we do not have to respond to the challenges and instabilities that spring from our life worlds. The comforts of a spurious epistemological certainty are traded for the uncertainties of hermeneutic transcendence. Despite its rigor and energy, the attempt of the will to method to subject *Sein* to the narrow horizons of what can be knowingly grasped cannot hide what its efforts betray. They betray a withered sensibility, blindness to other kinds of certainty and a nihilistic *Lebensmüdigkeit* that can no longer respond to the stimuli of the unexpected and the different. Nevertheless, it is not the woeful insensitivity of methodological consciousness that distresses philosophical hermeneutics. It is the claim of methodological consciousness that any insight that does not meet with its rigorous epistemological criterion for truth or reasonableness is irrational or inadmissible. In the eyes of philosophical hermeneutics, the rejection by methodological consciousness of the other and different is indicative of its profound nihilism.

Gadamer's worries about the nihilistic tendencies of method find an echo in Iser's remarks about the tendency of the will to method to colonize subject matters as its own. Now, philosophical hermeneutics views interpretation as making the difference that generates the need for further understanding. Interpretation opens an ineliminable space between the register in which a subject is received and the register into which it is to be translated or applied. For Iser, as we have seen, this ineliminable space drives further interpretation. For Gadamer, it is the differences and tensions within the subject matters themselves that are instrumental. He speaks of ideas occurring to us, of being drawn to and led by ideas as they manifest themselves within our linguistic horizons. Referring to Hegel's *Logik*, Gadamer implies that "the way of thinking" is not to pursue a method but to submit to the action of the thing itself (TM, 464): "Certainly the thing does not go its own course without our thinking being involved, but thinking means unfolding what consistently flows from the subject matter itself." Thinking in a speculative manner is, then, not the methodic activity of the subject but is something that thought "suffers": it is the activity of the thing itself that guides the thinker. Being drawn into what presents itself is not a matter of following a proof but of acknowledging the weight of its self-evidence. Gadamer insists that the thoughts that occur to one when one submits to the movement of a subject matter have a force, a persuasiveness, and a reasonableness of their own.

> The thing itself compels us to speak of an event and an activity of the thing. What is evident is always something that is said—a proposal, a plan, a conjecture, an argument, or something of the sort, The idea is always that what is evident has not been proved and is not absolutely certain, but it asserts itself by reason of its own merit within the realm of the possible and the plausible . . . what is evident is always something surprising as well, like a new light being turned on, expanding the range of what we can take into consideration. (TM, 486)

A thought that occurs to us or strikes us seems plausible or convincing not because it strikes us ex nihilo carrying its own epistemological credentials as it were, but because we recognize it as another or different aspect of a subject matter we have a past acquaintance with. The new thought is persuasive because it foregrounds what was held within a known contextual background. The new thought reconfigures the subject matter we were previously acquainted with, permitting it to be understood in a new way. The sense of certainty with which we are seized when we see that a new idea "fits" by making new sense of what went before, is not the certainty of method but the certainty of life, the certainty of that which *shows itself* to be the case. Furthermore, although it is the *subject matter* that shows itself, it nevertheless shows itself *to us* and, in so doing, is able to transform our understanding of it. In other words, individual subjectivity cannot be eliminated from the disclosure of subject matters: thoughts occur *to us*, insights strike *us*, ideas speak *to us*. The subjective element within such a cognitive process cannot be removed. Speculative thinking in the way that Gadamer understands it involves, then, a becoming *gebildet*, an attuning of oneself to the many voices of subject matters, a being prepared for the genuinely educative challenge of listening to and responding to their claims and a willingness to change accordingly.[77] The cost of not doing so would atrophy the horizons of meaning that initiate our self-understanding and would thereby also diminish the possibilities of hermeneutic translation and transcendence. Preserving such possibilities, however, depends upon a willingness to submit to the movement of *die Sachen* and to listen to what the movement of ideas discloses. Gadamer's hostility to the universalization of method focuses on what might be termed as the nihilistic threat of hermeneutic *stasis*, of bringing the movement of *die Sachen* to a stop. Iser, once again, gives us a valuable insight into the nature of Gadamer's concerns.

For Iser the ineliminable space between the register in which a subject is received and the register into which it is to be translated drives further interpretation. For Gadamer the opening of such a space allows for the movement of die *Sache* itself. Iser observes, however, that whenever the presuppositions of the receiving register are superimposed on the subject matter, the liminal space is colonized by the concepts brought to bear.

> Such a colonization converts interpretation into an act that determines the intended meaning of the subject matter. When this happens interpretation ceases. The colonization of the liminal space therefore sacrifices translatability and with it the chance to embrace more than was possible before the superimposition.[78]

The capacity of method to colonize experience is something Gadamer is clearly fearful of. The imposition of method's own presuppositions on a subject matter is not a model of hermeneutic engagement. It is an act concerned with the strict imposition of what according to its own premises constitutes a legitimate claim to truth or, in Nietzsche's phrase, what should count as true. In effect, the restricting and restrictive scope of method serves to eliminate difference and to hamper the movement of *die Sachen*. Interpretation (and opportunities for hermeneutic translation and transcendence) thereby cease. The anthroplogist Peter Duerr reveals an analogous dimension to this problem.

The tendancy of method to reduce everything to its own presupposition is characteristic for Duerr of those modes of translation which reduce the foreign to the norms of its own expectations.

> There are those who do not want to understand. They are satisfied to do nothing more than translate and subsume and incorporate. They have no desire to know *who* they are. All they want is to get heavier, or at least, to remain as they are . . . .[79]

> What is alien is supposedly understood when it is translated into familiar categories. . . . Strangeness is alienated and resettled at home and thus neutralized. Things are understood as soon as it can be shown that we have always virtually understood them. . . .[80]

> To *understand* is not the same as to *translate*. . . . To understand often means that instead of recognizing what is strange as if it were familiar (what Plato suggests with his model of cognition as "re-cognition"), we learn how a word is used in a strange context, how it functions in an unfamiliar environment.[81]

To understand, for Duerr, is in effect to be hermeneutically translated, to embrace difference and to become different to ourselves.

> If we want to see what it (the "werewolf" wheel) turns at home, how it "works" there, we need to go to where the "werewolf" walks about at night. We may then have to howl with the werewolves to understand how they howl.
>   What we then experience will not be easy to moor, load and take home. "Any one bent on an ocean voyage," says Jacob Grimm, "and able to man a ship, set sail and guide it to a distant shore, will still have to land where the ground is different and where a different wind blows."[82]

These arguments bring into focus two entailments within Iser's analysis of method as colonization. The first reminds us that without the moderation of other forms of intellectual sensibility, method has a tendency to operate as an imperial power. It tends to recognize the strange and foreign only once they have been made to fit a form that it can assimilate or handle. The second alludes to the fact that the emergence of imperious method is at the cost of what Duerr somewhat pejoratively describes as cultural annihilation. Although philosophical hermeneutics does not speak in such extreme terms, a similar disquiet is plainly apparent. As we have argued, philosophical hermeneutics is not fearful of method per se but of the idolization of method. It is fearful of such idolization because the latter castigates attuning oneself to the plural voices of subject matters as irrational subjectivism. It is in the pillorying of such sensitivity that philosophical hermeneutics senses the threat not of cultural annihilation but of cultural displacement. The nihilism implicit within unrestrained method induces an ever more profound deafness to the way tradition, *Sachen*, and the withheld within our language-horizons can address us. The spread of such insensitivity promotes an increasing indifference to the claims of hermeneutic transcendence within oneself. Atrophying the power of such claims limits the relevance and function of the subject matters themselves. Their movement is hindered and their power to disclose diminished. Here the link between Iser's and Gadamer's reasoning is at its strongest. Iser perceives how the capacity of method for colonization brings translation to a halt by suppressing the ineliminable space between subject matters and the registers into which they are to be transposed. For Gadamer it is precisely the ineliminable space that translation and understanding opens up that allows *die Sachen* to be kept in play and it is this play that is the basis of hermeneutic transcendence. The nihilism that philosophical hermeneutics detects in the will to method concerns the latter's suspiciousness toward change and instability. It aspires to control the spontaneous movement of thought and the play of *Sachen*, which animate thought. This highlights the substantial point of difference between philosophical hermeneutics and the aggrandizing tendencies of method. Reason and its methodical applications do not in themselves produce values and world outlooks. They betray the instrumentalist tendencies of what is in effect only one way of relating to the world. Philosophical hermeneutics shares with philosophers as various as Schopenhauer, Nietzsche, and Adorno that profound sense of unease about the limits of scientific rationality which is so ably expressed by Wittgenstein.[83] Indeed, philosophical hermeneutics shares with Nietzsche a deep worry about the potential cultural malaise that might follow once the pretensions of method become apparent. If the sources of cultural values, of *Bildung* and the transformative processes associated with it, become atrophied because of the ridicule the universalization of method heaps upon the subjective dimensions of knowing, what intellectual sensibilities can be turned to when method's empire recedes? Philosophical hermeneutics is haunted by the question of whether a culture that has had its inner sensibilities so damaged might ever be able to attune itself to the voices of *die Sachen* and of tradition ever again? Perhaps for the purposes of argument, the issue can be put even more starkly.

The divide between philosophical hermeneutics and scientific method involves a clash of sensibility. Hermeneutic consciousness orientates itself toward understanding as a mode of becoming. Its celebration of becoming subjects the interpreting subject to continual challenges, opening possibilities for transformation and transcendence. Methodological consciousness seeks stability and order and to subject the world to the norms of its own mode of enquiry. Philosophical hermeneutics, it must be stressed, is not involved in any grotesque denial of the unquestionable achievements of method in science and medicine. Neither is it concerned with those embarrassing claims made in arts-science debates about the superiority of one mode of reasoning over another. The issue for Gadamer and indeed for Iser and Duerr is simply that there is not one royal road to knowledge. Philosophical hermeneutics recognizes that cognition is multiform. Indeed, when the subject matter to be understood is constututed by a constellation of related fields of concerns, cognition must itself be perspectivally multiform. Philosophical hermeneutics does not demand the exclusion of method from cognition but only that the later should not monopolize cognition and subvert its multiform nature. For the will to method to deny the rights of *cortesia* to other routes to knowledge is to become party to the gradual silencing of the voices of inward cognition. To silence those voices and to cap the aquifers of inherited meaning from which they spring betrays in the eyes of philosophical hermeneutics a perturbing nihilism which is suspicious of the risks and challenges that our linguistic being affords. The defense of *Bildung* that philosophical hermeneutics argues for in such a sustained manner is precisely an attempt to acknowledge, to learn the ways of, and to remain open to not just the voices of inward cognition but to those of the different and the other. The practice of becoming *gebildet* is the practice of being able to respond to the challenges of translation and transcendence when they arise.

CONCLUSION

Far from being a romantic diversion, Gadamer's reflections on *Bildung* and the process of becoming *gebildet* are central to how philosophical hermeneutics articulates the ontological ground of understanding. The notion of *Bildung* is deeply implicated in the eleven theses concerning the nature of philosophical hermeneutics put forward in chapter 1 of this essay and extends them significantly. Thesis one proposes that understanding requires difference. Central to the discussion of *Bildung* is a consideration of the dynamics of hermeneutic encounter. Parties involved in such encounters require the difference of the other so as to become different to themselves. *Bildung* requires difference to achieve new formations of itself. *Bildung* entails the transformative process whereby we come to understand what we have understood differently. Thesis two contends that philosophical hermeneutics promotes a philosophy of experience. *Bildung* and its related terms *Bildung haben* and becoming *gebildet* are not connected to specific regimes of learning but rather to processes of experiential exchange. The notion of becoming *gebildet* is synonymous with the "negativity of experience" in which the challenge of the other forces a review of experiential expectancies. The tempering of *Bildung* is premised on a dialogical involvement with the other and is without prejudice as to what such engagement might give rise to. The concept of *Bildung* encapsulates Gadamer's conviction that "experience as a whole is not something that anyone can be spared" (TM, 356). Thesis three—philosophical hermeneutics entails a commitment to hermeneutic realism—is forcefully confirmed by *Bildung* conceived as a tradition. Engaging with tradition involves encountering the reality of interpretative frameworks that transcend subjectivity. The notion of becoming *gebildet* affirms the undeniable reality of the received past and the anticipated future. Thesis four—hermeneutics seeks otherness within the historical—is implicit within the argument that becoming *gebildet* demands an ear for the voice of the other and for the otherness that speaks through that voice. Thesis five—philosophical hermeneutics reinterprets transcendence—is embedded in the argument that becoming *gebildet* entails a willingness both to depart from one's initial interpretative expectancies and to recognize that any transformation of understanding is dependent upon dialogical involvement with the other. Hermeneutical transcendence does not seek to escape such engagement but to transform it. Thesis six—philosophical hermeneutics entails an ethical disposition—is endorsed by the argument that *Bildung* requires a sensibility for the other and otherness. The development of this disposition is central to the case for *cortesia*. The rites of *cortesia* acknowledge that the other has something to say and that what is held within the other's withheld are possibilities for understanding that are not presently ours. Thesis seven—hermeneutic understanding redeems the negativity of its constituting differential—finds its confirmation in the ontological argument that *Bildung* perpetuates and extends its being when the *Sachen* that constitute its being are engaged with and transformed accordingly. Thesis eight—philosophical hermeneutics affirms an ontology of the in-between—is confirmed by the argument that the process of becoming *gebildet* involves the acquisition of a mode of consciousnuess able to discern the space between different horizons of hermeneutic orientation. Thesis nine—philosophical hermeneutics is a philosophical practice rather than a philosophical method—is endorsed by the argument that becoming *gebildet* is fundamentally a practice in "sensibility," a practice dedicated to refining one's sensitivities toward the other and the different. Thesis ten—philosophical hermeneutics entails a negative hermeneutics—is sustained by the argument that becoming *gebildet* is to acquire sufficient experience to know that whatever present and future experience presents, no experience is definitive. This apparent negativity grounds the possibility of future learning. To recognize the limits of an experience is to acknowledge that there is always more to be said about it. Finally, Gadamer's approach to *Bildung* vindicates a central aspect of thesis eleven: philosophical hermeneutics affirms linguistic being as a *mysterium*. Philosophical hermeneutics does not appeal to a mystical conception of understanding unbounded by any limit. It appeals to that practical understanding which is synonymous with what becoming *gebildet* grasps. It is the always more to be said and the always more to be understood that is without limit.

The notions of *Bildung*, *Bildung haben*, and becoming *gebildet* both confirm and extend the eleven theses concerning philosophical hermeneutics stated above. That these three notions comply with these theses does not demonstrate that philosophical hermeneutics is a systems philosophy but rather that its arguments stand in systemic relation with the constellation of positions they establish. Yet the philosophical importance of *Bildung* for philosophical hermeneutics extends well beyond the theses outlined. Gadamer's elaboration of *Bildung* as the metaphysically groundless foundation of understanding is a central pivot in his case against nihilism. To turn one's back on the difficulty of finding words to express one's insights and to insist that propositional language is the only legitimate linguistic vehicle for expressing meaning is not just to impoverish the subtleties of experience but to spurn what life and learning depend on. It is to neglect the practice of becoming *gebildet*. It is to refuse the ceaseless endeavor to extend and deepen experience. However, whereas the analysis of *Bildung* considered above broadly deals with the exteriority of the process, it is to its interiority that we must now turn.

CHAPTER THREE

Intimations of Meaning
Philosophical Hermeneutics and the Defense of Speculative Understanding

Philosophical hermeneutics is *philosophical* in that it strives to discern objectivities within the subjective voice. The concern with tradition, with *Bildung* and with *die Sachen* endeavors to articulate the historical and ontological "truths" that inflect that voice. The articulation of a hermeneutic practice that strains to discern such objectivities in both the spoken and the written is integral to a conception of language as a world disclosive power. It is a fundamental claim of philosophical hermeneutics that though the practised communicator may know how to invoke them, the objectivities that emerge through his or her words are a linguistic event. An epiphany of meaning is not reducible to subjective intentionality. On this point, Gadamer is (unusually) emphatic.

> Words that bring something into language are themselves a speculative event. Their truth lies in what is said in them and not in an intention locked in the impotence of subjective particularity. (TM, 489)

Philosophical hermeneutics endeavors to chart those historical and linguistic "substantialities" which shape the subjective contrary to a subject's willing and doing. Philosophical hermeneutics does not seek to discredit the subjective but treats it as the site through which the hermeneutically "real" discloses itself. The stress that philosophical hermeneutics places upon the objectivities within the subjective is laudable enough. However, in its attempt to move away from the subjectivisms of romantic hermeneutics, philosophical hermeneutics overlooks a key function of subjectivity. The "truths" that are speculatively disclosed through speech or writing must be *subjectively* apprehended in order for them to become effective. Although the truth of a hitherto unperceived aspect of a *Sache* is not any the less true for not being apprehended, its hermeneutic appropriation by a subject is vital if that *Sache* is to function within a linguistic community and if it is to enable a subject to think differently about an issue. Gadamer appears to overlook this. He insists that when a subject matter discloses itself, "*it* asserts itself by reason of its own merit within the realm of the possible and probable . . . there is something *evident* in-itself." He even implies that an experience of the real is part of the reality experienced. He speaks of "experience that experiences reality and is itself real" (TM, 346). Nevertheless, the role of subjectivity within the *activation* of a *Sache* cannot be avoided. Who apprehends and for whom is a "truth" possible and probable? In short, philosophical hermeneutics must address the question of how a subject apprehends the claims of a subject matter as being true (TM, 411). Philosophical hermeneutics needs to confront the subjective dimension of its operation. It is one thing to discern the objectivities within the subject voice but quite another to show how the subject engages with those objectivities. Why is it needful that philosophical hermeneutics address this question? Why is it strategically vital that the interiority of hermeneutic experience be addressed?

It was noted in chapter 1 of this essay that philosophical hermeneutics has not always been its own best advocate. On matters of considerable importance, its arguments can seem frustratingly vague, indecisive, and opaque. Philosophical hermeneutics makes substantial claims about the specific nature of aesthetic, literary, and historical understanding and perceives the vital role of such understanding in the formation of a subject's sense of identity, individual narrative, and purpose. And yet, Gadamer's hermeneutics does not explicitly address the interior dynamics of what happens to us when a text or an artwork addresses us, even though philosophical hermeneutics clearly has the conceptual means to address this issue. The primary aim of this part of our essay is to demonstrate how a careful reflection on the notion of "speculative understanding" can successfully address the question of the interiority of understanding.

That philosophical hermeneutics does not *directly* address the question of the subject's apprehension of "truth" reflects, perhaps, Heidegger's unease about the romantic inheritance within the philosophy of subjectivity. Nevertheless, there are three clear reasons why philosophical hermeneutics *must* address the subjective dimension of hermeneutic experience. First, if philosophical hermeneutics does not address the question of a subject's apprehension of truth, it becomes vulnerable to its own criticism of Dilthey's hermeneutics. Dilthey's hermeneutics betrays a methodological distanciation (alienation) which seeks only to decipher or to read off a subject matter without becoming involved with it. Philosophical hermeneutics, however, lays claim to a phenomenological engagement with its subject matter as opposed to the detachment of a descriptive phenomenalism. Second, the understated concern of philosophical hermeneutics with subjective apprehension is, indeed, implicit within its treatment of application. Application is not subsequent to understanding but is intrinsic to its assimilative function. Understanding is, Gadamer, insists, concretization (TM, 334); it is the "very understanding of a universal—a subject matter—in concrete terms" (TM, 341). Application is not grasped as a mere carrying out of an order, as a dutiful application of a rule but as a knowing how to render for oneself what a text asks, a knowing how to translate into one's own terms what it asks of one. Gadamer openly concedes the need for a subject's involvement in what it apprehends when he states that hermeneutic understanding demands that the subject is kept in play.[1] Third, if philosophical hermeneutics were not committed to a view on a subject's involvement in what it apprehends, its defense of hermeneutical *experience* would collapse. What makes Gadamer's critique of aesthetic consciousness so powerful is its insistence that profound experience is not momentary in nature. Were such momentariness a genuine characteristic of aesthetic experience, we could only say that a work exists in a moment, in this "now" and is then no longer (TM, 95). Were this so, the temporal coherence of the work and of the person seeking to understand it would be destroyed. The continuity of meaning characteristic of both an artwork and a hermeneutic subject depends upon the ability to bring such moments in relation to others, past, present, of the same or different kinds. This requires memory and concerned involvement. Drawing comparisons between such moments would otherwise be vacuous. Philosophical hermeneutics can defend a continuity of understanding in self-narrative or in a tradition only if it can defend a continuity of *concern*, and that presupposes subjective engagement with what a subject matter discloses.

Despite being downplayed, the issue of the subject's role in activating the truth of an apprehended *Sache* is vital to any account of the dynamics of hermeneutic experience. This part of our essay explicates an approach to subjective apprehension consistent with the speculative nature of linguistic experience offered by philosophical hermeneutics. The importance of the subject's role in activating the "truth" of a *Sache* is made clear in Gadamer's account of the nature of speculative thinking. The issues involved in this account have an intimate bearing on why philosophical hermeneutics rejects the claim that subjective apprehensions of meaning are "groundless," why it seeks to found a philosophical humanism on *Sprachlichkeit*, and why it endeavors to refute Nietzsche's philosophy of language.

Before we embark upon a response to these issues, it should be remembered that the concern with the speculative involves more than the question of how a subject comes to be addressed by the truth claims of certain experiences. Such experiences are centripetal in nature, they have an element of self-implication in them which allows the subject to perceive an unnoticed continuity of meaning. Gadamer's emphasis upon the capacity of aesthetic experience to unify disparate strands of meaning into a whole—the transformation into structure argument—has prompted the criticism that his argument reverts to and reiterates a philosophy of identity. Unfortunately, Gadamer's choice of philosophical terminology (part-whole relationships) gives the charge credence. However, given its key philosophical commitments, it would be stranger still if philosophical hermeneutics were to collapse into a philosophy of identity. The emphasis given to the incompleteness of understanding and to the susceptibility of all understanding to the negativity of experience is quite at odds with a philosophy of identity. For the reasons outlined above, though philosophical hermeneutics addresses the centripetal moments of understanding, it is also concerned with the disruptive moments of understanding and, furthermore, with the relation between them. As we have argued, philosophical hermeneutics has not always been its own best advocate. What Gadamer fails to do is to properly articulate the dialectical nature of speculative understanding and to show that understanding renews and extends itself by virtue of the continual oscillation of its integrating and disintegrating moments. Though Gadamer may not achieve such an articulation, philosophical hermeneutics clearly has the internal philosophical resources to do so. The great merit of its approach to the speculative is its exploration of how our linguistic being puts us at the mercy of the continuous push and pull of linguistically born ideas. The importance of its enquiry into the speculative is not merely that it tries to establish the phenomenological conditions whereby the subject apprehends the truth or meaningfulness of an experience but that in so doing it also outlines the conditions that dissipate the meaningful. Precisely because philosophical hermeneutics approaches the subject's apprehension of the meaningful via a linguistic analysis of the speculative, that analysis also sets the conditions whereby the meaningful is dissolved as a prelude to its future renewal. As we shall see in the second half of this third part of this essay, this linguistic approach to the speculative dynamics within the meaningful establishes the basis for a major confrontation between Nietzsche and philosophical hermeneutics with respect to the philosophies of language they defend.

WHAT IS SPECULATIVE THINKING?

The importance of speculative thinking within philosophical hermeneutics was discussed in the previous chapter of this essay.[2] What specifically concerns us in this section is how Gadamer's account of speculative thinking illuminates the subject's role in bringing a subject matter to life. At the outset of our discussion, it is important to appreciate the ordinariness of what Gadamer's application of Hegel's account of the speculative directs us toward. Gadamer's account of speculative thinking attempts to articulate the dynamics of everyday thought, the way one idea passes to another and the way in which sometimes, contrary to our willing and doing, associations of ideas combine to provide new insights, throwing our previous understandings of a subject matter into disarray. Philosophical hermeneutics is not interested in speculative thinking because it offers a *method* of interpretation but because it attempts to articulate how we are continually at the mercy of the push and pull of ideas, images, and their associations. The interest of philosophical hermeneutics in the speculative is indicative of its interest in the life of hermeneutic consciousness itself. Philosophical hermeneutics is *philosophical* in that it seeks to enquire into experiences that we are all acquainted with at some level or other, experiences of being caught up in an idea and how it can unfold, and of being drawn along by a flow of thought toward an insight that we might initially only dimly perceive. Speculative thought tries to express something of what it means to be caught up in the motion of ideas and, indeed, what it means to be arrested by them. On a more formal level, philosophical hermeneutics offers two different but related accounts of the speculative. The first is a thinly disguised version of the language of Hegel's speculative logic and the second concerns an ontological rendering of the dialectical interplay of language and the language of images within speculative experience.

The Formal Elements of Speculative Thought

Gadamer states the formal features of speculative thought as follows.

> The word speculative . . . refers to the mirror relation. Being reflected involves a constant substitution of one thing for another . . . (TM, 465)

> A thought is speculative if the relationship it asserts is not conceived as a quality unambiguously assigned to a subject, a property given over to a given thing, but must be thought of as a mirroring, in which the reflection is nothing but the pure appearance of what is reflected, just as the one is the one of the other and the other is the other of the one. (TM, 466)

The relation between a subject and its predicate in an ordinary proposition is nonreflective. The predicates accumulate to inform us ever more about the subject. In so doing the predicates serve essentially as signs, always referring to the subject beyond them. There is no sense that such predicates operate like symbols embodying the presence of the subject. In a speculative proposition, however, the subject is recognized as being in its predicates. In Gadamer's phrase, "the subject passes over" into its predicates. The predicates no longer merely describe my attributes as a subject but I find myself, before myself, so to speak, embodied in the descriptive predicates themselves. Gadamer remarks,

> Starting from the subject, as if this remained the basis throughout, it finds that, since the predicate is rather the substance, the subject has passed into the predicate and has been superseded. And since what seems to be predicate has become the whole independent mass, thought cannot roam freely, but is stopped by this weight. Thus the form of the proposition destroys itself since the speculative proposition does not state something about something: rather it presents the unity of the concept. (TM, 466-67)

Gadamer explains this in the following way: "God is one" does not mean that it is a property of God to be one but that it is God's nature to be a unity (TM, 466). A better explanation can be obtained if we return to his argument concerning the ability to discern the substantive in all that is subjective. As will become apparent, speculative thinking concerns a moment of reversal in which the subject recognizes itself as itself in its predicates or attributes. Now, to be graspable as predicates of the self, such predicates have to be stated. Such statements accordingly objectify the predicates of the self. However, language does not merely objectify, it also reveals. In addition to objectifying or externalizing qualities of the subject as predicates, the linguistic act of stating such predicates *also* allows a sense of self to come to mind within the listening subject. The same act can summon up in the mind of the subject an image or likeness of itself. No longer does the linguistic act just separate the subject from its predicates but it also allows the subject to recognize itself—to see its likeness—embodied in the predicates. Bernstein takes up the theme of apprehending the substantive within the subjective.

Bernstein contends that speculative propositions are reflective elucidations of a sedimented substantiality.[3] They are forms of essentialist predication where the relation between subject and predicate begins to oscillate. In the reverse swing of this motion, the so-called predicate is revealed to be the actual substantial reality of the subject, so much so that the subject cannot be comprehended without it. For example, language is often taken to be an attribute of human subjects. Whatever the subject is, it is (supposedly) something more than language. Language is regarded as being at the disposition of the human subject. However, the substantiality that underwrites a subject's predicative awareness of language is, of course, language itself. It is, furthermore, our involvement in language that subjectivizes us. In short, whatever the subject is, it is inconceivable without the ontic priority of language. Thus, in Bernstein's phrase, the so-called predicate is revealed to be the substantiality of the subject such that the human subject cannot be thought without it. Like Hegel and Adorno, Gadamer is wedded to the conviction that because of the sedimented substantiality of human consciousness, whenever a subject seeks to elucidate its predicates or acts in such a way as to assume that its reality lies in its predicates (self-conceptions), it will suffer a "counter thrust."[4] By "counter thrust" Gadamer alludes to that "negativity of experience" in which the conscious subject is forced to consider renouncing some of its self-conceptions because the self, which begins to be speculatively configured within the predicates of its self-description, is at odds with the subject's preconceptions of itself. Speculative thinking, it would appear, is tragic.[5] The subject can only come to itself by losing itself, by coming to recognize its substantiality in an external other. The negativity of speculative experience involves "reflective self-dispossession."[6] Yet that moment of self-dispossession is a moment of hermeneutic transcendence, a moment when the subject recognizes its dependence on a substantive reality, which extends beyond its being. Such a moment of speculative recognition is centripetal in nature. Having considered some of the formal characteristics of speculative thought, we shall now pass to its phenomenological dynamics.

The Speculative Motion of Hermeneutic Experience

The insights that speculative experience affords have both a centrifugal and a centripet moment. In coming to realize that its substantiality is of a nature different to its previous self-conceptions, a subject is thrown beyond itself, forced to abandon previous subjective self-understandings (the centrifugal), and, in the light of what is newly revealed to it about its substantiality, made to reconfigure its self-understanding (the centripetal). The oscillation between the centrifugal and the centripetal aspects of understanding is central to Gadamer's approach to speculative experience.

Gadamer's phenomenological approach to speculative experience assumes that in our experiences of music, art, and literature, something speaks to us: "The first thing with which (aesthetic) understanding begins is that something speaks to us"[7]; we recognize "that there is something clearly true about . . . (what) is said" to us.[8] The experience of being open toward what is said constitutes the universality of hermeneutics' truth claim.[9] This does not allude to a universal truth-content which hermeneutics is privileged to uncover but to a shared experience concerning how artworks address us, albeit each in our own way[10] The speculative truth claim clearly contains a moment of *self-implication* in it. Such claims are not merely statements about "what is the case" but are statements that we grasp as truly illuminating our experience of their object. They seize us in such a way as to make it difficult for us to turn away from them: they make too much sense for us to deny them. Philosophical hermeneutics reflects a central claim of Hegel's phenomenology. The "principle of experience carries with it the unspeakably important condition, that in order to accept and believe any fact, we must be in contact with it; or, in more exact terms, we must find the fact united and combined with the certainty of our own selves."[11] Humboldt, too, grasps these moments of understanding as directly addressing our being: "I now understand fully how one can know nothing of mankind, of life and of the world that one has not brought to birth deep in one's own being, or rather, that one has not proved upon oneself."[12] The issue of the speculative truth claim of art is not strictly epistemological. It does not primarily concern the truth value of the way the world is represented in art.

What it concerns is the phenomenological fact that when art or literature addresses us in a profound and penetrating way, we know that we are truly being addressed. We recognize that our own self-understanding is potentially at stake, that our self-conception is at risk. In effect, the experience of knowing that there is something clearly true about what an artwork claims is already to have undergone a speculative reversal. It is to know that we are not the judges of art but that it is we who are susceptible to art's judgment. What provokes this susceptibility?

If the speculative experience of truth entails recognition of self-implication, a process of recognition must be involved. If recognition is entailed, remembrance is implied, and if remembrance is suggested, so too is forgetfulness. These conceptual associations point to the fact that the speculative experience of truth with its centrifugal and centripetal motions is driven by the dialectical tensions between *anamnesis* (forgetfulness), *mimesis* (the recognition of the same), and *mynemosyne* (memory or recall). Philosophical hermeneutics follows Heidegger in denying that the latter are merely psychological categories. They manifest themselves in the hermeneutic subject but as key aspects of its understanding. They reflect different aspects of our substance, those of our *being*, of our cultured "placedness" or "thrownness" (*Geworfenheit*) and of our linguisticality (*Sprachlichkeit*). Once again we can see a key motif of philosophical hermeneutics operating in the argument, namely, the struggle to discern objectivities within the subjective voice. However, we should not be misled by Gadamer's invocation of such terms as *mimesis* and *anamnesis*. They do not indicate a diverting meditation upon pre-Socratic thought. To the contrary, he deploys them in order to achieve a mythopoeic inversion. In talking of these Greek concepts he is trying to identify the phenomenological structure of our own speculative experiences.[13] We shall now approach the speculative dynamic of hermeneutic experience more closely.

The hermeneutic experience of being addressed, of grasping that there is clearly something true about what is being said, involves, first: recognizing something that one was already acquainted with but had not fully grasped, and, second: in reappropriating what had not been initially grasped, coming to realize its significance for the first time. Hermeneutical experience of a speculative nature is genuinely educational. The recognition of the truth of that which was not initially grasped as true, involves a becoming different toward oneself. Speculative experience involves the interplay of repetition and difference. Insofar as it brings a change within a subject's self-understanding, speculative experience involves a moment of hermeneutic transcendence. This is not an intimation of some other

nonphenomenal realm but involves, in Danto's words, the "transfiguration of the commonplace,"[14] a transfiguration of experience, which
Gadamer identifies as a "transformation into structure."

> The transformation is a transformation into the true. It is not
> enchantment in the sense of a bewitchment that waits for the
> redeeming word that will transform things back to what they
> were, but it is itself redemption and transformation back into
> true being. . . . The world of the work of art . . . is in fact a
> wholly transformed world. By means of it, everyone recognizes
> that this is how things are. . . . From this viewpoint "reality" is
> defined as what is untransformed art as the raising up of this
> reality into its truth. (TM, 112–13)

Speculative experience does not entail the recovery of some other order
of awareness but a recognition, a realization that what we have unknowingly experienced as the everyday has been transformed. It involves a phenomenological shift from absentmindedness to mindfulness, and, for
Gadamer, it is the Greek goddess *Mnemosyne* who presides over this shift.

> *Mnemosyne* rules everything: to keep in memory means to be
> human. . . . Plato informs us with a decisiveness which it
> appears to me, we are always forgetting—that the human
> essence and knowledge can only be realised through practice,
> through *meletan*, only through always new creation, continual
> re-acquisition, continual renewing or continual re-creating
> does the stable come to be. The Greek expression for the re-
> tention of memory, *mneme*, connoted for the Greeks some-
> thing from *menein*, from remaining, from becoming stable.[15]

The passage implies that "speculative" knowledge does not occur ex
nihilo but emerges from hermeneutic labor, from hermeneutical engagement with the different and the other. Gadamer's invocation of
Mnemosyne as the muse of such practice is certainly telling. *Mnemosyne* was
also the name given to one of two springs in the cavern of Trophonios at
Lebadeia. The spring *Lethe* (forgetfulness) named the waters of the Un-
derworld and was closely connected with the idea that those who are to
be reborn must drink its waters in order to forget their former existence.
Pilgrims also drank from the spring *Mnemosyne* so that they might forget
ordinary matters and yet remember what was revealed to them by the or-
acle.[16] Now, it would appear that *Lethe* (forgetfulness) is bound up with

the word *aletheia* (truth) and thereby implies that an apprehension of truth involves not just a forgetting of the immediate (Gadamer sometimes describes the speculative in terms of the ability to pass over the transient and the superficial) but also a remembering of the forgotten. *Mnemosyne* is then connected to *aletheia*, to a truth that is reappropriated from its hiddeness, from what Gadamer also refers to as the withheld. What, then, is the hidden and untransformed which we ordinarily forget but nonetheless recognize when it confronts us within hermeneutic experience?

If the circle of speculative experience brings a moment of self-recognition and if, analogously, hermeneutic experience translates us not into another but into our own transformed world, the premise of this cycle must be a certain forgetfulness, an unknowing *ekstasis*, a being outside ourselves both innocent and unreflective. Such *ekstasis* can be grasped as follows. The speculative element in philosophical hermeneutics views the subject as an element in a sedimented substantiality. For Gadamer too, words are always documents of some collected, sedimented experience. Words betray a key aspect of our linguistic being: we are always other and much more than we know ourselves to be, and what exceeds our knowledge is our real being. Although we find our selves sedimented into a particular language world, every such linguistically constituted world is always open to other possible insights and can, thereby, expand its own world-picture, becoming available to others (TM, 448). Gadamer's language ontology has, it would appear, a certain Leibnizian dimension. Whereas for Leibniz, "each monad represents the whole universe," Gadamer suggests that each and every use of language expresses a particular relation to Being: every spoken word is capable of resonating the infinity of unspoken meaning that constitutes the virtuality of language (TM, 469). However, though as subjects we are sedimented into the substantiality of language in unreflective consciousness, we are unaware of our substantive actuality. We are, in our innocent beginnings, beings who are essentially both outside and more than ourselves. We neither know that everything we might think or express lies virtually within that linguisticality which stretches beyond our subjective consciousness, and even more disconcerting, nor do we have any awareness that the very words we now use can point to what will befall us. Already inscribed in the virtuality of language, are those combinations of words that will articulate our future fate. What will occur to us is already written on language's wall. This innocent unreflective mode of being tends to accept that its horizon is the world rather than seeing that its perspective is one of many shaped by a wider world of horizons. However, though an unreflective subject may falsely regard its horizon as being the world, ontologically speaking, that horizon is the point of access to the wider world of other languages, other histories, and other cultures. In this condition, the unreflective subject is not so much forgetful of its rootedness in what lies beyond it, as unaware of it. Our ontological *ekstasis*—our being outside ourselves—is hidden by the blindness and forgetfulness of our initial linguistic "thrownness." The truth that is hidden is not hidden from us because it is a noumenal entity. To the contrary, such a truth is plain for all to see who can see it. Indeed, the transition from being unaware of our connectedness to the linguistically constituted "world-in-itself" to becoming aware of that truth, does not affect the truth of that truth. The "power of the immediate," the innocent acceptance of the horizons of our culture as being the horizons of our world, or the forgetting the true extent of our linguistic being all blind us from seeing what in fact lies before our eyes. This gives a specific twist to the term *aletheia*.

Lethe (forgetfulness or concealment) is contained within *aletheia* itself. What is disclosed is, before the moment of its disclosure, not so much hidden as passed over as insignificant. Only when the significance of the passed over is revealed, do we perceive the oversight and see—for the first time—what that failure of perception has led to. The recognition of the oversight is more a recollection or transformation of what was overlooked rather than recalling a forgotten state of affairs. The experience of remembering or re-cognition (*anamnesis*) over which Mnemosyne presides involves a sense of a truth dawning more than of a truth being recovered. The revelatory nature of a speculative truth is not a bursting forth from a noumenal realm but a sudden shift of perspective that allows us to see that which we had not anticipated even though the elements of what we now know stood before us albeit in a fragmentary way. The hermeneutic experience of being addressed is educative in that the recognition of the truth of that which was not initially grasped as true, involves becoming different toward oneself. What we recognize with not inconsiderable shock is that the ordinary, which we daily overlooked and took for granted, was, indeed, far from ordinary but mediated by innumerable hermeneutic perspectives, which reach beyond what our previous horizons enabled us to see. *Ekstasis*—the forgotten ontological condition of our actually always being beyond ourselves—is the precondition of a speculative insight into our linguistic sedimentation. Indeed, the speculative insight does not represent or reformulate the truth of our *ekstasis*: it allows its truth as the forgotten and the withheld to be disclosed to the hermeneutic subject for the first time, hence, the poignancy of *Lethe* (forgetfulness or concealment) being contained within *aletheia*.

Given that the forgetfulness of linguistic *ekstasis* is the formal precondition of speculative experience and that, in effect, speculative experience transforms our understanding of the commonplace, what economy of experiential elements triggers the switch from the isolated innocence of linguistic *ekstasis* to a reflective awareness of the hermeneutical nature of our linguistic being? Philosophical hermeneutics contends that is our *participation* in language that makes us vulnerable to such shifts of insight. The indeterminate character of meaning within language renders any centripetal insight vulnerable to disruption from the centrifugal. Hermeneutic insight into the nature of our linguistic being does not take place because we are able to acquire a speculative as opposed to a propositional mode of language. It is, much rather, that propositional language has a speculative dimension and that speculative uses of language also have propositional elements. Forgetting the speculative dimension of language makes us vulnerable to its sudden irruption and to what such interruption discloses.

Ekstasis entails a forgetting or an ignorance of the speculative dimension of language. Such forgetfulness fosters the illusion that the world is, indeed, how we speak about it. We "really think," as Nietzsche observes, "that in language we possess knowledge of the world and that in language we are expressing supreme knowledge of things."[17] For Heidegger such beliefs indicate the cultural dominance of *apophantic* (propositional) language that presumes that the essence of a thing can be contained within propositional form.[18] Gadamer's concern is not with *apophantic* discourse per se but with the way its successful deployment in technology and science tends to displace the subtle and quieter "speculative" dimension of language where something shows itself *through* rather than *in* what is stated. Unlike Heidegger, who in effect asserts the phenomenological priority of speculative over propositional language, Gadamer regards the living actuality of language as involving a constant interplay and tension between its speculative and *apophantic* dimensions. This is evident in his remarkable attempt to fuse the speculative dialectic of Hegel with the dialogical dialectic of Plato. The dialectic of language does not just involve proposition and counterproposition. It also entails the disruption of argument by the emergence of unexpected insights that transform its direction. Philosophical hermeneutics insists that nodialectical engagement is immune from the speculative "play" of language. No matter how we might be ensnared in the illusion that words picture things, the actual words we speak retain their "speculative" relation to linguistic being irrespective of whether we are aware of it or not. As we are linguistic beings, we are always prone to the constant "speculative" movement of words and their meaning. It is our being in language that makes us unavoidably vulnerable to having our everyday grasp on the relationship between word and thing questioned. How might the challenge of the speculative be thought of?

Within unreflective consciousness we readily assume that the conceptual denotation of a word means no more than what is named and that the particulars named are definitive and exhaustive instances of a given meaning. We remain, in other words, blind to the fact that words can always mean more than they state. Unexpected experience can, however, disrupt such unreflective assumptions. A speculative irruption can break our unreflective horizon in two. A transformative difference between the conceptual dimension of a word and the ability of that word to invoke objects and associations within our immediate horizon can be opened up. In everyday consciousness I can use "rose" to refer to (1) the plant by my gate, without connecting it to (2) the botanical and (3) the spiritual implications of the word even though within *Sprachlichkeit* all three meanings of "rose" are connected. Nevertheless, despite that connection, the biographical world of a word's association and the realms of its conceptual reference can be experienced as utterly disparate: the one appearing as immediate, particular but utterly contingent (the rose by my gate) and the other (the realms of botanical taxonomy and spiritual imagery) as alien, abstract, and general, though not entirely arbitrary. The conflict initiated by the slippage of linguistic meaning between denotation and connotation, between particular and universal, initiated by the slippage of linguistic meaning, establishes the paradigmatic ground for hermeneutic endeavor.

In the essay "Aesthetic and Religious Experience," Gadamer comments, "The hermeneutic art is in fact the art of understanding something that appears alien and unintelligible to us."[19] The evident immediacy of the rose before me seemingly questions the legitimacy of any conceptual claim that the meaning of what is in front of me is in fact beyond me. On the other hand, knowing that linguistic reality extends beyond the sensuously immediate weakens the claim of the immediate particular to be the sole reality. Accordingly, philosophical hermeneutics commences with the problem of the alien and strange (TM, 374), with a placing of what the rose is in question. And yet, far from being negative, the essence of placing something in question allows us to become more open to what the rose might be in its full complexity. The more I question the rose and move into issues of genus, soil type, and climate or learn to perceive the white rose as a medieval English image of innocence and experience, the more it *occurs* to me that what seemed remote and abstract has been a formative influence upon my sense of landscape and flora and that, furthermore and much to my surprise, something of the long tradition of English spirituality embodies itself at the foot of my gatepost. What initially appears as abstract shows itself to have something to do with my very substance: what seemed apart from me now appears as a part of me. Such recognition always implies that we have come to know something more authentically than we were able to do when caught up in it in our first encounter with it.[20] It is this mode of recognition that enables the "truths" which are speculatively disclosed through speech or writing to be *subjectively* apprehended and thereby become effective within a subject's horizon. In such moments of recognition a speculative reversal takes place: something that I took to have nothing to do with my immediate reality—the determinations of rose that have a bearing on English landscape and spirituality—reveals itself as having a very real bearing (application) upon my very substance, so much so that I can no longer think of myself without reference to it. Such reversals can potentially transform what one has understood of one's identity and narrative. Philosophical hermeneutics does not suggest that such speculative revelations disclose a *definitive* or *final* meaning, only that what is revealed *transforms* what we have understood of ourselves so that, as a result, we become different to ourselves. In such moments, the hermeneutic subject recollects itself from the *ekstasis* of its ontological dispersal and becomes "more essentially more what it is." We shall return to this quasi-Platonic theme in Gadamer's thinking.

We have asked what triggers the speculative motion of language? The starting point appears to be immersion in the assumption that words correspond to actual things, an assumption that blinds us to the speculative nature of language. The flux of experience and the slippage of meaning forever threaten to disrupt this assumption and when the rupture occurs, we experience the bifurcation of the word, which then points us simultaneously toward the two worlds of the phenomenal and conceptual. The breaking of the bond between word and thing emerges as the starting point of hermeneutic questioning. To bring something into question is both to admit that we do not understand it and, at the same time, to quest after it. The very the slippage of meaning that initiates hermeneutic questioning is the selfsame slippage of meaning that enables unassociated concepts and intuitions to suddenly fuse (as in the case of the idea of spirituality linking with the phenomenally experienced rose) and thereby bring about a transformative speculative insight. In awakening to the greater and initially alien world of *Sprachlichkeit*, I find that not only is there a world beyond my subjectivity but that that very world constitutes me and that I am in every sense "illumined from beyond."[21] In the essay "Hegel and Heidegger," Gadamer speaks of the very impetus toward transcendence within language: "Speaking always transcends the linguistically constituted realm within which we find ourselves. . . . The hermeneutic virtuality of discourse . . . surpasses at any moment that which has been said."[22] However, what is it about the form or transcendent or speculative insight that enables the subject to apprehend its truth? Two lines of thought are pertinent. One concerns a notion of aesthetic wholeness or narrative completeness and the other involves completing a circle of meaning, the so-called transformation into structure argument. Both indicate why a speculative centripetal insight can induce such surprise.

Concerning the question of wholeness, Gadamer speaks of structures "which hang together," with everything within them in place, containing nothing conventional or stale.[23] The speculative insight, whether achieved through the languages of art or philosophy, does not discover a preexistent whole but, rather, makes whole. The dispersed and fragmented, that which is outside itself, appears mended and is made whole. The speculative insight forges a wholeness of experience which when experienced throws the hermeneutic subject back on itself. It is in these moments that the speculative reversal takes place: the hermeneutic subject is dispossessed of its ability to make assertions about the world and finds itself made subject to an assertion about itself and its world. When Gadamer speaks of the "truth" claims of art or of tradition he is not concerned with questions of epistemological legitimacy but with the fact that we find ourselves truly addressed by such claims. Contrary to our willing and sometimes contrary to our expectancies, they call to us. Irrespective of the question of whether what they claim is true, we acknowledge them as true claims because they truly claim our attention. We cannot turn aside from them, sensing that our very being is implicated in their claims. What the speculative insight reveals, therefore, is a claim, a way of looking at the world, a narrative completeness that stands on its own, confronts us, and addresses us as if it were a subject and we were predicated to it, subject to its claims. Gadamer's "transformation in structure argument" articulates the nature of this speculative reversal. Here, then, is a major element of the answer to the question posed at the outset of this part of this essay: What are the phenomenological dynamics at play when a hermeneutic subject is addressed by the truth claim of an artwork or text?

The first stage of Gadamer's argument presumes what we earlier described as the *ekstasis* of ontological dispersal. In unreflective consciousness Gadamer argues that "reality" invariably stands for us "in a horizon of the future of observed and feared or, at any rate undecided possibilities . . . lines of meaning scatter in the void" (TM, 112). Visual or literary art forms, on the other hand, form a meaningful whole from the incomplete and undecided possibilities of the everyday such that "no lines of meaning " disperse (TM, 112–13). Lines of meaning that in actuality remain incomplete, art can complete and fulfill. Gadamer comments,

> The being of all play (art) is always realisation, sheer fulfilment, *energeia* which has its *telos* within itself. The world of the work of art, in which play expresses itself fully in the unity of its course, is in fact a wholly transformed world. By means of it everyone recognizes that that is how things are. . . . *From this viewpoint "reality" is defined as what is untransformed, and art as the raising up of this reality into its truth.* (TM, 113; emphasis added)

The "transformation into structure" claims that by means of art and the speculative insights it affords, the reality of what it deals with becomes more what it is. Instead of reality or a subject matter being the object of a hermeneutic subject's address, transformed reality subjects the hermeneutic subject to its address. How can this moment of self-recognition or self-implication within the speculative reversal be articulated?

Anamnesis—the moment of recollection in which the hermeneutic subject finds itself implicated—is more to do with a sense of a truth dawning than with reappropriating a fixed truth from a condition of loss. By means of recollection, *Mnemosyne* shows us not how things were, since, as we have seen, recognition does not return us to a fixed identity, but reveals "how things actually are," or rather, allows us to see what they have become. Gadamer argues,

> But we do not understand what recognition is in its profoundest nature, if we only see that something that we know already is known again, i.e. that what is familiar is recognized again. The joy of recognition is rather that more becomes known than is already known. In recognition what we know emerges as if through an illumination, from all the chance and variable circumstances that condition it in its essence. (TM, 114)

Recollection is not repetition but annunciation. Inverting the standard interpretation of Plato, Gadamer contends that "imitation and representation are not merely a second version or copy but a recognition of the essence . . . they are not merely repetition but a bringing forth" (TM, 114). Artistic representation does not depart from or distort an otherwise independent truth (Plato) but allows that which is virtual within actuality to be realized, that is, to become such that it can truly speak and speak truly. Here we have a clue as to why the speculative insight can be such a shock.

By closing a circle of possible meaning, a visual or literary artwork is able to disclose that circle as a circle for the first time. The indeterminacy of meaning in actuality means that there is no knowing how an experiential sequence will develop or resolve. Lacking that insight means that we do not know whether that sequence is a sequence. The brilliance of an artwork's speculative revelation is that can enable us to perceive a circle of meaning where prior to the insight we saw none. The shock of speculative recognition is in suddenly seeing events and experiences, which we assumed disparate and unconnected, as connected and as moving toward an unanticipated fulfillment of meaning. Yet it also involves being brought to recognize our own blindness. By illuminating that which was before our eyes, the speculative insight reveals the fact of our former blindness. However, the real force of Gadamer's argument perhaps lies elsewhere.

Speculative insight involves, as we have argued, a moment of reversal. Whereas in everyday discourse, the subject regards the world and its objects as being subject to its will and judgment, the speculative insight reverses the situation. The subject and its self-understanding become *subject* to the judgment of the visual or literary artwork. Before this reversal, what the artwork is deemed as being, how it is understood, and how it is esteemed is seemingly dependent upon the judgment of the subject. However, once the reversal has taken place and the speculative object acquires its own voice, it is the subject who is put in the position of awaiting the judgment of what the work reveals. Our self-understanding and sense of narrative identity are placed in the balance. Both wait on what the speculative voices of art, philosophy, and literature judge us to be. As hermeneutic beings, we always stand under the sentence of *Mnemosyne's law. Let us summarize.*

At the beginning of this part of our essay, we asked what it is about the experience of an artwork and its subject matter that enables the hermeneutic subject to feel that it is being addressed by a truth. We embarked upon a discussion of the nature of speculative understanding on the premise that the latter revealed certain of the objective structures within subjective experience that philosophical hermeneutics attempts to identify. The concern of speculative thought is to express something of what it means to be caught up in the motion of ideas and what it means to be arrested by them. The key formal feature of speculative understanding concerns a moment of reversal in which, much to its surprise, a hermeneutic subject recognizes something of itself in its own predicates or attributes. The so-called predicate is revealed to be the actual substantial reality of the subject, so much so that the subject cannot be thought without it. In this sense the understanding is *speculative*: the hermeneutic subject finds itself being reflected back from its outward objectifications. Though speculative understanding can be formally characterized as such a moment of reversal, it is clear that this form of understanding is experiential and involves participation in a dynamic of self-dispossession and retrieval. The initial movement of this dynamic concerns *ekstasis*, a forgetting of the speculative dimension of language, which blinds us to how deeply implicated we are in the construction of linguistic representations of the world. The second movement involves the "negativity" or the shock of "experience," which disrupts the illusions of *ekstasis*. It is a moment of reversal in which we are brought to recognize ourselves within what we took to be independent of ourselves. Such reversals entail a movement into what Gadamer describes as the "transformation into structure," a moment of understanding in which our previously fragmented understanding of our world and ourselves is temporarily transformed. The moment of transformation involves a recognition of "truth" in the sense that we cannot turn away from it without denying what we have understood ourselves as having become. Speculative experience involves, then, an interplay of repetition (moments of return and of mimesis) and difference (moments of hermeneutic transcendence in which we become different to ourselves). It is important to stress, however, that philosophical hermeneutics is not committed to regarding such moments of speculative understanding as enabling the hermeneutic subject to resolve all elements of its being into a permanent identity. To the contrary, moments of hermeneutic transcendence change the hermeneutic subject's relation to its world and in so doing, they expose the subject to yet further cycles of speculative experience. We will expand on this later.

In conclusion, what our account reveals of both the formal character and the dynamics of speculative experience is fourfold. (1) It gives substance to Gadamer's claim that there are objective structures within subjective experience. (2) The structured dynamics of speculative experience indicate why Gadamer insists that subjective experiences of art's truth claims are not to be rejected as arbitrary and groundless. (3) They

show why the account of understanding given by philosophical hermeneutics does not collapse into a Hegelian philosophy of identity. Understanding can generate a strong and disturbing sense of difference and not just a
sense of completeness. (4) The account of speculative experience exposes a
fundamental difference in the account of the relation between language
and experience as offered by philosophical hermeneutics and by philosophers such as Nietzsche. We shall now address these claims.

THE DEFENSE OF SPECULATIVE UNDERSTANDING

Why is Gadamer so keen to defend the claims of speculative understanding? He wishes to demonstrate that speculative insights, especially those
within the humanities, should not be dismissed as "groundless" and "subjective." One of the unstated achievements of philosophical hermeneutics is that it places the entire debate concerning the differences between
the *Geisteswissenschaften* and the *Naturwissenschaften* onto a sensible footing. Gadamer is harsh in his condemnation of Dilthey's hermeneutical
psychologism and severe in his rejection of any attempt to appropriate a
distinct method for the humanities. It is clear, however, that Gadamer
fails to appreciate the niceties of detail that embroider debates about the
completeness of scientific proof, and, as a consequence, he does not perceive the extent to which the sciences have themselves been hermeneuticized. However, as we have argued, the fact that language can operate
both propositionally and speculatively makes the *either/or* debate between
humanistic and scientific traditions ill-founded. Forcing a choice between
one and the other is not the issue. What is in question, however, are
those cultural prejudices that would persuade us that propositional discourse is the only legitimate model for knowledge. Philosophical
hermeneutics is concerned that the quiet voice of speculative understanding should not be smothered by the public discourses of science and
technology. Philosophical hermeneutics does not oppose the spread of
science but only that cultural veneration of technology that encourages
an increasingly profound deafness to the speculative dimensions of language and a denigration of its insights as "groundless." As we have
argued, speculative understanding is not groundless but founded on a
commonwealth of shared practice and tradition. Speculative insights are,
clearly, subjective occurrences but that they are so does not mean that the
objectivities they disclose (*ekstasis*, forgetfulness, thrownness, and mimesis)
are rendered subjective because they are subjectively perceived. There are,

however, a number of other concerns that prompt philosophical hermeneutics to defend speculative understanding.

The dominance of propositional discourse tends to substantiate a mode of thinking that promotes the will of a knowing subject rather than challenging its assumptions. Of course, a research project can collapse and force a subject back on its prior assumptions, but other than in such cases, propositional discourse tends to sustain the interests of a subject. The successful defense of a point of view is often viewed as seeing off the challenge of otherness. Propositional discourse tends to remain locked within its own assumptions. This leaning to enclosure disturbs philosophical hermeneutics. *Bildung*, becoming *gebildet*, and the spirit and well-being of one's own understanding depend upon movement within and between horizons. They require becoming subject to the address of the other and, as a consequence, becoming different to oneself. Hermeneutic vitality—preserving one's openness to the different—requires a willingness to remain immersed in the play of language and to remain vulnerable to its speculative turns and ruptures. It is not sustained by attempts to control, regulate, or methodize the use of language. This is not to denigrate the latter but to observe that the enthusiastic celebration of what propositional discourse can achieve in the realms of science and medicine should not blind us to esteeming the speculative vitality of language upon which the life of *Bildung* and individual insight depend. The close connection between Gadamer's defense of the speculative and his advocacy of a hermeneutical humanism becomes apparent.

The Speculative and the Humanistic

In *Truth and Method*, Gadamer observes,

> Experience as a whole is not a thing that anyone can be spared. [It] involves inevitably many disappointments of one's expectancies and only thus is experience acquired. . . . Every experience worthy of the name runs counter to our expectation. Thus the historical nature of man contains as an essential element a fundamental negativity that emerges in the relation between experience and insight. (TM, 356)

Elsewhere, he observes that *Mnemosyne* is the mother of the Muses and, hence, of speculative insight. She presides over those ways "of confronting ourselves in which we become mindful of ourselves . . . [for] . . . to keep in memory means to be human." Now, Gadamer's opposition to technology and propositional discourse is not indicative of a philosophical Ludditism. Rather, it questions the Promethean arrogance that appears to fuel propositional discourse, that is, a knowing subject's belief that it can reduce the world to a mode of its own representation, a belief Schopenhauer characterizes in the statement, "The world is *my* representation."[24] Gadamer follows Nietzsche and Adorno in their suspicion that what appears to be the universal reasonableness of propositional discourse disguises the operation of a distinct will to power. In short, he fears that propositional modes of discourse can feed humanity's habitual and arrogant beliefs that it is godlike and that the world is a mere resource for the satisfaction of its purposes.

Gadamer is well aware, however, that the gods' true gift to humanity is something of the reverse order, namely, an insight into what it means to be human. Speculative insights and revelation are linked to an experience of human finitude on two counts. They reveal, first, that we are not possessed of divine comprehension: as linguistic beings we are vulnerable to those plays of language which disclose that the world can always be different to expectancy. They show, second, how we are guilty of all too human failures of perception. The shock of the speculative insight has in part to do with the *shame* of realizing that reality contains truths we failed to anticipate albeit that the evidence for them was before our very eyes. The speculative insight not only marks out for us our fragile humanity but allows us to become more human. The negativity of speculative experience reveals that both the world and we can always be other than how we presently appear.

The relationship between speculative experience and the emergence of a very human sense of limitation and finitude touches on an important and productive tension in the nuances of Gadamer's argument. The conceptual associations tied to each element in this relationship appear to be at odds with each other. On the one hand, the speculative character of aesthetic experience is linked to notions of completeness while, on the other, experiences of limit and finitude intimate notions of incompleteness. Rather than suggesting a contradiction in Gadamer's stance, this tension is a fundamental part of his argument: the experience of aesthetic wholeness, the completion of a cycle of meaning, does not absorb us into its unity but sets us at a distance from ourselves. We become the completer as human beings by being shown and becoming reconciled to our incompleteness. Gadamer's account of aesthetic experience is much more radical in orientation than its customary reception suggests. The speculative dimension of aesthetic experience generates difference; it promotes a becoming different to ourselves whereby the apparition of beauty and completeness forces us to acknowledge the forgetfulness of *ekstasis*, our hermeneutic blindness, and our ignorance of the play of meaning before our very eyes. Rather than achieving an integration of self, speculative experience sets the self at a distance from itself. The argument is an integral element of the claim the hermeneutic subject is a subject whose being is always in question. This is a line of reasoning to which we shall return.

Speculative Insight and the "Unfounding" of Experience

To argue that speculative experience sets the self at a wise and painful distance from itself is consistent with Gadamer's description of religious experience as an experience of finitude. What it is not consistent with is the romantic language of much of Gadamer's analysis of aesthetic consciousness. The romantic overtones of the transformation into structure argument are ill-judged and, at times, misleading. The uses of such terms as "whole," "completion," and "realization" evoke notions of aesthetic fulfillment. The employment of concepts of mimesis and recognition in the context of arguments concerning both the completion of circles of meaning and the subject becoming more itself, have undeniable overtones of a Hegelian philosophy of identity. Without denying the *centripetal* element within hermeneutic experience, it is, nevertheless, a gross distortion of philosophical hermeneutics to conclude that speculative experience only culminates in a unifying moment. The suggestion undercuts the thesis that speculative experience sets us at a distance from ourselves. Given the romantic nature of some Gadamer's terminology, the case for the centrifugal (disruptive) moment of speculative experience is not an easy one to put. Perhaps the influence of the Hegelian conception of aesthetic experience of *Geborgenheit* (foundation or security) has too much of a hold upon Gadamer, so much so that it is difficult for him to make a convincing case for the disruptive element of speculative understanding. Can philosophical hermeneutics avoid the charge that its defense of the speculative implicitly leads to a philosophy of identity?

There is no denying that the speculative dynamics that animates Hegel's phenomenology of spirit strives to achieve a deep level of unification. It posits a process whereby the hermeneutic subject is impelled toward reappropriating the alien as its own. As a consequence, the subject becomes both "more" itself and consciously bound to the horizons that sustain it. Gadamer's conceptual language invites a Hegelian reading. In Heidegger's thought, too, a similar conservative element can be

discerned. The profound aesthetic insight is a "founding" moment bind-
ing the hermeneutic subject to the cultural projects that ground its consciousness. Aesthetic disclosure permits the isolated subject a prodigal
return, a rediscovery of itself within the historical world that has all along
nurtured its being. The hermeneutic subject achieves a speculative recognition of itself in that which has brought it into being. Such a line of argument suggests that a form of identity also marks Heidegger's aesthetics
of disclosure. As we saw in chapter 1, *Geborgenheit* implies a conscious
reintegration into the world sustaining one's being. Now if *Geborgenheit*
were for philosophical hermeneutics the only outcome of speculative experience, the consequences for Gadamer's position would be disconcerting. Does not Gadamer's thinking claim to be driven by a "negativity of
experience" that disrupts rather than reintegrates the expectancies of the
hermeneutic subject? Furthermore, his defense of speculative insight aims
to ensure that the hermeneutic subject does not succumb to the illusion
that any text corresponds to its expectancies. Were this defense of the
speculative no more than an apologetics for a philosophy of identity, the
hermeneutic subject would not have its unreflective presuppositions challenged, nor would it be put in the position of having to become other to
itself in order to think differently about itself. The possibility of an "unfounding" experience in which the subject is put at a distance from itself
is thereby disrupted. As a consequence, the dynamics of hermeneutic
translation and transcendence could not operate and Gadamer's claim
that the speculative insight contains the injunction to "alter thy life"[25]
would be deprived of its force. Alteration implies change but change does
not imply endorsement of the same. However, we contend that despite its
romantic language, the account given of the speculative by philosophical
hermeneutics does not necessarily collapse into a philosophy of identity
whereby the same is repeatedly played out. We suggest that there is a clear
centrifugal moment in speculative experience that can set the hermeneutic subject at a distance from itself.

     In his essay "Art as Oscillation," Vattimo makes a persuasive case for
the view that Heidegger's account of aesthetics should not just be read as
an apologetics for a Hegelian form of *Geborgenheit*.[26] Though Heidegger
links his aesthetics of disclosure with a process of communal bonding,
Vattimo suggests that Heidegger gives *equal* stress to the disruptive unfounding element of speculative experience. According to Vattimo's reading of Heidegger, the artwork "is like an encounter with someone whose
view of the world is a challenge to our own interpretation." The "art work
does not simply slot into the world as it is but purports to shed new light

upon the world."[27] Its speculative insight can entail an "experience of estrangement, which then requires re-composition and readjustment." However, the aim of this is not to reach "a final recomposed state . . . but towards keeping this *disorientation* alive,"[28] Without denying the unifying function of the centripetal moment of speculative understanding, Vattimo's appraisal of the disruptive element in Heidegger's aesthetics leads us closer to what philosophical hermeneutics has to defend in the speculative. The position that philosophical hermeneutics adopts is quite distinct from Heidegger's variation on *Geborgenheit*.

Within the tradition of aesthetic insight associated with *Geborgenheit*, there is no moment of speculative disorientation that forces us to think differently of ourselves. The moments of return and self-recognition celebrated by *Geborgenheit* clearly presuppose a perception of a fall, of loss, of not belonging to, and of being estranged from the world one finds oneself within. In other words, the *Geborgenheit* model of speculative experience assumes a single prodigal narrative: the hermeneutic subject falls away from and then returns to the single narrative that defines its hermeneutic community. However, because of its commitment to a linguistic ontology, philosophical hermeneutics is not of the view that humans are enclosed within a single cultural narrative. It acknowledges more openly than Heidegger, that human existence partakes in and is characterized by a great variety of personal, communal, national, historical, and religious narratives. The plurality of linguistic being is, we suggest, the primary reason why all speculative insights are susceptible to being disrupted. Although a hermeneutic subject may be the nodal point of an individual narrative, individual narratives are far from enclosed.[29] The fluidity of etymological networks gives ample evidence of how one word's meaning can lock into the meaning of others. As Bahktin aptly observes, "The word in language is half someone else's."[30]

The hermeneutic capacity of a word to pass beyond its immediate meaning is not only the basis of hermeneutic transcendence but also of the way in which meanings associated with one narrative cross over into another. Words do not have a single meaning. Each word is wired into a variety of semantic circuits. It is this plurality that gives a word its weight and resonance. Similarly, individual narratives are rarely singular. As linguistic phenomena, narratives cannot but incorporate the self/other relation. My narrative will include references to others just as I will figure in the narratives of others without knowing it. In other words, the interconnectedness of language and narratives makes possible the disruptive emergence of the other and otherness within my narrative, an emergence able to transform my individual self-understanding. The appearance of such otherness establishes the possibility of dialogue and sets the ground for hermeneutic translation and transcendence. That languages and narratives cross over and become mutually implicated in each other establishes the precondition whereby the other can emerge unintentionally within a subject's seemingly stable horizon of understanding and disrupt it.

Too often, subjects within a dominant linguistic or cultural horizon can forget their self-implication in the other. For many Europeans, it is a shock to discover that the benefits which economic development brings to their community inflict poverty upon others. The other emerges not as the reassuringly grateful recipient of philanthropic aid but as the distressing victim of imperious economic greed. In an analogous way, a writer may be astonished to discover that the lively and expressive idioms of speech she uses are shot through with the language of sexual inequality. When such collisions occur, it is not merely a case of one narrative meeting with another. Collisions per se do not constitute hermeneutic engagements. That there are different and mutually opposed narratives is not what is at issue here. The substance of the matter is what the collision of narratives enables. The aesthetic insight, the speculative understanding, the narrative of the other can be unfounding inasmuch as their emergence can force an entirely different but nevertheless plausible rereading of my own narrative. This is integral to the "truth-claim" of such experiences. Whereas the aesthetics of *Geborgenheit* brings endorsement and redemption, the unfounding character of some speculative experiences is such that I cannot turn away from the change in self-understanding that they demand. It is not that I adopt the other's narrative or abandon my own but that I am enabled to see my narrative transformed in such a way that I can see myself as the other might see me. For philosophical hermeneutics this is not the conclusion of a process of understanding but the recommencement of its continual transformation.

The disorientation prompted by such speculative unfounding is not the same as the shock or surprise associated with *Geborgenheit*. *Geborgenheit* (the moment of prodigal return) does not induce a fundamental review of a subject's understanding. It does not prompt the subject to become different to itself. More important, insofar as *Geborgenheit* marks a return home and the reunion of the self with itself, it does not promote dialogue or conversation. *Geborgenheit* marks the end of and indeed redeems disorientation and distanciation. Yet, the disorientation that for philosophical hermeneutics comes with the transformative power of speculative insight, does not mark a point of culmination or closure but one of opening and departure. Conversation and dialogue as philosophical hermeneutics conceives them are formally possible because, ontologically speaking, different narratives are always mutually entailed within and/or cross over each other. Genuine conversation and dialogue commence once the participants come to recognize that in the other they meet the other and the different of themselves. The speculative insights that concern philosophical hermeneutics are those that initiate disorientation and difference between hermeneutic subjects and their narratives. Transcendence—the hermeneutic subject becoming different to itself as a result of the disorientating impact of a speculative insight—takes place within the linguistically sustained "mutuality of the self and other, and not beyond it."[31] As we shall presently claim, it is precisely the linguistic basis of the speculative understanding that forever renders its insights susceptible to change and challenge. However, before the dialectical nature of speculative understanding is discussed, let us briefly reconsider another aspect of the aesthetics of *Geborgenheit* and its relation to the question of Gadamer's alleged romanticism.

In the Romantic tradition of aesthetics, *Geborgenheit* marks a return home and a reunion of the self with itself. It redeems disorientation and distanciation. Because of its references to completing lines of meaning, Gadamer's transformation into structure arguments seems to fall within this tradition. If this were the case, the embarrassment for Gadamer's hermeneutic project would be obvious. A philosophy that proclaims, on the one hand, the finitude of understanding, the openness of all meaning, and the impossibility of any final interpretative judgment cannot assert, on the other hand, that the power of aesthetic experience is such that it can bring a circle of meaning to completion. In order to avoid this impasse, Gadamer should have been more sensitive about the nuances within his choice of philosophical language. Nevertheless, the transformation into structure argument suggests philosophical tools able to overcome this difficulty. When a hermeneutic subject experiences what is for it a completion of meaning, Gadamer insists that the subject is set at a distance from that cycle of meaning, a distance that precludes practical or goal-oriented participation in that cycle. This distance, or what Gadamer also terms aesthetic distanciation, is "aesthetic distance in a true sense: it signifies the distance necessary for seeing and understanding" (TM, 128). The transformation of structure that allows a subject to see its world differently and to become different to itself also sets the hermeneutic subject at a distance from itself. It would not be inappropriate to use a Japanese idiom to describe this setting of a hermeneutic subject at a distance from itself as the *sadness* of understanding, that is, to describe it as an expression of understanding's finitude. When philosophical hermeneutics speaks of transformation into structure as the disclosure of meaning within a given cycle of events, it does not mean that the transformation reveals *the* essential meaning of that cycle. Such a transformation displays a meaning that, in relationship to the interests and concerns of the hermeneutic subject, reveals that cycle to be a cycle for the first time. As soon as a set of disparate events becomes perceptible as a coherent whole, what was incomplete and fragmentary emerges as a meaningful whole. This is not to say that the *true* meaning of that cycle has been uncovered, only that the elements have come together in such a way as to enable the hermeneutic subject to make sense of its place within them in a way it could not do before. In this respect, the hermeneutic subject becomes different to its (former) self. The very meaningfulness that brings a sense of coherence and unity to a hermeneutic subject also threatens to disrupt that subject's new won understanding of itself. The sadness of understanding resides in the fact that the advent of meaning conspires in the conditions of its own dissipation. As soon as something becomes discernible as meaningful, as having a distinct coherence or identity, it becomes something interpretable. Insofar as it becomes interpretable, it is at risk of losing its coherence. The traditional part-whole relations that form the transformation into structure argument and which many commentators take as evidence of the conservatism of Gadamer's position, demonstrate this. The meaningful emerges when disparate events are brought together and show themselves to be parts of a coherent whole. As has often been remarked, "The operation of the circle between parts and whole is the overarching framework of hermeneutics." Iser suggests that "the part/whole circle governs all interpretive activity insofar as the whole is understood from its parts, so the parts can be understood only from the whole."[32] But then, if the parts are only discernible as meaningful in relationship to the whole, and if the whole is perceivable as meaningful because the parts that form it are shown to be elements in a cycle, the meaningful opens a distinction that dissipates the force of its illumination. As Iser notes, the circularity of the meaningful brings out two things at once: "(a) something general is made ascertainable against the backdrop of a changing array of particulars; (b) the particulars gain salience by being set off from the general, a distinction which can never be obliterated."[33] In other words, as soon as the hermeneutic subject tries to grasp the meaning that appears to makes the disparate parts of its being whole and to see how that meaning is manifest in the particular elements of its being, an ineliminable space opens, dissolving the initial unifying meaning but driving the quest for a new synthesis. Hence, the sadness of understanding: as soon as the hermeneutic subject attempts to grasp or interpret what has become clear to it in speculative insight, the emergent meaning loses its clarity and the hermeneutic subject is once more set at a distance from itself. Philosophical hermeneutics is, then, quite unlike a philosophy of identity. It does not invoke aesthetics of *Geborgenheit*. What it recognizes within the transformation into structure argument is not the redemptive return of the self to itself but the ever-present possibility of the self losing what it has understood and of becoming different to itself once again. What the transformation into structure argument demonstrates is that the emergence of the meaningful conspires in the conditions of its own dissipation. Yet it is this very loss that drives the quest for further hermeneutic translation and transcendence. As we shall see in the next section, the waxing and waning of understanding itself prevents Gadamer's transformation into structure argument from collapsing into a form of *Geborgenheit*.

Language and the Dialectic of Speculative Experience

Speculative insight is formally possible because of the interconnection of different etymological and narrative networks. It occurs when one circuit of meaning is illumined by another. This reveals something of the temporal nature of hermeneutic experience. Though a speculative experience may be a transformative experience within an individual narrative, its temporal nature means that it will inevitably fade in intensity and relevance. Hermeneutic experience oscillates between the emergence and dissipation of meaning in essentially the same way as aesthetic experience does. That it does so indicates that for philosophical hermeneutics there can be no final closure of meaning. What differentiates philosophical hermeneutics from its deconstructive counterpart is its belief in the possibility of further meaningfulness arising out of the collision of different circuits of meaning. Such collisions clearly disrupt any one circuit of meaning regarded as privileged or as holding *the* meaning to a given cycle of experience. For philosophical hermeneutics, seeking to discredit the belief in foundational meaning or to discover alternative vistas of meaning to those we presently cherish is important but not the vital issue. Deconstructive tactics serve as (the perhaps necessary) prelude to what is hermeneutically pressing. The hermeneutically urgent issue is to be *responsive* to the collision of different sets of meaning rather than to stand back from that collision and regard it as evidence against foundational meaning. Philosophical hermeneutics does not despair of such collisions. The emergence of opposing and different viewpoints permits us new and unexpected ways of thinking about our own narratives and hermeneutic commitments. The issue does not just concern the completion of or a return to an established cycle of meaning (*Geborgenheit*) as Gadamer's transformation into structure argument suggests, but the transformation of a way of thinking we are committed to, a transformation that because of its power of illumination strikes us as both credible and probable. That such a new way of thinking addresses us in this way does not mean that it is not subject to further interpretation and analysis, as would be the case if hermeneutics resolved into a philosophy of identity. Philosophical hermeneutics is too close to Nietzsche and philology to forget that interpretation never arrives at a final, definitive meaning. Insofar as it opens an ineliminable space between itself and its subject matters, the interpretive process of applying new horizons of meaning to those to which we are accustomed guarantees the impossibility of such closure. The centrifugal dimension of interpretation certainly disrupts the possibility of securing *the* meaning of a subject matter, but the absence or postponement of such a meaning does not displace the future possibility of centripetal meaningfulness per se. Indeed, such postponements can be regarded as the very condition of if not a spur to arriving at new configurations of meaningfulness. As we have stated, the issue is not whether a hermeneutic subject secures *the* meaning of a subject matter but whether the speculative insight afforded by the emergence of a different perspective or narrative illuminates my own in a new, plausible, and informative way. To deny the meaningfulness of such insights on the ground that they do not secure *the* meaning of a subject matter is fatuous. To ask for the definitive meaning of a subject matter is to ask for our temporal experience of that subject matter to come to an end. To ask for that is to ask that learning and transcendence also come to an end. Catherine Pickstock has noted such a necrophiliac element within Derrida's thinking.[34] In the context of our present discussion, her comments merit reflection.

The association of meaning with that which is unattainable and beyond experience introduces an untenable opposition between life and death. It could be argued that it is death's perpetual entry into life that both constitutes the temporality of experience[35] and facilitates the narrative "becomings" that constitute our sense of being an identifiable subject. Pickstock suggests that Derrida disallows any sense of meaning as non-ideality, for he denies it as an inhabited, developing occurrence. Derrida presents meaning as an absent ideal that does not permit the slightest degree of participation. The consequences of such prohibitions render a subject's claim to meaning pure illusion and place subjectivity on an utterly negative basis. Philosophical hermeneutics clearly sets itself against such nihilism. Philosophical hermeneutics does not even have to explicitly argue against Derrida's equation of death and meaning. If meaning-in-itself did exist, it would be of no consequence, for as temporal beings we could not relate to it. If meaning-in-itself does not exist, it is also of no consequence, for what matters are the contingent, malleable, inhabited meanings that shape our narratives and horizons. Gadamer's concern is with the devaluation of subjectivity that follows from Derrida's inverted metaphysical rationalism.

To regard subjectivity and its interest in what draws it out of itself as worthless is to undermine the horizons of meaning that manifest themselves in subjectivity and that enable subjectivity to orientate itself toward its world. Philosophical hermeneutics is implacable in its resistance to such devaluation. Hence, its insistence upon the contingency of inhabited meaning. The emphasis philosophical hermeneutics places upon the speculative underscores the centripetal capacity of language to allow the circuitries of meaning that are deferred by its centrifugal capacities to flow back into the sign and fill it with a temporary meaningfulness. By no means does philosophical hermeneutics resist or deny the capacity of words to defer their meaning. But it *also* emphasizes the living actuality of the reverse movement: the ability of those networks of meaning beyond the sign (i.e., the withheld) to flow back into the sign and to body it forth so that it can also function as a symbol of the beyond (the withheld). Though signs can be emptied by what they defer to, what they defer to can also well up within them. The centrifugal and centripetal dynamics of linguistic signs emphasize the oscillating, unstable nature of hermeneutic experience. Although philosophical hermeneutics speaks of a language world, it is obvious that that world consists not of one language but of a myriad of different linguistic perspectives. Such a plurality facilitates a virtually infinite set of points where individual and collective narratives can meet and transform each other. The challenge of the other's counternarrative can, on the one hand, expose the withheld in a hermeneutic subject's prejudices and, on the other hand, inform that perspective with resonances of its own. Such chance collisions are the very stuff of literary, philosophical, and musical *exchange*. Indeed, philosophical hermeneutics insists that since our very being is sustained by language, such sudden inflows of meaning from one narrative to another are the very stuff of hermeneutic exchange. Such expansions of meaning within and between horizons are not necessarily to be associated with moments of return

(*Geborgenheit*). A perspective may indeed become "more" because of its encounter with another but it also becomes different to its former nature and, as a consequence, can conceive itself differently. Thus, a former way of thinking or a former configuration of meaning can, in a certain sense, pass away or, much rather, be surpassed. The temporal pathways of experience are waymarked by such deaths. Yet the passing of past possibilities of meaning is the condition for the emergence of new configurations of meaning. New configurations permit the narrative "becoming," which grounds the constellar identity of a given hermeneutic subject, to become different to itself and to unfold in new and unexpected ways. *Geborgenheit* is, therefore, not the necessary outcome of speculative insight. Indeed, by allowing parts of its former self to pass away and become past, the hermeneutic subject can enter into dialogical relationship with its past self, a relationship that hitherto would not have been possible. However, just as language facilitates the chance fusion of narratives and perspectives, so does it make the collision of perspectives and the disruption of stable meanings unavoidable. The closure of a cycle of meaning—a transformation into structure—is, after all, never in isolation. It takes place in the context of other such cycles and will come to be viewed differently in the light of the impact it has on those other cycles.

What is in question here is not the simple recognition of other and different perspectives, but the speculative insight that one is deeply implicated in what one thought was other and different, an implication that when brought to light prompts one to think quite differently about one's own perspective. Philosophical hermeneutics is insistent that it is the multiple play of language that makes vulnerability to such disruptions of understanding unavoidable. No English person can be immune to the challenge that Welsh, Scottish, or Irish historical narratives make to established notions of English national understanding. What language reveals is, as Williams points out, that "my publicly identifiable history, the story that can be told of me, does not belong exclusively to me." Concerning this narrative, he continues,

> I can set out to reorder it, to rewrite it in various ways, but I don't in fact control it. My actions have had effects and meanings I never foresaw or intended; even the meanings I did intend have now become involved with speech and the story of the other lives. I cannot (any longer) separate my biography as a thing in itself.[36]

The disruption of understanding occurs because of the linguistic fact that the term *English* can turn different wheels in different narratives. Insofar as it is connected to a set of meanings and associations that contribute to my sense of self, I am deeply vulnerable to what that term can mean in other narratives. An unexpected argument or a chance encounter with a piece of historical research can bring me to realize that the term *English* does indeed turn different wheels, and the implication of this for my self-conception can be profound. The naiveté of a former self-understanding may have to be renounced: I can no longer think of my Englishness in the same way. A previous self-conception dies as I begin to adjust my narrative in the light of having become different to myself. Several points arise from this.

First, philosophical hermeneutics articulates the temporality of experience, that is, the dialectical shifts of understanding over time in terms of the conflict of linguistic and historical perspectives. It suggests that moments of speculative insight mark the pivotal turning points around and through which personal and collective narratives unfold. Second, philosophical hermeneutics does not advocate a deeper principle of unity whereby the differences between conflicting narratives are to be resolved and their oppositions overcome. The recognition that the other's narrative challenges my own and forces me to think differently about myself is the basis on which genuinely dialogical exchange can occur. However, there is little evidence to indicate that Gadamer agrees with the conviction of Habermas that language is driven by a desire for consensual agreement. Philosophical hermeneutics suggests that on the basis of reciprocal difference we engage in conversation for the sake of those unpredictable speculative instances whereby we are brought to understand ourselves differently. The play of language and its inherent slippages of meaning ensure that no understanding is fixed or privileged. For this reason philosophical hermeneutics eschews any attempt to resolve the differences between perspectives into a higher unity. To seek a philosophical transcendence of difference and otherness denies the temporality of experience and undermines the possibility of hermeneutical transcendence. To dissolve the irreducible dialecticity of language brings death to understanding, for, paradoxically, it is the perpetual challenge of the other, the unavoidable speculative disruption of our narratives, and the inescapable negativity of experience which is the lifeblood of understanding's movement. Third, on the basis of what has been argued above, it can be argued that it would be a grotesque travesty of philosophical hermeneutics to see in its advocacy of speculative insight, an attempt to shore up a view of understanding as *Geborgenheit*. The discussion of its defense of speculative insight reveals that philosophical hermeneutics eschews both the absolutism of Hegel's attempt to bring opposition and contradiction into a transcendent principle of identity and Derrida's disruption of the identical and the same in his affirmation of absolute difference. Philosophical hermeneutics refuses to transcend language by absolutizing one aspect of its dialectical vitality as an overriding philosophical principle. To be sure, the living inhabited realm of linguistic meaning, which philosophical hermeneutics defends, has a centripetal impetus toward identity but that impetus is always vulnerable to the centrifugal impetus toward difference and negation. *Io ipso*, difference and negation tend toward identity in that they do not merely challenge a hermeneutic subject's identity but reconfigure it in new and unexpected ways. In its defense of the contingency of inhabited meaning, philosophical hermeneutics discerns within language not only the constant impetus toward identity and difference but also that the power of identity is marked by the negativity of difference and the power of negativity by identity. The impetus toward identity, as in the case of the transformation into structure argument, is marked by negativity in that its emergence is only possible by virtue of the alteration of previous forms of self-understanding. Similarly, the impetus toward difference is driven by a tendency to identity, that is, toward reconfiguring a subject's understanding in new ways. This constant interplay of the tendencies toward unification and disruption maintains the inherent temporal instability of language, an instability that guarantees the vitality of understanding. The absolutization of either impetus puts meaning beyond our reach. However, recognizing that both impetuses coinhere guarantees that the meaningful occurs within an accessible a temporal frame. Temporal instability allows meanings to be meaningful precisely because of what they open and close us toward. The temporal instability of linguistic meaning also underwrites the possibility of learning and transcendence. We shall return to a discussion of these themes in the next part of this essay.

The defense of inhabited meaning mounted by philosophical hermeneutics amounts to a decision in favor of the vitality of language as opposed to the abstract claims of philosophy. Philosophical hermeneutics in effect stands in between philosophies of identity, which affirm the presence of meaning in itself, and philosophies of difference, which dissipate all meaning. The poignant claim of philosophical hermeneutics is that both aforementioned philosophical approaches amount to the death of the meaningful. On the one hand, philosophies of identity fix meaning in the identity of self-presence. Such a fixity of meaning amounts to a denial of the temporality of experience and, thus, frustrates the possibility of learning and transcendence. On the other hand, philosophies of difference achieve, curiously enough, a similar result. The dissolution of meaning and its removal from the temporal denies or renders illusory those temporary constellations of meaning that give the meaningful its shape. Philosophical hermeneutics insists, however, that inhabited meaning requires contingent limits, definition, and shape. Without such limits, narratives lose their temporal form and structure. Philosophies of difference thereby also threaten the temporality of experience and the possibilities of learning that arise within it. Against the positions taken by philosophies of identity and philosophies of difference on the question of meaning, philosophical hermeneutics defends the view that language's vitality depends on the constant oscillation and mutual limitation of its dual impetuses toward centripetal identity and centrifugal difference. The absolutization of either inaugurates the death of the meaningful. Gadamer recognizes that "hermeneutics has to see (its way through) the dogmatism of meaning-in-itself" and, we might add, the dogmatism of the absence of meaning too (TM, 473). What makes meaning both meaningful and inhabitable is in fact its very instability and uncertainty.

What lays claim upon us as meaningful gains its credibility and poignancy only in relationship to other such claims. The force of such a claim—its ability to assert itself and negate other meanings—only makes sense in terms of what its emergence illuminates, namely, other related networks of meaning. To paraphrase Hegel, a meaning is what it is only in and by reason of its limit.[37] Insofar as a speculative insight illuminates something of the withheld—the prejudices and pre-understandings of a subject's horizon—the insight gains its weight or resonance in relation to what it illuminates. Furthermore, its meaningfulness is limited or bounded by what it reveals. It can be argued that the meaningful is indeed marked by an inherent negativity. Not only does the emergence of such an insight displace previous understandings but the meaning of what emerges is also dependent on what limits it. Its meaning is relative, that is, dependent upon its relationship to related networks of meaning. The inherent "negativity" within the meaningful is, arguably, precisely that which drives the temporality of hermeneutic experience. That a meaning is able to displace others, allows the *temporality* of experience to unfold. But the achievement of a new perspective or understanding does nothing to make it immune from the threat of displacement by the emergence of another, more plausible view. That the meaningfulness of a new perspective depends upon its relation to other networks of meaning implies that any alteration in the related field will alter the meaningfulness of that perspective. In short, philosophical hermeneutics recognizes that it is the very instability and uncertainty of meaning that enables the emergence of the meaningful. Speculative insight and, hence, the possibility of hermeneutic translation and transcendence stand on the living coinherence of identity and difference within language. However, as we shall now see, it is by way of contrast with Nietzsche's philosophy of language that further pertinent aspects of philosophical hermeneutics' defense of the speculative can be brought into light.

NIETZSCHE, PHILOSOPHICAL HERMENEUTICS, LANGUAGE, AND THE MARKET PLACE

Nietzsche remarked, "Of what is great one must either be silent or speak with greatness."[38] He was fearful of the banality of ordinary language and its tendency to sully the new and unexpected, hence his injunction to find new ways of speaking with greatness or of remaining silent. In a similar but inverted vein, Adorno was genuinely concerned with the tastelessness of speaking and writing about of such horrendous calamities as the Holocaust in certain idioms of poetic language. Gadamer takes an opposite view to Adorno: it is precisely the greatness of catastrophic events that demands that poetry speak of them. What is at issue here is a set of conflicting assumptions about the relationship between language and experience. Is experience too delicate or too intense to be spoken about? Does speaking about such experiences defile their nature? Or, is it precisely because words cannot capture the complexities of experience that words are needed to fathom its depths, in short, to enhance and to extend experience, to allow experience to find its voice? In the following section, the philosophical issues raised by the contrasting approaches taken by Nietzsche and Gadamer on the question of the relationship between language and experience will be explored. The contrast between the two philosophers is all the more striking because of a common cause.

Nietzsche's critique of *Fach-Philologie* makes a significant and often overlooked contribution to the *Naturwissenshaft* and *Geisteswissenshaft* debate that shaped the direction of hermeneutic thinking in the later half of the nineteenth century. What is remarkable about *The Birth of Tragedy* is not that it argues for a distinctness of method within the humanities but that it puts a case for the intuitive. It defends those intelligent intuitions that drive one toward beauty and wholeness (the Apollinian) or those that impel one toward the destructive (the Dionysian). Such intuitions, Nietzsche argues, should not be displaced by the superficial optimism of Alexandrian rationalism with its demand for argued grounds for each and every action. It is a travesty of Nietzsche's subtle arguments to say that *The Birth of Tragedy* is an apologetics for irrationalism. What he discerns are the limits of scientific reasoning. Science cannot make itself rationally explicable to itself and it fails to offer an alternative to what it displaces, namely, those speculative Dionysian insights into life's horrific finitude which nevertheless inspire a desire for life in all of its precarious beauty. Nietzsche's nightmare is that after having ridiculed, slandered, and brought subjective intuitions into disrepute, Alexandrian rationalism will have so atrophied the powers of the aesthetically intuitive that when it collapses, such powers will no longer be capable of mustering a response to the advent of meaninglessness. Like Gadamer, Nietzsche's argument is not with scientific reasoning per se but with its displacement of those aesthetic cum speculative sensitivities upon which our orientation toward the questions of meaning depend. However, the approach that both thinkers adopt toward language and its relation to experience reveal sharp differences in their understanding of the aesthetic, the speculative, and the subjective. Let us, first, consider the question of the relation of spoken and written language to experience.

Despite the fact that Nietzsche's aphoristic idiom and Gadamer's hermeneutical perspectivism share the aim of getting the reader to think differently, Nietzsche is a skeptic concerning the relationship of language to experience and Gadamer is not. Nietzsche is among those writers, such as Plato and Iris Murdoch, who believe that writing does not engage with the truth of the real but only disseminates secondary reconstructions of the actual. Not only is linguistic representation at a remove from actuality but it can propagate secondary and artificial views of the real as if they were the real. Heidegger too was notably perturbed by the ability of writing to cheapen the intense and the harrowing: writing just "passes the word" along without any involvement in the full resonance of what was originally experienced. Indeed, the written word tempts us to comment upon experiences we have never had.[39] Worse still, dwelling solely in the written word can be a way of absenting oneself from the intensities of immediate experience or, indeed, mask one from recognizing one's lack of it. For Plato, however, truth and wisdom are neither communicated nor are they to be found in the written but only in what we undergo. Unlike our enormous capacity to forget what we read, there is little danger, as Murdoch observes, of somebody forgetting the truth once it has been seized evidentially.

Nietzsche's doubts about the ability of words to capture the complexities of actuality are based on two principal arguments: words do not represent the outer world as it is, and words are not delicate enough to convey the inner intensities of experience. With regard to the first argument, Nietzsche suggests that it is because of words and concepts that we are continually misled into imagining things as being are simpler than they are.[40] Linguistic means of expression are useless for expressing becoming; it accords with our inevitable need to preserve ourselves to posit a crude world of stability, of things.[41] Words do not refer to things but to fictions, that is, to a simplified perceptual world created by us. We can scarcely help construing the world in terms of things and subjects: "Every word and sentence we utter speaks in favour" of this prejudice but "there are no things: that is our fiction."[42] With words we operate with referents to what does not exist. An objection to Nietzsche's stance has some bearing on how the approach of philosophical hermeneutics to the speculative surpasses this linguistic skepticism. It might be conceded that linguistic means of expression are useless for describing becoming. Yet without the ability of language to contrast the difference between process and being, we would not be able to intuit what the word *becoming* alludes to. That we cannot put into words what the word *becoming* refers to does not diminish the value of words but calls for a more delicate, careful, and subtle use of them. To this point we shall return.

Nietzsche maintains that with words we deal with a world of epistemological fictions. This does not speak against the efficacy of such fictions insofar as they reflect a species need to communicate, to reduce the complexities of the phenomenal world to a regularized schema in which we can live. We have arranged for ourselves a linguistically structured world, which in its articles of grammatical faith (the belief in subjects and objects) betrays our survival needs. Such an argument clearly demarcates Nietzsche's philosophy of language from that defended by philosophical hermeneutics. Heidegger's and Gadamer's anti-instrumentalist linguistic ontology necessarily suspends any debate about the origin of language. The impossibility of standing outside language renders questions about what language is for redundant. Philosophical hermeneutics is concerned with what *happens* within and what happens because of linguistic experience. Gadamer is quite clear in his rejection of Nietzsche's condemnation of language as being incommensurable with the nature of actuality.

> We cannot look at the things referred to and criticise the words for not correctly representing them. Language is not a mere tool we use, something we construct in order to com-

municate and differentiate. [We cannot] . . . start from the existence and instrumentality of words and regard the subject matters as something we know about previously from an independent source. (TM, 407)

Such a theory starts "too late." Nevertheless, Nietzsche's instrumentalist conception of language is at the root of his skepticism concerning the ability of language to express the complexity of experience.

Language, for Nietzsche, expresses only the common and the average. "All communication by words is shameless; words dilute and brutalize; words depersonalize; words make the uncommon common."[43] With regard to what is rare and exceptional, "words lie in the way." As Danto has noted, J. L. Austin inadvertently illustrates precisely the point that concerns Nietzsche. Austin argues, "Our common stock of words embodies all the distinctions men have found worth drawing, and the connections they have found worth marking in the lifetimes of many generations."[44] But for Nietzsche everything worth marking within a *common* stock of knowledge is only the "shallow, small, relatively stupid, general signs—herd signs." If language, like consciousness, has developed from a need to communicate, words must convey what is the same, what is common, and, thus, what can be readily understood. For something to be communicable, it must be experienced as *adapted*, as recognizable.[45] For Nietzsche, then, language represents an impetus toward conformism, toward thinking in a collectivist fashion and within common predictable patterns. There is no doubt that for Nietzsche language is tied to relations of power within society. In the early essay *On Truth and Lies in an Extra-Moral Sense*, Nietzsche shows how language in effect is socially established. Its grammatical rules and their related logical prejudices originate in a random fixing and hardening of metaphors and establish themselves arbitrarily as a legitimate conceptual scheme.[46] Vattimo remarks in this respect, "Society comes into being when one system of metaphors wins through against the others and becomes the publicly prescribed and accepted way of characterizing things."[47] Nietzsche sees in this a subtle attempt on the part of the "mediocre" and herd-like to control the different and exceptional. Not only do simplified concepts and "big words" reflect the common prejudices of the marketplace but the insistence that shared words must be the basis of communication carries with it an injunction that one make oneself knowable to the community. As Shrift comments, "To make such a self-disclosure, we must become self-conscious, which amounts to making what is individual and unique about our experience 'average' and capable of being communicated."[48] Two points arise from these observations. The first concerns Nietzsche's hostility to philosophical tradition, and the second relates to the ability of words to express the intimate.

Nietzsche's hostility to philosophical tradition is structured by his view that language tends to endorse metaphorical systems that privilege the general, the same, and the common. It is no surprise that he should express an "absolute scepticism towards inherited concepts."[49] Quite unlike philosophical hermeneutics, Nietzsche does not regard tradition as a dialogical other to be engaged with. To the contrary, insofar as they embody a restrictive and reductive ideology of the commonplace, tradition and the marketplace of language must be broken away from. Nietzsche's skepticism concerning the ability of words to express the varieties of perception also extends to the difficulties of expressing inner experience.

> Alas, and yet what are you, my written and painted thoughts! It is not long ago that you were still so many coloured, young and malicious, so full of thorns and hidden spices you made me sneeze and laugh—and now? You have already taken off your novelty and some of you, I fear, are on the point of becoming *truths*: they already look so immortal, so pathetically righteous, so boring! And has it ever been other wise? For what things do we write and paint, we mandarins with Chinese brushes, we immortalisers of things which let themselves be written, what alone are we capable of painting? Alas only that which is about to wither and is beginning to lose its fragrance. Alas, only storms departing, exhausted, and feelings grown old and yellow! Alas, only birds who have strayed and grown weary in flight, who now let themselves be caught in the hand—in our hand. We immortalize that which cannot live and fly much longer, weary and mellow things alone![50]

For Nietzsche there is a vital immediacy, a *frisson*, to intense experience which particularizes and makes it intensely individual. To objectify such experiences in language is not only to cheapen and sully them but to dull them. In *Beyond Good and Evil* he comments, "One no longer love's one's knowledge enough when one has communicated it."[51] Again, in the *Twilight of the Idols*, we read,

> We no longer have a sufficiently high estimate of ourselves when we communicate. Our true experiences are not at all

garrulous. . . . In all talk there lies a grain of contempt. Language it seems, was invented only for what is average, medium and communicable. With language, the speaker immediately vulgarizes himself.[52]

The use of words to objectify intense experience is as culpable in Nietzsche's mind as the philosopher's use of concepts: it kills and mummifies experience.[53] Let us now turn to the problems Nietzsche's stance poses and to how they can be addressed from within philosophical hermeneutics.

In his defense of the intensity of rare experience, does Nietzsche seek to break free from language and bow down, silent, before the awesome and the inarticulable? The issue is not whether there are such experiences. Nietzsche clearly believed in them and in their transformative power.

Life consists of rare individual moments of the highest significance and countless intervals in which at best the phantom of those moments hover about us. Love, spring, a beautiful melody, the mountains, the sea—they all speak truly to our heart only once: if they ever do in fact truly find speech.[54]

Can such moments be put into words? Contrary to Nietzsche's position, Gadamer holds that the "true being" and "reality" of such moments only becomes apparent when we do strive to speak about them (TM, 430, 431). Nevertheless, Nietzsche's hesitancy about bringing such experiences into language is understandable. Words carry a heavy burden of meaning and association, which can be difficult to set aside. If one speaks, for example, of intense experiences as "revelatory," no matter how plain one's motives, the sheer weight of tradition can prove insurmountable. Even though one might only wish to talk of what is phenomenologically revealed in experience, traditional theological overtones will be discerned in one's description. Nietzsche's caution about translating intense experience into the common frameworks of language is perhaps understandable. Yet does his hesitancy justify the view that such experience is sullied when spoken about? If Nietzsche adheres to a quietism, what protects his stance from Gadamer's charge of aestheticism? Furthermore, if Nietzsche wishes to isolate intense experience from being contaminated by language, how are such experiences to be thought of as significant? The issue is not whether there are or are not nonlinguistic experiences or whether there are experiences that cannot be satisfactorily articulated verbally. Experiences of intense excitement and delight are nonverbal experiences. Experiences of joy or of grief share a complexity that escapes easy linguistic expression. Yet, these experiences are not *beyond* words. The difficulty lies in trying to find the right words. But the difficulty must not be shirked, for the key point remains, profound experience only assumes significance once brought into language spoken or thought. In Gadamer's phrase, we need to find the "right language" for these experiences if they are to speak at all (TM, 397). Language and thinking about experience are bound together (TM, 417), so much so that

> [e]xperience is not wordless to begin with, subsequently becoming an object of reflection by being named, by being subsumed under the universality of the word. Rather experience itself seeks and finds words that express it. We seek the right word—i.e. the word that really belongs to the thing (or experience) so that in it the thing comes into language. (TM, 417)

The consequence of this viewpoint for Gadamer is plain: "Not only is the world *world* only insofar as it comes into language, but language too has its real being only in the fact that the world is presented in it" (TM, 442). The use of the verb presented is significant. Gadamer is *not* saying that only that which can be objectified in propositions belongs to the world. Were he to do so, his speculative theory of language would be nonsensical. However, he is, as we have seen, committed to the view that the power of language resides in its ability to disclose subject matters and insights over and above what is actually spoken. Two things follow from this. First, if Nietzsche is guilty of proposing a straightforward opposition between the privacy of experience and the public world of language, how can Nietzsche make these exceptional experiences thinkable to himself? If, as Nietzsche grants, it is our relationship with the outer world that has developed our consciousness, and if what is thinkable is thinkable only in relation to the public world of language, then the privacy of such experiences collapses. In the pithy words of Strawson, "if *only* mine, then not mine at all."[55] In other words, it is only because Nietzsche already participates in the public world of language that he can think about his experiences at all. The division between an inarticulable *privacy* of experience and a public world of language collapses. We can but conclude that if Nietzsche is able to *think* about his experiences, he cannot prevent them from being contaminated by what he regards as the language of the "herd." The second point follows on directly. It is our participation in language that enables us to acquire a sense of what is rare and difficult to express. However, it does not follow that because the division between an inarticulable privacy of experience and a public world of language is indefensible, the division between inarticulable experiences and articulable experiences is unsustainable. The experiences of not having found the right words, of being dumbfounded and of being lost for words are not indicative of a linguistic incapacity or malfunction. Neither are such experiences exterior to language. To the contrary, they are indicative of our participation in language. Acquiring a sense of the limits of a certain style of thinking or of the expressive capacities of a language is dependent upon being placed within a language world. On occasion Nietzsche seems to grasp this. Prefiguring Ernst Gombrich's argument that artists only paint what their stylistic skills permit them to, he observes that "we always express our thoughts with the words that are to hand. Or to express my whole suspicion: we have at any moment only the thought for which we have to hand the words."[56] Later, Nietzsche remarks that "we cease to think when we refuse to do so under the constraint of language; we barely reach the doubt that sees this limitation as a limitation."[57] Nietzsche's understanding of how both grammar and the social dimensions of communication influence the structure of thought makes him intensely aware of language's constraints. This understanding drives his impatient stylistic experimentalism. In touching the limits of a given linguistic framework, he knows he is approaching the gateways to other, less neurotic ways of thinking. Nevertheless, the crucial point remains: though Nietzsche may try to escape the language of the marketplace, it is only because he trades in that language that he is able to press it to its limits hoping to discern the possibilities of other ways of thinking. Hermeneutic transcendence does not entail transcending language so that the uniqueness of experience can be inwardly refined. To the contrary, philosophical hermeneutics engages with the linguisticality of experience precisely in order to transcend and extend it by touching on what limits it.

Contrary to Nietzsche's stance, philosophical hermeneutics argues that there is nothing about intense experience that in principle makes it *incommensurable* with linguistic expression. The difficulty resides in the finitude of the *word* itself: "No word can express our mind completely" (TM, 425). The challenge presented by an intense experience is that we can be unclear as to what we think about it. Our thoughts about what we undergo can be so rapid, various, and contradictory that it is difficult to be clear about what we are experiencing. A rare experience is difficult to express not because of any inherent incommensurability with language but because our thinking about it remains unclear and incomplete. Gadamer comments,

> The variety of words does not mean in any way that the individual word has some remediable deficiency, in that it did not completely express what the mind is thinking, but because our intellect is imperfect—i.e. is not completely present to itself in what it knows—it needs the multiplicity of words. It does not really know what it knows. (TM, 425)

If this is right, language is not hostile to intense experience but is a means of deepening and extending it. After all, is it not such a conviction that drives philosophical hermeneutics to its defense of speculative experience? Thus, contrary to Nietzsche's view that language distorts experience, philosophical hermeneutics contends that the sensitive use of words brings to light what is held within intense experience and thereby opens the possibility of extending it. Philosophical hermeneutics maintains therefore that if Nietzsche's concern is to enhance and intensify profound experience, his purpose would be better served by the challenge of bringing it into language rather than placing it in linguistic quarantine. The more such experience is brought into language, the clearer and more distinctive it can become.

For philosophical hermeneutics, dialogical engagement with the other and with the different forces us to think differently about our understanding and to extend if not multiply the hermeneutic perspectives available to us. Given that one of Nietzsche's declared philosophical aims is to increase the perspectival range of understanding, dialogical confrontation with the other and different would surely serve his purposes. Accordingly, his disdain for the marketplace of language renders his attempt to preserve the purity of rare insight rather precious. If the intelligibility and significance of experience depends upon its intrinsically linguistic nature, the ability to plumb its depths and to acquire additional perspectives requires a willingness to enter the marketplace of language. What is it that is so precious about intense experience that Nietzsche is unwilling to risk it in dialogical exchange? Isn't Nietzsche open to the charge of dishonoring such intense experience by refusing to share it no matter how risky hermeneutic engagement might be? Or is it that such exchange threatens to alter his own understanding of these experiences and to alter his self-understanding? Why should the latter be protected from public discourse? Is this a case of the all too youthful rather than of the "all too human"? Even if his grasp on difficult experience is tenuous, is it not precisely dialogical exchange that can ease any difficulty of expression by revealing alternative ways of articulation. Is it not dialogical exchange that permits such experiences to become "more"? Is it not dialogical exchange that permits the rare and exceptional in experience to be better articulated and understood? Why then should this pose a problem for one of Europe's greatest philosophical advocates of becoming?

Nietzsche is undone by one of his own metaphors. Philosophical hermeneutics reverses the metaphor of the marketplace to telling effect, exposing the substantial difference between its celebration of language's speculative capacity and Nietzsche's suspiciousness of its expressive capacity. The linguistic "marketplace" is not just a site for the herd and the commonplace. It is also a place of exchange, a place where everything I can construe about my self-understanding is dependent upon entering into a process of dialogical encounter. It is, furthermore, a place where different linguistic "trade" routes converge. Linguistic exchange in the marketplace lights up the presence of what lies beyond it, namely, the actuality of alternative linguistic perspectives. The linguistic marketplace is not, therefore, a site of limitation and constraint. It is a site that both exhibits and makes make hermeneutic translation and transcendence possible. The marketplace may be a site where common diseases are transmitted but it is also a place to obtain cures and remedies. As Williams suggests, "My health is in the thinking or the sensing of how I am not one with myself, existing as I do in time (change) and language (exchange)." Not to acknowledge this dependence and, instead, to enclose the other within a linguistic ghetto so as to confine all risk of contamination is surely a recipe for "inner dislocation" and "dysfunction."[58] To refuse such exchange is to shackle the speculative dynamic of language and reflection. To shun linguistic exchange is to reject precisely that which makes the self conscious of itself. This brings us to several other points of conflict between Nietzsche and philosophical hermeneutics.

Defenders of Nietzsche might suggest that his dispute with the commonplace does not take issue with language per se but with a dominant set of metaphors that has monopolized both how the world is represented and how we think of ourselves. Vattimo contends that Nietzsche wishes to free the inventive powers that generate metaphors. Nietzsche's purpose is not to refute the metaphorical nature of language but to embrace it. He seeks to free the original impulse toward creating metaphors, to allow art to deploy it in its struggle to gain mastery over life and to thereby open new ways of describing the world.[59] Nietzsche regards this creative impulse as an unconscious one. His declared intent is "to give back to men the courage of their natural drives."[60]

Because Nietzsche regards the language of the everyday as indicative of the dominance of one set of metaphors over other possible ways of describing things, he is *not* interested in engaging with the philosophical canonical or the traditional. The dominant canon represents an impetus toward conformism and hence to making oneself recognizable within an imposed collectivist way of thinking. As we have seen, there are sound reasons to sympathize with Nietzsche here. As Heidegger and Derrida have discovered, it is extraordinarily difficult to embark upon a critical engagement with the tradition of the Western metaphysical tradition without becoming tainted by its metaphors and assumptions. Nor is it easy to inject new meaning into long-established terms without such creative hubris being punished. No matter how justifiable it might be to baptize philosophical hermeneutics as a genuinely innovative form of rhetoric, the historical weight of the latter term is so burdened with negative associations that any (laudable) attempt to rejuvenate rhetoric hermeneutically (still) remains difficult and untimely. Because Nietzsche chaffs at the yoke such conceptual burdens place around the neck of the thinker, his modernist desire to sunder the dominant regime of philosophical metaphors with a new range of expressive devices is understandable. The question remains as to whether such a strategy is justifiable.

Philosophical hermeneutics strives to heighten the reflective difference between the canonic texts of the past and our own philosophical horizons. Nietzsche's thought moves in an opposing direction. His equation of the emergence of consciousness with the need to communicate suggests that any enhancement of conscious reflection acquiesces to prevailing linguistic metaphors of the commonplace. Therefore, "not an increase in consciousness is the aim, but enhancement of power,"[61] a freeing of those Dionysian creative drives that are able to forge new ways of forming a world. Once again, it is possible to have sympathy for Nietzsche's view. Whether we are talking of the power of prevailing metaphors or of the expectancies of a cultural horizon into which new works are delivered, there is no doubting the sheer weight established norms place upon thinkers. It can exert pressure to conform, to comply, and to become "recognizable." Nietzsche knows that artists and thinkers must diminish their conscious awareness of the norms of critical convention and trust to their own creative instincts (judgment) if they are to find their voice. Insofar as he venerates the unconscious powers of free invention from which metaphor springs, it is not inappropriate for him to argue against the (secondary) powers of reflective consciousness in favor of the Dionysian impulses that underlie conscious activity. Yet the question remains: Is such a romantic view of creative subjectivity hermeneutically plausible?

From the perspective of philosophical hermeneutics, Nietzsche's attempt to force a break with philosophical tradition and to invest in the creative unconscious powers of the subjective is indeed implausible. Philosophical hermeneutics would argue that the all-encompassing onto-logical horizon of language means that no thinker can step aside from the conceptual stock that enables his or her thinking in the first place. Nietz-sche is no exception to this. Not only is his entire philosophy permeated by traditional questions concerning the good and the true but his attempt at a "revaluation of all values" is also the outcome of a deeply pious pur-suit of intellectual integrity worthy of philosophical tradition at its best. Philosophical hermeneutics insists that underlying subjective conscious-ness are not just unconscious instincts but also the substantial influences of language and tradition, which enable and mold our thinking some-times contrary to our willing and doing. No thinker can escape such sub-stantialities without abandoning the intellectual inheritance that enables their project in the first place. It is, after all, the problems inherent in Christian morality and metaphysics that circumscribe the importance of Nietzsche's thought and not vice versa. However, against the argument that if we cannot escape the endowment of our linguistic and intellectual horizons, Nietzsche might ask (as Habermas was to), are we simply to ac-quiesce to the prejudices and distortions of understanding inherent within our heritage? If so, does not the attempt to breach tradition with new and inventive modes of thought appear attractive after all? Philo-sophical hermeneutics offers two points in reply. First, the attempt to break away from linguistic and intellectual tradition is not an option. To do so would be to abandon those objective and substantive issues that en-able us to define the subjective in the first place. Second, and more im-portant, to accept that we cannot escape the endowment of our linguisitc and intellectual horizons does not mean that we acquiesce to its preju-dices. How then does philosophical hermeneutics make good the claim that to acquiesce to tradition does not mean that we are committed to accepting its prejudices?

A defense of tradition does not entail a descent into intellectual bad faith, that is, the adoption of pat answers to ethical or religious questions. Traditions when vital always embody, as MacIntyre puts it, continuities of conflict.[62] The practices and narratives that sustain a tradition are logi-cally open-ended and can therefore sustain *different* anticipations of wholeness and completeness. Gadamer, following Heidegger, senses that the truth of a tradition lies ahead of itself and is, historically speaking, still open. As Pannenberg has perceived, the anticipation of different narrative outcomes or "transformations of structure" can have the critical function of "refuting" the temporally conditioned understandings of a given tradition. The ability of a tradition to go beyond its own subjective meaning in the light of different anticipated totalities of meaning can be justified, according to Pannenberg, by understanding the projective nature of meaning. It does not require, as Habermas famously insisted against Gadamer, going outside a traditional narrative to another level of critical reflection altogether.[63] Critical transcendence is therefore possible within a tradition. Precisely because of its inherent critical ability to project an anticipated wholeness for its narrative against received anticipations, traditions can surpass "the temporally conditioned form" of their subjectively intended meanings.[64] To recognize this, however, is to recognize not merely that vital traditions embody continuities of conflict but also that they do not provide set answers to inherited questions. Traditions offer different ways of anticipating what such answers might be. Traditions are indeed difficult spaces. However, it is the ability of tradition to interrogate the present that attracts philosophical hermeneutics. To discuss this point, we shall briefly turn to Heidegger.

In *Being and Time*, Heidegger comments that " every enquiry is a seeking [and that] every seeking gets guided beforehand by what is sought."[65] Heidegger knows, however, that in order for him to recapture a primordial experience of being, he has to strip away that which has infiltrated our understanding of being, namely, all those traditional theories and opinions that blur our immediate apprehension of being. His theory of *Destruktion* attempts to rid our understanding of historically acquired philosophical prejudices in order for us to reacquire a sense of the majesty and mystery of being. Heidegger's *Destruktion* constitutes an unbuilding (*abbauen*) or dismantling of philosophical tradition in order to recover a fundamental phenomenology of being. Nietzsche would of course question whether there was an original recoverable phenomenological essence to religious or metaphysical experience. He would object that the device of *Destruktion* only serves to phenomenologically purify a tradition of religious or metaphysical thought rather than to critically engage with it. These points notwithstanding, the substantive issue concerns something else. Heidegger's conceptual archaeology endeavors to recover a pre-Christian meaning to metaphysical categories so that we might think anew and more immediately about the nature of our existence. In contrast, Gadamer's etymological talents are not deployed to retrieve a lost sense of wonder but to remind us that embedded within words are worldviews capable of supplementing and extending our own. The existence of such embedded worlds is not always readily perceived. Against the subtler residues of previous speech-created worlds, any contemporary language horizon is advantaged by the force of immediacy and thereby possesses the distorting capacity of an ideology. What Gadamer describes as the dogmatism of the immediate can blind us to alternative meanings and modes of feeling that flow, historically, into our contemporary world. It can also shroud us in the illusion that the world contained within our immediate speech world is *the* world and not one of many possible language worlds etymology reveals we are in fact connected to. Once we develop an ear for what lies within words, the spell of immediacy's force and its prejudices can be broken. The importance of this philological tactic is not merely that it retrieves past meanings but that in so doing it frees us from having to feel and think solely in terms of our present speech world and its assumptions. The liberating aspect of this tactic concerns the uncovering of other logically possible ways of thinking, looking, and feeling.[66] The full force of Gadamer's commitment to engaging with the otherness of the other (tradition) becomes clear.

Gadamer does not attempt a phenomenological *Destruktion* to return us to a primal experience of wonder underlying an ancient metaphysical text (Heidegger). He deploys the Aristotelian tactic of strengthening the arguments of his opponents, in this case, ancient texts. The task is to allow the text's voice to assert its alterity against the blind expectancies we normally bring to our readings.

> A hermeneutically trained consciousness must be, from the start, sensitive to the text's alterity. But this kind of sensitivity involves neither neutrality with respect to content nor the extinction of one's self, but the fore-groundings and appropriation of one's own fore-meanings and prejudices. The important thing is to be aware of one's own bias, so that the text can present itself in all its otherness and thus assert its own truth against one's own fore-meanings. (TM, 269)

However, the point of this stratagem is not merely to allow a text's alterity to come forth but to bring it forth so as to become different to ourselves. The purpose is not merely to present the text in its alterity. Thinking differently about the text is not itself of any purpose unless it forces us to think differently about the presuppositions that have governed our reception of such a text and, more important, to think differently about ourselves. Bringing a text's voice to a point where it can express its alterity clearly is of a piece with Gadamer's commitment to the hermeneutic positivity of the "negativity of experience": "Experience in this sense inevitably involves many disappoinTMents of one's expectations and only thus is experience acquired. . . . Every experience worthy of the name thwarts an expectation" (TM, 356). Yet the outcome of such experience is not mere negation. True, it forces a distanciation between our previous and present understanding of both a text and of ourselves but insofar as it does so, such negation prompts a new communion between the other and oneself. In a successful albeit painful hermeneutic engagement, the assertion of a text's alterity, the assertion of its own truth, and the process whereby that assertion brings us to a more truthful understanding of ourselves are bound together. As Gadamer argues, "to reach an understanding" in a dialogical engagement with an other or with the otherness of a text, " is not merely a matter of putting oneself forward and successfully asserting one's point of view, but [of] being transformed into a communion in which we do not remain what we were" (TM, 379).

The argument put forward by philosophical hermeneutics makes clear that acquiescing to the enabling horizons of tradition does not constitute blind acceptance of its norms. "Tradition," Gadamer insists, "is not simply a process that teaches us to know and govern; it is language—i.e. it expresses itself like a thou" (TM, 358). As such it puts questions to us.

> The voice that speaks to us from the past—whether text, work, trace—itself poses a question and places our meaning in openness. In order to answer the question put to us, we the interrogated must ourselves begin to ask questions. (TM, 374)

The dialogical conception of hermeneutic engagement with tradition does nothing to perpetuate the sameness of our conception of the past or the sameness of the received text itself. Such engagement strives to bring about a differential space between the alterity of the text and our received preconceptions of it. It seeks to increase the difference between how we understood ourselves while in the thrall of our preconceptions and how we understand ourselves subsequent to a revelation of their limitations. There can, of course, be no full transparency with regard to the nature and operation of our preconceptions but, then, there never could be. At least, the negativity of hermeneutic experience disabuses us of some of those preconceptions. The clear strength of philosophical hermeneutics is that its dialogical engagement with received values creates encounters in which the differences between a subject matter and our received views of it are brought out. The purpose is to think differently about ourselves and our inherited subject matters. Philosophical hermeneutics can make good the claim that to acquiesce to tradition does not mean that we are committed to accepting its prejudices. How do these arguments affect the plausibility of Nietzsche's case?

In his critique of philosophical and moral values, Nietzsche deploys a genealogical rather than philological tactic. His "critique of big words"[67] presupposes that key moral and philosophical concepts can be shown to have their origins in dispositions and orientations other than those that they proclaim. The concept of "truth" emanates from a will that something should count as true while the concept of good emerges from cruel and brutal modes of social regulation. Nietzsche's genealogical tactic attempts to disburden the present of the absolutist claims of certain forms of epistemology and morality. He literally *deconstructs* such claims by employing an archaeological critique that reveals their origin to be in impetuses and values other than what they proclaim. Nietzsche's own genealogical tactic certainly succeeds in showing how "something can emerge from its opposite," but the question concerning this deconstructive operation is not whether it is insightful or not (for it clearly is) but how extensive its range of hermeneutic application is. First, we can observe that a moral claim can be shown to have its roots in practices that are far from moral, but this does not necessarily invalidate the claim unless it is supposed that its meaning depends solely and exclusively upon what was once intended by it in bygone communities. However, not just philosophical hermeneutics but also thinkers such as Habermas insist that because of its linguistic nature the meaningfulness of a claim will always transcend or be in excess of the circumstances in which such a claim was first made.[68] Second and far more telling is the question of whether Nietzsche sought to subject his own thinking to the challenge of alterity and difference. The tracing back of one mode of thinking to another is not necessarily to engage with it in such a way as to enter into a dialogical relationship with it and be interrogated by its alterity. Nietzsche's genealogical tactic undoubtedly disrupts the conventions of epistemological and moral thought but there is no occasion where he allows such conventions to disrupt his own presuppositions about the origins of truth and morality.

There is little evidence that for the purposes of dialectical engagement Nietzsche attempted to strengthen the case for traditional morality. Such a ploy might have tested the plausibility of his initial assumptions about the nature of values. Trying to make the case for the position one opposes does not entail embracing it. It attempts to draw out the "withheld" within such a position, seeing what one did not see in it or in one's assumptions about it. Irrespective of whether such a stratagem would have strengthened or weakened his assumptions, Nietzsche would have been forced to review his thinking about the claims of morality and his own view of those claims. There is little evidence that Nietzsche subjected the terms of his own revaluation of morality to being interrogated by the "subject matter" itself. If these observations are right, it would follow that Nietzsche was not interested in dialogically sustained difference and being challenged to think beyond the terms of his own critique but only in displacing the traditional claims of morality with another set of values (the will to power). Although he aimed to fragment and disrupt the claims of traditional morality (and thus to accelerate humanity's creative becoming), he remains vulnerable to the charge of not wanting to amend or alter the terms of his own critique. Nietzsche often remarked on the danger of oppositional (as opposed to dialectical) thinking. The danger does not lie in having to risk one's thoughts but in becoming dependent on precisely that which one would oppose. In Nietzsche's later language, one needs such resistances in order to overcome them. Once again, his language is telling. Overcoming implies the displacement of one thought regime by another. It does not imply the transformation of one's own thinking. This exposes Nietzsche to the charge that despite his avowal of becoming, he is evidently reluctant to risk his own assumptions by opening them to the challenge of the truly different and other. Philosophical hermeneutics insists, to the contrary, that our language being is such that we are constantly exposed to the risk of confrontation with the other and the different. Does Nietzsche not fall victim to another of his favored metaphors? The abilities to wage war, to struggle, and to oppose are not necessarily indicative of health, power, or the desire for a fuller affirmative life. As Nietzsche's critique of herd morality suggests, such abilities can equally betray a defensive posture. They can be indicative not of a desire to become and to transform but of a wish to remain the same. Philosophical hermeneutics grasps to Nietzsche's discomfort that with the word one is never alone. Philosophical hermeneutics also understands that if one is never alone with the word one can never remain the same either. Nietzsche's wilful determination to avoid the contamination of the linguistic marketplace and his stratagems of affirmation and negation, as opposed to those of dialogical openness, isolate him from one of the central insights of philosophical hermeneutics. Dialogical engagement exposes and opens one to insights beyond one's *willing* and *doing*. The opportunities for extending one's own philosophical and spiritual journey—the chance of becoming truly different to oneself in how one thinks and understands—depends upon a dialogical openness to hearing what the other has to say. In turn, the willingness to risk becoming subject to the address of the other stands upon the understanding that one's own position is never definitive but always capable of becoming more. The ability to "become more" depends, it would seem, upon a willingness to enter the marketplace of language.

ENTR'ACTE

Philosophical hermeneutics accepts that understanding is possible, that artworks and texts address us. When artworks "speak," a truth claim is imposed upon us such that we cannot turn away from it. The power of such claims is that as a consequence of their assertion, we think of ourselves differently. Philosophical hermeneutics stands upon a rigorous philosophy of subjectivity. What arrests the subject in its experience of art does not lack objectivity. It is the objectivities within the intensities of subjective experience that matter. This part of our essay has explored the objective dynamics of speculative understanding, which body forth the structures of phenomenological (aesthetic) experience. The occasion of speculative insight may be arbitrary but its structure is shaped by the dynamics of forgetfulness and recognition.

The primary structure of speculative disclosure is linguistic. Philosophical hermeneutics expresses something of what it is to be caught up within the commotion of ideas and what it is to be seized by them. Philosophical hermeneutics conceives the traffic of ideas as being essentially speculative. Speculative understanding involves the ability hear what is said beyond the spoken and to see in the visible something of the invisible. The revelatory nature of speculative insight has a clear structure involving a cycle of forgetfulness and self-recognition. In the unresolved flow of meanings that constitute the "everyday," the possible truth (*aletheia*) of an as yet unrealized line of meaning remains hidden (*lethe*), overlooked, or unforeseen. A speculative understanding involves a moment of centripetal insight. By means of illusion or fiction, the commonplace is transformed. An unrealized line of meaning is fulfilled, allowing us to see in the artwork the hidden coherence of everyday experience, a coherence that lay incomplete or unseen until the work's intervention. That which was forgotten is experienced in its truth for the

first time. The hermeneutic subject is addressed or shocked by the speculative not merely because of a moment of self-implication in the disclosed
but because the artwork reveals how the subject's lack of foresight has
conspired to prevent it from seeing the truth latent within the everyday.
Gadamer's phenomenological economy of the speculative uncovers the
objective dynamics that drive interior understanding.

Gadamer's exploration of the speculative strives to unfold the objectivities that animate the inward voice. His enquiry confirms thesis one of
our discussion. Hermeneutical understanding requires difference. Speculative insight enables us to think of ourselves and what is around us in an
unfamiliar way. Insofar as speculative truths are disclosed to us rather than
being arrived at by methodological enquiry, Gadamer's account of the
speculative supports our second thesis, namely, that philosophical
hermeneutics promotes a philosophy of experience. Speculative truths
may emerge because of an objective dynamic with language but they disclose themselves to *subjects*. The occasion of such disclosure affirms thesis
three, which states that philosophical hermeneutics is committed to a
hermeneutic realism. Speculative disclosure confirms that what is experienced by the subject is not always a matter of its willing and doing.

Gadamer's examination of the speculative offers a formidable philosophical analysis of the objective conditions governing a subject's experience of art's truth claim. It is an analysis that brings the dialectical nature
of language to light. The dialectic concerns the mutual opposition of the
centrifugal and centripetal aspects of linguistic experience as well as the
insight that the conditions that appertain to the emergence of the meaningful (the perception of limit, of wholeness and completeness), are also
the conditions that *dissipate* the meaningful. This prevents Gadamer's account of the speculative from collapsing into an apology for *Geborgenheit*.
Each reconfiguration of meaning permits the narrative becoming that
grounds the constellar identity of a hermeneutic subject to become different to itself and to unfold in unexpected directions. Openness to
chance collisions of meaning and to the transcendence they afford is the
very stuff of hermeneutic exchange. A commitment to such openness
drives philosophical hermeneutics in its resistance to nihilism. Avoiding
the marketplace of "common language" for the sake of preserving the
purity of individual experience declines the invitation to become uncommon, to become different to oneself. The implicit nihilism of Nietzsche's
sanctimonious aestheticism is found out by philosophical hermeneutics.
However, in exposing the dialectical structure of speculative understanding, philosophical hermeneutics reveals something difficult within the

character of hermeneutic exchange itself. The difficulty appertains to the status of *difficulty* within understanding itself. Have we not just suggested that to grasp the conditions that facilitate a perception of the meaningful is to perceive the conditions that can dissipate it? To pose the question another way, if speculative insights can be disrupted by chance collisions of meaning of the same order as those that bring them into being, are we not saying that to understand is to understand that understanding is always in difficulty? If we know that an apparition of the meaningful is one aspect of a *Sache*, do we not simultaneously perceive that we stand in a relationship to a *Sache* that is simultaneously *near* and *far*? Does not understanding place us in a relationship to a *Sache* that is one of hermeneutic proximity *and* distance? Is this what is *hermeneutical* about hermeneutic understanding? Such questions have a direct bearing upon our theses concerning both the constituting differential and the in-betweenness of hermeneutic understanding. Approaching them offers an appropriate hermeneutical *entr'acte* between this part of our discussion and the next.

Hermeneutical consciousness *knows* that understanding is always in difficulty. Understanding both draws near to its object and places that same object at a distance. As we have seen, Iser argues that interpretation does not dissolve but generates difference. This suggests that the end point of "hermeneutical" scholarship is not understanding per se but the disclosure of the "hermeneutic" task. Its aim would not be to resolve debate but to start it, to clarify what is at issue, and to define the differences between the horizons of a text and those of its interpreter. Hermeneutical understanding, it would appear, resolves nothing. The aim of philosophical hermeneutics is to initiate a conversation, to set it going and not to end it with a final interpretation. It does not remove hindrances to communication allowing conversation "to go on" free of disruption and obstacle. To the contrary, hermeneutical scholarship would set the task which hermeneutic conversation would subsequently negotiate. A hermeneutical consciousness is aware that "the exchanges of conversation and negotiation are the essence of what is going on. . . . Difficulty is inherent in what is being done."[69]

Difficulty sets us at a distance. It places us between expectation and outcome. In Latin, *dis* + *facultas* conveys a sense of reversal, of meeting an obstacle that throws one back on oneself. The negative nuances of the term are not at odds with claims of philosophical hermeneutics. Gadamer speaks of how distance is the condition of understanding (TM, 298). Hermeneutics, he claims, is rooted in the in-between. Tradition is recognized as a continuity of conflict, as a process that conserves difficulty by passing on the questions that each age must confront in its own way. Philosophical hermeneutics proposes that all understanding is finite and subject to disruption by new configurations of the meaningful. Furthermore, the arguments in favor of strengthening the position of an opponent and allowing a text to speak in its own terms against our presuppositions extend the distance between ourselves and the object of our understanding. These remarks support the thesis that philosophical hermeneutics is a negative hermeneutics. What then of the status accorded to the transformation into structure argument?

In the light of the above, the transformation into structure argument and its case for the completion of meaning seem at odds with the *via negativa* of philosophical hermeneutics. Neither are many of the key motifs within Gadamer's writings consistent with it. We note, first, that succumbing to an artwork's completion of meaning may transform our understanding but the experience hardly challenges understanding's presuppositions. Does not *reverie* dissolve distance? Second, is it not the case that Gadamer insists that such epiphanic moments are necessarily finite? Language's centrifugal impetus is always at odds with the centripetal? Third, does not the transformation into structure argument place hermeneutical consciousness in an unsatisfactory light? Does it not suggest that understanding becomes aware of its difficulties only when it meets a limit or point of resistance? This implies that consciousness becomes "hermeneutical" not because of an interpretative practice but because of what limits that practice. Fourth, if hermeneutic awareness only emerges because of what frustrates it, interpretative practice is cast in the role of blithely pursuing a completion of meaning, which, in turn, implies that interpretation only seeks to de-problematize meaning and render it transparent. However, Gadamer opposes any Diltheyean conception of understanding. What has happened? Why have we arrived at this impasse? Are Gadamer's arguments in this respect inconsistent and self-contradictory?

The difficulties under discussion emerge from an opposition. They spring from the supposition that the transformation into structure argument and the *via negativa* spirit of philosophical hermeneutics are in conflict. What, however, if the *via negativa* were implicit within the transformation into structure argument? What if an intimation of meaning were not the opposite of a deconstructive dissipation of meaning but bore the mark of its own dissolution? What if the centrifugal and centripetal aspects of language coinhered? What follows from such reasoning is precisely the thesis we are arguing, namely, that the "hermeneutic" nature of understanding resides precisely in an awareness of its difficulty, in its constituitive in-betweenness. To support this, we need to make brief reference to Hegel, to Heidegger, and to the closing sections of *Truth and Method*.

For Hegel, "Nothing can be understood in isolation."[70] "A thing," or a meaning, "is what it is only in and by reason of its limit. We cannot regard the limit as only external to being which is then and there."[71] Although a perception of meaning might be aesthetically and psychologically immediate, ontologically speaking, it does not stand alone. It always relates to that which "limits" it and to that which is beyond it. Yet, as we have seen, the "transcendent" elements of meaning remain inherent with singular perceptions of meaning. A singular perception of meaning is edged with that which it is not, namely, that virtuality of meaning which, though it surpasses any single perception of meaning, coinheres with it. Such an entailment links directly with Heidegger's conception of the withheld. Referring to Heidegger, Gadamer remarks that a work of art not only brings something meaningful to experience that was not known before, but that in so doing brings something new into existence. It is not simply that an artwork lays bare a truth.[72] In speaking to us, it reveals something; it "brings something forth from unconcealedness." Yet the emergence into light is not the annihilation of concealedness per se but the revelation of a continued sheltering in the dark. There is a clear tension between the emergence and the sheltering that constitutes the form *niveau* of a work. The work's "truth" is not constituted simply "by laying bare its meaning but rather by the unfathomable depth of its meaning. Thus by its very nature the work of art is a conflict between . . . emergence and sheltering."[73] The artwork's revelation of emergence and sheltering is a disclosure of "the essence of Being itself," for the conflict of revealment and concealment is "the truth of every being."[74] This is reminiscent of Adorno's conception of the enigmatic quality of art: "Art . . . hides something while at the same time showing it."[75] Heidegger does not articulate the conflict of revealment as an enigma but as that "which comes to stand," a "standing-in-itself." What comes to stand in an artwork is a thing or world that is sufficient unto itself. The autonomy of the artwork resides in its ability to reveal the extent to which it also remains concealed within in itself. The phrase "coming to stand" invokes a fullness of being in which fullness is not a laying bear of its meaning but a revelation of what has yet to be revealed. Coming to stand does not indicate a condition of disclosure as opposed to a state of hiddenness but the process whereby a thing—precisely because it partially comes forward into disclosure—also reveals the extent to which it remains undisclosed. Coming to stand does not therefore oppose the intelligible dimensions of a thing against its mysterious aspects. As Adorno rightly contends, the task of understanding dissolves and yet preserves art's enigmatic quality.[76] In Heideggerian terms, it is precisely because certain aspects of a work are intelligible that the unseen presence of the full mystery of a work can be brought to light. As he remarks in the essay "On the Origin of the Art Work," the sayable "brings the unsayable into the world."[77] Thus, the disclosed and the withheld are not opposites. The disclosed enables us to discern the presence of the withheld. Without the disclosed, the withheld would be deprived of its promise. It would have no presence as the "as yet to be disclosed." Referring back to Hegel, we can argue that that which limits or negates a meaning and that which transcends that meaning but is not uttered by it (the withheld), is not external to that meaning but is discernible in the very *relatedness* of that meaning. Such relatedness does not concern the relationship between language and what is outside it but between the disclosed and the withheld within language. This is substantiated by the closing sections of *Truth and Method*.

The closing arguments in *Truth and Method* do not mention Heidegger's conception of the withheld and yet, somewhat appropriately, it is implicit within Gadamer's notion of the self-presencing of language. Being, Gadamer writes, is self-presentation and all understanding is an event of being (TM, 484). Being "is" the events in which it presents itself. Being "is" its appearances, its images, its interpretations,[78] and, as he asserts elsewhere, "Being that can be understood is language" (TM, 474). However, the decisive point is not stated by Gadamer, namely, that the event of being which language facilitates involves the bringing forward of the withheld. The essential being of language is also self-presentation. When, accordingly, something is stated in language, something is brought forward (a meaning or a *Sache*) and yet what is brought forward is more than the stated for what is stated can only be stated because of the efficacy of the withheld, that is, that incalculably large and complex network of traditional meanings and associations that underlie and enable our deliberations. Thus, the event of being that language facilitates brings forward not just the disclosed but also the withheld. The withheld manifest in the disclosed would have no presence were it not brought forward by the disclosed. The disclosed and the withheld are not opposites but coinhere in one another. There is, in this respect, no openness on the one hand and closedness on the other. To the contrary, a perception of meaning acquires its clarity, resonance, and allure precisely because it intimates the presence of the withheld. It is both vague and distinct, near yet far. Furthermore, it is the intimation of the withheld that allows a perception of meaning to open toward its own depths. Without its ground in the withheld, a perception of meaning could not open to what is both beyond it and more than it. As Heidegger suggests, is it not language that first provides the possibility of standing among the openness of entities?[79] To conclude: to perceive a meaning as disclosed is to perceive that it is limited by what is withheld and that, as a consequence, the disclosed is always vulnerable to the otherness within the withheld. This implies, as we have argued, that understanding is always in difficulty. Hermeneutical consciousness senses the in-betweenness of understanding. Because it discerns the withheld within the disclosed, it knows that any understanding is inconclusive, incomplete, irresolvable, and always renegotiable. However, it also knows that such vagueness shades what is understood and gives it definition. Once again philosophical hermeneutics senses the positivity that is inherent within the finitude that renders all experience of meaning seemingly negative.

The foregoing is a response to the observation that the transformation into structure argument with its emphasis upon completeness conflicts with the *via negativa* of philosophical hermeneutics and its rejection of closure. If, however, the disclosed and the withheld are not opposites but are bound to each other by their mutual coinherence, it follows that the *via negativa* of philosophical hermeneutics is indeed implicit within the transformation into structure argument. There is clear symmetry between the different elements in Gadamer's reasoning. The conceptions of something "coming-to-stand," of the process of "self-presencing," and of the "event" that is an artwork are openly allied to the argument that the withheld is made manifest in the disclosed and would have no presence were it not for that which is disclosed. The disclosed and the withheld are not opposites. Nietzsche makes the point.

> You will know that I love shadow as much as I love light. For there to be beauty of face, clarity of speech, benevolence and firmness of character, shadow is as needful as light. They are not opponents: they stand, rather, lovingly hand in hand, and when the light disappears, shadow slips away after it.[80]

The argument for coinherence suggests that the hermeneutical awareness of the meaningful is not the opposite of a deconstructive dissipation of meaning. Rather, it is an awareness of that which can potentially dissipate, limit, or negate such meaning as being present within the emergence of the meaningful. It is the hermeneutical equivalent to what Blake perceives as "the sickness of the rose." To understand (as Heidegger might argue) that time is a condition of beauty's coming forth is to understand that the very time that brings beauty forth is also the time that impels it to fade. For Gadamer it is not time but the instability of language that is at the center of the argument. To understand that the withheld (be it articulated as tradition or as implicitly understood networks of meaning) is the condition of the meaningful coming forth is also to understand that the very fusions of meaning that enable the meaningful to emerge can also generate the conditions of its disappearance. Hermeneutic consciousness knows that understanding is always in difficulty. Yet the *via negativa* of philosophical hermeneutics demands that the central point also be asserted positively. Is it not the case that that which makes understanding difficult—the ability of the withheld to disrupt, defer, or dissipate the meaningful—is also that which gives the meaningful its depth, its resonance, and its weight? From these observations, several issues arise. The first concerns a paradox similar to that posed by the transformation into structure argument.

If the intertwining of the withheld and the disclosed is the ontological foundation for a meaning always meaning more than itself, why does Gadamer insist on *strengthening* an opponent's viewpoint rather than proposing dialectical alternatives? The tactic, it would seem, pursues a closure rather than an expansion of meaning. Yet, this apparent paradox reveals the force of Gadamer's strategy of strengthening an opposing argument in relation to the mutual coinherence of the withheld and the disclosed. Given the intertwining of the latter, the implication of refining an opponent's argument is not closure but drawing nearer to what is withheld within an argument and, therefore, to what will change our understanding of it. This is consistent with Iser's argument concerning interpretation and the hermeneutical differential. Because of its particular setting within a withheld, refining an interpretation of an opponent's argument will expose the interpreter to other readings of the argument. Indeed, the *practice* of interpretation, the attempt to clarify an opponent's argument, is precisely the process that generates possibilities for understanding it differently. Hermeneutic *cortesia* involves, then, not merely listening to the argument of the other but listening for what is other within it, for intimations of what would push the argument beyond itself. Refining the argument of the other is not a pursuit of closure but an attempt to discern the presence of the different within the disclosed. Hermeneutic tact entails an openness to the other and to those possibilities for transcendence the other opens out onto. Hermeneutic *cortesia* embraces the disinterested involvement reminiscent of *theoria*. The attentive listener, the discerning viewer, or the careful reader seek to be outside themselves.

> Being outside oneself is the positive possibility of being wholly with something else. This kind of being present is a self-forgetfulness to what one is watching. Here self-forgetfulness is anything but a private condition, for it arises from devoting one's full attention to the matter at hand, and this is the spectator's own positive accomplishment. (TM, 126)

This giving oneself up to the argument of the other is an act of attentiveness, an attending to something that enables "one to forget one's own purposes" (TM, 124). Seeking a dialectical alternative to an argument is, however, a deliberate "self-determination of the subject" and as such is never quite free of the suspicion of being self-interested (TM, 124). On the other hand, giving oneself over to the argument of the other is not an instance of what Nietzsche descried as philological positivism. It is not merely an attempt to fix the other's text as a text-in-itself and for-itself. The intent is dialectical and the form is dialogical. By giving one self up to the text of the other and to its independent nature, the distance between one's own horizons and those of the text is sharpened. By allowing the text of the other to become more itself we achieve that spectorial distance that brings us closer to the other precisely because the difference between the other and ourselves is emphasized. Pursuing the text's distinctiveness also exposes us increasingly to what is indistinct about it, to how it is set within and set off by its withheld. It is the achievement of such differences that problematizes our initial assumptions. Here, hermeneutic consciousness comes to its real task. It is where understanding *begins*, where *what is at issue* between the other and ourselves becomes clear. In effect, hermeneutical understanding starts when it becomes *dialogue*, that is, when it ceases to be a merely individual or subjective operation. The difficulty of dialogue is not to be underestimated. Dialogue demands the *recognition* that, in relation to the other, our assumptions are indeed questionable. Dialogue requires that its participants not only risk becoming open to each other but also that they be willing to become difficult to themselves as a consequence. The hermeneutic communion is not one of consensus. Rather, it bonds those who both realize that understanding is difficult because difficulty is inherent in what is being done and know that without the risk and challenge of such difficulties, the opportunities for translation and transcendence are diminished. The hermeneutic communion is one that is open to what is held within the withheld. It is *attentive* to difficulty.

This philosophical *entr'acte* further establishes the status of the in-between, the withheld, and the difficult within philosophical hermeneutics. Its arguments offer positive confirmation of thesis seven (hermeneutic understanding redeems the negativity of its constituting differential), thesis eight (philosophical hermeneutics affirms an ontology of the in-between), and thesis ten (philosophical hermeneutics is a negative hermeneutics). Insofar as this *entr'acte* has stressed *attentiveness* to the withheld, the discussion consolidates both thesis nine (philosophical hermeneutics is a philosophical practice rather than a philosophical method) and thesis two (philosophical hermeneutics promotes a philosophy of experience). Indeed, the claim that "hermeneutical understanding starts when it becomes *dialogue*" returns us appropriately to thesis eleven (philosophical hermeneutics proposes that linguistic being is a *mysterium*), for thesis eleven is pertinent to themes this *entr'acte* has led us to, namely, *difficulty, dialectic,* and *dialogue*. The next part of our discussion will approach these themes in relation to thesis eleven as this particular constellation of arguments has an important bearing upon a major corollary of thesis three; namely, that philosophical hermeneutics embodies a substantial response to the challenge of Nietzsche's nihilism. We shall explore this claim by considering Werner Hamacher's criticism that a key difficulty posed by philosophical hermeneutics is that "understanding is in want of understanding."[81]

CHAPTER FOUR

Understanding's Disquiet

The position of Hermes was truly unenviable. On the one hand, he had to translate the wishes of the gods into terms that mortals could understand, and on the other he had to transpose the language of humans into an idiom that the immortals might grasp. Hermes was in genuine difficulty. Though he could communicate with both gods and humans he could not communicate his particular predicament of being caught in between in terms that either party would understand. The language of myth is, as Gadamer perceives, often the language of mytho-poeic inversion. Hermes' predicament expresses an all too human hermeneutical predicament. Only too often do we find ourselves caught between and unable to reconcile first-person understandings of ourselves with the understandings others have of us. Yet such negativity is precisely the constituting differential of hermeneutic consciousness. It is the difficulty of the in-between that drives understanding toward new configurations. It is, then, to the difficulty of hermeneutics and its alleged philosophical difficulties that we now turn.

THE WANTONNESS OF UNDERSTANDING

> wanton: something immodest or promiscuous, growing profusely, to be playful, to be rebellious, to lack discipline.[1]

In the essay "Premises," Werner Hamacher charges that "understanding is in want of understanding."[2] This is an important charge and is worthy of some consideration. If the claim that "understanding is in want understanding" means that since there is always more to understand, understanding is always incomplete, Hamacher's remark is not at odds with philosophical hermeneutics but is consistent with one of its central claims. If, furthermore, understanding is always in want of understanding because of its capacity to mean more, Hamacher's comment might imply that understanding is *wanton* in its excess. However, as we shall see, Hamacher's thesis takes another direction, one that concerns the fundamental possibility of what he takes to be understanding. We shall contend that because of a serious confusion between language and reason, Hamacher's case is flawed. Nevertheless, Hamacher's arguments are instructive. Exposing their underlying confusion concerning *logos* as word and *logos* as reason not only brings forth central points about philosophical hermeneutics but also establishes in a clear and decisive manner the nature of its case against nihilism.

Hamacher's thesis concerns the very possibility of understanding and cleverly invokes the Kantian theme of critique. In *The Critique of Pure Reason*, Kant concerns himself with the indispensable *possibilities* of experience.[3] Gadamer too seeks to demonstrate how hermeneutic experience is possible: "How is understanding possible?" (TM, xxx).[4] It would be a mistake to suppose, however, that Kant and Gadamer are concerned with the same kind of possibility. Whereas Kant is concerned with the necessary epistemological conditions of experience, Gadamer pursues the ontological conditions of understanding. Despite the Derridean overtones of his arguments, Hamacher is inclined (perhaps inadvertently) to a Kantian notion of possibility: understanding is impossible since it cannot articulate that upon which its possibility rests (tradition, linguistic being). The disruptiveness of Hamacher's charge is largely deceptive as it rests on the questionable assumption that understanding is possible only if it rests upon a necessary ground. The Kantian inflection lies in the implied suggestion that the possibility of understanding has more to do with the conditions of reason than with the dynamics of language. Despite its Derridean sophistication, we shall argue that Hamacher's criticism is undone by its Kantian connotations. If understanding rests upon language rather than reason, then, as Gadamer remarks, "Does what has always supported us need to be grounded?" (TM, xxxvii). We shall see that this question invokes the key difference between *logos* as reason and *logos* as word.

Hamacher's claim about the impossibility of understanding is not an unfamiliar one. Iser, for example, argues that understanding is "impossible" in the sense of it being unable to complete itself: it can never fully grasp its object because the act of interpreting a subject matter opens an ineliminable space between reception and application. This positions understanding in its in-betweenness, between what we have already grasped of a *Sache* and what we have yet to make of it. Hamacher is not concerned with whether the practice of understanding continually defers or postpones its object but with whether it is marked (or rather disrupted) by an ineluctable want or lack of its own possibility.

> "Understanding is in want of understanding" means first of all that understanding is not only concerned with understanding things but must itself be understood whenever anything is to be understood. . . . If the determining moments of understanding remain in the dark, if it is not even understood that there are such moments—both historical and structural—then the subject matter to be understood also remains obscure.[5]

> That understanding is in want of understanding . . . [is a] . . . proposition [that] speaks also of the impossibility of understanding and thus the impossibility of this very proposition.[6]

As will become apparent, Hamacher's argument promotes an oppositional mode of thought which fails to do justice to the in-betweenness of understanding. This aside, Hamacher makes several salient points.

First, Hamacher notes that understanding produces effects and, what is more, remains incomplete without an understanding of such effects.[7] Understanding is never a relation between two already given immobile entities that remain untouched by this relationship. It is a relation in and by means of which each term constitutes itself. Understanding is a procedure of reciprocal affection and alteration.[8] Second, as a procedure of reciprocal affection and alteration, understanding is a process of change and alteration that cannot be arrested or contained by stable patterns of transformation. Third, as a consequence, understanding can never passively absorb the understood into a vessel of concepts or expectations. Understanding is a process in which the self and other are altered in ways impossible to anticipate. Understanding is a *standing before* (*ver-stehen*) exposure and exposition. Understanding must stand before what will expose its presuppositions and what will prompt it to become different to itself and to others (exposition).

It is plain that in many respects, these three points are consistent with positions defended by philosophical hermeneutics. Where Hamacher's arguments differ from those of philosophical hermeneutics is in the degree to which they depend upon sets of formal opposites that simultaneously enable and yet limit the possibility of understanding. In the context of our discussion of depth and disquietude within philosophical hermeneutics, the value of Hamacher's arguments stems from the emphasis they place upon the role of *negativity* within understanding.

Hamacher observes that understanding means "to be able," "to have the capacity," to "take something upon oneself" and "to be in charge of it."[9] These suggestions are innocent enough, but difficulties arise when it becomes clear that in addition to the Kantian overtones of his thesis, Hamacher sympathizes with Adorno's critique of instrumentalist reasoning.

It is not unreasonable to hold that a good understanding of a discipline requires a command over what one knows. Hamacher argues,

> It is one of the remarkable features of the movement of understanding that the incomprehensible, the foreign and the irreducibly other—each of which sets understanding into motion in the first place—can be bought to rest at the end of this movement (but it is precisely this end that is at issue here), can be stabilised into an account of representation, thematized by a subject, and thus made into a cognised, controlled reduced other of this subject. Understanding does not start by referring to objects; rather, objects constitute themselves in the act of understanding. Once they are constituted (and this final constitution is, once again, in question) the movement of understanding comes to a halt and turns into a certification of the object and a self-securing of cognitive reason.[10]

Yet, as we have seen, this is precisely the caricature of understanding that Duerr and Iser resist. Understanding is not conceived by philosophical hermeneutics as a referring back to, a taking control of the strange and usual within what one already knows. Understanding in the sense of making oneself open to the suffering of another does not constitute an "ability to take control" of what one is open to (though it does imply the self-control of the Samaritan to resist the temptation of noninvolvement). Hamacher insists, however, that understanding always orientates itself toward the other. Philosophical hermeneutics would concur with this claim if it meant that understanding needs the other not as a stimulus to its will to power (Nietzsche) but for those unexpected and unpredictable insights that the encounter with the other can give rise to. It is precisely those unpredictable insights that challenge understanding's assumptions, especially those held about the other. Yet this is not what Hamacher is arguing. He insists that understanding longs for the other and wants to be understood by another.[11] Yet here, of course, lies the rub. Longing for complete and fulfilling communication with the other is a longing for what is impossible. The *ecstasy* of such hermeneutic consummation would render communication impossible. It would dissolve the differentiation between the subject and object of understanding, a differentiation that enables the perception of the other as *other* in the first place. Furthermore, given Hamacher's description of understanding as "taking control" and his characterization of that control as "a process of certification by self-securing reason," understanding would destroy the very otherness it sought an encounter with. It seems, then, that in longing for both the other and the other's understanding, understanding longs for the impossible. On the one hand,

> The path of language goes towards the otherness of one "turned into a You, so to speak," and it thus goes out into an opening that cannot be occupied or invested by methods and topics; the impossible. . . . It is the path of understanding toward the siteless, the unsecurable, toward the otherness of understanding (itself). . . .[12]

And yet on the other hand,

> Longing for another must mean longing for something "impossible," since this longing strives to break through the categorial forms of subjectivity that dominate every experience of the other and distort every other into a replica of the self: the other must be impossible, the one beyond all possibilities of the subject—the *other* other—if the I is going to be able to discharge itself in this other and come free. The language that turns itself toward this other can no longer conform to the communicative codes in which an egologically structured society comprehends itself. Indeed, this language must be impossible, incomprehensible—and in its incomprehensibility it must allow, as Adorno writes, that sudden flash that in language itself, under the conditions of its impossibility, is other.[13]

Hamacher's powerful and telling observations demand some reflection.

FOUR RESPONSES TO DECONSTRUCTIVE CRITICISM

First: it should be noted that the terms of Hamacher's general discussion assume the epistemological mode of argument from which the language ontology of philosophical hermeneutics endeavors to escape. Following Adorno, Hamacher speaks of the "I," of the subject, which tries to break free of its subjectivity in its engagement with the "other." Hamacher's argument reveals little awareness that the language ontology of philosophical hermeneutics renders this a false opposition. As language speakers, the "other" (the implicit network of linguistic and cultural connections embedded in our language) is *already* in us just as we are in the "other."

Second: Hamacher's argument tends to assume a unitary conception of the "I" whereas philosophical hermeneutics adopts a "constellar" view. The notion of a "closed" subjectivity tends to assume that there is a single narrative that grounds the "I's" self-understanding, which, in Hamacher's words, the other is forced to replicate. However, the actuality of our linguistic being demonstrates that the "I" can be the subject of several narratives. Furthermore, the fact of my being with others within language means that I figure in many other people's narratives. Such configurations can make me appear other to myself and disrupt my own sense of narrative cohesion. Because of a shared language ontology, the other's narrative is always capable of reflecting back to me not a narcissistic mimesis of my desired self-projection but an image of myself that is deeply estranging and capable of placing my self-understanding into crisis.

Third: it is notable that the epistemological model of Hamacher's reasoning impels him to an instrumentalist view of subjective understanding that it is driven to *subsume* the other, "to dominate every experience of the other and distort every other into a replica of the self." Hamacher follows Schopenhauer, Nietzsche, and Adorno in assuming that the knowing subject is impelled by a noumenal will to reduce the world "to its own." In contrast, the language ontology of philosophical hermeneutics insists that the hermeneutic subject is never "its own" in the first place. Issues of *subsumption* and radical alterity do not arise, since what is in question is how a subject negotiates both the other held within in its own self and the other of itself held within the other's narrative. The issue for philosophical hermeneutics is neither the subsumption of the other nor ecstatic self-forgetfulness within the other, but the movement of understanding itself. The issue concerns that hermeneutical motion or event by means of which both negotiating parties exchange and transform their understanding by virtue of the fact that the linguistic being of each penetrates that of the other.

Fourth: the next point relates to Hamacher's epistemological approach to the question of the alterity. So long as the knowability of the internal nature of another ego is articulated as an epistemological issue, grasping alterity remains impossible. If understanding is a matter of experiencing mental states, I can never distinguish between "experiencing" my own mental state and that of another. The possibility of knowing the other as other is denied by the epistemological solipsism embedded in this line of reasoning. The language ontology of philosophical hermeneutics avoids this difficulty not merely by contending that the other is already within my linguistic horizon but by insisting that because the other presents itself in language, alterity can never be absolute but always the subject of hermeneutic exchange and negotiation. Referring to the work of Quine and Putnam, Hans Herbert Kögler observes that the alterity of different language horizons does not mean that they are incommensurable. If the other is recognized as other because of the otherness of her language, her language is nevertheless recognized as a language. If the other's language is recognized as a language, it is possible to engage with it. This suggests to Kögler that the incommensurability thesis is incoherent. The understanding of another language as a language already implies in principle that conceptions within that language relate to similar subject matters within my own.[14] However, it is important to qualify these remarks in two respects. Kögler's sympathy for Putnam's rejection of the incommensurability thesis does not necessarily collapse into the view that the other's domain is essentially reducible to the home language of knowing subject. Duerr argues, as we have seen, that the meaning of understanding is not reducible to reductive translation. *Pace* Wittgenstein, understanding involves understanding what wheel turns what in the language of the other. Understanding entails learning to operate within the horizon of the other rather than reducing that horizon to our own or, indeed, forgetting our own.[15] Furthermore, and contrary to Putnam's rejection of incommensurability, there are a host of words and phrases that do not have an equivalent in the English tongue. Howard Rheingold's research into the phenomenon of the untranslatable provides numerous examples: *tirare la carretta* (to slog through the everyday dirty work), *Radfahrer* (one who flatters superiors and browbeats inferiors), *amaeru* (to presume upon another's love), and *faux frais* (items likely to be forgotten in the drawing up of budget) are but a few.[16] Though there are no English equivalent to these terms, that they cannot be directly expressed in English does not mean that they are *beyond* understanding. Rheingold's lengthy descriptions of many such terms offer a constellar perspective that speculatively infers how their content might be grasped. They open a space whereby difficulty and difference are discernible within linguistic experience rather than being external to it. The difficulties of translation do not constitute the Achilles' heel of linguistic understanding, rather, they are indicative of the difficulties inherent in all understanding. The emergence of difficulty and difference within linguistic experience clears a space whereby the presence of the withheld and its intimations of the as-yet-to-be-understood can come forth. The difficulties of translation are therefore not exceptional. They are characteristic of understanding itself and are, as such, the very basis of hermeneutic transcendence. Philosophical hermeneutics does not diminish alterity and difference: it insists that both are fundamental to our linguistic experience of the world. Rather than seeking to diminish alterity by diluting and "distorting it into a replica of the self," philosophical hermeneutics offers a courteous attentiveness toward the difficult and the untranslatable and the possibilities for transcendence they offer. It is easy to see why. The path of language that goes toward the other is strictly speaking, as Hamacher claims, an impossible one. I certainly cannot become the other. But why is it supposed that understanding entails becoming the other? Surely, confronting alterity, difference, and the untranslatable *does not* mark the impossibility of understanding and the ending of its aspirations, for in recognizing that which challenges and potentially frustrates understanding, there is, as Gadamer perceives, something of a beginning. Is it not the shock of alterity's proximity and the collision with difference that jolts consciousness toward a form of hermeneutical awareness? Is it not the negativity of such experience that discloses what is at issue between the other and ourselves? In short, rather than standing in the path of understanding, is it not such difficulties that set the terrain that understanding must negotiate? Do not these difficulties articulate the space of in-betweeness in which the presence of the withheld in everything that is understood can be discerned? If so, then, the confrontation between alterity and ourselves is both formative and constitutive of hermeneutic consciousness itself. Philosophical hermeneutics openly acknowledges its dependence upon an insight that Hamacher's critical thesis obscures, namely, that if the other is genuinely impossible, then, so am I. The epistemological tenor of Hamacher's critique gives rise to further difficulties.

PHILOSOPHICAL HERMENEUTICS AND
THE QUESTION OF ALTERITY

Hamacher emphasizes the reality of the ego and the absolute alterity of the other in order to stress the unreality and incompleteness of the transactions between them. Philosophical hermeneutics, however, asserts the primacy of linguistic interaction and maintains that the subject and the other have no reality in themselves: they do not exist apart from language. Their reality derives from the ontological primacy of the linguistic interactions that constitute their being. This is not to say, for example, that a child does not exist before it acquires language, but it is to argue that a child's consciousness of itself as a subject depends upon becoming a subject of address. The child must acquire a *name* to become a subject of address. Subject and other do not exist prior to linguistic interaction. It is, rather, linguistic interaction that *subjectivizes* both subject and other. Philosophical hermeneutics reverses Hamacher's argument: subject and other are *impossible* without the actuality of linguistic engagement. According to Hamacher, however, although language reaches toward the other, such longing is impossible. A subject cannot break thorough the forms of subjectivity that enfold its experience of the other. Understanding between the two is supposedly impossible. However, philosophical hermeneutics insists that the subject would not have any sense of itself as a subject were it not *already* engaged with the other. In other words, the impossibility of subject and object existing apart from one another renders understanding *possible* though in an incomplete, unstable, and ever-changing form.

Hamacher's claims concerning the inarticulable otherness of the other rest upon an epistemological model of reasoning that places alterity outside what would be linguistically intelligible to a subject. Philosophical hermeneutics argues that, to the contrary, alterity and otherness are not alien to language but embedded within it. The interconnectedness of different etymological and conceptual frameworks within language means that as linguistic subjects we are all in part other to ourselves. In addition, language is always more than what is stated within it. That something cannot be stated does not mean that it is not part of language. This observation has a considerable bearing on the question of the relationship between alterity and language.

Hamacher's view that the otherness of the other cannot be grasped by linguistic understanding places otherness on the other side of language. No matter how understanding may strive to embrace it, otherness will escape. If a dialectical engagement between subject and other is

impossible, then so is dialogical understanding. In contrast, philosophical hermeneutics' insistence that understanding always occurs *within* a
language, suggests that alterity does not stand outside language. In
Hamacher's view, this is to deny alterity altogether. Now, on one level,
Gadamer's allegiance to Heidegger's axiom that "Language is the house
of Being" appears to support Hamacher's suspicions. It is important,
then, that we get to grips with what is meant by Gadamer's dictum, *"Sein,
das verstanden werden kann, ist Sprache"* (TM, 474). Is it the case that an otherness that is not articulable in language has no being and, furthermore,
has no being in language?

Gadamer's use of the phrase, "Where the word breaks off, no thing
may be" (*Kein Ding sei, wo das Wort gebricht*) (TM, 489), might be taken to
mean that where words fail, that which escapes description has no being-
for-us. On one level Gadamer clearly is saying this. Yet such a position does
not commit him to saying that that which is not spoken of has no being.
There are numerous star clusters neither named nor known. Yet their not
being spoken of has no bearing on their actual existence. Gadamer's point
is simply that for something to become relevant to us it has, in principle,
to be brought into and figure within our language world.

> Language is not just one of man's possessions in the world;
> rather, on it depends the fact that man has a world at all. The
> world as world exists for man as for no other creature that ex-
> ists in the world. But this world is verbal in nature. . . . Not
> only is the world *world* insofar as it comes into language, but
> language has its real being only in the fact that the world is
> presented in it. (TM, 443)

If this contention is understood as saying that the limits of *our* world are
determined by what can be said in language, Gadamer's view is allied to
Foucault's account of *epistémes*: those schemas of discursive practice and
epistemological networks that characterize and even articulate the outlook of a given historical period. Foucault claims that such schemas determine what is and is not thinkable within their framework. Though it
is absurd to deny that molecular activity occurred in the early Celtic
world, it is plain that the Celtic *epistéme* could not recognize such activity
just as the Viking *epistéme* cannot accommodate Early Christian notions
of the sanctity of all persons. There is a clear sense, then, that what is not
articulable within in a given language marks a limit to that language
world and has no being within it. However, the phrase, "Where the word
breaks off, no thing may be," can also be read in such a way as to imply

neither that the unsayable is something noumenal on the other side of language nor that it exists apart from language.

Language for Gadamer is always more than what can be stated within it. Language is not merely a process of objectification: it has a generative and formative capacity. Philosophical hermeneutics is concerned with language as "event." It reflects on *what comes into being by means of language.* Consistent with what we have argued above, a sense of difficulty and the presence of the withheld are two of the entities language brings into being. Language does not therefore stand opposed to a realm of the unsayable. To the contrary, *it is language that allows the unsayable to have its place in a given speech world.* This conception is central to Gadamer's speculative theory of meaning. Every word, he argues, carries with it the *unsaid:* "The living virtuality of speech brings a totality of meaning into play, *without being able to express it totally*" (TM, 458, emphasis added). Whether its form is philosophical or poetic, the illuminating power of speculative language stems not from what it objectifies in predicate form. Rather, it springs forth from that which the said lights up of what is not said. The speculative charge of language depends upon the way unuttered meaning and nuance feed into and lead away from what is actually said. It is the speculative that reveals the presence of the withheld within the said, demonstrates that interpretation has no closure, and exposes the essentially *enigmatic* nature of linguistic being. The speculative allows the unsayable its place within language. It summons that which lies beyond what is the stated and brings it to presence within language. In short, the unsayable does not exist apart from language. It is precisely the sayable that allows the unsayable to come forth.

The unsayable is not a *noumenal* entity beyond language: there is no element *within* the unsayable that cannot in principle be put into words. Each association of meaning, each philological connection lying beyond what is immediately said can in principle be articulated. Each new perspective that can be brought to bear on an artwork can be linguistically expressed. What cannot be objectified, however, is the whole, that is, the huge complexity of possible perspectives that surround a given work. The speculative dimension of language points to that complexity. Yet the fact that such a complexity cannot be expressed is neither indicative of an intrinsic opposition between language and the unsayable, nor of a failure of language. What it reveals is the finite nature of language. Though language can evoke a totality of possible meaning, it cannot articulate it. Yet such finitude is, hermeneutically speaking, an asset. Were the unsayable not within language, and if the unsayable did not light up the presence of the always more to be said, what motive would there be to say anything more? If language could not illuminate the presence of the unsaid, how could hermeneutic transcendence be possible? In conclusion, to place alterity, difference, and the unsayable beyond language dissolves the living interplay of otherness, difference, and the unsayable within language. More important is the fact that to disrupt the speculative interplay of the sayable and the unsayable, is to disrupt the play of understanding itself. Plainly, then, what divides philosophical hermeneutics and Hamacher is the question of nihilism, for, as we shall see, the specter of nihilism arises whenever the movement of understanding is threatened.

NIHILISM AND THE LIFE OF UNDERSTANDING

Hamacher could insist that Gadamer's dictum that "Being that can be understood is language" prevents philosophical hermeneutics from acknowledging that genuine alterity which escapes being said. However, being unsayable is not something that is strange to philosophical hermeneutics. The complex constellar nexus of any meaningful phenomenon is not something that can be articulated as such. This does not place it beyond language, for its presence is only approachable via the perspectival nature of interpretation. All meaningful phenomena contain an element of an instrinsic otherness insofar as that which is meaningful always points beyond itself. Furthermore, Gadamer qualifies his dictum that "Being that can be understood is language" in a significant way. In the same paragraph he goes on to remark that "we speak not only of a language of art but also of a language of nature—in short, of any language that things have" (TM, 475). Now, it is clear that the apparition of an other's face or the warmth of an other's touch, have an intensity and immediacy that places them beyond instant verbal or written capture. Yet Gadamer's remarks suggest that silent looks and speechless gestures speak. They *mean*. Insofar as they mean, they reach out to us. That which is beyond verbal articulation touches us and reveals that we belong to a sphere of meaningfulness larger than we can give utterance to. These looks and gestures are readable not in the sense that they are translatable into spoken or written form but because they have a language of their own. Visual expression can involve extraordinarily complex and shifting configurations of facial planes. We learn that different configurations mean different things in different circumstances. These configurations constitute a simple language in the sense that like spoken language, their different patterns bring something into being. A certain look bestows forgiveness, another grants acceptance or approval. We understand such gestures not because we translate them into a spoken idiom but because we understand their status as clear nonverbal expressions of the other. Looks and glances can operate like a language in that they can bring something to pass. This does not mean that a nonverbal gesture means something in its own right. If it means anything it will point beyond itself. In other words, nonverbal gestures can be enigmatic not because they are outside spoken language but precisely because they are part of a language and thus part of a communicative structure that has its own withhelds and undiscloseds. The alterity of the other, the enigma of art or the unfathomable nature of the withheld do not therefore stand outside language but, to the contrary, disclose themselves in and through the hermeneutic relations language (in the broad sense of the word) makes possible.

Philosophical hermeneutics is committed to the view that hermeneutic transcendence is possible because of the language relations we stand within. Insofar as these relations enable the enigmatic and the withheld to come forth, their emergence drives the always-more-to-be said. Their coming forth drives the impetus toward hermeneutic transcendence and toward the becoming different to ourselves which engagement with the different and the other makes possible. For Iser, it is the fact that we always stand within interpretative relations that generates the ineliminable spaces of the yet-to-be-said, spaces which in their turn provoke the self-proliferation of interpretation. In short, understanding and interpretation function within the spaces opened and generated by the relations that constitute our linguistic being. The specter of nihilism arises whenever the closure of these spaces and the movement of understanding that they facilitate is threatened. As we have seen, Hamacher does not regard otherness and difference as being generated from within the interpretative relations that constitute language. He postulates otherness and difference as being entities that confront and dumbfound language from the outside as it were and it is precisely this that threatens to disrupt the movement upon which understanding and the possibility of transcendence depends. Contrary to the negative nuance that Hamacher gives to understanding's wanton nature, it is the very wantonness of understanding that is important. Unlike reason, understanding does not seek wholeness or completeness but ever-new interpretative relations. It is precisely upon the generation of new interpretative tensions which understanding's resistance to nihilism's entropy depends.

In contrast to nihilism's *stasis,* the vitality of hermeneutic understanding resides in maintaining the inherent tension of its constitutive inbetweeness. Understanding is inherently unstable. Any moment of understanding moves from what *has been* understood toward that which has yet to be understood. Understanding more of that which we thought we understood can change our understanding of what we thought we understood, and changing our understanding of that can change our sense of what has yet to be understood. What guarantees the living movement of understanding is the irresolvable tension of its in-betweeness. The being or rather the movement of understanding is upheld. It is upheld, on the one hand, by the constitutive relations of what constantly comes to be within it (the disclosure of what has yet to be understood) and, on the other hand, by what constantly passes away within it (configurations of understanding that have been surpassed or displaced). If language is the being of all understanding, it is a being that, in Nietzsche's words, neither becomes nor passes away, "or rather, it becomes, it passes away but it has never begun to become and never ceased from passing away—it maintains itself in both" (WP, 1066). As an ontological phenomenon, understanding is the simultaneity of that which comes into being and passes away within it. If one element of this relationship is hypostasized at the cost of the other, the vitality of understanding is threatened. If tradition is privileged over yet to be realized determinations of meaning or if anticipated meanings are given greater value than those acquired from the past, the tensions that animate understanding are diminished. Such diminishment gives rises to the specter of nihilism. If the life of understanding depends upon continuous movement then, unlike reason, understanding does not seek wholeness or completeness. To aspire to being like reason, would involve understanding seeking to end the constant transitions on which its being depends. Understanding is indeed wanton. It seeks ever-new transformations of itself in order to maintain itself. For understanding to aspire to wholeness and completeness, would be for understanding to seek its end. Becoming whole and complete would involve understanding stepping outside the ever-changing relationships between the withheld and the disclosed, relationships that constitute its being. In this respect, understanding and reason are at odds. Returning to Hamacher's argument will establish the point.

Hamacher argues that "understanding remains an unfulfillable promise, always behind and ahead of itself at the same time . . . for understanding . . . the whole remains a necessary but unredeemable project."[17] The "project of a fundamental hermeneutics . . . collapses at its limit, at the very place where it was supposed to have secured the completeness of understanding and therefore its own wholeness."[18] Understanding, according to Hamacher, is forced to face its own incomprehensibility. Michal Markowski pursues a similar line of reasoning: "What has to be interpreted is still hiding itself beyond an endlessly receding horizon of time. Unlike explanation, interpretation does not tend toward something we have already known."[19] The origin and *telos* are not the possible world, but an impossible one: "impossible to be (in the) present, but demanding presence all the time."[20]

Understanding, it seems, *desires* an object (the whole or the complete) that cannot itself be an object of interpretation. Now what is discernible in Hamacher's and Markovski's arguments is a subtle sleight of hand whereby the sense of understanding passes from a process of linguistic/hermeneutic engagement to understanding as a mode of philosophical reasoning. Understanding as a hermeneutic practice is not required to be grounded in anything other than a practice, but understanding as a mode of reason demands that it be grounded in fundamental concepts.[21] To present understanding as a mode of reason steps outside and transgresses the relationships that both generate hermeneutical insight and keep language in play. Philosophical hermeneutics insists to the contrary, that the experience of meaning is essentially dialogical and is concerned with the interplay of relationships within language. Gadamer states that meanings must not be thought of as concepts: there is no meaning-in-itself. "Meanings, too, are like a space in which things are related to one another" (TM, 433). Something is meaningful because of the interconnectedness of disclosure and hiddenness within it. Each element in such a relationship only makes sense in relationship to the other. Nietzsche's note "New World Conception," cited above, exemplifies this line of thought. *Becoming* is not a halfway world caught between the fullness of Being and the abyss of non-Being. Being and non-Being only make sense in relation to each other. Becoming is the immanence of that relationship. Heidegger's conception of the relationship between the withheld and the disclosed is similar. Neither are fixed opposites but each expresses something of the other. The being of becoming is the constant interplay of the withheld and the disclosed. For Heidegger (and even more so for Gadamer), a dialogical conception of the interrelatedness of such terms supplants those ways of thinking that demand that understanding be grounded in the fixity of concepts.

By emphasizing their absence, Hamacher's argument slides back into thinking about hermeneutics in terms of grounding concepts.

Conceptions of the "whole" and "complete" only have any meaning if they remain within the dialogical practices that generate them. The notion that understanding can always be more clearly implies that a given interpretation can be *more* complete or whole. However, the notion of a "more" to be understood is relational. The more-to-be-understood is a more that is "more" only in relation to what has been and what has yet to be understood. A completer understanding may be anticipated, but what is anticipated will be a mode of understanding that nevertheless remains in a dialogical relationship with past and future "understoods." Such understanding can always be "more" complete yet never complete.[22] When Hamacher argues that the completeness desired by understanding is unrealizable, he absolutizes the notion of the complete and places it outside the dialogical relationships that generate it. It becomes the lodestone against which the adequacy (or rather inadequacy) of finite understanding is measured. In short, Hamacher's critique extracts one element from a dialogical relationship, conceptualizes it as something in itself (a determinable whole that would complete understanding), and then deploys it to tyrannize the dialogical relationship from which it was taken. When *measured* against a concept of wholeness that claims it would complete understanding, dialogical understanding cannot but fail to fulfill any promise of completeness but then, it never could keep such a promise. However, *the task of understanding is not to fulfill concepts but to transform dialogical relationships.* Dialogical understanding could never make a promise of completeness. All it can promise is an understanding "more" complete than any previously achieved.

This is not to say that philosophical hermeneutics does not speak of completeness or wholes. Gadamer speaks explicitly of an anticipation of completeness that guides the reading of a text. Yet this does not mean that Gadamer *believes* in the possibility of acquiring such completeness. Though Gadamer's mode of expression is sometimes not as precise as it could be, it is clear that he does not *mean* to say either that understanding is grounded in a concept of completeness or that a fixed totality of meaning underwrites each and every hermeneutic invocation of meaning. Were this his intended meaning, Gadamer would concede Hamacher's principal point: the fulfillment of understanding would induce its own death. In other words, by fulfilling the *concept* of wholeness, understanding would have moved beyond the dialogical relations that made it possible in the first place. Now we can see why Gadamer insists that as a dialogical way of thinking, hermeneutics must see through the dogmatism of meaning in-itself. The human word is, indeed, essentially incomplete (TM, 425). It is in such incompleteness that the resonance and depth of the word becomes possible. Put another way, it is in the incompleteness of the spoken word that the withheld resides although it is precisely the spoken word that brings forth the withheld. In conclusion, "understanding is in want of understanding" not because hermeneutics lacks a plausible conceptual grounding but because of something Hamacher overlooks and something Gadamer could have stressed more emphatically. If the hermeneutic process entails dialogical as opposed to dialectical (conceptual) relationships, any attainment of understanding will only reveal a want of further understanding. Achieving a more complete understanding of a subject matter would neither bring the hermeneutic task to a close, nor make it any the less intense. It simply changes the scope and intensity of understanding. For example, acquiring a completer understanding of a thinker's work may make an understanding of another issue seem less complete and, as a consequence, prompt difficulties not seen before elsewhere. Understanding is here not so much wanting (lacking something that would give it a clear determinate concept) but wanton: the more complete its understanding, the more the yet-to-be-understood beckons. In short, understanding does not aspire to its own death (the realization of completeness) but seeks translation and transcendence *within* the ever-fluid nature of dialogical relationships.

In summary, if Hamacher were right and understanding were grounded in *concepts* of wholeness and completeness, then in its quest for self-explication understanding would aspire to grasp that which would be incomprehensible, namely, the *whole*. If the possibility of understanding presupposed a preexistent whole and if the essence of understanding required a conscious appropriation of that whole, understanding would indeed be impelled toward its own death. Yet this supposes that understanding requires an essential rational grounding. If the thesis were true, Hamacher's contention would also be true, to wit, understanding is committed to its own failure. As we have seen, however, Iser takes a different point of view. He argues that ascription of an essential nature to understanding circumscribes and limit its possibilities. As a process of unending interactive translation, understanding has no essence. Understanding and translation cannot stand outside the relations that enable them to function. Understanding is always ontologically *between* what has been understood of a subject matter and how that understanding might be applied in different circumstances. The activity of understanding generates of itself an ineliminable space between hermeneutic horizons, opening the possibility of yet further configurations of itself. The emergence of such an ineliminable space does not constitute a failure, a promise of completeness broken or a fatal contradiction at the heart of the hermeneutic endeavor. To the contrary, such incompleteness fulfills the hermeneutic promise not of a complete or final understanding but of the possibility of further understanding. Such a space does not mark the absence of a grounding concept. Rather, it is a space opened by dialogical interaction. The space is sustained by the tensions between what has been understood and what has yet to be understood of a subject matter. Iser's analysis of understanding implicitly exposes the nihilism that haunts Hamacher's arguments.

Nietzsche stressed that nihilism can be the consequence of disappointment, disillusion with the belief that the categories of reason can be applied to actuality.[23] Hamacher's argument betrays such disappointment. He speaks of the incomprehensible, incomplete, unfulfillable, and therefore hopeless nature of understanding and its aspirations. The nihilistic element in the argument is plain. The hermeneutic project is to no avail. To this philosophical hermeneutics can rightly object that understanding only seems pointless if the measure of its success is taken to be the extent to which it realizes any grounding concept. Yet this supposes that understanding is grounded in concepts rather than in the dialogical practices of language. To despair of understanding on the ground that it is a process that cannot realize and fulfill its grounding concepts is nihilistic. The life of understanding is not about completion but transformation. What matters is not that understanding complies with the fixity of a concept but that it remains in play, continuing to open possibilities of transformation and transcendence. To question the meaningfulness of this task on the ground that it cannot be completed is, as Nietzsche would argue, indicative of a desire that it *ought* to be completed. Yet this is to desire that the motions of understanding and the dialogical relationships that sustain it should come to an end or have a realizable end. This raises a difficult and awkward question. Is the desire for the motion of understanding to be stilled indicative of philosophy (Hamacher) using reason to take revenge on the constant shifts and transformation of meaning that constitute the very life of langauge? Philosophical hermeneutics may not side with Nietzsche's *Lebensphilosophie* but it does side with the life of language.

As we claimed, philosophical hermeneutics is a good deal more radical than is often supposed. In its opposition to Hamacher's reasoning, philosophical hermeneutics prioritizes the play of language over the fixity of ideas and concepts. It affirms a "dialectic of the *word*" as opposed to a "dialectic of *ideas*." This affirmation of the word is at the root of its resistance to Nietzschean nihilism. In short, philosophical hermeneutics is avowedly *logocentric,* that is, it centers itself on the dynamic of the word as opposed to the fixity of the concept. As a dialogical process, understanding springs from, perpetuates, and requires to remain within the centrifugal and centripetal play of language. We shall now consider this claim.

DIALOGUE AND DIALECTIC

Our claim that philosophical hermeneutics is *logocentric* is seriously meant. Philosophical hermeneutic centers upon the word (*logos*). The claim that it is *logocentric* seems playful precisely because of an ambiguity in the term itself. The ambiguity makes clear that words such as *logos* and *dialectic* have a double history. One of these histories tends to associate the *logocentric* with reason and the dialectic of ideas while the other associates it with language and the dialogue between words. Philosophical hermeneutics clearly emphasizes *logos* as word. It is this that saves it from the nihilism and the *aporia* of ideas that dog attempts to ground hermeneutics in fundamental concepts rather than in the wayward nature of linguistic practices.

Three meanings attach themselves to the term *logocentric.* The first equates *logos* with reason. Referring to Heraclitus, Henri Frankfort writes of *logos* as "a term so heavily laden with associations as to be an embarrassment whether we translate it or not. 'Reason' is perhaps the least objectionable rendering."[24] Not so, for phenomenology and philosophical hermeneutics: they emphasize both the priority of language over reason, and the historicity of rational thought.

The second meaning equates the *logocentric* with a specific philosophy of language that assumes words to be a fundamental expression of an external reality. Gadamer equates this with "the doctrine of the unity of expression and meaning": the meaning of a word achieves a presence within it.[25] Philosophical hermeneutics stands accused by Derrida of advocating just such a logocentricism. Close attention to Gadamer's thinking indicates, however, that he does not fall into it. In an early essay, *Amicus Plato Magis Amica,* Gadamer makes a key distinction between the thing spoken of and the thing that arises through the speaking of it. He notes that Plato "in no way disputes that all speaking is ultimately speaking about something which is" but then comments that "Plato, insofar as he analyses the *logos* as the *koinonia* of ideas, does not reflect upon this fact."[26] Implicit in this differentiation is the distinction between representation (*Vorstellungen*) and presentation (*Darstellungen*): do words represent, stand in for, and serve as signs for those things they refer to (the ideas) or do they allow that which is spoken of to come into being within language? Does language seek to objectify the things it refers to or is language a medium in which those things come to presence? It is clear where Gadamer's sympathies are. Nevertheless, his reasoning is complex. One the one hand, he agrees with Plato that words point beyond themselves: "All intentional speech points away from itself. Words are not simply complexes of sound but meaning gestures that point away from themselves as gestures do."[27] The hermeneutic defense of transcendence clearly depends upon such pointing away. However, on the other hand, Gadamer's philosophical orientation concerning what words point to is quite different to that of Plato. For Plato, words (*logoi*) point to the *eidos* of thought that antedate language. Words point to and give presence to a reality that is prior to language. Gadamer certainly conceives of words as pointing beyond themselves but not as pointing to anything that antedates language: words both refer to, address, and allow that which is beyond them to emerge within language. They point to *Sachen* (subject matters) but the being of these entities is linguistic; they do not antedate language. Whereas for Plato thought precedes language, for Gadamer thought turns to language for its own instruction in the stock of ideas language builds up (TM, 430). In the essay "Greek Philosophy and Modern Thought," Gadamer makes its clear that with the word (*logos*), "the world itself, is evoked by speech, lifted into presence, and brought into articulation and communicative participation."[28] *Logos* not only permits dialogue but allows everything we can exchange with one another to be laid down within language.[29] Although Gadamer is at odds with Plato concerning the ontological priority of ideas over words, he openly concurs with him about conversation (*dialegesthai*) and the dialectical use of question and answer as means to bringing that which is beyond words (*die Sachen*) to come forth within language. As Smith contends, Plato's dialectic as exemplified in Socratic *dialesthai* establishes a central point in Gadamer's hermeneutical theory. From Plato, Gadamer learns that an understanding of something is reached in a dialogical process and that understanding occurs not in subjective thought but in an interrogative discursive exchange *between* speakers.[30] Nevertheless,

Gadamer declines to follow Plato's metaphysics. Insofar as philosophical hermeneutics offers a *dialectic* of the word rather than a dialectic of ideas, it is not guilty of *logocentrism* in the second sense of the word. However, with regard to the third meaning of logocentric, Gadamer's philosophy is undeniably centered upon the dynamic of the word (*logos*). To this specific meaning of the term we shall now turn.

Strictly speaking, Gadamer's thinking is *logos*-centric as opposed to logocentric. This is reflected in his broad commitment to a language ontology. The characteristics of this mode of thought are difficult to grasp clearly partly because they run against the grain of received forms of thought. To get his point across effectively, Gadamer should have made a stronger distinction between *Sachen* and concepts. However, the power of philosophical tradition is in some respects against him. Whereas as he believes that it is "our historical fate to speak the language of concepts,"[31] we should in this context speak more of subject matters and less of concepts. The distinction between *Sache* and concept is central to Gadamer's *logos*-centric form of thought.

Gadamer's dialectic of the word insists that the word always points beyond itself. This is seminal to the thesis that language has a capacity for transcendence. However, what do words point to? That which words speak of are the *logoi* (the things spoken of) (cf.TM, 429). The *logoi* are names, generalizations, and concepts. Gadamer sees the generation of general terms and concepts as indicative of a natural formative capacity within language. In speaking of the world, language does not follow an antecedent logical order: "The natural concept formation that keeps pace with language does not always simply follow the order of things but very often takes place as a result of accidents and relations" (TM, 428). The ordering of our thoughts within orders of name, association, and structure exhibits a *natural* achievement of language (TM, 428). We acquire in language an entire framework of preestablished meanings, reference, and association. When we use words we implicitly invoke rather that reflectively apply such schema.

> Even if each particular case of speech involves subordinating what is meant to the pre-established verbal meaning, it is obvious that speaking cannot be thought of as the combination of these acts of subsumption through which something particular is subordinated to a general concept. A person who speaks—who, that is to say, uses the general meanings of words—is so orientated toward the particularity of what he is perceiving that everything he says acquires a share in the particularity of the circumstances he is considering. (TM, 428)

Application and translation (the bringing of a general preestablished meaning to particular circumstances) are inherent *within* speaking. Speaking too finds itself in the in-between, placed in the tension between the centrifugal and centripetal dynamics of language. Just as speaking grounds preestablished meanings in particular circumstances, so each application can enrich and extend the concept or meaning applied.

> [T]he general concept meant by the word is enriched by any given perception of a thing, so that what emerges is a new, more specific word formation which does more justice to the particularity of that act of perception. However, certainly speaking implies using pre-established words with general meanings, at the same time, a constant process of concept formation is going on, by means of which the life of a language develops. (TM, 429)

Speaking involves, then, the natural oscillation inherent within language between the centrifugal and the centripetal dynamics of the word. How does dialogue bring this play within the word into the open?

When we ask what a subject matter or *logoi* is, a dialogical process of question and answer commences. Gadamer insists that understanding occurs not just in the solitariness of subjective thought but in the interrogative discourse between speakers.[32] Dialogue is a means of finding out and bringing forth what is inherent in language about a given *logoi*. We engage in conversation to draw out what language holds about a given subject matter. What is revealed of the *logoi* in a dialogue "is neither mine nor yours" but "exceeds the subjective beliefs of the partners in the discussion to such an extent that . . . the leader of the discussion remains unknowing."[33] Engaging in the "dialectic" of words is envisaged not as a matter of conceptual analysis but as a discursive participation in which the participants set their expectations concerning a given subject matter to one side and open themselves to what the exchange may give rise to. In *Truth and Method*, Gadamer describes this form of "dialectic" as "the art of forming concepts by elaborating what is meant in common" (*gemeinsame Gemeinten*) (WM, 350; TM, 368). This might involve a shared experience of surprise concerning how a subject matter's meaning can spontaneously come forth within a dialogue contrary to the expectations of the interlocutors. The emergence of such hermeneutical unforeseens can alter what the participants understand by that subject matter. The play of dialogue allows the subject matter to become more itself and the participants to become different to themselves. This gives rise to an important question. If dialogue is the art of raising further questions and not of giving fixed univocal answers, does the question of what a subject matter is always remain open? This is the parting of the ways between Gadamer and Plato. Plato wants to close such questions. He wishes to pass beyond what is spoken of (the *logoi*). By means of dialectic he endeavors to move toward a purely intellectual apprehension of the ideas which allegedly inform the *logoi*. Gadamer does not make this move. For him, hermeneutics is about the dialogical capacities of language and not about the dialectical powers of reason. He keeps the question of what a subject matter is open by remaining within the play of language. As we have stressed, the transcendence philosophical hermeneutics aspires to is achieved within language and not beyond it.

Gadamer holds that the ability to generalize and unify is indicative of language's formative powers and not of language's ability to mimic a wordless order of ideas. For Plato, however, the true being of a thing can only be grasped by an intellectual apprehension of its idea. According to Gadamer, Plato regards the cosmos of ideas as the true structure of Being itself (TM, 430). This Gadamer does not accept. He grants that Plato cannot dispense with names and words in order to arrive at an inner apprehension of an idea but, then, if an idea is uniquely itself it must be distinguishable from everything else that exists. If, however, all that can be known and expressed stands in a network of relations, an idea outside such relations would be inexpressible. For Gadamer the *logoi*—the subject matters of speech that reside in speech—are indeed the "final repose of all human inquiry and understanding."[34] Just as there is no meaning-in-itself, there are no ideas outside expressible relationships. This argument clearly emphasizes the *logos*-centric character of Gadamer's thought. Nevertheless, a certain negative outcome seems unavoidable.

If there is no meaning-in-itself, the question of what something is (its essential form or idea) appears impossible to answer. Now, such negativity need induce epistemological nihilism only if it is assumed that the something that makes a thing distinctly what it is stands apart from all relations. Philosophical hermeneutics rejects this assumption not least because such a conception of uniqueness is unthinkable but because, even if it were thinkable, it would imply an end to understanding. The principal point is, however, that if the essence of what a thing is does not reside in a conceptual form antedating language, what it is will remain in question. This is another way of saying that the issue of what a thing is comes alive and maintains itself in the "dialectic of question and answer," a dialectic that oscillates between the questions of what a thing *is* and what it *is not*. It is not that the question of what a thing is is left hanging in the balance but rather that what the thing or subject matter is resides in the balance, shimmering as it were between the disclosed and the withheld. Philosophical hermeneutic is plainly committed to the thesis that rather than obscuring the nature of what a thing is, it is precisely the relations of the language-world that create the space for a subject matter to reveal itself. Once again, primacy is given to the generative space between words. In rejecting Plato's dialectic of ideas, Gadamer's argument affirms that his dialectic of question and answer has nothing to do with what lies beyond words (*logoi*) but with what emerges between them.

LANGUAGE, IDEAS, AND *SACHEN*

Gadamer's dialectic of the word emphasizes his clear commitment to a *logos*-centric manner of thought, a style of thinking that follows the "advance work" of language (TM, 430). His dialogical approach to the word emphasizes his doctrine of *die Sache selbst* and demonstrates why his *logos*-centric hermeneutics is not an instance of the second form of logocentrism outlined above. A further comparison between Gadamer's *Sache-selbst* and Plato's *ideas* will bring these contrasts into sharper relief.

In asking what a thing is, Plato believes that we are in some way guided by what we have forgotten or already have a dim apprehension of, namely, the idea or form that antedates our speaking about it. Gadamer holds that when we ask what a thing is we are guided by prejudices and expectancies that antedate our asking of the question. The elements of preunderstanding center around inherited projects or concerns and as fields of concern they are neither reducible to a given concept, nor do they predate language itself. The acquisition of such *Sachen* clearly entails inheriting a stock of assumptions about what things are or can be. As we have seen, Gadamer argues that language has a generalizing power: in bringing different perceptions together and giving them a common name, we build ever-stronger notions of what such unity (or thing) is. However, though our immersion in a language-horizon may prompt us to follow inherited paradigms of what a thing is conceived to be, that does not mean (as Plato believes) that language itself follows or imitates an intellectual template of thinghood that is prior to speech. Both Plato and Gadamer agree that the word strives to go beyond itself. However, whereas Plato believes that the word is drawn toward a realm of intellectual apprehension beyond words, for Gadamer the word is not drawn beyond language, but to a *saying* more which allows a subject matter to become more and to be understood differently. When we ask what a given subject matter is, we are not seeking to grasp it as an intelligible object beyond the horizon of language but to lay open its nature or, rather, to keep the question of its nature open to further questioning. Insofar as such questioning takes place in language, any understanding achieved will be tentative and provisional. Yet this is the point: precisely because such understanding is incomplete and ongoing it can be extended and in so doing become "more." For Plato every spoken description of a thing in some way falls away from and corrupts the purity of the thing as a purely intelligible object. Gadamer contends to the contrary that every linguistic description of a *Sache* potentially increases the being of that *Sache* within language. Plato's ideas are of course neither incomplete nor completable but complete in themselves. The price (if price it is) of Gadamer's dialectic of the word enabling *Sachen* to become more is that, at the same time, it prevents them from ever becoming complete. Because *Sachen* are brought forth and have their being within language, they cannot pass beyond language and therefore cannot and will not ever be fully understood. Yet this only serves to reaffirm the importance of the dialectic of the word (dialogue) and to emphasize that Gadamer's *logos*-centered thought is not logocentric in any conventional sense of the term. In summary, consider the following:

1. The speculative identities of *Sachen* are not fixed presences. Their historical nature hides elements of their being in past and future withhelds. Their temporal nature means that they can never be fully present.

2. The name of a given *Sache* does not denote a fixed entity. It refers to a constellar grouping of perspectives that denote common areas of concern or interest. Though these overlapping interpretative fields may form a provisional identity, they do not refer to an actual identity. The multiple and varied ways, for example, of studying English or German Literature suggest that there is something that is called English or German Literature, but, of course, there is no such permanently stable or identical subject matter. Taken together, such modes of studying suggest such a subject matter but the subject matter they allude to is a fluid perspectival construction, not a fixed identity.

3. Indeed, to raise the question of what English Literature as a scholarly discipline is puts the provisional identity of that

subject matter back into question. Raising the question already supposes some understanding of what such a *Sache* is, and it is precisely the accepted understanding of a *Sache* that is put at risk by asking the question. Asking the question allows the subject matter to be seen in a new light. What it was understood as being is itself changed and insofar as it is changed, what that subject matter may be seen to be is also changed.

4. Asking what a subject matter is, then, potentially defers what the subject matter is understood as being. First, the prising open of the always more to be said defers our grasp of what the subject matter has been understood as being. Second, insofar as raising the question of what a subject matter is opens the possibility of new interpretations, a completer understanding of that *Sache* is deferred into the future. Third, inasmuch as that completer understanding is put off (projected into the future), we are asked to put on one side what we presently understand as adequate. Insofar as we defer to both the possibility of completer understanding and the incompleteness of present understanding, we defer to or rather submit to the finitude of all understanding. The speculative identity of a subject matter (its constellar nature) is forever shifting, which guarantees that we are always in between what we have understood and have yet to understand.

5. Heidegger, Gadamer, and Adorno all insist upon the enigmatic nature of *Sachen*. In speaking to us, a *Sache* discloses something. It reveals something but such emergence is not the negation of concealment per se but a revelation of a continued sheltering in the dark. It is the coming into presence of the withheld dimension of a *Sache's* meaning that gives it weight, resonance, and enigmatic character. What Gadamer says of the work of art can also be said both of the *Sache* and the word.

> There is clearly a tension between the emergence and the sheltering that constitutes the form *niveau* of a work of art. . . . Its truth is not consituted simply by its laying bare its meaning but rather by the unfathomable depth of its meaning. Thus by its very nature the work of art is a conflict between . . . emergence and sheltering. (HW, 107)

6. Emergence and sheltering is at the heart of questioning. Every time we ask what a *Sache* is, the question can close lines of enquiry and allow others to be opened. Indeed, the intellectual weight of a *Sache* lies in its ability to reveal the extent to which part of it remains concealed. Thus, the "presence" of a *Sache* does not indicate a condition of disclosure as opposed to a state of hiddenness. Precisely because it partially comes forward into disclosure, it reveals the extent to which part of it remains undisclosed. In this respect, *Sachen* show something of the nature of linguistic being. Like the word, the fullness of its meaning does not reside in its being brought to exhaustive disclosure but in the fact that something of its meaning is withheld by virtue of other aspects of its meaning coming forward. Philosophical hermeneutics knows that the process of interpretation both dissolves and yet sustains the enigmatic quality of the word it seeks to understand.

The essential in-betweenness of interpretation and of *Sachen*, the resonance of which both depend upon the simultaneity of the shown and the withheld, demonstrate that Gadamer's thinking is far from being logocentric. Postponement, deferral, and difference of meaning are intrinsic elements of his dialectic of the word. In these specific respects, Gadamer's approach to language is not altogether dissimilar to Derrida's. In the essay "Hermeneutics and Logocentrcism," Gadamer claims that his argument "whoever understands must understand differently" obviously implies *difference*."[35] However, despite this similarity, Gadamer's philosophy of language manages to avoid the negativity of the deconstructive stance. How it does so reveals further aspects of the way philosophical hermeneutics resists the challenge of nihilism.

KEEPING THE WORD IN PLAY

Both deconstruction and philosophical hermeneutics agree that the finite nature of language and understanding suggest that "meaning-in-itself" is endlessly deferred. Neither recognizes a final solution to the question of meaning. Interpretation can never complete itself. However, philosophical hermeneutics insists that though there is no end to the question of meaning, the lack of such finality does not dissolve the possibility of meaningfulness. Philosophical hermeneutics maintains that questions of meaning resolve into questions of relation. Thus, the question of meaningfulness involves residing (albeit temporarily) in a *junction* between hermeneutic horizons. It is not a question of achieving a logical terminus to interpretation, of either returning to a lost meaning or arriving at an envisaged meaning. In contrast, Derrida's arguments, according to Pickstock, set language and interpretation into a false set of oppositions. Meaning-in-itself, she argues, is presented by Derrida as impossible, as something beyond experience. Any attempt to illumine the "meaningfulness" of the present by grounding it in a retrievable or anticipated meaning is rendered futile. This supposes that the end of interpretation lies beyond it and, hence, that interpretation is undecideable. In Pickstock's opinion, this suggests that meaning and death are separated from life and that the distinctly relational and provisional nature of the meaningful has been unjustifiably overlooked. Derrida is charged with implying that when we seek an interpretation, when we search for a meaningful insight into a text, we seek a meaning that would bring interpretation to an end. Now, because of its commitment to both the finitude of understanding and the historical nature of human existence, it is hardly plausible that philosophical hermeneutics should have such an aim. Arrival at such a terminus would, as Hamacher contends, bring the motion of hermeneutic understanding to a stop. It would require that we leave the world of relations upon which the vitality of language depends. What Derrida and Hamacher fail to see is that *what philosophical hermeneutics seeks is not an end interpretation but what interpretation does.* Philosophical hermeneutics is not in pursuit of the final interpretation but what interpretation gives rise to, that is, the lighting up of unseen and unexpected facets of our concerns and commitments with regard to a subject matter. It might be suggested that deconstruction forgets the contextual nature of interpretation and assumes that it is monological in nature: that is, that it seeks to decipher *the* meaning of a text or work. It overlooks the dialogical character of interpretation as an encounter and as a participation with a subject matter.[36] Hermeneutic interpretation does not seek methodological closure or the last word. It seeks the word that transforms and transfigures. The life of the word is therefore central to how philosophical hermeneutics negotiates the question of meaningfulness.

Hermeneutic interpretation is dependent on keeping the word in play. In fact the analogy of participating in a game, which Gadamer uses to articulate the nature of aesthetic involvement in the work of art, offers an equally poignant insight into the serendipitous nature of hermeneutic interpretation. It may be an activity that we intend to involve ourselves in, but once we become players, events can arise in the playing of the game that are quite contrary to our expectancies. This is because hermeneutic interpretation does not take place in a vacuum. It takes place within the language-world, which means that it plays with and against other practices that thematize a subject matter or narrative in different ways. Indeed, what makes an interpretation coherent and compelling is not just that it reveals hidden aspects of a given *Sache* but that in so doing it can also make us think differently about other commitments in unexpected ways. An interpretation can surprise us precisely because it can emerge from unpredictable collisions with other interpretations. In this sense, deconstruction is right: interpretation is wanton and in excess of itself, spilling out beyond the objects of immediate focus and informing other aspects of our understanding. Nevertheless, the substantial point remains. Critiques of hermeneutics that deny the possibility of interpretation because of the unobtainable nature of meaning-in-itself overlook the fact that what is compelling about an interpretation is not whether it attains a greater degree of (an anticipated) completeness but whether it throws other interpretative engagements into a new light. The connection between philosophical hermeneutics and the humanistic tradition of learning is explicit. One engages with or "reads" a subject matter not so much because one wishes to get to the alleged meaning at the "bottom" of it but because the very process of becoming involved with a subject matter is transformative. By seeking out what is in fact unattainable (the final interpretation) one inevitably collides with and becomes involved with unexpected perspectives capable of transforming how we understand ourselves. Philosophical hermeneutics entails an involvement in humanistic education. It probes subject matters not to attain the holy grail of interpretation, which it knows would still the word and put an end to understanding. Philosophical hermeneutics explores subject matters not in order to pursue the impossible but because it knows that in pursuing the impossible, it can induce those transformative events of understanding that "happen" as a consequence of one's engagement with a subject matter colliding with others. This emphasizes, once again, that hermeneutics is not a practice that takes place in a vacuum.

Something is meaningful not because a final interpretation has been reached but because something is brought to light by an unexpected conflict of interpretations. What is important in the case of reading (as in the case of Kant's reading of Hume or Gadamer's study of Plato) is not what a text-in-itself means but how engagement with that text transforms how we understand our own projects. The experience of meaningfulness therefore depends upon keeping linguistic horizons and perspectives in play. It does not rest upon appropriating the alleged meaning of a text, an appropriation that would, in effect, put the word out of play. This implies that language's vitality and the possibility of an experience of meaningfulness depends upon the ability of the word to pass continually in and out of different relationships. Closing the play of language implies the death of understanding. Hamacher's and Derrida's overt preoccupation with the absence of meaning-in-itself arguably drains language of its capacity to generate new configurations of meaning.

Pickstock suggests that by hypostatizing the unattainablity of meaning-in-itself, Derrida presents meaning as death-like, as something beyond our experience. Hermeneutics is characterized as a tragic endeavor questing for that which will stop its quest. That which enables its quest—the openness of language—is condemned as indefinite, finite, and contingent while that which supposedly justifies its quest—meaning-in-itself—would, if realized, destroy it. Such is the consequence of bringing the contingency and incompleteness of meaningfulness into a false opposition with meaning-in-itself. The negative hypostatization of meaning-in-itself bleeds the meaningful of its living content. This constitutes the nihilistic threat of both Hamacher's and Derrida's thinking to the vitality of the word and, hence, to hermeneutics. What these critiques deem important is not the degree to which an experience of the meaningful lights up new areas of insight but how it fills out a projected meaning-in-itself. This indeed makes it hard for Derrideans to refute the charge that they bear a *ressentiment* toward the living instability of the meaningful. How can they refute the charge that they are *revengistes*, that they revenge themselves upon the contingencies of language by imposing an unrealizable criterion of meaning? The confusion this sustains is the supposition that by pointing beyond themselves, words refer to that which they endlessly defer, namely, the pure presence of meaning-in-itself. Does this not imply that the stammerings of language can only be redeemed by an *event* that, though it is anticipated by language, cannot occur within language? Does it not suggest perversely that every experience of the meaningful is a lapse, a falling away, from an uninhabitable ideal meaning? Yet, surely, this is indeed churlish reasoning. Is it not like saying that since the only games worth playing are winnable ones, there is no point entering language and its wordplay? Philosophical hermeneutics in its resistance to such nihilism unequivocally supports the subjective, that is, the inhabited side of language. The event of the meaningful has nothing to do with filling in or bringing to realization a concept or schema of meaning, but it has everything to do with bringing contingent horizons of meaning into new and unexpected alignments. That there is no logical limit to such alignments does indeed demonstrate the formal undecideability of interpretation, but what makes one interpretation more compelling than another resides in its ability to offer new and unexpected insights. In other words, what deconstructive thinkers regard as the very impossibility of meaning (death) is, curiously enough, a condition of the meaningful, a condition of the living word and its vitality. This can be supported in a number of ways.

If language were like music and could be conducted, then *vivace* (keep it moving, keep it lively) would surely be written at the top of its score. However, the issue here involves a more fundamental equation of stasis and death. Because Hamacher and Derrida equate meaning-in-itself with a transcendent beyond the contingency of language, they nurture a false opposition which, though they inflict it on philosophical hermeneutics, is not in fact found within it. When Gadamer wrote, "Being that can be understood is language" (TM, 474), he implied that language is a totality of meaning and that, furthermore, this totality no longer demarcated the boundary between language and world. Language and all that it holds is grasped as world. The totality of this language-world can neither be transcended nor brought into expression. Nevertheless, it is implied in every linguistic expression and, furthermore, lends itself to an infinity of interpretations. The transcendent is not that which surpasses language. It is not an "impossible," as both Derrida and Hamacher imply. Rather, the transcendent is taken back into language and is inherent in every linguistic expression. As such, the transcendent disappears into an inexplicable but immanent totality of meaning. At this point philosophical hermeneutics adopts a position quite different to those of its critics. Meaning in the sense of a fixed totality becomes self-effacing. The more any hermeneutic quest seeks out meaning as something in-itself, the more the quest for meaning dissipates or defers itself. However, it is precisely the self-effacement of "meaning" in its hermeneutic quest of itself that occasions the emergence of meaningfulness within the contingencies of the language-world.[37] To put this another way, within the universality of the language-world, the more a specific interpretative tendency seeks out "meaning," the more it will collide with different and unforeseen horizons of meaning. In other words, it is precisely the impossibility of "meaning" within the world of *Sprachlichkeit* that permits the emergence of the meaningful. The fact that meaning can never be resolved into an in-itself permits a space in which the event of meaningfulness (the collision of different interpretations) can arise. The absence of meaning-in-itself opens a space in which different forms of interpretation can mix and collide. The vitality of inhabited, contingent meaning derives, then, from an ineliminable emptiness which is simultaneously being filled and emptied by the meeting of different hermeneutic perspectives. Iser forwards a similar argument. There is no essential subject matter underlying interpretation. For a subject matter to function within a contemporary horizon it has to be translated from the receiving language into the language in which it will be applied. This opens an ineliminable space between the understanding of how a subject matter operates in one linguistic register and how it might be applied in another. However, as we have already implied, it is not just translation that perpetuates such a space. Understanding too is dependent upon the existence of a space it can never close. This reinforces the claim that the emergence of the meaningful is dependent upon the absence of meaning.

If meaning were realizable in itself, if meaning could be completed and made final, nothing more need be said about it. The "to and fro" of further articulation and explication would end. The hermeneutical space of the in-between would be filled. There would be no difference between what had been understood of a subject matter and what had yet to be understood of that subject matter. The vitality of the word, and with it the motions of understanding, would cease. The realm of meaning-in-itself would, in other words, be uninhabitable. What makes the realm of lived, contingent meaningfulness habitable is precisely what prevents it from being a realm of meaning in itself. It is a space that is neither full nor empty but one that is constantly filled and emptied by different configurations of meaning. Any attempt to refine our understanding of what has come forth into that space seeks in effect to close it. Yet such attempts invariably make even starker the connections of the precise meaning pursued with other networks of meaning. Thus, the anticipated meaning dissolves in prominence as other unanticipated meanings come forth. The dialectic of the word is kept in motion by the constant inhalation and exhalation of associations of meaning. The centrifugal and centripetal aspects of language uphold the vitality of the word. It is the inherent instability of linguistic meaning that allows different configurations of the meaningful to simultaneously come forth and pass away.

In this respect Pickstock is surely right to argue that what makes inhabited meaning *vital* is not its opposition to *death* (death as conceived by Derrida as meaning-in-itself) but its immediate relationship with it (death conceived as the ever-present process of passing away). After all, there can be no emergence of the meaningful if the signs that communicate it do not themselves pass away in the process of communicating.[38] Derrida thinks of "death" as a meaning-in-itself beyond experience. Now, if it is supposed that *the* meaning of a text or utterance is what hermeneutics pursues, then death emerges as the absolute negation of the hermeneutic quest. However, upholding the living instability of contingent meaningfulness does not hypostatize emptiness and dying as "impossibles" beyond language, but places them at its heart. The signs of the spoken word must be allowed to pass away before the meaningfulness of what is said becomes apparent. The emergence of the meaningful must displace previous insights if what it communicates is to assert itself. Furthermore, the very condition of the meaningful emerging—the fact that not everything about a subject matter has yet been said—is also the condition of its passing away. The said is always vulnerable to the yet to be said. Death and negation are therefore essential to the vitality of the word. They are intrinsic to the very *being* of that which can be understood as language.

Meaningfulness is constituted by the constant play of linguistic *Entgehen* and *Vergehen*. No longer should the flux of the meaningful be conceived of as a purgatorial state that imprisons language between an unrealizable future-meaning-in-itself and an unredeemable past meaning. To suppose that language is stretched between the *being* of an unrealized meaning-in-itself and the *nonbeing* of lost or dissolved meaning is, once again, to impose on language a schema of opposites more characteristic of the rigidities of reason. *It is to succumb to that nihilism which denies the vitality of inhabited meaning by maintaining that the realization or redemption of language lies in an unattainable state of completeness.* Philosophical hermeneutics resists such nihilism by insisting upon the continuous fusion of genesis and extinction within language. It suggests that deconstruction's approach to language is in fact insufficiently dialectical. Deconstruction privileges the centrifugal dimension of interpretation and overlooks the centripetal movement, a privileging that once again disrupts the vitality of the word.

Deconstructive thought clearly emphasizes the centrifugal aspects of language. The more we try to retrieve what are imagined as past unities of meaning, the more we fragment them and capture only their traces. Equally, the more we move toward an anticipated meaning of a text, the more we dissolve what we would move nearer to. Such forms of analysis seemingly pose a challenge to hermeneutics because of their denial of meaning-in-itself. However, this denial threatens hermeneutics only if it is assumed that the Holy Grail of philosophical hermeneutics is meaning-in-itself. Once this assumption is rebuffed, philosophical hermeneutics is far from being disrupted. As we have contended, philosophical hermeneutics is not in quest of the *end* interpretation but in pursuit of what interpretation *does*, to wit, open unanticipated, overlooked, or new modes of meaningful involvement with a subject matter. The concern of philosophical hermeneutics is with achieving a plausible case for meaningfulness, not with making claims about meaning-in-itself. Returning to the point, why does deconstruction assume that meaning only recedes into an unrecoverable past or points toward an unrealizable future? Does not the notion of inhabited meaning or meaningfulness suggest something contrary to this assumption? If the notion of lived meaning is conceived as a temporary and illuminating configuration of meaning, the past and future need not be understood as points that recede into the what-was and the yet-to-come. As we shall see, because a configuration of meaning has become *past* does not mean that certain of its aspects can no longer travel toward us in the present.

Philosophical hermeneutics recognizes that a given contingency of meaning can always mean more or otherwise, and that there is no temporal restriction upon when it can come to mean more or otherwise. A given alignment of meaning holds within it future potential configurations of meaning all of which can never be realized. Just as we have seen Nietzsche and Dilthey argue that profound experience never comes to an end, so philosophical hermeneutics maintains that there is no way of saying when a tradition is truly dead. If meaning is indeterminate, it is impossible to claim whether a tradition is fulfilled or completely exhausted. The idea of the past transmitting to us unrealized hermeneutic possibilities for later actualization is intrinsic to Heidegger's arguments concerning historicity and authenticity. Moltman offers an ethical variation that strives to redeem and give sense to past sufferings by realizing what those who endured them were unable to bring to fruition.[39] In the case of philosophical hermeneutics, the ability of the past to act upon the present in unexpected and unpredictable ways is inherent within the very notion of hermeneutic engagement.

The nature of hermeneutic engagement is complex and dialectical. Determining the nature of past arguments and, indeed, seeking to strengthen them, can not only change our current thinking about a subject matter but also initiate shifts in the nature of contemporary concerns, which can bring to light previously unseen dimensions of the past. For example, Heidegger's existential phenomenology led Gadamer to discern in Platonic dialogue a dialectic of the word rather than a dialectic of ideas. In turn, disclosing unseen dimensions of the past induces alterations in contemporary understanding. Gadamer's reevaluation of the hermeneutic significance of Plato's dialogical procedures leads him to a new way of articulating Heidegger's philosophy of language and its poetics. Engaging with Platonic dialogue clears Gadamer's path to formulating Heidegger's notion of the "event" of language as conversation. That shifts in contemporary interests can allow previously unseen determinations of meaning within the past to come forth, emphasizes the relational nature of past and present and that the language-world is a realm of multiple becomings. Furthermore, that there is no meaning-in-itself but only endlessly changing and shifting patterns of meaningfulness suggests that within the realm of language, as within the realm of the spirit, nothing ever dies and nothing becomes fully present. As Nietzsche remarks, "*Es gibt im Geistigen keine Vernichtung*" (WM, 589). A configuration of meaning occluded by another, is not annihilated, but subordinated or displaced (WP, 589). There is always just a perceptible imbalance between meaning and utterance. As Steiner argues, "Other voices urge the disequilibrium, the loss of sterile poise, which triggers imagining into motion."[40] All language events are vulnerable to being unsettled by others. Certain alignments of meaning displace others while allowing unanticipated configurations to come forth. They, in turn, induce other comings-forth and other passings-away. The *being* of language is the endless interplay of the endless *Entgehen* and *Vergehen* of the meaningful. Maintaining the vitality of linguistic being is central to the case philosophical hermeneutics makes against the nihilistic aspects of deconstruction. Deconstruction tends to the nihilistic because its stress upon the centrifugal dynamic of language overlooks the formative centripetal capacity of language.

The "dialectic of the word" depends precisely upon the perpetual play of the centrifugal *and* the centripetal aspects of language within the meaningful. This implies that in language there are "no first and last things." Interpretation is unlike reason. It does not seek final judgments. In this respect Hamacher is right. To posit a unified wholeness of meaning that language has somehow fallen away from and can never return to is to posit a realm where language would be impossible. What Hamacher fails to note, however, is that this is not indicative of a failing on language's part. The failure is indicative of his confusion of language with reason. To criticize language for failing to achieve wholeness and completeness in its judgments is to criticize language for not being reason and, yet, though inherently reasonable, language is not reason. *The dialectic of the word is not a science of reason and cannot be judged as such.* To pass from language conceived as endlessly mutable fields of interconnecting meaning to the finality of "first and last things," is to pass from the vitality of language's intrinsic play to the rigidities of concepts. The passage from one to the other is facilitated by the common but nevertheless mistaken belief that, rather than pointing to other configurations' meaning, words point beyond themselves to the concepts and ideas they allegedly refer to. This confusion prompted Nietzsche's famous remark in the *Twilight of the Idols* about the common belief that language is tied to reason.

> Reason in language: oh what a deceitful old woman! I fear we are not getting rid of God because we still believe in Grammar. (TI, Reason in Philosophy, 5)

Insofar as grammar structures the way *we* speak about the world, we fall into the belief that the intelligible world is filled with entities that correspond to the popular metaphysics of language. As Nietzsche commented elsewhere, because we speak and think in terms of subject and thing we constantly mislead ourselves into thinking of beings simpler than they are.

> The word and the concept are the most obvious reason why we believe in this isolation of groups of actions: we do not merely designate things by them, we originally believe that through them we grasp what is true in things. Through words and concepts we are now constantly tempted to think of things as being simpler than they are, as separated from one another, as indivisible, each existing in and for itself. [Such is the] . . . philosophical mythology concealed in language.[41]

Philosophical hermeneutics contends that it is not *language* that deceives us but our misjudgments concerning the question of reference. Wittgenstein notes that language has a clear capacity to generalize and to classify phenomena according to the universals it formulates. Gadamer describes this capacity as the ability of language to form concepts. It does not, however, follow from the fact that language is capable to form general references, that what it loosely refers to as universals are actual universals. As a consequence, language cannot be condemned for being unable to fully formulate what is not there to be articulated in the first place. It follows that such a condemnation of language stands on a false premise, namely, that it refers to an intelligible realm of concepts beyond itself. It is clearly the case that language does have a transcendent reference: namely, subject matters (*Sachen*). As we have seen, *Sachen* transcend any particular utterance but they do not transcend or represent anything beyond language. They are not Platonic forms or unchanging essences. The central point in all this is clear. To condemn language for not being like reason, to censure language for not being able to definitely capture and express a meaning-in-itself, is to succumb to the profound nihilism inherent within what Nietzsche calls the metaphysics of grammar. To seek to pass beyond the interplay of different alignments of meaning within a discourse by attempting to clarify, to pin down, and to separate the concepts that inform it, is to stifle the play of indeterminacy upon which new determinations of meaning depend. Whereas for Nietzsche the philosophical pursuit of concepts dishonors the vitality of everything within the flux of becoming, for philosophical hermeneutics such a pursuit is dangerously nihilistic. In the name of reason, it devalues the play of words upon which the emergence of the meaningful depends. Any attempt to control the autonomous life of the word with its attendant but nevertheless expressive instability of meaning by forcing it into a rigid and controllable choreography of concepts, diminishes the possibilities for hermeneutic engagement, translation, and transcendence. In this respect philosophical hermeneutics can be defended against the implicit charge of its critics that its task is impossible because the object that it seeks is impossible. An affirmation of the vitality of language is central to the defense mounted by philosophical hermeneutics against Hamacher's nihilism. Nevertheless, is not the price for this defense rather dear? Does not philosophical hermeneutics' antinihilistic affirmation of the vitality of language and what it brings forth return us to the endless crosscurrents of undecidable meaning? If it does, what distinguishes philosophical hermeneutics from deconstruction? Does it in fact escape the nihilism it seeks to resist? An answer to these questions depends upon what is meant by decideadable meaning.

CHOICE WORDS

Speaking of hermeneutics, George Steiner puts the principal point admirably tersely: "Commentary is without end."[42] "Anything can be said and, in consequence, written about anything,"[43] and, "Talk can neither be verified nor falsified in any rigorous sense." Such "is the open secret which hermeneutics and aesthetics . . . have laboured to exorcise or to conceal from themselves and their clients."[44] In a related vein, Wittgenstein observes that there is no logical limit to interpretation: signs and symbols can always be interpreted this or that way.[45] However, like

Gadamer, he recognizes that we do not always reside in such undecide-ability. Wittgenstein observes,

> If I see the thought symbol "from outside," I become con-scious that it could be interpreted thus or thus: if it is a step in the course of my thoughts, then it is a stopping place that is natural to me, and its further interpretability does not occupy (or trouble me).[46]

But, then, he goes on to remark that such a stopping place is a *psychological* rather than a logical terminus.[47] Philosophical hermeneutics recognizes that there is no logical end to interpretation. The perspectival and finite nature of understanding prohibits a final interpretation (*endgültige Inter-pretation*). However, like Aristotle, Gadamer recognizes the evident claim of human practice. Philosophical hermeneutics accepts that despite (or in-deed because of) the logical indeterminacy of interpretation, decisions within human practices with regard to interpretation have to be made. For Nietzsche, such decisions are made with regard to their ability to enhance a life form's vital powers. Gadamer contends that is the human interest in the continuity of one's own or collective narrative that drives the decision in favor of one interpretation rather than another. For Wittgenstein, the decision is arrived at according to the extent to which an interpretation allows us to proceed with a given train of thought or communicative prac-tice. Wittgenstein's claim that the point where I do no more interpreting is a psychological and not a logical terminus invites the question whether such an end point is purely arbitrary? Is one such psychological terminus as good as any other? Now, it is, of course, precisely the view that the only correlative to a logical terminus for interpretation is a subjective and there-fore arbitary terminus, which philosophical hermeneutics seeks to resist. Philosophical hermeneutics insists that the factors that incline persons to-ward one interpretation rather than another involve matters that are not merely a question of personal psychological preference but ones that con-cern the cultural horizons we find ourselves within. No matter how logi-cally impeccable a given interpretation might be, it will not be persuasive unless it fits into or can be indexed by a schema of personal vision.[48] In Wittgenstein's terms, it is not a question of us stepping into an interpre-tation but of allowing it to step into us. How then do we decide upon a interpretation? What makes one view more convincing than another?

Gerald Bruns and Georgia Warnke suggest that a certain persua-siveness attaches itself to a "rationality of rhetoric" operating within

philosophical hermeneutics.[49] Bruns argues that Gadamer follows Plato
in arguing that whereas demonstrative reasoning from first principles is
possible in mathematics, it is not really appropriate to the contingencies
of the life-world. Accordingly, Bruns contends that rhetorical argument
with its dialectical structure must take the place of ultimate foundations
by constructing the grounds upon which interpretative decisions are arrived at.[50] Both Bruns and Warnke ask what guarantees the rationality of
rhetoric? The answer is: "Nothing, or anyhow, nothing fixed, at any rate
nothing that does not have to be got up on the spot. An argument cannot
be guaranteed by its form."[51] Bruns continues,

> In the "Hermeneutics of Suspicion," Gadamer has asked
> about the relation of the rationality of science to the rational-
> ity of life and his answer was that whereas the first has to be
> methodically produced, the second is given in language as a
> dialogue structured according to the interplay of the one and
> the indeterminate dyad. This givenness is not an ultimate
> foundation, however, because it is possible only in virtue of
> our participation in the give and take of the argument as it
> occurs in the situations in which we find ourselves. In life,
> Gadamer writes, *participation*, being-with or being-together,
> must do the work of *Letztbegründungen*.[52]

To seek to pass beyond the interplay of different alignments of meaning
in pursuit of the final interpretation is to smother the randomness and
contingency upon which new determinations of meaning depend. In the
name of foundation, the play of meanings from which the vitality of language springs is stifled. Gadamer's argument against the grounding of dialogue in "first principles" is clear. It parallels Searle's remarks about the
mistaken need for metaphysical foundations: "The real mistake of the
classical metaphysicians was not the belief that there are metaphysical
foundations, but rather the belief that unless there were such foundations, something is lost or threatened or undermined or put in question."[53] The continuous play of language and the logical undecidablity of
interpretation do not prevent defensible decisions being arrived at in
favor of one interpretation rather than another. That the play of language
prevents the issue of the decideability from being put beyond argument
guarantees that new insight, understanding, and the possibility of
hermeneutic transcendence can be kept within the bounds of discursive
exchange. Nevertheless, despite all the logical possibilities, we do opt for
or are drawn toward one interpretation rather than another. Such a

choice may seem, logically speaking, to be arbitrary and the result of random acts of subjective volition, but from a hermeneutic perspective such
acts are far from arbitrary. The field of hermeneutic assumptions that
form our horizons guides any opting for a certain interpretation. It influences what is judged fitting, plausible, or appropriate. It is not merely a
matter of an interpretation's internal coherence but of whether the interpretation coheres with and expands what we already know and take an
interest in. As Gadamer's transformation into structure shows, what is
grasped as meaningful is taken hold of not because it is the meaning-in-
itself but because it illuminates a nexus of meanings we are interested in
and involved in. This confirms a claim of philosophical hermeneutics,
namely, that it is the relational nature of linguistic meaning that makes
epiphanies of the meaningful possible.

New insight and further understanding come about because of the
play of the word. An accidental use of language can suddenly "wire up" our
involvement in a whole number of different existential, philosophical, and
social horizons in surprising and unexpected ways. Differently expressed,
further insight and understanding become possible when the reductive
quest for meaning-in-itself is renounced. The pursuit of *Letztbegründungen* is
in other words an expression of the nihilism inherent within the metaphysical tradition. Its pursuit smothers the life of the word and stifles the
creative uncertainty of interpretation upon which the movement of all understanding rests. A hermeneutic claim can be persuasive, then, partly because of its extensive and intensive capacity to show that it fits into and
illuminates a wider set of interests and allows us to reconfigure them in unexpected but entirely plausible ways. Overlooked alignments of meaning
appertaining to our self-understanding can suddenly make us think differently about ourselves. An alteration in how we think about ourselves can
alter how we relate to the outward or extensive aspects of historical and cultural meaning. This confirms that a condition of the experience of meaningfulness—what makes us opt for one interpretation rather than
another—is ontological. We can be inclined to select between interpretations on the basis of what they reveal about the complex and ever-shifting
alignments of social and cultural meaning we are already placed within.
Philosophical hermeneutics prioritizes the ontological placement of the interpreting subject in order to emphasize that the epiphany of meaningfulness is not an arbitrary subjective act. This suggests that it is participation
in language rather than consciousness that grounds the experience of
meaningfulness. How does this relate to the matter of one hermeneutic
insight being more plausible and more persuasive than another?

Philosophical hermeneutics holds that understanding is a *passion*. There is something revelatory about understanding: something *strikes* us, a thought *occurs* to us, we are *taken* by an idea.[54] However, it is not the phenomenological *force* of the revelatory experience that constitutes its persuasiveness. It is rather the shock recognition. The persuasiveness of the revelatory experience is that it makes sense of something in such a way that it seems we recognize it for the first time. As Gadamer's transformation into structure makes clear, it is not that we return to or recollect a meaning but, rather, we realize that a configuration of meaning that we now find compelling was already latent within what we were already acquainted with, though we did not recognize it at the time. The revelatory moment is not a reacquaintance with something forgotten but recognition of something as if for the first time. The full weight of why philosophical hermeneutics emphasizes the ontological priority of language can now be felt.

A given interpretation can convince when it involves a recognition that the interpretation emerges from and has been held unseen within what we were already acquainted with, when the interpretation is seen explicitly to be logically consistent with what were acquainted with and when that recognition transforms what we thought we previously understood. In such moments, understanding does not meet with a preestablished meaning but with a certain configuration of meaning, which is recognized as being implicitly present within what understanding was already unknowingly acquainted with. Thought recognizes its lameness, that is, its blindness to what was "obvious," to what was already before it and underway (*ob-viam*). This etymological twist demonstrates what is for Gadamer a pivotal point: *language is prior to thought*. In uncovering a certain plausible configuration of meaning, thought discovers that language was there before it. In *The Relevance of the Beautiful*, Gadamer argues that the word is "the advance achievement of thought."[55] *Truth and Method* makes a similar point: "Language has accomplished in advance the abstraction which is the task of conceptual analysis as such. Now thought needs only to utilize this advance accomplishment." Thought turns to the logical advance work that language has already undertaken (TM, 429–30). The reasonableness of an interpretation does not therefore lie solely in its internal consistency or in the cogency of its form abstracted from its hermeneutical context but in the extent to which it is consistent with, illuminates, and extends that context. It is persuasive not just because it fits with what we are already acquainted with but because it transforms such acquaintance in unanticipated ways. When we are inclined to such an insight, it is not really a matter of subjective preference that we take it up. It is the power of its very reasonableness that inclines us toward it. This reemphasizes why philosophical hermeneutics is inclined to a dialectic of the word rather than to a dialectic of the idea. It is not the use of reason per se that discloses the potential frameworks of thought that language holds within itself. To the contrary, it is being responsive to the ebb and flow of the word that allows the sea of language to give up the hidden configurations of potential meaning that lie not far below the surface. Philosophical hermeneutics discerns the threat of nihilism in any attempt to diminish the centrifugal and centripetal vitality of language.

Taking up an interpretation is not indicative of a methodological decision but of the fact that we are prone to the *reasonableness* of its claim when it addresses us. This is not a variation of Proust's dictum that the heart has its reasons which reason can *never* know. If an interpretation "fits" with what we already know and illuminates it in a new and consistent manner, there *are* clear and articulable reasons in its favor. Such reasonableness is analogous to the reasonableness of a case in a court of law. Reason cannot *prove* a case but it is quite reasonable to ask for the reasons that support it. Although no aesthetic or literary interpretation can be arrived at by virtue of reasoning alone, reasons in its favor can be given. That language is, in this respect, ahead of thought and that we are hermeneutically disposed toward one interpretation rather than another prior to rational decision, does not mean that such a disposition is beyond what Hume would call "good reason." There is indeed something "speculative" about such hermeneutic reasoning in that it sheds new light on *both* the known and what was, prior to the insight, the unseen or unknown. Adorno observes that the persuasiveness of hermeneutic insight has something of the musical argument about it: it operates "forward and backward" at the same time, changing our view of what we both understood and have now come to understand.

> Highly organised music too must be heard multidimensionally, forward and backward at the same time. Its temporal organizing principle requires this; time can be articulated only through distinctions between what is familiar and what is not familiar, between what already exists and what is new: the condition of moving forward is a retrogressive consciousness. One has to know a whole movement and be aware retrospectively at every moment of what has come before, the meaning of advergent repetition has to be evaluated, and re-appearance has to be perceived not merely as an architectonic correspondence but as something that has evolved with necessity.[56]

Adorno's passage suggests that Gadamer's privileging of the "voice" over writing has nothing to do with a return to a privileging of the authorial voice but everything to do with the power of a compelling and persuasive performance.[57] The vitality of the spoken word does not just derive from the singular power of its delivery but also from the power of that which comes to life in the speaking of the word.[58] What is persuasive about the spoken is not what is uttered per se but how what is said discernibly gains its sense from what it lights up of what is unsaid, from what we have previously been acquainted with or have ill-advisedly taken for granted. Such persuasive performance is by no means a matter of managing rhetorical effects: it is a matter of being able to summon or to discern the "good reasons" that incline us toward preferring one interpretation rather than another.

Against this the skeptic can still argue that as there is no logical termination to interpretation, then, no matter how reasonable one claim may be over another, a decision favoring one remains subjective and is therefore beyond argument. Philosophical hermeneutics can counter this objection by pointing out that the *Letztbegründungen* demanded by the skeptic amounts to an inappropriate insistence upon achieving the last word which would silence all argument. However, paradoxical though it may seem, the strongest defense that philosophical hermeneutics has against the skeptic is that *no matter how powerful the subjective inclinations toward a given interpretation, the reasons in support of that interpretation are never beyond argument.* Philosophical hermeneutics recognizes that the power of counterargument is unlikely to persuade the iconoclast or ideologue to abandon their convictions. Attacking an interpretation in a purely dialectical manner invariably prompts the adherent of an interpretation to reassert and defend it all the more tenaciously. However, it is perfectly possible that an iconoclast or ideologue can be brought to think differently about their position. This is not a matter of proving that a given perspective is wrong but rather of showing that when viewed alongside other interpretations, it appears somewhat differently. Philosophical hermeneutics knows that it cannot refute interpretations. However, by aligning contrasting interpretations that potentially realign or reconfigure the meaningfulness of a cherished perspective, the adherent of an interpretation can be induced in a perfectly reasonable way to think differently about their position. The advantage of this is that the ideologue is not browbeaten into a change of view but is enabled by the proximity of contrasting viewpoints to change or widen his own perspective. Difference is not presented, as in the case of a counterargument, as an affront to an

opposing perspective but rather as offering a self-empowering opportu-
nity to alter, change, and perhaps even to abandon an initial interpretation. Philosophical hermeneutics understands that reasoned dialogue
is not the same as the dialectic of reason. In conclusion, the claim that
there is no final ground to choose between perspectives does not deprive hermeneutic exchange of its linguistically inherent reasonableness. In language, nothing is ever beyond being talked about.

If, then, there is nothing that is ever beyond being talked about and
there is no logical end to dialogue, it may seem that in relation to
"method" hermeneutic exchange is indeed indecisive and never free of
ambiguity. However, philosophical hermeneutics deliberately aligns itself
with the irresolvable tensions and ambiguities of language and does so because it knows that it is not the rigidities of reason's concepts that expose
us to the ever-open possibilities of understanding but the restless play of
language. If, then, philosophical hermeneutics does not aspire to methodological closure, what does it aim at?

THE POISE OF THE IN-BETWEEN

On one level, it is obvious that in deciding in favor of one interpretation
rather than another, a closure of sorts is sought. It may not be the definitive closure of method but insofar as the adoption of a preferred interpretation resolves something not previously understood, it permits us, as
Wittgenstein might say, to "carry on" with a given discourse. A local difficulty in a communicative practice is resolved, allowing normal activity
to resume, as it were. However, philosophical hermeneutics entails a lot
more than resolving localized ambiguities in a text or communicative
practice. As we have argued, philosophical hermeneutics is a philosophy
of experience. It is wedded to the conviction that understanding has a
transformative capacity. Understanding potentially "changes one's whole
knowledge" (TM, 353) so that one cannot return to a practice or a discourse and "carry on" as one once was. Gadamer writes of such experience in the following way.

> The nature of experience is conceived in terms of something
> that surpasses it; for experience itself can never be a science.
> Experience stands in an ineluctable opposition to knowledge
> and to the kind of instruction that follows from general theo-
> retical or technical knowledge. The truth of experience always
> implies an orientation toward new experience. (TM, 355)

The notion that hermeneutic experience is conceived in terms of something that surpasses it relates to the argument that there is always something more to be said and that, furthermore, even though one may settle on a given interpretation, one is at the same time settling for a new orientation toward the unexpected openings in one's horizons that the adoption of a new interpretation brings. This suggests that the discipline of hermeneutics is shaped by a philosophical practice that endeavors to maintain a certain reflective or spiritual tension. Such tension constitutes that mode of consciousness which is genuinely *in between*, in between a past that we cannot return to because understanding has transformed our relationship toward it and those yet-to-be-realized transformations of ourselves which our present understanding projects us toward. Such in-betweenness is explicitly emphasized in Gadamer's remark that "genuine experience is experience of one's own historicity" (TM, 357): a transformation of one's understanding of the past also transforms one's understanding of one's future possibilities. The "event" of such transformation is "negative" in the sense that "every experience worthy of the name thwarts an expectation [and] . . . implies a fundamental negativity . . . in the relation between experience and insight" (TM, 356). Yet, being tempered by experience also inclines one toward new experience.

> A person who is called experienced has become so not only through experiences but is also open to new experiences. The consummation of his experience, the perfection that we call "being experienced," does not consist in the fact that someone already knows everything and better than anyone else. Rather, the experienced person proves to be, on the contrary, someone who is radically undogmatic; who, because of the many experiences he has had and the knowledge he has drawn from them, is particularly equipped to have new experiences and to learn from them. *The dialectic of experience has its proper fulfilment not in definitive knowledge but in the openness to experience that is made possible by experience itself.* (TM, 355, emphasis added)

Gadamer understands the negativity of experience—the disruption of one's expectancies by the emergence of unexpected insights—as a form of "religious insight": "Real experience is that whereby a person becomes aware of their finiteness and experience"; "What a person has to learn through suffering—*pathei mathos*—is not this or that particular thing, but insight into the limitations of humanity" (TM, 357). Thus, with regard to the three questions, "What inclines philosophical hermeneutics toward one interpretation rather than another?," "What does philosophical hermeneutics aim at?," and, "What is the philosophical practice that philosophical hermeneutics upholds?," we can say the following. First, it is the degree to which an interpretation opens new ways to past and future understanding that is decisive; second, residing in the openness such betweenness affords is precisely the attentive poise that philosophical hermeneutics aims at, and third, remaining "radically undogmatic" and remaining in an open and settled disposition toward the risks of new experience, which immersion in the play of language exposes us to, is the philosophical discipline that philosophical hermeneutics seeks to uphold. There remains, however, something unsaid in Gadamer's position and it relates to the openness and uncertainty the play of language affords.

THE GIVING WORD

To abjure the certainty of concepts for the sake of the play of language exposes one's understanding to those unexpected shifts of perspective that Gadamer's dialectic of experience articulates so well. At the core of this dialectic is the experience of learning through suffering (*pathei mathos*): we become wise through suffering and our knowledge of things is corrected through deception and undeception (TM, 356). Yet it is not suffering that is prior here but something else. It is that which makes us vulnerable to such suffering in the first place, that which gives us the resolve to endure it and to remain open to the future no matter the hurt it might contain. The stress philosophical hermeneutics places upon the word always striving to go beyond itself and upon experience seeking to surpass itself, suggests that it is indeed a conception of love that animates the desire for hermeneutic translation and transcendence. Hans Waldenfels offers an illuminating parallel between the ontological primacy of language and certain notions of divine love.

In his remarkable study of Keiji Nishitani, a Japanese philosopher with whom Gadamer was acquainted, Waldenfels speaks of God as the continual self-emptying incarnation, a constant dying toward being, a groundless, selfless, and motiveless coming-into-being which continually and radically points away from itself and yet is selfless in its perpetual dissolution of itself.[59] Love is understood as the "total surrender" to this silent outpouring. Indeed, the theologian Ratzinger speaks of the "pure relatedness" and "non-substantiality" of this process.[60] Rahner writes of God's self-utterance, of "his word" as being "given out lovingly into the void [*Leere*—emptiness] of godless nothing"[61] despite the seeming futility of the act. There might be understandable unease about applying a term such as *love* to the play of language. Love gives of itself? How does language give of itself? Yet, do we not speak of speech *acts*? Speech acts can be synonymous with changes in the world. To follow on from this, we can note that philosophical hermeneutics emphasises the "event" of language and the ability of language to "bring" a world into being. Being is *language*, thus, *self-presentation*. Whether such a *self-presenting* can be named as "love" is not the point. What is notable is that in this respect certain descriptions of divine love are equally applicable to the *play* of language. Language is "an endless giving out of worlds into the void," a "metaphysically groundless opening out of itself," seemingly purposeful but without knowable purpose, nonsubstantial, a constant emptying of internal possibilities, always pointing away from itself and dissolving itself. In these respects, the world-grounding and world-dissolving play of language share some of the miraculous attributes accorded by theologians to divine love. Yet the use of the word *miraculous* does *not* imply a divine agency, merely that the generative capacity of language is a *miraculum*: an object of wonder (*mirus*—"wonderful"), an irreducible mystery, the *fons et origo* of our being. Though philosophical hermeneutics does not recognize the authority of either the "first" or the "last word," it upholds the *phenomenological* truth of the assertion: *in principium erat verbum*. Another connection between the play of language and the notion of love is relevant.

Philosophical hermeneutics celebrates language's divine-like powers of world creation. It understands how the play of language guarantees that thought never achieves congruence with its desired object and is, accordingly, kept in motion. For the skeptic, presenting language in this way generates the view that there is no final (logical) terminus to interpretation: the meaning of words remains enigmatic, never fully disclosed and always partly withheld. However, philosophical hermeneutics understands that it is precisely the enigmatic nature of language and meaning that draws us out of ourselves. Attempts to straitjacket linguistic meaning and to impose rigid conceptual schemas upon experience, diminish the ability of the enigmatic to take us out of ourselves. Philosophical hermeneutics contends that because it is linguistic in nature, self-consciousness is never self-presence. Self-consciousness is never self-possession since the full extent of its linguistic grounding is hidden from it.[62] Our linguistic-being means that we do not and cannot fully belong to ourselves. While Bakhtin remarks that "[t]he word in (my) language is half someone else's," Sartre observes that it is the other in me (that) makes my language.[63] Hermeneutically aware consciousness is a divided consciousness: it knows that it is not merely what it knows itself to be and that what it does not know itself to be is in many respects what it is. Dialogical engagement with the other brings out some of what is presently withheld in a subject's consciousness. Such engagements open pathways to insight, which one is rarely done with. Hermeneutic consciousness bears comparison with the Socratic Eros: "a divided consciousness, passionately aware that it is not what it ought to be. It is from this feeling of separation and lack that *love* is born."[64] Gadamer does not speak directly of *love* but a notion of *eros* is evident in his thinking. He frequently talks of *being drawn into* a meaning, of being *captivated* by a desire for completeness. The crucial point is, then, that it is the susceptibility to being drawn-toward and drawn into that interpretation that promises a greater completeness and inclines us toward one interpretation rather than another. This is also part of Iser's argument: the quest to achieve a greater completeness drives interpretation to fill the ineliminable space that animates understanding. Understanding, then, is a passion and is passionate, something that we both passionately care about and are drawn toward.[65] The passionate nature of understanding is reflected in the latter's centripetal and centrifugal aspects. The centripetal aspect of understanding that disrupts our presuppositions involves *suffering* (*passio*) those insights that challenge our grasp of our narrative identity. Linguistic being places us within determinate historical horizons. Not only do we *suffer* such thrownness but we are deeply vulnerable to and must endure alterations in or attacks upon its content. The centrifugal aspect of understanding, which reveals an unexpected and telling insight, reflects the active (*passionate*) nature of *pathos*. It impels us toward what we love or harken to. Thus, the centripetal and the centrifugal aspects of understanding are related. The pain of disappointed expectancies mirrors the extent to which we have been drawn to something. This suggests that what philosophical hermeneutics aims at is to keep the centripetal and centrifugal play of language in motion. The dialectic of the word is a dialectic of constant expectancy and disappointment. Yet it is only by seeking out and residing within the oscillation of the centrifugal and centripetal aspects of understanding that translation and transcendence can be guaranteed. Philosophical hermeneutics does not pursue closure. To the contrary, it seeks the disciplined and attentive poise of openness, ever open to the risk of having its presuppositions challenged and ever open to the arrival of new ways of thinking and seeing. Hermeneutical consciousness is thus in a permanent condition of difficulty, perpetually poised between conditions of arrival and departure, hope and loss, expectation and renunciation. Needless to say, however, it is precisely such tensions that maintain the possibilities of hermeneutic translation and transcendence.

LANGUAGE AND *WITHOUTENNESS*

There is a tendency among protagonists and critics of hermeneutics to assume that the stock of knowledge we inherit within our fore-understandings, or which is communicated to us through tradition, is relatively *fixed* and stable. This tendency is strengthened by both Heidegger's and Gadamer's inclination to affirm what might be termed as the contingent certainties of the hermeneutic horizons we find ourselves placed within, as opposed to the necessary uncertainties that attach to the (nihilistic) quest for *Letztbegründungen*. Indeed, Heidegger's description of language as being the *house* of being suggests something abiding, a place within which we may dwell. Images of the security, reliability, and trustworthiness of the "at-hand" are juxtaposed to the uncertainty generated by the *aporias* of metaphysics. The issue is, however, whether Heidegger and Gadamer underplay and, worse, overlook the inherent instabilities of language. The continual shifts and elisions of meaning within language mean that no matter the nature of our hermeneutic inheritance, so long as it is framed within language, it is always prone to disruption and displacement by other perspectives. In *Truth and Method*, Gadamer comments that no one can be exempted from experience: "Experience as a whole is not something anyone can be spared . . . only through negative instances do we acquire new experiences" (TM, 356). Given the linguisticality of our being, then, *whatever* the perspective or table of values we abide by, its stability will be challenged by the inherent play within all language. The challenges are by no means predictable. The vitality of language cannot be controlled: what emerges in the play of conversation cannot be anticipated. As linguisitic beings we have to endure and, indeed, suffer (*passio*) the disruptive twists of language. Yet even this description is not, strictly speaking, accurate. It suggests that relatively fixed perspectives and alignments of meaning suddenly find themselves being displaced by another perspective or undone by the deconstructive tendencies within language itself. However, this description is misleading. Because each is a linguistically communicated framework, no transmitted tradition or inherited horizon of meaning is inherently stable or identical with itself. The inherent play of language suggests that no meaning was or will be resolved into meaning-in-itself. Just as it is impossible to predict what unforeseen alignments of meaning a dialogue might give rise to, so too is it difficult to be aware of all the entailments of meaning within a received perspective. Furthermore, if all meaning is relational, all linguistically communicated perspectives will have an inherent instability. It is precisely this instability that makes them vulnerable to the unexpected emergence of new alignments of meaning. The intellectual traditions that provide us with our initial cultural orientation are by no means free of conflict and tension. The vitality and robustness of a tradition does not entail a resistance to change, nor the power to suffer change, but rather the creative ability to transform itself in and through change. As in dialogue, controversy, challenge, and disagreement sustain the vitality of a tradition and enable its rejuvenation. MacIntyre accordingly refers to traditions as "continuities of conflict."[66] In a related way, Adriana Cavarero in her book *Relating Narratives* suggests that historical traditions have the characteristics of a narrative: they address the question "Who am I?" and seek a narrative structure able to offer a answer. These stories are also inherently unstable. They are invariably incomplete. What has been understood as going before can be completely transformed by twists in a narrative that have yet to emerge and, furthermore, the narrative can be told in many different and unpredictable ways. Cavarero points out that

> a unique being is such in the relation, and the context, of a plurality of others, which likewise unique themselves, are distinguished reciprocally—the one from the other. The story of a unique being is obviously never the monotonous and monolithic story of an *idem*, but is always the unpredictable and muti-vocal story of an *ipse*.[67]

A story can not only change in its telling but can change the sense of identity of the community about which it is told. The inevitable finitude of such narratives—their incompleteness and their capacity to metamorphose in the telling—leaves the question of "Who am I?" in the open. Culture frameworks, linguistic inheritance, memory, and experience clearly respond to the question. Yet far too much is assumed by defenders and critics of hermeneutics alike about the supposedly homogeneous and singular nature of received narrative identities, collective or individual. If identities are narrative-dependent, identity is not made whole until the final judgment of the tale. Yet the final word of the tale is not the point of its telling. For philosophical hermeneutics, there is no last word that completes and redeems such a narrative. In addition, the openness of historical horizons suggests that though, for example, the material power of the Roman Empire has long declined, its story and the story of the telling of it is far from over. From an ontological point of view, Borges's claim that "any life, no matter how long or complex it may be, is made up essentially of a single moment—the moment in which a man finds out, once and for all who he is" may have a certain theological credence to it but it remains a literary fiction.[68] Though we acquire everyday identities from our social and cultural involvements, strictly speaking the point remains: the question of self identity always remains open. The point is conceded by Cavarero who comments that "autobiography does not properly respond to the question 'who am I?' Rather it is the biographical tale of my story, told by another, which responds to the question."[69] The self's sense of identity is kept open, for each telling of my story either by myself or by an other can potentially destabilize how that identity is grasped. Iser's arguments are once more relevant. If a listener strives to discern the nature of his identity or her character by listening to a third-person rendition of his or her tale, the listener must transpose the self represented in the narrative to the self he or she inwardly recognizes. Yet the gap between third-person representation and first-person understanding can never be closed. For Iser, translating a third-person narrative into first-person terms opens an ineliminable space between how we are seen and how we see ourselves. The point here is not that that the emergence of such an ineliminable space endlessly postpones an answer to the question "Who am I?" but rather that it keeps the question open and reminds me that the provisional answers that my history and experience have allowed me to acquire, are just that—provisional answers. Who we are will always remain in part an enigma. This returns us to our earlier comments on the connections between understanding, love, and being drawn out of oneself by what one would understand.

The hermeneutic dynamics of love are ancient. In philosophical hermeneutics, the dynamics are ontologized. Understanding knows that the completeness it is both in quest of and beholden to is in a certain sense outside itself. If the process of self-understanding is beholden to a *withoutenness* (and we mean by this that that which we are is in part hidden within or withheld by the different historical and personal biographical narratives that constitute our present self-understanding), then, as linguistic beings we will, like the word, strive to go beyond ourselves and thereby be drawn out of ourselves.[70] We sense that in the *withoutenness* of how we appear in the other's narrative, there is some clue as to how we might come to understand ourselves differently and, perhaps, more completely. A fascination with the historical and linguistic horizons that form us, an enduring respect for the voices that truly speak to us, and a love for the other who reveals one's own mystery to oneself, express with differing degrees of intimacy that sense of being indebted to and yet of being drawn toward the ontological *withoutenness* of the beloved, of the history, and of the language that sustains our being. The capacity to be drawn by the *withoutenness* of our being and the yearning to discern ourselves in what is immediately beyond us, is inseparable from having an acute ear for what is at play within the inexhaustible vitality of language.

LANGUAGE, AFFIRMATION, AND NEGATION:
A RESUMÉ

Before we approach the final stages of our discussion, a brief recapitulation of the principal points in the debate between Hamacher and philosophical hermeneutics is appropriate. Hamacher's critique of philosophical hermeneutics charges that "understanding is in want of understanding" and because of that "want" lacks a credible conceptual grounding. Hamacher's criticism is important both in its own right but also for its shortcomings. Discussing these has strengthened support for several of the key theses defended by this essay. Thesis one contends that hermeneutical understanding requires difference. Thesis two proposes that philosophical hermeneutics embraces a philosophy of experience. Thesis three suggests that philosophical hermeneutics is committed to a hermeneutic realism and that this commitment is central to its critique of nihilism. Thesis seven argues that hermeneutics is dependent upon a negative differential and thesis eight claims that philosophical hermeneutics affirms an ontology of the in-between. Discussing Hamacher's criticisms has brought to light the fundamental differences over the nature and status language that differentiate deconstructive thought from philosophical hermeneutics. Not only does the hermeneutical defense of the vitality of language constitute a *riposte* to Hamacher but it also strengthens each of the theses outlined above.

Hamacher contends that "understanding is in want of understanding."[71] Philosophical hermeneutics does not so much deny the objection as ask why a description of understanding's actual nature—its irresolvable in-betweenness—should constitute an objection to it? Philosophical hermeneutics contends that what guarantees the living movement of understanding is the irresolvable tension of its in-betweenness. We have argued that understanding depends upon continuous movement. Unlike reason, it does not seek wholeness or completeness. Were understanding like reason, understanding would seek an end to the constant transitions on which its being depends. The wantonness of the life of "the word" is generic to the possibility of understanding and its movement. For philosophical hermeneutics, any restriction upon the vitality of "the word" and its movement and, indeed, any bewailing of that movement, amounts to a form of nihilism. Hamacher's critique inadvertently slides back into thinking about hermeneutics in terms of grounding concepts. When he argues that the completeness desired by understanding is unrealizable, he absolutizes the notion of the complete and places it outside the dialogical relationships that generate it. However, philosophical hermeneutics insists that the lack Hamacher perceives is a virtue. The human word is essentially incomplete. It is in such incompleteness that the resonance and depth of the word becomes possible. The life of the word is not about completion but transformation. Thus, strictly speaking, philosophical hermeneutics is *logos*-centric rather than logocentric. It is concerned with maintaining the play of the word, with upholding the dialogical capacities of language as opposed to the dialectical powers of reason. Accordingly, philosophical hermeneutics does not seek an end-interpretation but what the play of the word *does*, that is, light up hitherto unseen and unexpected insights. It is the very play of the word—the constant tension between the centripetal and centrifugal aspects of language—which allows for the continuous waxing and waning of the meaningful. That the said is always vulnerable to the yet to be said suggests that affirmation and negation are intrinsic to the very vitality of the word. As we have argued, to suppose that language is stretched between the *being* of unrealized and unrealizable meaning-in-itself and the *nonbeing* of lost or dissolved meaning imposes on language a rigid schema of opposites, which is characteristic of reason, not of language. Philosophical hermeneutics insists that to argue that the realization or redemption of language lies (or ought to lie) in an unattainable state of completeness, is to succumb to that nihilism that denies the vital tensions and transitions of inhabited meaning. In conclusion, Hamacher's attack on philosophical hermeneutics is ill-conceived. The arguments that "understanding is in want of under-standing," that "the play of language" is irresolvable, that there is no end interpretation, and that there is no *Letztbegründung* for understanding do not demonstrate the impossibility of understanding. To the contrary, what they illuminate are the conditions that keep "the word" in play. They point to the vital instabilities that guarantee the unpredictable emergence of new alignments of meaning.

That philosophical hermeneutics embraces the vital instabilities of language rather than the rigidities of reason does not have the negative consequences deconstructive critics suppose. It does not suggest that there can be no grounds to prefer one interpretation to another. As we have argued, the claim that there is no final ground to choose between interpretations does not deprive hermeneutic exchange of its linguistically inherent reasonableness. Hermeneutics is not committed to achieving an end interpretation. It recognizes that no matter how powerful the subjective inclination toward a given interpretation, the reasons in support of an interpretation are never beyond argument. Philosophical hermeneutics cannot in principle seek the "last word." What it endeavors to induce is a change of perspective, that is, that while conversing about the virtues of opposing interpretations we are brought to think differently about the assumptions that govern our initially preferred interpretation. Philosophical hermeneutics pursues an attentive poise. It strives to remain radically undogmatic in order to remain open to and be accepting of the excitements and the suffering that new insights held within the play of language will expose us to. We are both drawn to and prepared to affirm the possibility of such negativity because we know that in the play of language resides something of ourselves that we have yet to discern.

In conclusion, its critics too readily assume that the denial of meaning-in-itself destroys the cause of philosophical hermeneutics. We have argued, to the contrary, that it is precisely the indeterminacy of language, the enigmas of meaning, and the instability of meaning that underwrite the shifting configurations of hermeneutic understanding and which, indeed, inflame its passion. It is indeed the play of language that drives the endless need to translate experience from one idiom to another and—insofar as those changes make us think differently about ourselves—it is the play of language that grounds the possibility of hermeneutical transcendence. The connection between the ontological indeterminacy of language and being drawn into a deep involvement in its otherness (its withholden mystery) suggests that the type of openness

philosophical hermeneutics advocates is of a different order to that
which its critics often assume it is defending. It is to the question of
openness that we shall now turn.

THE OPEN AND THE EMPTY

Hermeneutical openness has been presented as a disguised will to
power, an openness that is only open to opportunities for imposing
one's own sense of meaning and purpose upon the environment. In so
many words, the otherness of the other is not responded to. The other
is only a pretext for the aggrandizement of one's own perspective. This
charge is fundamentally flawed. It rests upon a key confusion. It assumes that interpretation is an epistemological schema or projection
and not a process of involvement or engagement. Those who propagate
the charge invariably adopt a Nietzschean view of interpretation that
has little to do with the openness at the heart of philosophical
hermeneutics. The concept of interpretation as an epistemological projection lacks the intrinsic openness (vulnerability) that animates the
pathos of hermeneutics. That the intrinsic openness of hermeneutics
should be confused with interpretation as an epistemological schema
is indicative of another confusion. Just as the play of words and their capacity to point beyond themselves can be mistaken for their pointing to
a wordless world of concepts, so the fact that philosophical hermeneutics concerns itself with dialogue between different world views and
perspectives makes it seem as if understanding is concerned with discovering or indeed imposing a schema of understanding beyond difference. However, such confusions can be dispelled.

If interpretation were merely the imposition of one dominant conceptual scheme upon another, there would be no change of self-understanding within the imperious subject. As Hegel well understood,
imperviousness shades into imperiousness. In this context, Gadamer's
stipulation that to understand another means to understand ourselves
differently must lose all purchase. For Iser too, interpretative understanding is definitely not a matter of colonization. In *The Range of Interpretation*, he writes,

> [A] caveat seems to be necessary regarding the elimination
> of the liminal space by certain types of interpretation.
> Whenever, the pre-suppositions of the register are superim-

posed on the subject matter, the liminal space is colonized
by the concepts brought to bear. Such a colonization of the
liminal space therefore sacrifices translatability and with it
the chance to embrace more than was possible before the
superimposition.[72]

In this passage, Iser dissects the workings of the imperious (colonizing)
mode of interpretation. Attention to the dynamics of understanding suggests that despite any imperious gloss, the actual process of interpretation
disrupts its own attempt at the superimposition of any schema of meaning. Whereas Gadamer contends that it is the play of language that is disruptive, Iser holds that it is the process of interpretation that generates
difference and the emergence of the unpredictable: "Whenever interpretation occurs, something emerges, and this something is identical neither
with the subject matter nor with the register into which the subject-
matter is to be transposed."[73] In other words, it is the very dynamics of
the process of interpretation itself which disrupts the view that interpretation is an imperious epistemological schema. Every time an interpretation attempts to fit a foreign subject matter to its own presuppositions, it
disrupts its own ambition.

Interpretation is basically performative in character. It makes
something happen, and what arises out of this performance
are emergent phenomena.
. . . the residual untranslatablity . . . is not a feature of the
subject-matter to be interpreted but is produced by interpretation itself . . .
The performative character of interpretation is brought out
by the fact that it generates its own power, that is, the ineliminable residual untranslatability drives the performance.[74]

The serendipitous effect of interpretation therefore frustrates any attempt
to impose a schema on the other.
  The claim that hermeneutic interpretation fails to recognize and
that, indeed, marginalizes the otherness of the other, overlooks the intrinsic vulnerability of the domineering perspective. The view that interpretation involves an imperious imposition assumes that the
colonizing schema is well grounded and robustly formed. However,
philosophical hermeneutics is deeply aware that such schemas are far
from immune to the challenge of the other. When Gadamer argues
that an intellectual practice is always more than it knows itself to be,

he is not merely arguing that within it there are a number of unreflected fore-understandings which shape and guide it. The argument implies something more telling and, potentially, more disruptive. There is a clear sense in which any interpretative practice is both blind to what lies within it and vulnerable to the play of language circumscribing its outlook. The point here is that insofar as an interpretative practice is formed within language, its ground will not lie in any fixed or stable set of concepts. It will lie in what are certain loose and unstable alignments of meaning, which, because of their linguistic nature, will be implicitly connected to other such configurations of meaning. There is no way of anticipating what all these connections are or how, when, and where they will be revealed. The vulnerability of all forward planning is not just to unexpected events but to the hidden limitations of the presuppositions that guide our thinking, limitations that it falls to the unexpected to expose.[75] The negativity of past experience should forewarn us of the possibility of such embarrassment. However, we should not lose sight of the principal point. It is the language-being of both the interpreting subject and the interpreted other that makes the individual perspectives of both parties deeply vulnerable to each others' dialogical interventions. The vulnerability is made clear in the following terms.

An interpreting subject's perspective is always inherently and potentially unstable in that it is incomplete, has unrealized potentialities of meaning within in it, and is capable of being reconfigured in unanticipated ways. These three factors enable the expressions of the other (often quite unintentionally) to bring an interpreting subject to think about its own perspectives in a transformed and transforming way. There is no predicting when such disruption and transformation can occur. However, that the subject and the other participate in the same speculative infinity of language, enables such shifts in perspective to occur. Philosophical hermeneutics emphasizes the ontological primacy of language and its play. It insists that the interpreted subject and the interpreted other both participate in that play and are, as a consequence, vulnerable to an alteration of perspective because of such *exchange*. These points reveal the shallowness of the charge that philosophical hermeneutics is a thinly veiled will to power.[76] In conclusion, the defining difference between the imperious model of interpretation and that advocated by philosophical hermeneutics is plain. Whereas the former is based upon a commitment to imposing a reductive regime of concepts that marginalizes difference, the latter is committed to engagement and participation to the end of achieving a transformation of understanding with all its attendant risks. Once again, whereas the former is committed to the minimization of difference, the latter is open not only to the difference of the other but to the difference that the other is able to open within ourselves. That philosophical hermeneutics defends the latter notion of interpretation also questions the view that the *openness* of philosophical hermeneutics amounts to little more than a liberal *tolerance* of other points of view.

The suggestion that hermeneutical openness amounts to no more than a liberal tolerance of different perspectives can be read in two ways. First, it might be suggested that hermeneutical openness is a form of Faustian fascination with the exotic and the unusual, a pursuit of cultural distractions born of a deep weariness of one's own knowledge and outlook.[77] Second, the notion of tolerance might imply an indifference towards the other, a laissez-faire willingness to let the other *be* because the being of the other does not impinge upon one's interests or concerns. It is, however, somewhat ludicrous to suggest that philosophical hermeneutics is guilty of perpetrating either view. First, the Faustian reading implies that hermeneutic openness amounts to nothing more than an existential distraction, a pursuit of cultural difference as an entertaining displacement activity which postpones the need for critical engagement with one's own or with the other's horizon. However, in the case of philosophical hermeneutics, it is precisely a deep involvement with the tensions and ambiguities of one's own horizon and a willingness to be drawn out by them that impels one to open toward the other and to the genuine risks that such openness entails. The Faustian position seeks forgetfulness while philosophical hermeneutics journeys for the sake of discovering the hidden, the forgotten, and the overlooked. Second, the claim that hermeneutic openness amounts to an indifference toward the other assumes that hermeneutic subjects seek (ideally) to unfold their individual life-narratives in such a way so as not to inhibit or interfere with the ability of others to do the same. This view ignores the participatory nature of our linguistic being, which is such as to make it impossible for us to disassociate our individual narrative from those of another. Williams makes the point: "Every 'telling' of myself is . . . an act, with consequences, like other acts in the world and speech of others."[78] It is not merely that we participate with others in a common linguistic being but that we are sometimes drawn toward a deep involvement with others contrary to our own willing and expectations. As we have argued, the fact that we inhabit individual and cultural narratives does not mean that such narratives are resolved, free of contradiction, or, indeed, internally consistent. The finitude of our being ensures that from an individual's perspective, his or her narrative is always open-ended and on-going. Immersion in the play of language guarantees that narratives can alter their poignancy or significance and, furthermore, "every telling of myself is a re-telling and the act of telling changes what can be told next time."[79] Indeed, it is this very instability that can draw us toward the other. A dialogical exchange, an unexpected remark or encounter may suddenly intimate a different way of thinking about ourselves, may reveal something not fully understood or something unresolved in our narrative, and may even point to new and unanticipated ways of configuring the tensions within how we think of ourselves. No wonder that we might be drawn to, become deeply involved with, and offer ourselves up in love to the other. It is not in the gift of the other to make us whole or complete. It is in the gift of the other to completely reconfigure what we have understood ourselves as being. The other, then, can make us other to ourselves in both a positive and negative sense. By virtue of our both participating in linguistic being, the other can transform or disrupt my self-understanding by bringing its individual elements into a new alignment of meaningfulness. Even the positive and loving exchange between the self and other is not without its difficulties and challenges. The narratives we inhabit are rarely singular. That an other is able to offer me a transformation of my self and to bring to fruition aspects of my being that were present within me and yet withheld from me does not necessarily mean that I will travel the particular path they open. The cost of so doing for those whose narratives are deeply intertwined with my own, may be too great. Genuine hermeneutic openness has to brave its risks and hurts. The intensity of what such openness demands brushes aside the accusation that hermeneutic openness amounts to an indifference toward the other. Hermeneutic openness may lead toward the possibilities of translation and transcendence but such a path cannot be taken without the risk of transforming one's self-understanding and hence one's relations with others. Liberal indifference risks nothing. It does not have the capacity or willingness to be drawn toward or to be open toward the other. It lacks the courage or desire to confront what the other will inevitably expose as the ambiguities and insecurities within one's self-understanding. Such indifference is indicative of that nihilism which philosophical hermeneutics abhors.

UNDERSTANDING AND THE DISQUIETING
OF THE SELF

That philosophical hermeneutics has its foundations within the play of language suggests that understanding involves not just an openness toward the unusual and the foreign but also entails an acceptance of risk and, indeed, a willingness to endure the negativity of experience at its most challenging. Hermeneutic exchange may bring with it the promise of translation and transcendence but precisely because it does so, it also brings with it the inevitability of disorientation and disquietude. Two issues are relevant here: first, the inseparability of self-awareness from its hermeneneutical dependence upon the other, and, second, the intimation that the self is a certain "nothingness" as the full extent and depth of its relational nature is unfathomable.

Concerning the inseparability of self-awareness from its hermeneutical dependence upon the other, the argument is part of the wider case that self-understanding is initially shaped by the formative powers of the linguistic and cultural horizons the self finds itself located within. Even the self's name is given to it by others and in being named we thereby become someone who can be addressed and absorbed within a certain language horizon. Yet, as we have been at pains to point out, the biographical and historical social narratives we are placed within are ontologically open. They can contain unresolved tensions and the future they anticipate is resonant with possibilities. As Davis argues, the self I know is a self not at one with itself: it is moving and changing. Such a self even gains its self-awareness from being a being whose very being is to be in question.[80] Now, philosophical hermeneutics insists that it is toward the dialogical other that this self must look in order to gain a transformative insight into what it might become. Indeed, the very *desire* for self-understanding concedes the point. Such a self may deeply yearn for self-insight but the energy of that longing and the hermeneutic movement it initiates presupposes that that self is already irretrievably dispersed in a multiplicity of unstable affiliations and relations.[81] Not only is the self in all its incompleteness dependent for the understanding it does possess upon both the other and the otherness of language and tradition but it is also dependent upon the dialogical other for bringing to realization the hidden potentialities of meaningfulness within itself. Such a self is doubly dependent upon what is beyond itself. Firstly, the configuration of the self's present inwardness is beholden to the outer horizons of its language and culture, horizons that extend into the withheld of the past. Secondly, how the tensions and ambiguities within that present configuration unfold depends upon what future encounters the self may become involved in. This suggests, in effect, that the boundaries of the self are limitless, which is to say that what the self is and has yet to become is limitlessly dependent upon what is beyond it. This amounts to the claim that self's inner apprehension of itself is unthinkable other than in terms of the dialogical relations that shape both its past and future. Given the unpredictable nature of those relationships, a hermeneutic awareness of self must entail an awareness of its ontological dependence upon language and its speakers. This, in turn, suggests that a hermeneutic awareness of self must also embrace an awareness of its own mystery, a sense that it is grounded in the ever-ungrounding play of language. The self cannot be disassociated from the otherness of language. There is and always will be something more to say about such a self. Such a linguistically formed self has no finality to it. It can always be understood differently. This notion of self is disquieting for its strikes against the individualism inherent in much post-romantic thought. Not only does the mystery of the self reveal the depths of our dependence upon the past and future but also it demands that we acknowledge that with regard to what we are and have yet to become, we are beholden to what is beyond us, beyond our willing and beyond our doing.

Hermeneutic understanding intimates that the self is a certain "nothingness." The suggestion rests on the argument that the full extent and depth of the self's relational nature is unfathomable. Several things can be said about this. The disquieting recognition that the self is irretrievably dispersed in a multiplicity of unstable affiliations and relations suggests that the self is, in certain respects, a nothingness in that it has no essence apart from those affiliations and relations. Furthermore, insofar as those affiliations and relations are limitless, the self is dissolved into what appears as an abyss of nothingness and interminable difference. If such a self lacks an intrinsic essence, it is nothing. Such a self has no depth or bottom to it. There is no *End station* to its being, no point where it can step outside the relations that constitute it and see itself as something in and for itself. Hence, whatever it is, and whatever it might become, is constituted in a potentially endless set of perspectival shifts. Behind these shifts there is no noumenal self hidden or withheld, but only an overlooked or unanticipated element within a given perspective or, indeed, another perspective presently excluded from the one we might presently occupy. However, the hidden perspective does not have an ontological status different from one we might presently occupy. It too exists in the language world but because of the nature of our current perspective, we might not be aware of its presence. To return to the main point, the *nothingness* of the self enables it to be fully relational in that nothing in its essence prescribes what relation it may or may not enter. For the essentialist, however, such a view is nihilistic. It presents the self as if something profound were absent or missing. As a consequence, it is perhaps more appropriate to speak of the self as an emptiness, an emptiness that creates the possibility of the self entering into a wide range of cultural and linguistic relations. There is, perhaps, a more mundane way of speaking of the self, as a nothingness that can bypass the confusions the language of "metaphysics" can sometimes promote. We need to return to an aspect of Iser's argument.

Self-understanding is acutely dependent upon the relations the self enters into. It is these relations that allow the self to reach beyond its immediate horizon into the withheld. Thus, the hermeneutic subject is a self whose fundamental nature is to be in between, in between what it presently understands of itself and what the other understands of it. The disquiet prompted by the tensions and contradictions within the hermeneutic subject's present mode of self-understanding drive it toward other as yet unrealized configurations of itself past or future. As language beings we *are,* and precisely because we are language beings, we are not immediately available to ourselves but find ourselves dispersed in the web of language and how it binds us to the narratives of others. This implies that self-understanding is, in part, a matter of hermeneutic translation: the self in pursuit of a fuller understanding of itself has to relate its self-conception to how others see it. We are not immediately available to ourselves because we are, as language beings, quite properly outside ourselves. The self has to make the other's understanding of itself function within its own. Yet as Iser notes, such translation is not without consequence. It opens an ineliminable space within the self. If the constellar nature of self demands that cognition of the self has to be multiform, that which moves ever nearer to a completer grasp of the self also displaces that self into a plethora of new relations. This opens a space that can never be eliminated.[82] Thus, the disquiet that arises from the self not being fully available to itself propels it into engaging with the other whether it be the otherness of the past, of a different culture, or with the other of ourselves, which lies in the eye of another. Yet the very interpretative nature of this engagement is such that what makes it possible—the self-understanding that springs from the perceived difference between the self and the other—also prevents that understanding from ever being completed or closed. The life-affirming character of the word is clear.

To conclude that the ever-open and irresolvable nature of self-understanding is life-affirming may seem perverse. Iser's conception of understanding being based upon an ineliminable space between interpreter and interpreted might be taken to convey the same pessimism within Schopenhauer's and Nietzsche's account of the *principium individuationis*. It would seem that for Iser, hermeneutic consciousness is based upon an ineliminable space. For Schopenhauer and Nietzsche, however, the irresolvable tension between the subject of knowing and the object of knowledge articulates the pain of self-consciousness. The estrangement within self-consciousness—the fact that as language beings we are not fully available to ourselves—is akin to Williams's description of the wound of knowledge,[83] a wound that for Nietzsche and Foucault never heals, for there is no final word or end-interpretation to absolve or redeem its pain. Yet such pessimism is the pessimism of the concept, a yearning for fixity and resolution. It is a pessimism that is alien to the vitality of the word. Compared to Hamacher's nihilism, the ineliminable nothingness that prevents understanding from understanding itself has consequences both serene and humane. In Iser's words,

> Interpretation indicates what it might mean to lead a conscious life that is permeated by (an) awareness of the unfathomableness out of which it arises. Such a view tends to prevent us from lapsing into another master narrative of the human condition, because unending interpretation unfolds in fleeting configurations, during the course of which either is modified or canceled by what is to follow. . . . Life . . . is basically unrepresentable and can therefore only be conceived in terms of the transient figurations of interpretation.[84]

Furthermore, it is precisely the unending nature of interpretation—the very life of the word—that guarantees and affirms what Iser calls, after Rosenzweig, "the selfication of the self." Because of the ineliminable space, which is both produced by and generates further interpretation, the self in quest of its self in the other can never "consolidate into an identifiable, let alone ultimate shape."

> It [the self] never consolidates into an identifiable, ultimate shape. Instead, it passes through endless configurations of itself. None of these becomes its property. Even what is its very own, its character, its peculiarity, it retains in name only. In truth no recognizable portion of it remains to it in its passage

> through the configurations. Thus, the "selfication" of [the] self,
> proliferates into continual reconfiguration. Each individual
> manifestation of such an unfolding sequence of "selfing" is
> nothing but a transition, leading to another shape of the self.[85]

Thus, paradoxically, it is in the patterns of the self "forever dispersing
into a differential of itself" that the empty self does indeed become
available to itself as *something*, that is, as the ever-changing configurations
of its self-understanding. To put it another way, it is in the endless reconfigurations of itself, which the play of language inflicts upon the
hermeneutic self, that the *being* of such a self is upheld and kept vital. In
conclusion, whereas for Hamacher the endless play of language empties
this self of meaning and the possibility of self-understanding, for philosophical hermeneutics it is precisely the play of language that allows the
self which is nothing to be something, to understand itself in its transi-
tional forms and thereby to afford it the possibility of translation and
transcendence. This argument may dissolve the threat of nihilism; it does
not dissolve the difficulty of being such a self.

The emptiness of the self can be thought of as a generative space. A
self constituted by its hermeneutical relationships lacks a fixed essence.
Such emptiness is not a vacuous abyss but a fullness of transitions that
allows the self to be what it essentially is, a process animated by the constituting practice of understanding. This practice is animated by the tensions inherent within the interpretative process itself. The practice entails
a continuous emptying-out of previous understandings and a continuous
arising of new understanding. The latter is made possible by both the unrealized potentials within past understanding and the fact that changes to
one's present understanding draw one toward yet further unrealized future configurations of understanding. Thus, for philosophical hermeneutics it is the sheer *play* or the *event* of language that drives the continuous
Entgehen and *Vergehen* of self-understanding. This amounts to saying, in
Iser's terms, that it is interpretation, that it is what the self *does*, that animates the transitions of understanding. This is compatible with Gadamer
arguing that interpretation is a process that induces unpredictable events
of understanding beyond our willing and doing. Emergence is the hall-
mark of interpretation.

> Interpretation is basically performative in character. It makes
> something happen, and what arises out of this performance
> are emergent phenomena. The performative nature of inter-

pretation is brought out by the fact that it generates its own power, that is, the ineliminable residual untranslatability drives the performance.[86]

The view that we as hermeneutic beings are able to respond to emergent phenomena and assimilate them within our understanding, strengthens the argument that as selves we are without a defining essence. To say the same thing differently, if we are nothing, then what we are is what we do. What we do is what we practice. We are, essentially, an interpretative process and are what that process has made us. As performative beings without a defining essence, we can rely only upon what we learn by virtue of the practices we are engaged in. Iser observes appropriately,

> As the system has no essence, it must avail itself of . . . previous behavioral patterns and process potentially all the efforts it has made to ensure self-maintenance, thus giving rise to its internal "recursive history."[87]

We are what we do and what we do is to enter into dialogical practices. Philosophical hermeneutics is plainly committed to the view that the emptiness of the self allows it be more fully what it is, a dialogical self, formed and transformed in hermeneutical relations. Though this argument constitutes a powerful riposte to Hamacher's nihilism, it can still invoke a pessimistic response.

The nothingness of the self is compatible with the hermeneutic notion of the self as a generative space. What is generated in this space is constantly challenged and amended. The hermeneutic self is entwined within a continuous ebb and flow of moments of productive confluence and moments of dispersal and disruption. As Dilthey understood, there is no goal outside the movement of understanding.[88] However, this does not render the movement meaningless, as deconstructive critics of hermeneutics assume. What, in fact, is nihilistic is any attempt to bring that movement within a fixity of purpose and thereby to restrain the possible configurations of self-understanding. The claim that the movement is meaningless without such a goal is guilty of the same nihilism. To lament the absence of purpose reveals a wish that the movement of self-understanding should be constrained. Philosophical hermeneutics is, however, more affirmative in its stance. While it recognizes that all understanding is subject to challenge, it also contends that it is precisely such negativity, precisely the fact that the self is nothing, that opens the self to all the inherent possibilities for its being within the language world.

Philosophical hermeneutics can also respond to the pessimist challenge by asking why we should feel that being subject to the continuous *Vergehen* and *Entgehen* of hermeneutic configurations *condemns* us to an interminable flux? If the play of language is the singular but ever-shifting ground of our being, rather than speaking in condemning fashion of understanding's endless indeterminacy, would it not be more appropriate to speak of the ceaseless transformations of understanding? Is it perhaps the unquiet spirit of metaphysics, which still whispers in the pessimist's ears, invoking the old wish for a *Letztbegründung* of understanding. But to be subject to such suggestions is to wish that the play of language should be stilled with the rigid schemas of concepts. The nihilism of such a wish is explicit. To still the movement of language would be to still the movement upon which understanding depends. Perhaps, then, it is because the pessimist has not stopped his ears to the sirens of metaphysics that he remains subject to the nihilistic tendency to revile the openness of language as meaningless rather than reveling in the language world's eternally open possibilities for translation and transcendence. The pessimist's stance indicates that there are also other issues at play.

To regard existence in the vicissitudes of the language world as a form of damnation betrays an oppositional mode of thinking in which *Entgehen* and *Vergehen* are represented as autonomous processes forever seeking to *displace* one another. The actuality of hermeneutic engagement suggests a more complex set of interactions. It is misleading to think of emergence and withdrawal within the play of language as equivalent to a power relation whereby the rise of one eclipses the other. Emergence and withdrawal would then denote a sequence of events and not an ontological process. Hermeneutic relations are not a matter of different outlooks displacing each other. The passing of one configuration of meaning opens us toward different oncoming alignments of meaning, and their approach may, in turn, induce changes in how we previously understood ourselves. The interconnectedness of the emergent and the declining is evident in how our understanding of the past alters how we grasp the future while alterations in how we anticipate the future can equally change our perception of the past. This reemphasizes that the in-betweenness of our self-understanding cannot be articulated in terms of oppositions. We find ourselves held in between a *past* which while it withholds something of our being nevertheless opens that being to a certain set of possible futures, and a *future* which while it too withholds what we will become nevertheless disposes us to certain views of the past. Though this argument does not displace the nihilistic challenge to hermeneutics it does hint at how the understanding of that challenge can be transformed.

The arguments we have presented in this part of the essay reveal how a number of ideas cluster around each other. The notion that a hermeneutic subject or self is essentially an emptiness coincides with the relationality of that subject's mode of existence. Such a relationality entails an in betweenness. Hermeneutic consciousness comes to itself not so much as an awareness that finds itself between one *Sache* and another but as being that in betweenness itself. In its turn, such being in-between facilitates the distance that constitutes hermeneutical consciousness. The motif of distance is important to philosophical hermeneutics. Not only does it draw to itself ideas that have been vital to our discussion—the notions of experience, of transcendence, of ethical responsiveness, of the withheld, of engagement, of becoming *gebildet*, and of difference—but it also brings them into a remarkable reconfiguration, which gives Gadamer's claim to hermeneutical universality an unusual twist. The motif of distance can be approached with the question, "Does our inescapable being within language make confrontation with the negativity of experience inherent in the play of language, unavoidable?" The answer is yes. If we are linguistic beings grounded in and moved by the vitality of language, then no one can be shielded from the experience of valued meanings being challenged. Yet recognizing the universality of the negativity of experience and the sense of distance it implants within the hermeneutic subject constitutes a far from negative response. In order to explore the affirmative quality of the negativity of experience, we must return to the interconnectedness of Gadamer's arguments concerning the in-between, the withheld, and distance.

DI-ALOGUE AND DI-STANCE

In *Truth and Method* Gadamer argues that "hermeneutic work is based on a polarity of familiarity with strangeness" (TM, 295) and that "the true locus of hermeneutics is this in-between." Gadamer has a clear sense of the poignancy of the notion of distance for hermeneutic consciousness. After having stated that the true locus of hermeneutics is "this in-between" he implies that in-betweenness is a fundamental condition of hermeneutic consciousness.

The true locus of hermeneutics is this in-between.

> Given the intermediate position in which hermeneutics oper-
> ates, it follows that its work is not to develop a procedure of
> understanding, but to clarify the conditions in which under-
> standing takes place. (TM, 295)

To explore the poignancy of these remarks we must enquire into the
theme of temporal distance and its significance for understanding.
Gadamer states,

> Temporal distance obviously means something other than the
> extinction of our interest in the object. It lets the true mean-
> ing of the object emerge fully. But the discovery of the true
> meaning of a text or a work of art is never finished: it is in fact
> an infinite process. (TM, 298)

In these and other such passages, "true meaning" does not refer to the
epistemological value attributed to a given meaning but to the ability of
that meaning to truly step forward and assert itself as something coherent and distinct in its own right. In effect, we begin to understand a text
when it begins to assert itself *against* our expectancies, thereby enabling
us to understand it and ourselves differently: "It is enough to say that we
understanding in a different way, if we understand at all" (TM, 297).
Strictly speaking, then, hermeneutical consciousness does not define itself over and against that which is temporally distant from it but, rather,
emerges from within the space that distanciates the outlook of the text
from that of our contemporary horizon. Hermeneutical consciousness is
born of spanning this distance and indeed seeks to refine and articulate
it. We have seen that philosophical hermeneutics regards *Bewusstsein* ontologically, that is, it articulates consciousness as *consciousness* of this difference. Etymology supports the suggestion on two levels. Consciousness
seems to be related to the idea of bringing different ways of knowing together (L. conscius, f. *com* CON + *sci-*, base of *scīre*–know).[89] If, indeed,
a text asserts itself against one for the first time and one realizes both
how the text was in part withheld from one and how the blinding nature
of one's own expectancies was also withheld from one, then one begins
to see one's own expectancies and those of the text differently.
Hermeneutic consciousness is indicative of a becoming "privy to a thing
with another or within oneself."[90] Hermeneutic consciousness is therefore grounded in distance, a distance that allows the difference between
one's own horizon and that of the text to assert itself. It is this distance

that allows one to become different to oneself. Gadamer believes that the tension that constitutes hermeneutic consciousness can never be resolved. Resolution implies that the "withhelds" within the horizons of both the text and one's own understanding could be fully known. Without doubt, hermeneutic consciousness emerges as a site of difficulty and contra-diction (speaking against). It points to an *agon*, to an agony, which must be endured. As that which is grounded in the *pathos* of differentiation and distance, hermeneutic consciousness comes to itself only when its prereflective outlook is challenged by texts or by others asserting themselves against it. The implicit paradox is that hermeneutic consciousness comes into being because of a distance that, though it might wish to, it cannot close without destroying itself. In other words, in-betweenness and the *spaces* of difference establish the environment within which hermeneutic consciousness resides. They point to "the distance within which we live."[91] Indeed, insofar as hermeneutic consciousness becomes aware that it resides in a distance that is impossible to close, it gains an awareness of the irony of its own being. Only by being separate from what it strives to understand does hermeneutic consciousness become aware of itself. Furthermore, in seeking to understand that which is different and distant, hermeneutic consciousness perpetuates the distance between itself and that which it would understand. Hermeneutic consciousness cannot but be a problem for itself. Each of us in our own way is privy to the nature of its quality. The anguished quality of hermeneutic consciousness is reminiscent of Gadamer's comments on Böhme's use of the word *Qual*, meaning agony or anguish.

> Böhme interpreted "quality" as *Qual* because quality is what distinguishes one existence from another. The being of each particular thing is characterized by the isolating pain or anguish that is unique to it. It perseveres in being in its own special way, gives itself form and so unfolds its own particular way.[92]

The dialectical nature of *Qual* is important in demonstrating the positivity of the negativity of experience, but to establish the point we must pass beyond Gadamer's use of the word *distance* and probe its general relevance for philosophical hermeneutics.

The notion of space or distance that in holding horizons apart also holds them together is a *leitmotif* in a number of areas within philosophical hermeneutics. Consider the following:

Distance structures hermeneutic consciousness in that it knows that it is placed between what it knows and what it does not know. It knows that what it knows is dependent upon what it does not know, namely, the withheld preunderstandings of tradition that uphold what it knows.

Distance and the difference it affords is implicit in the self-awareness of the hermeneutic subject. The hermeneutic subject is a being whose being always remains a being-in-question. In discovering that the linguistic other is hermeneutically opaque in that his or her intended meaning is always, logically speaking, capable of receding from us, we discover that our own self-understandings are far from transparent. Williams comments on the difficulty eloquently. In a manner that is reminiscent of Nietzsche, he argues that the self is not a substance one unearths by peeling away layers until one gets to the core, but an integrity one struggles to bring into existence.[93] What we are is held in what constitutes us. Whereas Gadamer speaks of a shared language ontology in this respect, Williams refers to a world of exchange and of converse.[94] The integrity Williams speaks of parallels exactly the in-betweenness that is characteristic of Gadamer's hermeneutic ontology. Noting the temporal nature of understanding, Williams argues,

> My sense of the hiddenness of another is something I develop in the ordinary difficulty of conversation and negotiation. I don't follow; I don't know how to respond in such a way that what I want can be made clear and achieved. Conversation and negotiation are of their nature unpredictable, "unscripted"; their outcome is not determined. Thus I develop the sense of the other speaker/agent as obscure to me: their motivation or reasoning is not transparent, not open to my full knowledge but always waiting to be drawn out clarified. In this process I develop correspondingly the sense of myself as obscure. . . . I discover that I am far from sure what it is that I can say, I become difficult to myself, aware of the gap between presentation and whatever else it is that is active in my acting.[95]

Williams effectively dismantles the illusion that what stands between self and other is not a consequence of the distorting effects of language (Habermas), for there are no intrinsically transparent self-presences for language to stand between.

The exchanges of conversation and negotiation *are* the essence
of what is going on, not unsatisfactory translations of a more
fundamental script. The difficulty is inherent in what is being
done.[96]

A hermeneutic subject's sense of interiority emerges as a relational outcome of linguistic exchange. The play of language will necessarily make
the other obscure to me and in so doing bring me to an awareness of my
own obscurity. Hermeneutic consciousness involves not just an other becoming *distant* to one's understanding but, in consequence, becoming
distant from one's own self-understanding. Though seemingly negative,
there is a positive dialogical turn within Williams's argument concerning
the difference between the hermeneutic subject and its other.

The Ethical Distance. That the other's distance from my understanding is capable of making me distant to my own self-understanding
emphasizes my ethical dependence upon the other. The difficulty of understanding the other leads me to sense the difficulty of understanding
myself. However, it is in the continuing work of conversation, negotiation, and exchange with the other that other ways of understanding myself can emerge. The other can not only problematize my self-understanding but can also assist in its reconfiguration. Williams's position not
only displays the centrifugal and a centripedal aspect of hermeneutic understanding but questions the view that philosophical hermeneutics does
not recognize the otherness of the other. To the contrary, as we have seen,
it is precisely because the other is an *other*, is one who is opaque and who
does not succumb to my way of thinking, that the other emerges as *distant*. Insofar as the other's distance reveals my own distance from myself,
I am not put in the position of attempting to reduce the other to my interpretative schema. This suggests an ethical dependence upon the *otherness* of the other. It is only in relation to the difference of the other that
the hermeneutic subject gains a consciousness of its own difference. Indeed, it is only because the other sees me differently that I can begin to
see myself differently. The awareness and articulation of distance is integral to the process of becoming *gebildet*. To its credit, Williams's argument
allows for the full reciprocity of hermeneutic exchange. Insofar as the
other allows me to see myself differently, I become different to the other
and in becoming different to the other, I can enable the other to become
different to him- or herself. Gadamer rightly insists the effects of a profound conversation are mutual. The "event" of understanding, which

participation in conversation facilitates, cannot not be monopolized by the parties within the exchange, and yet what emerges in that conversation is capable of bringing its participants to a point where each in their own way begins to see themselves differently. Successful conversational exchange is not imposing an epistemological schema upon the other. Yet the labor of conversation, negotiation, and exchange is always without end and without an end. In conclusion, hermeneutic translation and transcendence are possible precisely because of the distance between the other and myself. However, that distance—the ineliminable space that drives translation and transcendence—is never removed, only altered and transformed. In conversation and exchange, then, difficulty, distance, risk, and vulnerability are of the essence. But then, whoever supposed that hermeneutic exchange was easy. Eagleton certainly does not.

In *After Theory*, Eagleton recognizes that being with others "is a taxing, technical business," one that "does not flow from the heart."[97] "Fellow subjects," he argues, "can reveal to us their otherness, and in that act disclose to us our own."[98] What is interesting about Eagleton's remarks is that they are set in a framework of argument that locates the difficulty of converse and negotiation at the heart of the formative dimensions of hermeneutic practice. In a suggestive fusion of Marxist and Aristotelean thought, he proposes that self-realization concerns the realization and the flourishing of a subject's capacities but that this "is not just an individual affair."[99] It cannot be an individual matter for, "nobody who was not open to dialogue with others, willing to listen, argue honestly and admit when he or she was wrong could make real headway in investigating the world" and their part in it.[100] Yet dialogue is an arduous, fatiguing business requiring patience, honesty, courage, and persistence in order to delve through dense layers of self-deception.[101] Thesis three of this essay—philosophical hermeneutics entails a commitment to hermeneutic realism—is firmly endorsed by Eagleton: "Others are the paradigm case of objectivity . . . other persons are objectivity in action."[102] What, however, is striking about Eagleton's stance is the way it articulates thesis nine of our argument, namely, that philosophical hermeneutics is a philosophical *practice* rather than a philosophical method. Eagleton's comments unintentionally illuminate an important aspect of the ontology that underwrites philosophical hermeneutics. This aspect involves, as we shall see, an unusual refraction of Vico's dictum *verum ipsum factum*. Eagleton observes that Aristotle believed that "there was a particular way of living which allowed us, so to speak, to be at our best for the kind of creatures we are."[103] Philosophical hermeneutics, however, is inclined to the view that we are not an essential natural kind naturally disposed to a certain way of life. Iser and Varela also defend the view that we have no fixed essence or nature. However, philosophical hermeneutics does not draw the Nietzschean conclusion that for a creature without a defining essence *everything* is possible. For a creature without the capacity for predetermined responses, learning from accumulated experience in both the individual and collective sense is imperative. There is nothing else for it to rely on. This view sits well with philosophical hermeneutics. It is consistent with Heidegger's conception of understanding as being a specifically human mode of being, with Gadamer's notion of human *being* as being fundamentally a linguistic being and, indeed, with Habermas's view that communicative practice is central to our mode of existence. The relevance of Vico's dictum is generic. Humanity is what it has made itself. Humanity's "truth" lies in the fact that its communicative practices have shaped the nature of its being. We are what our cultural and linguisitic practices have made us. Everything that we have become and everything that we will yet become is shaped by linguistic being and its inherent practices. As we have argued, an individual subject cannot step outside the linguistic, cultural, and historical relations that constitute it. Whatever it is for itself, it is only because it is both in and for another. Whatever it presently understands itself to be and whatever it may yet become is constituted in a potentially endless and shifting set of perspectives. Thus, the realization or fulfillment of a subject's project cannot be solely an individual matter. The nature of our linguistic being means, as Eagleton puts it, that "we become the occasion for each other's self-realization."[104] This is a double endorsement of thesis six of this essay, namely, that philosophical hermeneutics entails an ethical disposition. Not only is the difference of the historical and linguistic other endorsed in that it is only through the otherness of the other that I can become other to myself but the argument also responds to the question concerning what particular way of life—what practice—is best suited for the kind of creature we are. Our fundamental mode of being is understanding. Understanding is essentially dialogical. The question becomes, what particular way of life allows us to flourish as dialogical beings and what particular way of life can enhance the possibilities for translation and transcendence? The ethical implication is clear. The hermeneutical practice of tact and *cortesia* is precisely the practice—the way of life—appropriate to the type of hermeneutical creature that we are. Eagleton intimates that "sympathetic listening" is indeed the practice demanded of us. Following Nussbaum and Murdoch, Hampson also indicates that proper "attentiveness" is "an ethical stance, and one which is closely allied to . . . spirituality. It involves listening to and watching both oneself and others."[105] In a manner that echoes our previous comments about becoming *gebildet*, the in-betweenness of hermeneutic poise and *cortesia*, Hampson observes that "attending involves not being swallowed up by circumstances but keeping a certain critical distance, while also being deeply involved, in the sense of caring for that to which one attends."[106] Attentiveness involves, then, a fundamental openness (TM, 324) but openness not just to the other. It requires openness to involvement, to self-discipline, to partaking in the hard and sometimes uncomfortable business of negotiation. As Davies remarks, the "rhythms of understanding and relating must always act upon the stability of our conceptual understandings, so that the latter are themselves always revisited in deepening reflection and understanding in the context of the relations of conversation with others."[107] Hermeneutic practice is not easy: it is a practice through which the one who attends to the other, changes.[108]

Interpretation and Distance. The concept of distance is inseparable from the process of interpretation itself. Iser's analysis of hermeneutic engagement shows how the translation of a *Sache* from one hermeneutic register to another establishes an ineliminable distance or difference between how it is received and how it's applied. The issue is not whether there can be translation without loss but whether there can be translation and application without the generation of difference. The difference between the original and its application will always remain to haunt and challenge the hermeneutician. Yet in seeking to close the very distance that drives interpretation, the hermeneutician perpetuates it.

Distance emerges as being fundamental to hermeneutic consciousness, to hermeneutical self-awareness, to the work of conversation and exchange, and to the process of interpretation itself. Distance, differentiation, and difference preside over understanding and its intimacies. The courteous formalities of greeting, of allowing the other to be other and to be comfortable in that otherness, establishes not a cold distance but a space that enables intimate exchange. An intimate appreciation of the otherness of the other makes us attend to ourselves differently. Thus, in its very in-betweenness, philosophical hermeneutics seeks to refine and tune the tensions that keep distance and closeness in relationship to each other. Nevertheless, in all that has been said about the positivity of distance we do not yet appear to have arrived at a positive conclusion whereby the negativity of experience can itself undergo a positive turn.

We have argued that hermeneutic self-awareness is possible so long as the difference and distance between the hermeneutic subject and the other is perpetuated. Insight into the self and the other remains possible so long as difference and distance is perpetuated. Nevertheless, whatever the positivity distance and difference might have for understanding, distance and difference will always undo understanding. Disquiet afflicts the hermeneutic consciousness. Can such negativity be overcome? Is hermeneutical consciousness another case of Hegel's unhappy consciousness? Though it would be a mistake to argue that such negativity can be overcome, it would not be mistaken to suggest that it can be transformed. What transforms the negativity of experience is the character of hermeneutical experience itself.

What is invariably overlooked in the debates about hermeneutic experience is the cumulative nature of that experience. Analysis normally focuses upon the nature of the interchange between artwork and viewer or between text and reader. Philosophical hermeneutics centers around the question, "What happens to us, in our experience of a work or text?" However, such experiences are not just of a *Sache* or of the foreign and the strange. They are also experiences of our experiences. If this were not the case, hermeneutic experience could not become the bedrock of an interpretative practice. What makes a practice a practice rather than a method is precisely the fact that it is based upon acquired and accumulated experience. The acquisition of discernment, judgment, and insight is based not so much upon what comes to us in a given experience but upon what comes to us by involvement and participation in a whole number of experiences. The negativity of experience, as Gadamer presents it, is "a form of religious insight" into the limited and finite nature of our aspirations (TM, 357). Real experience may indeed be a matter of recognizing finitude and historicity (TM, 357) but becoming experienced (practised) involves memory and demands that we adjust what we know and expect according to what the negativity of experience has taught us. Experience of this order affords a wisdom. Such wisdom is based upon attaining a disciplined distance from our hermeneutical engagements, which at the same time enables us to attach to them more understandingly. Basing philosophical hermeneutics upon the play of language may seem to the pessimist to condemn every new insight and configuration of meaning to eventual fragmentation and dispersal. Yet the slippage of meaning which fragments insights is also the condition of their reconfiguration. The experienced hermeneutic practitioner knows that no matter how enthralling a new configuration of meaning might be or no matter how powerful a transfiguration of actuality it might achieve, that configuration is always marked by the finitude of language. It is marked by the fact that there is always more to be said about it and insofar as there is always more to be said about it, it is marked by the inevitable slippage of meaning. In other words, the experienced practitioner knows not to become too attached to a given alignment of meaning because it will be disrupted by the very play of the word that gives it life. The experienced practitioner, in effect, transcends the desire for hermeneutic transcendence. The hermeneutic practitioner knows from experience that despite the increased insights it affords, the desire for transcendence and the fuller understanding that attends it will always meet with the negativity inherent in the play of language. Yet to seek detachment from any desire for a completer understanding seems a nihilistic response to the negativity of experience. It seems quite contrary to the spirit of phenomenological involvement that animates philosophical hermeneutics. However, the distance the practised hermeneutical self places between itself and the wish for hermeneutical transcendence is born not of disappointment or frustration but of the hope that accompanies any involvement in dialogue and exchange. On what is such hopefulness grounded?

If all configurations of meaning are prone to being dissolved by the play of language, from whence comes the hope for new configurations of meaning? The answer is clearly that *experience* itself teaches that wherever there is a negativity of experience, there is also the hope for a reconfiguration of meaningfulness. Experience brings with it its cumulative disappointments and failures. Experience knows how within a lifetime, valued frameworks of interpretation are undermined by shifts in language and history. Yet experience also brings with it the lesson that no matter how bleak the loss of an interpretative framework might seem, negativity is always of itself limited and never absolute. Negations as well as affirmations of meaning always leave more to be said. There is always within the negation something that is withheld or has been overlooked and that when uncovered is capable of inaugurating a new configuration of meaningfulness. There is no philosophical or theoretical justification for such a hope. The only justification for such hope is experience itself, namely, the fact that we have experience of past withhelds disclosing themselves to us. In other words, what transforms the negativity of experience and indeed the challenge of deconstruction is the character of hermeneutical experience itself.

The cumulative experience of prolonged dialogue, negotiation, and interpretation forms a hermeneutical disposition, a hermeneutical wisdom and poise. Such a comportment does not succumb to the illusions of metaphysical transcendence or of achieving an *End-Interpretation*. It knows that all hermeneutic transfigurations of understanding are finite. It does not give in to disillusion and disappointment, because it knows that understanding can never be complete. It also knows that the fragmentation and negation of a given framework of meaning is necessarily finite. Such negation hides and withholds other possible configurations of meaning which unexpected twists in history or the serendipitous play of language can suddenly bring to light. Hermeneutic wisdom knows that a priori argument neither establishes nor justifies the hope that in the wake of a collapse of a given framework of meaning, another configuration will emerge in its wake. Only the experience of past withholds becoming disclosed justifies such a hope. The distance that such experience affords allows the practitioner to transcend the negativity that is both in the blind desire for hermeneutic transformation and in the disappointment accompanying the failure of a perspective. Experience teaches the practitioner that within the play of language, each is the other of the other. In the blind wish for transformation there is a hidden promise of emptiness and disappointment and in the negativity of disappointment there is the promise of unattained transformation and insight. Redemption from the play of hope and disappointment is not attained by achieving a false detachment or by disengaging from that play. To pursue either would be nihilistic. Rather, redemption is achieved when the distance that experience affords us allows us to see that both the disappointment born of hope and the hope born of disappointment are inseparable. The wisdom or poise that prolonged hermeneutic experience develops, recognizes and holds fast to this unity within the play of linguistic being. The hermeneutic poise does not entail a rejection or negation of either the impetus toward closure (the centripetal drive of understanding) or the impetus toward disruption and fragmentation (the centrifugal drive of understanding). Hermeneutic wisdom recognizes the interdependence of both. The poise of the attentive hermeneutician stems from the recognition that the life of understanding resides in the constant movement and exchange of converse. There can be no understanding without the risk of disappointment and rejection. Yet in all disappointment and rejection there is always the hope for new understanding and insight. The experienced practitioner does not reject this tension but affirms it. Philosophical hermeneutics "knows" the tension to be irresolvable and thereby breaks through to its redemptive insight. But it is only because of the constant "cost and difficulty" attached to this irresolvable tension that the hermeneutic practitioner is drawn despite all uncertainty and disquiet into a deeper understanding of herself and of the other.[109] The pessimism inherent in the hermeneutics of suspicion is answered. The dynamic inherent within the "negativity of experience" impels the hermeneutic practitioner toward both a knowing affirmation of and a willing participation in the mystery of linguistic being. Philosophical hermeneutics is a philosophy that springs from the disciplines of experience. It is a philosophy born of an experience of language, not an experience born of philosophy.

AFTERWORD

What is in a word? Within the word for Gadamer lies "an experience of linguistic being." To experience linguistic being is to experience and partake in the vital movement of the word and its dialogical dynamics. Philosophical hermeneutics is grounded in such an experience of language. It reveals why dialogue is central to philosophical hermeneutics. The unpredictable and uncontrollable turns of a conversation give rise to insights that catch its participants unaware. The movement of a conversation has its own autonomy: its insights can prompt its participants to question the assumptions they bring to it. The consciousness of such a "limit" can force a participant to think differently about his self-understanding. The experience of linguistic being is, in other words, an experience of translation and transcendence, an experience of becoming different to oneself. Philosophical hermeneutics resists the formal claims of method for the sake of remaining loyal to this fundamental experience of linguistic being. Such loyalty reveals much about the open nature of philosophical hermeneutics and why it seeks not an end-interpretation but what interpretation *does*. It is not methodological closure or the last word that philosophical hermeneutics pursues but the word that transforms and transfigures.

It would be insensitive to the nature of philosophical hermeneutics to claim that chapter 4 of this essay has "demonstrated" the eleven theses this essay has defended. However, chapter 4 offers additional ways of thinking about them and adds to their plausibility. Chapter 1 of this essay argued that though the practice of philosophical hermeneutics cannot be conceptually captured, its nature can be discerned among the spectrum of philosophical refractions which a variety of interpretative perspectives bring to light. To this end, the essay forwarded eleven theses about philosophical hermeneutics. They were: philosophical hermeneutics (1) requires difference, (2) promotes a philosophy of experience, (3) entails a commitment to hermeneutic realism, (4) seeks otherness within the historical, (5) reinterprets transcendence, (6) entails an ethical disposition, (7) redeems the negativity of its constituting differential, (8) affirms an ontology of the in-between, (9) is a philosophical practice rather than a philosophical method, (10) constitutes a negative hermeneutics, and (11) recognizes the *mysterium* of linguistic being. These theses are interlocked by a key theme. Philosophical hermeneutics is *philosophical* in that strives to discern the objectivities within the subjective voice and *hermeneutical* in that it enquires into how the subject experiences and engages with those objectivities. On the basis of this claim, chapter 2 explored the objective *Bildungsprozess* that underwrites hermeneutic experience and chapter 3 examined the speculative structure of hermeneutic experience. It was noteworthy that the objective and subjective elements of hermeneutic experience were both inflected with the further themes of instability, inbetweenness, and difficulty. One the one hand, chapter 2 discussed how tradition is marked by a continuity of conflicts, how the *Sachen*, which sustain a tradition, are ontologically unstable, and how the process of becoming *gebildet* required an ability to reside in between different horizons of hermeneutic orientation. On the other hand, chapter 3 showed how hermeneutical consciousness knows that understanding is always in difficulty, that it never truly grasps its object, that it is always caught in between what it has and what it might yet understand, and also that whatever it believes it does understand is always prone to disruption from the negativity of experience itself. Chapters 2 and 3 explored the oppositions within the ontological structures sustaining hermeneutic consciousness and how they were mirrored in the in-betweenness of hermeneutic consciousness and vice versa. The question both parts of the essay moved toward was whether that which made understanding difficult—the ability of the withheld to disrupt, defer, and dissipate the meaningful—was also that which gave the meaningful its depth, its resonance, and its weight. In short, the question both chapters 2 and 3 posed was whether difficulty, difference, and distance was constitutive of hermeneutic consciousness itself. To address this question, chapter 4 turned to a consideration of Hamacher's argument that understanding is want of understanding.

Discussing Hamacher's deconstructive arguments alongside those of philosophical hermeneutics reveals how misleading it is to think of philosophical hermeneutics as being incommensurable with many of the central tenets of deconstruction. As thesis one claimed, philosophical hermeneutics requires *difference*. Without acknowledging difference in the other, I cannot become different to myself. Philosophical hermeneutics radicalizes this difference. Assisting the other to become more resolutely other allows the other to put greater pressure on the adequacy of my self-understanding. The enhancement of difference lies at the heart of the transformative experiential process that constitutes the *Bildungsphilosophie* defended by philosophical hermeneutics. Nor does the impossibility of achieving a final interpretation render philosophical hermeneutics untenable. For understanding to aspire to wholeness and completeness would be for philosophical hermeneutics to renege on its commitment to translation and transcendence.

Thesis two claims that that promotes a philosophy of experience. Philosophical hermeneutics agrees with Hamacher's claim that one is never in charge of what one understands. However, Gadamer's commitment to the negativity of experience does not dissipate the possibility of understanding. What debates about Gadamer's account of hermeneutic experience often overlook is what comes to us by virtue of our involvement in a whole range of experiences. What makes philosophical hermeneutics a practice rather than a method is the fact that it is based on acquired and accumulated experience. The practice demands not that we claim to be in charge of what we understand but that we continually adjust what we know and expect in the light of what the negativity of experience has taught us. That we cannot predict or control the negativity of experience reconfirms thesis three, namely that philosophical hermeneutics entails a commitment to hermeneutic realism.

Thesis four contends that philosophical hermeneutics seeks otherness within the historical and the cultural and is directly challenged by Hamacher's claim that hermeneutics distorts the experience of the other into a replica of the self. However, as we have claimed, philosophical hermeneutics does not endeavor to subsume otherness within itself. To the contrary, philosophical hermeneutics strives to open and articulate the spaces of such otherness. It offers a courteous attentiveness toward the difficult and the untranslatable precisely because of the possibilities for transcendence they offer. Thesis five—that philosophical hermeneutics reinterprets transcendence—is confirmed once more.

The unwarranted charge that philosophical hermeneutics attempts to reduce the other to the dominating language of the interpreting subject loses sight of the fundamentally dialogical nature of hermeneutic engagement. It is the language-being of *both* the interpreting subject and the interpreted other that renders the individual perspectives of both parties deeply vulnerable to the dialogical intervention of the other party. This gives further support to thesis six, namely, that philosophical hermeneutics entails an ethical disposition. This disposition can be articulated as a form of *tact* and *cortesia* toward the other. It also expresses the fact that as a linguistic being, I am undeniably bound up with the being of the other. The narratives we inhabit are rarely singular. I also exist in the narrative of others. Thus, it can be in the gift of the other to completely reconfigure what I have understood myself to be. Indifference to the other is an indifference to what I can yet understand of myself. Hermeneutical self-understanding is not an individual matter.

Hamacher's criticism that "understanding is in want of understanding" accuses philosophical hermeneutics of being unable to establish a *Letztbegründung* upon which the possibility of understanding could stand. The criticism fails to perceive that, as thesis seven claims, philosophical hermeneutics redeems the negativity of its constituting differential. Philosophical hermeneutics senses that the quest for a *Letztbegründung* constitutes a nihilistic attempt to stifle the vitality of language and the insights its dynamic gives rises to. Deconstruction fails to see that understanding and interpretation are performative in character. They generate an ineliminable space between how a subject matter is received and how it is applied. Yet, as we have seen Iser argue, it is precisely the ineliminable space at the heart of understanding (its constitutive in-betweenness, as thesis eight suggests) that drives understanding toward ever-new configurations of itself.

Thesis nine suggests that philosophical hermeneutics is a philosophical practice rather than a philosophical method. We have seen that philosophical hermeneutics is wedded to the thesis that understanding is essentially dialogical. This suggests that philosophical hermeneutics embraces an ethics of practice. The hermeneutical practice of tact and *cortesia* is precisely the practice—the way of life—appropriate to the type of linguistic creatures that we are. This argument reenforces thesis ten, namely, that philosophical hermeneutics constitutes a negative hermeneutics. It requires a practised openness to the negativity of experience. It demands a willingness to sacrifice the stability of our conceptual understandings to the sometimes uncomfortable demands of hermeneutic engagement. Though difficult, the practice assures the one who is attentive to the other and to otherness, the possibility of transcendence.

The arguments presented in chapter 4 culminate in a defense of thesis eleven. Philosophical hermeneutics recognizes the *mysterium* of linguistic being. It is not a logocentric mode of thought but is unequivocally *logos* (word) centered, centered upon the play of the "word." *The task of understanding is not to fulfill concepts but to transform dialogical relationships.* Philosophical hermeneutics affirms the "dialectic of the word" as opposed to the "dialectic of ideas," and it is this affirmation that sustains its resistance to both Nietzsche's and Hamacher's nihilism. Philosophical hermeneutics is not interested in grasping what lies beyond words (*logoi*) but in the possibilities for transcendence that emerge between them. Remaining loyal to an experience of linguistic being—to the experience of language as a *mysterium*—commits philosophical hermeneutics to keeping the word in play. All can never be said and therefore we can never be done with saying. One of Nietzsche's aphorisms comes uncannily close to expressing a genuine truth about the dialogical nature of philosophical hermeneutics, its eventual character, its difficulty and its ethical responsibilities,

> One times one. One is always in the wrong but with two, truth *begins*.[110]

Notes

PREFACE

1. "Only linguistic analysis believes that one can say everything that one means or knows." See Hans-Georg Gadamer, *On Education, Poetry, and History: Applied Hermeneutics*, ed. D. Misgeld and G. Nicholson (Albany: State University of New York Press, 1992), 69.

2. Hans-Georg Gadamer, *A Century of Philosophy, A Conversation with Riccardo Dottori* (New York: Continuum, 2004), 76–77.

3. Ibid.

4. Ibid.

5. See Gianni Vattimo, "Gadamer and the Problem of Ontology," in *Gadamer's Century, Essays in Honor of Hans-Georg Gadamer*, ed. J. Malpas, U. Arnswald, and J. Kertscher (Cambridge: MIT Press, 2002), 304.

CHAPTER ONE. PHILOSOPHICAL HERMENEUTICS: NAVIGATING THE APPROACHES

1. Gadamer comments, "Essential to an experience is that it cannot be exhausted in what can be said of it or grasped as its meaning. . . . The mode of being of experience is precisely to be so determinative that one is never finished with it. Nietzsche says, 'all experiences last a long time in profound people' (*Gesammelte Werke*, Musarion ed. XIV 50). He means that they are not soon forgotten, it takes a long time to assimilate them, and this (rather than their original content as such) constitutes their specific being and significance." *Truth and Method*, ed. Weinsheimer (London: Sheed and Ward, 1989), 67, hereafter referred to as TM. With regard to the inexhaustible nature of telling experience, Gadamer is indebted to Dilthey's concept of *Erlebnis*. Dilthey writes, "Elements

253

in my awareness of . . . experience draw me on to elements which, in the course of my life—though separated by long stretches of time—were structurally connected to them . . . linked to them in the far distant past are the events through which they originated. Another element leads into the future. . . . Because living through an experience calls for ever new links, we are carried along in this way." W. Dilthey, *Selected Writings*, ed. H. P. Rickman (London: Cambridge University Press, 1979), 185.

2. The most recent of Gadamer's political critics is Richard Wolin who, like Habermas and Caputo, falls for the simplistic equation that a critique of the Enlightenment is synonymous with an irrational legitimization of tradition and authority: see R. Wolin's "Untruth and Method," *The New Republic* 4, no. 432 (May 2000): 36–45. For comments on other recent work on the political dimensions of Gadamer's life and work, see Robert Dostal, "Gadamer, The Man and His Work," in *The Cambridge Companion to Gadamer*, ed. R. Dostal (Cambridge: Cambridge University Press, 2002), 13–35.

3. Derrida describes hermeneutics as the endeavor that yearns to come to a stop "in the decoding of a meaning or truth": see J. Derrida, *Limited Inc.* (Evanston: Northwestern University Press, 1997), 21. Foucault claims that hermeneutics "dooms us to an endless task . . . [as it] . . . rests on the postulate that speech is an act of 'translation' . . . an exegesis which listens to the Word of God, ever secret, ever beyond itself," a word which "for centuries we have waited (for) in vain": see M. Foucault, *The Birth of the Clinic, An Archaeology of Medical Perception*, trans. A. M. Sheridan Smith (New York: Vintage, 1975), xvi–xvii.

4. The word *radical* is used here in the sense of implying a far-reaching or thorough change in a framework of established ideas: see *The New Oxford Dictionary of English* (1998), 1528.

5. "*Patere legem, quam ipse tulisti*," Nietzsche, *Genealogy of Morals*, Third Essay Section 27, ed. Kaufmann (New York: Vintage, 1969).

6. Gadamer's principled commitment to the historical incompleteness of understanding is consistent with Ernst Cassirer's view that the creator of a philosophical concept cannot anticipate all of its future historical determinations: see Ernst Cassirer, *The Philosophy of Symbolic Forms*, trans. R. Mannheim (London: Yale University Press, 1980), 1. Cassirer argues, "The history of philosophy shows us very clearly that the full determination of a concept is very rarely the work of that concept who first introduced that concept. For a philosophical concept is generally speaking rather a problem than the solution to a problem—and the full significance of this problem cannot be understood so long as it is in its first implicit state" (ibid.). It is noteworthy that he is alluding to a passage in Kant's *Critique of Pure Reason*. Referring to the ambiguities within Plato's expression "idea," Kant comments, "I need only remark that it is by no means unusual, upon comparing the thoughts which an author has expressed

in regard to his subject, whether in ordinary conversation or in writing, to find that we understand him better than he has understood himself. As he has not sufficiently determined his concept, he has sometimes spoken, or even thought, in opposition to his own intention": see Immanuel Kant, *Critique of Pure Reason*, trans. N. K. Smith (London: Macmillan, 1970), A314, 310.

7. See for example Wilhelm Dilthey who contends that "the personalities of the interpreter and his author do not confront each other as two facts which cannot be compared: both have been formed by a common human nature and this makes common speech and understanding among men possible": see *Dilthey Selected Writings*, 258.

8. See Anthony Savile, *The Test of Time* (Oxford: Clarendon, 1982), 84.

9. "I too affirm that understanding is always understanding-differently [*Anders-verstehen*]," and, "Who ever understands must understand differently if he is to understand at all." See Hans-Georg Gadamer, "Letter to Dallmayr" and "Hermeneutics and Logocentricism," in *Dialogue and Deconstruction; The Gadamer Derrida Encounter*, ed. D. P. Michelfelder and Richard E. Palmer (Albany: State University of New York Press, 1989), 96 and 118.

10. The secular reappropriation of transcendence as a moment of transformation within a phenomenology of experience suggests that philosophical hermeneutics follows Heidegger in attempting a *Destruktion* of not just metaphysical but also religious terminology.

11. "The essence of what is called spirit lies in the ability to move within the horizon of an open future and an unrepeatable past": see Hans-Georg Gadamer, *The Relevance of the Beautiful and Other Essays* (Cambridge: Cambridge University Press, 1986), 10.

12. The term *dialecticity* is used in order to stress that though hermeneutic experience entails experiences involving the negation of one's expectancies, it is not systematically dialectical. Furthermore, achieving an understanding does not necessarily imply the resolution of differences.

13. This has something of Wilhelm Humboldt about it. Humboldt writes of a loving relationship in the following terms: "The effectiveness of all such relations as instruments of cultivation, entirely depends on the extent to which the members can succeed in combining their personal independence with the intimacy of the association; for while, without this intimacy, one individual cannot sufficinetly possess, as it were, the nature of the others, independence is no less essential, in order that each, in being possessed, may be transformed in his own unique way. On the one other hand, individual energy is essential to both parties and, on the other hand, a difference between them, neither so great as to prevent one from comprehending the other, nor so small as to exclude admiration for what the other possesses, and the desire to assimilate it into one's own

character." Wilhelm von Humboldt, *The Limits of State Action*, ed. J. W. Burrow (Cambridge: Cambridge University Press, 1969), 17.

14. Hans-Georg Gadamer, *Hermeneutics, Religion, and Ethics*, trans. J. Weinsheimer (New Haven: Yale University Press, 1999), 16.

15. See Julian Roberts, *German Philosophy, An Introduction* (London: Polity Press, 1988), 263.

16. Martin Heidegger, "On the Origin of the Art Work," in *Poetry, Language, and Thought*, trans. Albert Hofstadter (New York: Harper and Row, 1972), 42. Insert and emphasis added.

17. "From the Aristotelian doctrine of catharsis to the free play of the Kantian faculties, to the beautiful as the perfect correspondence of inside and outside in Hegel, aesthetic experience seems always to have been described in terms of *Geborgenheit*—security, 'orienation' or 'reorientation'." See G. Vattimo, *The Transparent Society* (London: Polity, 1992), 52.

18. "If we . . . regard experience in terms of its result, we have ignored the fact that experience is a process. In fact, this process is essentially negative. . . . We call this kind of experience dialectical" (TM, 353).

19. Wolfgang Iser, *The Range of Interpretation* (New York: Columbia University Press, 2000), 154.

20. Ibid., 60.

21. See also Nicholas Davey, "Between the Human and the Divine: On the Question of the In-Between," in *Between the Human and the Divine, Philosophical and Theological Hermeneutics*, ed. A. Wiercinski (Toronto: Hermeneutic Press, 2002), 88–96.

22. See R. Williams, *On Christian Theology* (Oxford: Blackwell, 2001), 240. Related arguments are discussed at length in my article "The Subject as Dialogical Fiction," in *Rethinking Communicative Interaction*, ed. Colin Grant (Amsterdam: John Benjamin Publishing, 2003), 53–68.

23. See *The Construction of Reality*, ed. M. A. Arbib and Mary Hesse (Cambridge: Cambridge University Press, 1986), chapter 9 and Paul Feyerabend, *Farewell to Reason* (London: Verso, 1987), chapter 3.

24. Dilthey for example writes, "A work must be understood from individual words and their combination but full understanding of individual parts pre-supposes understanding of the whole. This circle is repeated in the relation of an individual work to the mentality and development of its author, and it recurs again in the relation of such an individual work to its literary genre." *Dilthey Selected Writings*, 259.

25. Gordon Leff was among the first English hermeneuticians to advance such an argument in the case of historical objectivity. He writes, "Nor is history peculiar in being partial knowledge. Every problem entails limiting the area and the kind of knowledge to be considered." The issue for Leff is the extent to which a historian is aware of his or her intellectual limitations and acts in a manner that is consistent with that consciousness. See Gordon Leff, *History and Social Theory* (London: Merlin Press, 1969), 122.

26. Gadamer comments that his real philosophical interest concerned "what happens to us over and above our wanting and doing" (TM, xxviiii).

27. "This characteristic of Dasein's Being—this 'that it is'—is veiled in its 'whence' and 'whither,' yet disclosed in itself all the more unveiledly; we call the 'thrownness' of this entity into its 'there'. The expression 'thrownness' is meant to suggest *the facticity of its being delivered over*." Martin Heidegger, *Being and Time* (Oxford: Blackwell, 1960), 174. See also pages 219-24.

28. Iser, 60.

29. Ibid., 153.

30. Joel Weinsheimer, *Gadamer's Hermeneutics. A Reading of Truth and Method* (New Haven: Yale University Press, 1984), 12.

31. "The object . . . exists only for the subject": Arthur Schopenhauer, *The World as Will and Representation*, trans. E. F. J. Payne (New York: Dover, 1969), Vol 1, 11.

32. See TM, 238.

33. See TM, 506.

34. The notion of *Sache* is discussed at length in chapter 2 of this essay. Gerald Bruns offers a detailed discussion of the nature of the subject matter as it is presented by Gadamer. See Gerald Bruns, *Hermeneutics, Ancient and Modern* (New Haven: Yale University Press, 1992), 62-63.

35. Gadamer's worries about the language of the statement clearly derive from Heidegger's concerns about apophantic language. See *Being and Time*, 200-201.

36. Gadamer says of the speculative, "Language itself . . . has something of the speculative about it . . . as the realisation of meaning, as the event of speech, of mediation, of coming to an understanding. Such a realisation is speculative in that the finite possibilities of the word are orientated toward the sense intended as toward the infinite" (TM, 469).

37. Iser, 46.

38. Nicholas Davey, "The Hermeneutics of Seeing" in *Interpreting Visual Culture*, ed. Ian Heywood and Barry Sandywell (London: Routledge, 1999), 9.

39. See Nicholas Davey, "A Response to Christopher Smith," in *Gadamer and Hermeneutics*, ed. H. Silverman (London: Routledge, 1991), 42-62.

40. Hermeneutics is not free from such a tendency itself. Gadamer perceives in Dilthey's philosophy an overt emphasis upon deciphering words as signs. See TM, 231-34.

41. "Language . . . [is] . . . an instinctive pre-figuring of logical reflection" (TM, 469).

42. See Bruns, 223.

43. See Hans-Georg Gadamer, *Philosophical Apprenticeships*, trans. R. R. Sullivan (Cambridge: MIT Press, 1985), 55-61. See also Fred Lawrence, "Gadamer, the Hermeneutic Revolution and Theology," in *The Cambridge Companion to Gadamer* (Cambridge: Cambridge University Press, 2002), 167-200.

44. See John D. Caputo, ed., *The Religious* (Oxford: Blackwell, 2002).

45. D. E. Cooper, *The Measure of Things. Humanism, Humility, and Mystery* (Oxford: Clarendon Press, 2002), 364.

46. Andrew Louth, *Discerning the Mystery* (Oxford: Clarendon, 1989), 139.

47. See Iser, 105.

48. Werner Hamacher, *Premises, Essays on Philosophy and Literature from Kant to Celan* (Cambridge: Harvard University Press, 1996), 1.

49. For a recent and very lucid account of this debate, see Andrew Ford, *The Origins of Criticism, Literary Culture, and Poetic Theory in Classical Greece* (Princeton: Princeton University Press, 2002).

CHAPTER TWO. PHILOSOPHICAL HERMENEUTICS AND *BILDUNG*

1. T. J. Reed offers some interesting insights into how Goethe and Schiller apply the idea of *Bildung* (self-education). It is clear, however, that the German Romantics tied the conception of *Bildung* to a notion of improving or perfecting the self. This notion of perfectibility is completely missing from Gadamer's conception of *Bildung*. See T. J. Reed, *The Classical Centre, Goethe and Weimar* 1775-1832 (Oxford: Clarendon Press, 1986), especially 14. Gadamer's more Hegelian approach to the notion of *Bildung* is made clear in TM. See TM, 9-19. The question of *Bildung* has received much attention in the philosophy of

education. See the special issue "Educating Humanity: *Bildung* in Postmodernity," *Journal of Philosophy of Education* 36, no. 3 (August 2002).

2. A. G. Baumgarten, *Texte zur Grundlegung der Ästhetik* (Stuttgart: Felix Meiner, 1983), 4-6.

3. See Feyerabend, *Farewell to Reason*, 112-88.

4. Ernst Cassirer, *The Logic of the Humanities* (London: Yale University Press, 1974), 117.

5. John D. Caputo, *Radical Hermeneutics, Repetition, Deconstruction, and the Hermeneutic Project* (Bloomington: Indiana University Press, 1987), 96-97.

6. Alistair MacIntyre, *After Virtue, A Study in Moral Theory* (London: Duckworth, 1993), 187-94

7. See Jean Grondin, *Sources of Hermeneutics* (Albany: State University of New York Press, 1995), 111-24.

8. Iser, *The Range of Interpretation*, 84.

9. Richard Rorty, *Philosophy and the Mirror of Nature* (Oxford: Blackwell, 1980), 357.

10. See my essay "On the Other Side of Writing: Thought's on Gadamer's Notion of Schriftlichkeit" where this is discussed. Refer to *Language and Linguisticality in Gadamer's Hermeneutics*, ed. L. Schmidt (New York: Lexington Books, 2000), 77-114.

11. Adrian Marino, *The Biography of the Idea of Literature from Antiquity to the Baroque* (Albany: State University of New York Press, 1996), 16.

12. Ibid., 69.

13. Hans Peter Duerr, *Dreamtime, Concerning the Boundary between Wilderness and Civilization* (London: Blackwell, 1985), 125-33.

14. Gadamer's notion of subject matter (*die Sache selbst*) is discussed at length in section seven of chapter 2.

15. See Wolfhardt Pannenberg, *Theology and the Philosophy of Science* (London: Darton, Longman and Todd, 1976), 196-98.

16. "However thoroughly one may adopt a foreign frame of mind, one still does not forget one's world view and language-view" (TM, 442).

17. MacIntyre, 222.

18. Iser, 84.

19. TM, 353–57.

20. Marino, 17.

21. See J. A. Barash's essay "Heidegger's Ontological 'Destruction,'" in *Reading Heidegger from the Start: Essays in his Earliest Thought*, ed. T. Kisiel and J. van Buren (Albany: State University of New York Press, 1994), 112.

22. On the question of the difficulty of self-presence, see Williams, *Christian Theology*, 240 and W. Davis, *Inwardness and Existence, Subjectivity in/and Hegel, Heidegger, Marx, and Freud* (Madison: University of Wisconsin Press, 1989), 105.

23. Varela's arguments in his book *The Tree of Knowledge: The Biological Roots of Human Understanding* (Boston: Shambhala, 1992) are discussed at length in chapter 4 of Iser's *The Range of Interpretation*.

24. Iser, 105.

25. "The essence of what is called spirit lies in the ability to move within the horizon of an open future and an unrepeatable past." *The Relevance of the Beautiful*, 10.

26. H-G. Gadamer, *The Enigma of Health* (London: Polity, 1996), 143.

27. Ibid. p. 59.

28. For a lengthier development of these themes see my essays "Between the Human and the Divine" and "The Subject as Dialogical Fiction."

29. Italo Calvino offers one such definition of a classic. He writes, a "classic is a book to which you cannot remain indifferent, and which helps you to define yourself in relation or even in opposition to it. . . . [W]hat distinguishes a classic is perhaps only a kind of resonance we perceive emanating from an ancient or a modern work." See his book *Why Read the Classics* (London: Vintage, 1991), 7.

30. In the essay "The Origin of the Artwork," Heidegger also argues that "the (art) work belongs, as work, uniquely within the realm that is opened up by itself. For the work-being of the work is present in, and only in, such opening up." See *Poetry, Language, Thought*, 41.

31. For Heidegger's distinction between *Welt* and *Erde* see "The Origin of the Artwork" in *Poetry, Language, Thought*, 49.

32. This charge is discussed at length in the volume *Dialogue and Deconstruction, The Gadamer Derrida Encounter*, ed. D. P. Michelfelder and R. E. Palmer (Albany: State University of New York Press, 1989), see especially 162–75.

33. Of transcendence, Havel writes, "to give up on any form of transcending oneself means, *de facto*, to give up on ones own human existence." See Václav Havel, *Letters to Olga* (London: Faber and Faber, 1998), 237.

34. Gadamer remarks that "the hermeneutical experience also has its own rigour: that of uninterrupted listening. A thing does not present itself to the hermeneutical experience without an effort special to it i.e. keeping one's initial prejudices at a distance" (TM, 465).

35. Iser, 46.

36. Ibid., 154.

37. This ambiguity concerning *die Sache* is implicit in Gadamer's statement that "the thing does not go its own course without our thinking being involved, but thinking means unfolding what consistently follows from the subject matter itself" (TM, 464).

38. Friederich Nietzsche, *The Will to Power*, trans. W. Kaufmann and R. J. Hollingdale (London: Weidenfeld and Nicolson, 1968), section 515. WP refers to this work in the text.

39. Edmund Husserl, *The Crisis of the European Sciences and Transcendental Phenomenology* (Evanston: Northwestern University Press, 1970), 112.

40. Henry Staten, *Wittgenstein and Derrida* (London: University of Nebraska Press, 1984), 143.

41. The passage cited does not deal with the language-world per se but with the notion of "the world, apart from our condition of living in it." Nietzsche is, of course, insistent that such a world does not exist as a world-in-itself but is essentially a world of relations.

42. Edmund Husserl, *Logical Investigations* (New York: Humanities Press, 1970), Introduction Section 2, 252–54.

43. Staten, 143.

44. Hirsch as cited by Staten in *Wittgenstein and Derrida*, 143.

45. Julian Young, *Heidegger's Philosophy of Art* (London: Cambridge University Press, 2001).

46. Theodor Adorno, *Negative Dialectics* (London: Routledge, 1973), 33. See also T. Eagleton, *The Ideology of the Aesthetic* (Oxford: Blackwell, 1990), 346.

47. Adorno, *Negative Dialectics*, 162.

48. Ibid., 162–63. Elsewhere Adorno argues, "Constellation is not system. Everything does not become resolved, everything does not come out even, rather, one moment sheds light on the other, and the figures that the individual moments form together are specfic signs and a legible script." See Adorno's *Hegel, Three Studies* (Cambridge: MIT Press, 1993), 109.

49. Adorno, *Negative Dialectics*, 149.

50. Eagleton, 346.

51. Iser, 195.

52. Adorno, *Negative Dialectics*, 150.

53. Ibid., 150, 151, 157.

54. Hans Belting, *Likeness and Presence, A History of the Image before the Era of Art* (London: University of Chicago Press, 1994), 153. Gadamer also refers to John of Damascus in note 249 of TM, 141.

55. See Karl Popper, *Objective Knowledge, An Evolutionary Approach* (Oxford: Clarendon Press, 1974), 163.

56. See Nicholas Davey, "Sitting Uncomfortably: Gadamer's Approach to Portraiture," in *Journal of the British Society for Phenomenology* 33, no. 3 (Oct. 2003).

57. Popper, 161.

58. Ibid., p.159.

59. Ibid., p.110.

60. Ibid., p.162.

61. It is the case that Baird invented the television and with that invention the subject matter of television was brought into being. The embrace of that subject matter and the extent to which it has transformed visual culture has hardly been exhausted. The significant point, however, concerns how an invention and creation is explored and elaborated once it has been received and adopted within a given community. In this sense, Baird's creation transcends his own understanding of it.

62. George Steiner, *Real Presences: Is There Anything in What We Say?* (London: Faber and Faber, 1990), 147.

63. Ibid., 148.

64. Karlheinz Stierle, "Translation Studii und Renaissance," in *The Translatability of Cultures, Figurations of the Space Between*, ed. S. Budwick and W. Iser (Stanford: Stanford University Press, 1996), 66.

65. Edward Said argues for a humanist notion of "hospitality." He observes that "I have called what I try to do 'humanism', a word I continue to use stubbornly despite the scornful dismissal of the term by sophisticated modern post-modern critiques." Central to this practice is the invocation of philology that is alive with "a sense of the density and interdependence of human life." Said's key remark is that "rather than alienation and hostility to another time and another culture, philology as applied to *Weltliteratur* involved a profound humanistic spirit deployed with generosity and, if I may use the word, hospitality. Thus,

the interpreter's mind actively makes a place in it for a foreign "other." And this creative making of a place for works that are otherwise alien and distant is the most important facet of the interpreter's mission." See Edward Said, *Orientalism* (London: Penguin, 2003), xix.

66. Iser, 154.

67. Gadamer alludes to this point when he comments that "certainly the thing does not go on its own course without our thinking being involved, but thinking means unfolding what consistently follows from the subject matter itself" (TM, 464).

68. Friedrich Nietzsche, *The Twilight of the Idols*, trans. R. J. Hollingdale (London: Penguin, 1968), "How the Real World at Last Became a Myth," section 4, 40.

69. Nietzsche, *The Will to Power*, section 55.

70. Young, 131.

71. Searle argues that "the real mistake of the classical metaphysicians was not the belief that there are metaphysical foundations, but rather the belief that somehow or other such foundations were necessary . . . that unless there were such foundations something is lost or threatened or undermined or put in question." According to this argument the philosophical nihilist turns out to be an apologist for metaphysics: to assert the absence of meaning is to lay down the criteria of what it would be for something to be meaningful. John Searle, "The World Turned Upside Down," *New York Review of Books* 30, 74–79 cited in Susan Hekman's *Hermeneutics and the Sociology of Knowledge* (London: Polity, 1986), 194.

72. For a critique of the nihilistic aspects of deconstruction, see Nicholas Davey, "Beyond the Mannered: The Question of Style in Philosophy or Questionable Styles of Philosophy," in *The Question of Style in Philosophy and the Arts*, ed. C. van Eck, J. McAllister, and R. van de Vall (London: Cambridge University Press, 1995), 177–200.

73. Young, 132.

74. Ibid.

75. Ibid.

76. Steiner, *Real Presences*, 82–83.

77. "The hermeneutical experience also has its own rigour: that of uninterrupted listening. A thing does not present itself to the hermeneutical experience without an effort special to it. . . ." (TM, 465).

78. Iser, 151.

79. Duerr, 129.

80. Ibid., 126.

81. Ibid., 129.

82. Ibid., 129.

83. "We feel that even when all possible scientific questions have been answered, the problems of life remain completely untouched." Ludwig Wittgenstein, *Tractatus Logico-Philosophicus* (London: Routledge, 1969), section 6.52.

CHAPTER THREE. INTIMATIONS OF MEANING

1. Of the sciences, Gadamer writes, "Understanding is possible only if one keeps oneself out of play. This is the demand of science" (TM, 335).

2. See chapter 2.

3. J. M. Bernstein, *The Fate of Art, Aesthetic Alienation from Kant to Derrida and Adorno* (London: Polity Press, 1992), 258.

4. Ibid. Also see TM, 467. Refer also to Hans-Georg Gadamer, *Hegel's Dialectic, Five Hermeneutical Studies*, ed. P. Christopher Smith (New Haven: Yale University Press, 1976), 95–99 and 115–16.

5. Bernstein, *The Fate of Art*, 258.

6. Ibid.

7. H-G. Gadamer, "On the Circle of Understanding," in *Hermeneutics Versus Science: Three German Views*, trans. and ed. J. M. Connolly and T. Keutner (South Bend: University of Notre Dame Press, 1988), 77.

8. See H-G. Gadamer, "Aesthetics and Hermeneutics," in *Philosophical Hermeneutics*, trans, D. Linge (London: University of California Press, 1966), 95–104. Also see TM, 442.

9. See H-G. Gadamer, "The Universality of the Hermeneutic Problem," in *Philosophical Hermeneutics*, 1–17.

10. The failure of Habermas to pick up this nuance in Gadamer's argument suggests that his critique of the universality of hermeneutic's truth claim is based on a misunderstanding.

11. Hegel, cited by Adorno in T. W. Adorno, *Hegel: Three Studies*, trans. S. W. Nicholson (Cambridge: MIT Press, 1993), 59.

12. Wilhelm von Humboldt, *The Limits of State Action*, ed. J. W. Burrow (London: Cambridge University Press, 1969), xviii.

13. "All poetic discourse is myth, that is, it certifies itself through nothing more than its being said. It tells a story or speaks of deeds and yet gains credence—but gain it it does—only to the extent that we ourselves are the ones who encounter ourselves in these actions and sufferings of gods and heroes. That is why, right down to the present, the mythical world of the ancients stimulates poets ever anew to revitalise it for the purpose of contemporary self-confrontation. . . . In all such cases the principle of understanding is founded on an inversion; what presents itself as the action and suffering of others is understood as one's own suffering experience." See H-G. Gadamer, "Mythopoetic Inversion in Rilke's Duino Elegies," in *Hermeneutics versus Science*, 122.

14. A. C. Danto, *The Transfiguration of the Commonplace* (London: Harvard University Press, 1981), 208.

15. Gadamer, *On Education, Poetry and History*, 89 and 88.

16. For such information I am indebted to Robert Graves, *Greek Myths* (London: Cassel, 1955) and to H. J. Rose, *A Handbook of Greek Mythology* (London: Methuen, 1965).

17. F. Nietzsche, *Human All Too Human*, trans. R. Hollingdale (London: Cambridge University Press, 1986), Section 11.

18. For Heidegger's view of the primordiality of the *aletheic* as opposed to the *apophantic* function of language, see *Being and Time*, sections 33–34.

19. H-G. Gadamer, *The Relevance of the Beautiful*, ed. R. Bernasconi (Cambridge: Cambridge University Press, 1986), 141.

20. Gadamer, *The Relevance of the Beautiful*, 47.

21. David Levy, "Europe, Truth, and History: Husserl and Vöglin on Philosophy and Identity in Europe," in *Man and World* (Amsterdam: Kluwer Academic Publishers, 1996), Vol. 26, 170.

22. Gadamer, *Hegel's Dialectic*, 115.

23. Gadamer, *The Relevance of the Beautiful*, 113–14.

24. Schopenhauer, *The World as Will*, Vol. 1, 3.

25. Gadamer, *Philosophical Hermeneutics*, 104.

26. Gianni Vattimo, *The Transparent Society* (London: Polity Press, 1992), 45–61.

27. Ibid., 50.

28. Ibid., 51.

29. Anthony Giddens questions this single narrative assumption with some force. See his *Modernity and Self-Identity* (London: Polity, 1991), chapter 3.

30. Bakhtin, in Gavin Flood, *Beyond Phenomenology, Rethinking the Study of Religion* (London: Cassel, 1999), 199.

31. Oliver Davies, *A Theology of Compassion* (London: SCM Press, 2001), 38.

32. Iser, *The Range of Interpretation*, 52.

33. Ibid., 53.

34. "One could argue that because, for Derrida, the meaning of the written sign is always postponed, and is therefore identified with death—that which one can never experience—in a certain way he makes meaning *complete*, just as the written text itself, in all its distance and assumed authority, would seem also to present knowledge as accomplished and to impose a gulf between subjectivity and meaning." See Catherine Pickstock, *After Writing: On the Liturgical Consummation of Philosophy* (London: Blackwell, 1998), 115.

35. Ibid., 114.

36. Rowan Williams, *Lost Icons, Reflections on Cultural Bereavement* (Edinburgh: T. & T. Clark, 2000), 104.

37. See Adorno, *Hegel: Three Studies*, 7. Gadamer makes a similar observation: "Everything alive is bound to its 'other,' the world around it, in the constant exchange of assimilation and secretion." See his *Hegel's Dialectic*, 58.

38. Nietzsche, *The Will to Power*, section 1, 3.

39. See John Richardson, *Existential Epistemology* (Oxford: Clarendon Press, 1986), 31.

40. Nietzsche, "The Wanderer and His Shadow," in *Human All Too Human*, section 11.

41. Nietzsche, *The Will to Power*, section 715, 380.

42. See Arthur C. Danto, *Nietzsche as Philosopher* (New York: Macmillan, 1970), 86.

43. Nietzsche, *The Will to Power*, section 810, 428.

44. J. L. Austin, "A Plea for Excuses," in *Philosophical Papers* (Oxford: Oxford University Press, 1962), 130, cited by A. C. Danto in *Nietzsche as Philosopher*, 121.

45. Nietzsche, *The Will to Power*, section 569, 306.

46. See Gianni Vattimo, *Nietzsche, An Introduction* (London: Althone, 2002), 28.

47. Ibid.

48. Alan Schrift, *Nietzsche and the Question of Interpretation* (London: Routledge, 1990), 136.

49. Nietzsche, *The Will to Power*, section 409, 220.

50. Friedrich Nietzsche, *Beyond Good and Evil* (London: Penguin, 1973), section 296.

51. Ibid., section 160.

52. Friedrich Nietzsche, *Twilight of the Idols* (London: Penguin, 1968), Part 9, section 26.

53. Ibid., Part 3, section 1.

54. Nietzsche, *Human All Too Human*, section 586.

55. P. F. Strawson, *Individuals: An Essay in Descriptive Metaphysics* (London: Methuen, 1959), 109.

56. Friedrich Nietzsche, *Daybreak* (Cambridge: Cambridge University Press, 1982), section 257.

57. Nietzsche, *The Will to Power*, section 522, 283.

58. Williams, *Lost Icons*, 152.

59. Vattimo, *Nietzsche*, 28.

60. Nietzsche, *The Will to Power*, section 124, 76.

61. Ibid., section 711, 378-79.

62. MacIntyre, *After Virtue*, 222.

63. Pannenberg, *Theology*, 198.

64. Ibid., 197.

65. Heidegger, *Being and Time*, 24.

66. Davey, "The Hermeneutics of Seeing," 6.

67. Nietzsche, *The Will to Power*, section 80, 50.

68. Jürgen Habermas, *The Philosophical Discourse of Modernity* (London: Polity Press, 1987), chapter 9.

69. Williams, *On Christian Theology*, 241.

70. Adorno, *Hegel*, 100.

71. Ibid., 77.

72. Hans-Georg Gadamer, *Heidegger's Ways* (Albany: State University of New York Press, 1994), 105.

73. Ibid., 107.

74. Ibid., 108.

75. Theodor Adorno, *Aesthetic Theory* (London: Routledge, Kegan and Paul, 1984), 178.

76. Theodor Adorno, *Aesthetic Theory* (London: Routledge, 1984), 177.

77. Heidegger, "The Origin of the Art Work," in *Poetry, Language and Thought*, 74. See also Cristina Lafont, *The Linguistic Turn in Hermeneutic Philosophy* (Cambridge: MIT Press, 1999), 63.

78. Joel Weinsheimer, *Philosophical Hermeneutics and Literary Theory* (New Haven: Yale University Press, 1991), 123.

79. Heidegger, "Origin of the Art Work," 73.

80. Nietzsche, *Human All Too Human*, Part Two, "The Wanderer and his Shadow," 301.

81. Hamacher, *Premises*, 1.

CHAPTER FOUR. UNDERSTANDING'S DISQUIET

1. See *want, wanting,* and *wanton* in *The New Oxford Dictionary of English* (Oxford: Oxford University Press, 1999).

2. Hamacher, *Premises*, 1.

3. Immanuel Kant, *Critique of Pure Reason*, trans. N. K. Smith (London: Macmillan, 1970), 45.

4. Gadamer immediately distinguishes the philosophical manner of his approach to this question from that of Kant. "This is a question," he writes, "which precedes any action of understanding on the part of subjectivity. . . . Heidegger's temporal analytics of *Dasein* has, I think, shown convincingly that understanding is . . . the basic being-in-motion of *Dasein*" (TM, xxx). Gadamer of course refines Heidegger's notion of being-in-motion and articulates understanding as an action of linguistic being, of tradition, and of linguisticality. Though he proposes the latter as the *ground* of understanding, he comments appropriately, "Does what has always supported us need to be ground?" (TM, xxxvii).

5. Ibid.

6. Hamacher, 1.

7. Ibid., 2.

8. Ibid.

9. Ibid.

10. Ibid., 5.

11. Ibid., 39

12. Ibid., 43.

13. Ibid., 40.

14. Hans Herbert Kögler, *The Power of Dialogue, Critical Hermeneutics after Gadamer and Foucault* (Cambridge: MIT Press, 1996), 162.

15. Gadamer remarks that "[i]f, by entering foreign language worlds, we overcome the prejudices and limitations of our previous experience of the world, this does not mean that we leave and negate our own world. Like travellers, we return home with new experiences. Even if we emigrate and never return, we still never wholly forget" (TM, 448). Duerr offers a similar argument. He maintains that "not *all* facts become apparent in every language. . . . Not *all* wheels turn *everywhere*. The 'werewolf' wheel hardly turns anything at all in our modern civilization, and even if it were to turn something, it would not be the same thing that it moves where it is 'at home.' . . . If we want to see what it turns 'at home', how it 'works' there, we need to go to where the werewolf walks about at night. . . . At times we will have to howl with the wolves, and that means that we have to forget somethings that are familiar, especially those things that prevent us from understanding strange contents. This in no way suggests that we will forget *everything* for all times, as implied by a consistent relativism. The anthropologist returns home changed but he is not going to be an entirely different person, for in that case, it would not be *he* who had gained the insight. . . . What we then experience will not be easy to moor, load and take home. . . . Will we then be able to describe what we experienced, what it was like to be a werewolf?" (Duerr, *Dreamtime*, 129). The experience of being in an alien language may not be translatable into a mother language but what emerges in the mother tongue as a sense of difficulty with regard to the other language is not alien to langauge but remains an experience within the mother tongue. That experience of limit and difficulty is itself subject to expression. The mother tongue may not be able to describe the world as it is perceived within the alien language but as with all opaque foreign terms, though it is not possible to obtain a direct equivalent for them, it is possible to get an approximate fix on them by triangulating them with other related terms. For example, Hans Waldenfels knows that it is impossible to find a precise meaning in English for the Japanese term *mu* (nothingness) but by relating it to the Sanskrit *sunyata* (a moral sense of emptiness), the Chinese *kun* (sky or the vault of heaven), and other Japanese terms such as *kyomu* (negativity) and *ku* (the vast and empty) he manages to convey something of the philosophical complexity of the term. Waldenfels shows what it is to give a "constellar" or "speculative" meaning to such a term. By offering various epistemological coordinates, he allows, in

Gadamer's words, something to come into being within (his) language "which had not existed before and that exists from now on" (TM, 462). Waldenfels's difficulty is not extralinguistic. His difficulty is that difficulty of understanding which always appertains to what takes place within and between languages. Experience of such difficulty is central to the formative connations of hermeneutic *Bildung* and emphasizes once again that philosophical hermeneutics is a philosophy of experience.

16. See Howard Rheingold, *They Have a Word for It, A Lighthearted Lexicon of Untranslatable Words and Phrases* (Louisville: Sarabande, 2000).

17. Hamacher, 26.

18. Ibid., 34.

19. Michal Pawel Markowski, "Desire, Time, and Interpretation," in *Between the Human and the Divine: Philosophical and Theological Hermeneutics*, ed. Andrzej Wiercinski (Toronto: The Hermeneutic Press, 2002), 540.

20. Ibid.

21. See Jeff Malpas, "Gadamer, Davidson, and the Ground of Understanding," in *Gadamer's Century*, 206–207.

22. See Pannenberg, *Theology*, 196–98.

23. Friederich Nietzsche, *The Will to Power* (London: Weidenfeld and Nicolson, 1968), sections 12A and 12B, 12–14.

24. Henri Frankfort, ed., *Before Philosophy, The Intellectual Adventure of Ancient Man* (Baltimore: Penguin Books, 1971), 256.

25. Michelfelder and Palmer, *Dialogue and Deconstruction*, 116.

26. Hans-Georg Gadamer, *Dialogue and Dialectic, Eight Hermeneutical Studies on Plato*, trans. P. Christopher Smith (New Haven: Yale University Press, 1980), 199.

27. Gadamer, "Composition and Interpretation," in *The Relevance of the Beautiful*, 69.

28. Hans-Georg Gadamer, *The Beginning of Knowledge* (New York: Continuum, 2002), 12.

29. Ibid.

30. P. Christopher Smith, "Plato as Impulse and Obstacle in Gadamer's Development of a Hermeneutical Theory," in *Gadamer and Hermeneutics*, ed. H. J. Silverman (London: Routledge, 1991), 37.

31. *Dialogue and Dialectic*. Gadamer comments that "[i]t is our historical fate to speak the language of concepts." See page 101 of aforementioned text.

32. Smith, "Plato as Impulse," 37.

33. Ibid., 37.

34. Ibid., 35.

35. See Gadamer's remark in Michelfelder and Palmer, 118.

36. Gadamer places this very accusation against Dilthey. "Dilthey ultimately conceives inquiring into the historical past as deciphering and not as historical experience" (TM, 241).

37. For comments on how the self-effacement of meaning can become "its arrival" as trace, see Davies, A Theology of Compassion, 129.

38. Catherine Pickstock, After Writing (Oxford: Blackwell, 1998), 129.

39. See Jürgen Moltman, On Human Dignity (London: SCM Press, 1984), chapter 6.

40. George Steiner, Grammars of Creation (London: Faber and Faber, 2000), 73.

41. Nietzsche's Zarathustra cited by Gary Shapiro in his article, "In the Shadows of Philosophy," in Modernity and the Hegemony of Vision, ed. D. M. Levin (Berkeley: University of California Press, 1993), 140. No reference given.

42. Steiner, Real Presences, 39.

43. Ibid., 53

44. Ibid., 61.

45. Ludwig Wittgenstein, Zettel (Oxford: Blackwells, 1967), paragraphs 231-35.

46. Ibid.

47. Ibid.

48. Charles Taylor, Sources of the Self (Cambridge: Cambridge University Press, 1989), 510.

49. Gerald Bruns, "The Hermeneutical Anarchist: Phronesis, Rhetoric and the Experience of Art," in Gadamer's Century, 45-76.

50. Ibid., 56.

51. Ibid., 56.

52. Ibid., 56.

53. See John Searle, "The World Turned Upside Down," New York Review of Books, 30, 74-79, cited in Susan Hekman's Hermeneutics and the Sociology of Knowledge (London: Polity, 1986), 194.

54. The themes of *pathos* and *passio* in hermeneutics are discussed in my article, "Educative Passions," in *The Welsh Journal of Eucation* 6, no. 1 (1997): 56–68.

55. "We should never underestimate what a word can tell us, for language represents the previous accomplishment of thought." Gadamer, *The Relevance of the Beautiful*, 12.

56. Theodor W. Adorno, *Hegel, Three Studies* (Cambridge: MIT Press, 1993), 136.

57. Hamacher contends that for Gadamer "primacy and privilege are reserved for the spoken word": "the actual and authentic hermeneutic task is the backwards transformation of writing into speech." See *Premises*, 49 and 50.

58. Davey, "On the Other Side of Writing," 88.

59. Hans Waldenfells, *Absolute Nothingness, Foundations for a Buddhist-Christian Dialogue* (New York: Paulist Press, 1980), 160.

60. Ibid.

61. Ibid., 158.

62. Michelfelder and Palmer, 95.

63. Bakhtin cited by Gavin Flood, *Beyond Phenomenology, Rethinking the Study of Religion* (London: Cassel, 1999), 199. See J. P. Sartre, *L'Idiot de la famille* (Paris: Gallimard, 1971), 23ff.

64. Pierre Hadot, *Philosophy as a Way of Life* (Oxford: Blackwells, 1995), 163.

65. See Nicholas Davey, "The Hermeneutics of Passion: Nietzsche and Gadamer on the Subjectivity of Interpretation," *International Journal of Philosophy* 2, no. 1 (September 1993): 45–64.

66. MacIntyre, *After Virtue*, 222.

67. Adriana Cavarero, *Relating Narratives, Storytelling and Selfhood* (London: Routledge, 1997), 43

68. Ibid., 44.

69. Ibid., 45.

70. For the English term *withoutenlesse*, see Robert Fayrfax's madrigal, "Sumwhat musyng," Robert Fayrfax, *Missa O quam glorifica*, The Cardinal's Musick, Gaudeamus CD GAU 142. The related term *outsideness* plays a prominent role in Bakhtin's account of the relationship between an author and his characters. See Michael Holquist, *Dialogism* (London: Routledge, 2002), 30–32.

71. Hamacher, 1.

72. Iser, 151.

73. Ibid.

74. Ibid., 153.

75. See Gadamer's essay, "Notes on Planning for the Future," in *On Education*, 165–80.

76. The experience of the British Empire in India is a case in point. Given the astonishing and haunting influence both Hindhu and Mughal aesthetics have had upon the British imagination and given the influence British academic studies of ancient Hindhu texts had upon the formation of Indian nationalist consciousness, the imperial model of hermeneutic translation fails to acknowledge the actual and lasting intricacies of hermeneutic exchange between the two cultural constellations.

77. Friedrich Nietzsche puts forward a similar argument in *The Birth of Tragedy*, section 18.

78. Williams, *Lost Icons*, 144.

79. Ibid.

80. Walter Davis, *Inwardness and Existence, Subjectivity in/and Hegel, Heidegger, Marx, and Freud* (Madison: University of Wisconsin Press, 1989), 98. See also Williams, *Lost Icons*, 14.

81. Ibid., 145.

82. Iser, 185.

83. Rowan Williams, *The Wound of Knowledge* (London: Darton, Longman, and Todd, 1979).

84. Iser, 158.

85. Ibid., 133.

86. Ibid., 153.

87. Ibid., 105.

88. "Life does not mean anything other than itself. There is nothing in it which points to a meaning outside it." Dilthey, *Selected Writings*, 236.

89. *The Oxford Dictionary of English Etymology*, ed. C. T. Onions (Oxford: Clarendon Press, 1976), 206.

90. Ibid.

91. Gadamer, *The Enigma of Health*, 58.

92. Ibid., 155.

93. Williams, *On Christian Theology*, 240.

94. Williams's use of the term *converse* may be indebted to Michael Oakeshott. Oakeshott writes, "Conduct is encounters of reciprocity in which agents converse with one another, and the postulate of these encounters is a relationship in which *this* converse may be understood to take place. . . . Nor do agents merely 'communicate' or 'connect' with one another, or 'trigger' one another's reactions; their relationships with one another are not syndromic. On the contrary. They speak to one another in words and gestures and are understood by one another; their responses to one another are in terms of understandings. Thus, the relationship postulated in conduct *inter homines* is an understood relationship, capable of being engaged in only in virtue of having being learned. And further, it must be a relationship which prescribes conditions for, but does not determine, the substantive choices and perfomances of agents. In short, what joins agents in conduct is to be recognized as a 'practice.'" *On Human Conduct* (Oxford: Clarendon, 1991), 55.

95. Williams, *On Christian Theology*, 240.

96. Ibid., 241.

97. Terry Eagleton, *After Theory* (London: Penguin, Allen Lane, 2003), 125.

98. Ibid., 139.

99. Ibid., 127.

100. Ibid., 133.

101. Ibid., 132.

102. Ibid., 138.

103. Ibid., 122.

104. Ibid.

105. Daphne Hampson, *After Christianity* (London: SCM Press, 2002), 260.

106. Ibid.

107. Davies, 289.

108. Hampson, 261.

109. Williams, *The Wound of Knowledge*, 182.

110. Friedrich Nietzsche, *The Gay Science*, Section 260, *Kritische Studienausgabe* (Berlin: de Gruyter, 1980), Band 3, s. 517.

Bibliography

GADAMER BIBLIOGRAPHIES

Two Gadamer Bibiographies are worthy of note. Lewis Edwin Hahn's *The Philosophy of Hans-Georg Gadamer* (Chicago: Open Court, 1993) has a "Selected Gadamer Bibliography" with five sections: (1) Gadamer's books and monographs in German with their English translations, (2) books in English that are collections of Gadamer's articles, (3) published articles and their English translations, (4) interviews and videos: published interviews and archival tapes, and (5) secondary sources, bibliographical resources, book length studies, and essay collections. The second bibliography is the recently extended edition of Etsuro Makita's excellent *Gadamer Bibliographie* (Frankfurt: Lang, 1995).

PRIMARY LITERATURE

In German

Gesammelte Werke. Tübingen: J. C. B. Mohr Siebeck, 1993. 9 Bände.

Wahrheit und Methode. Tübingen: J. C. B. Mohr, 1975.

Kunst als Aussage. Gesammelte Werke. Tübingen: J. C. B. Mohr (Paul Siebeck), 1993, Band 8.

Das Erbe Europas. Frankfurt: Suhrkamp, 1990.

In English

Hegel's Dialectic, Five Hermeneutical Studies. New Haven: Yale University Press, 1976.

Philosophical Hermeneutics. Ed. D. Linge. Berkeley: University of California Press, 1976.

Dialogue and Dialectic, Eight Hermeneutical Studies on Plato. New Haven: Yale University Press, 1980.

Reason in the Age of Science. Cambridge: MIT Press, 1981.

Philosophical Apprenticeships. Cambridge: MIT Press, 1985.

The Relevance of the Beautiful. London: Cambridge University Press, 1986.

Truth and Method. London: Sheed and Ward, 1989.

On Education, Poetry, and History. Albany: State University of New York Press, 1992.

Heidegger's Ways. Albany: State University of New York Press, 1994.

Literature and Philosophy in Dialogue. Albany: State University of New York Press, 1994.

The Enigma of Health. London: Polity, 1996.

Praise of Theory, Speeches and Essays. New Haven: Yale University Press, 1998.

Hermeneutics, Religion, and Ethics. New Haven: Yale University Press, 1999.

The Beginning of Philosophy. Trans. Rod Coltman. New York: Continuum, 2000.

Gadamer in Conversation. Ed. Richard E. Palmer. New Haven: Yale University Press, 2001.

The Beginning of Knowledge. Trans. Rod Coltman. New York: Continuum, 2002.

A Century of Philosophy, A Conversation with Riccardo Dottori. London: Continuum, 2004.

SECONDARY LITERATURE

Theodor Adorno. *Aesthetic Theory.* London: Routledge 1984.

———. *Negative Dialectics.* Trans. E. B. Ashton. London: Routledge, 1971.

———. *Hegel, Three Studies.* Cambridge: MIT Press, 1993.

Roberto Alejandro. *Hermentics, Citzenship, and the Public Sphere.* Albany: State University of New York Press, 1993.

Karl-Otto Apel. *Towards a Transformation of Philosophy.* London: Routledge, 1978.

Michael A. Arbib and Mary B. Hesse. *The Construction of Reality*. Cambridge: Cambridge University Press, 1986.

Annette Barnes. *On Interpretation*. Oxford: Blackwell, 1988.

Alexander G. Baumgarten. *Texte zur Grundlegung der Ästhetik*. Stuttgart: Felix Meiner, 1983.

Hans Belting. *Likeness and Presence, A History of the Image before the Era of Art*. London: University of Chicago Press, 1994.

Jay Bernstein. *The Fate of Art, Aesthetic Alienation from Kant to Derrida and Adorno*. London: Polity Press, 1992.

Richard J. Bernstein. *Beyond Objectivism and Relativism*. Oxford: Blackwell, 1983.

Gerald Bruns. *Hermeneutics, Ancient and Modern*. New Haven: Yale University Press, 1992.

S. Budwick and W. Iser. *The Translatability of Cultures, Figurations of the Space Between*. Stanford: Stanford University Press, 1996.

Italo Calvino. *Why Read the Classics*. London: Vintage, 1991.

John D. Caputo, ed. *The Religious*. Oxford: Blackwell, 2002.

John D. Caputo. *More Radical Hermeneutics*. Bloomington: Indiana University Press, 2000.

———. *Radical Hermeneutics: Repetition, Deconstruction and the Hermeneutics Project*. Bloomington: Indiana University Press, 1987.

Thomas K. Carr. *Newman and Gadamer*. Atlanta: Scholars Press, 1996.

Adriana Carvarero. *Relating Narratives, Storytelling and Selfhood*. London: Routledge, 2000.

Ernst Cassirer. *The Logic of the Humanities*. London: Yale University Press, 1974.

———. *The Philosophy of Symbolic Forms*. Trans. R. Mannheim. London: Yale University Press, 1980.

Rod Coltman. *The Language of Hermeneutics, Gadamer and Heidegger in Dialogue*. Albany: State University of New York Press, 1998.

J. M. Connolly and T. Keutner. *Hermeneutics versus Science: Three German Views*. South Bend: University of Notre Dame Press, 1988.

David E. Cooper. *The Measure of Things*. Oxford: Clarendon Press, 2002.

Arthur Danto. *The Transfiguration of the Commonplace*. London: Harvard University Press, 1981.

——. *Nietzsche as Philosopher*. New York: Macmillan, 1970.

Nicholas Davey. "A Response to P. Christopher Smith." In Hugh J. Silverman, *Gadamer and Hermeneutics*. London: Routledge, 1991.

——. "Mnemosyne und die Frage nach dem Erinnern in Gadamers Aesthetik." In Figal, Grondin, und Schmidt, *Hermeneutische Wege, Hans-Georg Gadamer zum Hundersten*. Tübingen: Mohr Siebeck, 2000.

——. "The Enigma of Art." In *Gadamer Verstehen*, hrsg. Mirko Wischke. Darmstadt: WBG, 2003.

——. "Hans-Georg Gadamer's Aesthetics." In *Key Writers on Art*, ed. C. Murray, 130–36. London: Routledge, 2002.

——. "Hermeneutics and Art Theory." In *A Companion to Art Theory*, ed. Paul Smith and Carolyn Wilde, 437–47. London: Blackwells, 2002.

——. "Between the Human and the Divine: On the Question of the In-Between." In *Between the Human and the Divine: Philosophical and Theological Hermeneutics*, ed. A. Wiercinski, 88–97. Toronto: The Hermeneutic Press, 2002.

——. "The Subject as Dialogical Fiction." In *Radical Communications: Rethinking Interaction and Dialogue*, ed. Colin Grant, 9–31. Amsterdam: John Benjamins, 2003.

——. "On the Other Side of Writing." In *Language and Linguisticality in Gadamer's Hermeneutics*, ed. L. Schmidt, 77–112. New York: Lexington Books, 2000.

——. "Signs of Faith: Gadamer on Authenticity, Art and Religion." In *Performance and Authenticity in the Arts*, ed. S. Kemal, 66–94. Cambridge: Cambridge University of Press, 1999.

——. "The Hermeneutics of Seeing." In *Interpreting Visual Culture, Explorations in the Hermeneutics of the Visual*, ed. Ian Heywood and Barry Sandywell, 3–30. London: Routledge, 1999.

——. "Beyond the Mannered: The Question of Style in Philosophy and Questionable Styles of Philosophy." In *The Question of Style in Philosophy and the Arts*, ed. C. van Eck and R. van de Vall, 177–200. Cambridge Studies in the Arts. London: Cambridge University Press, 1995.

——. "Sitting Uncomfortably: Gadamer's Approach to Portraiture." *Journal of the British Society for Phenomenology* 33, no. 3 (Oct. 2003).

——. "Towards a Hermeneutics of Attentiveness." *Renascence*. New York, 2004.

——. "Hermeneutics and the Challenge of Writing: Gadamer and Cixous on Speaking and Writing." *Journal of the British Society for Phenomenology* 33, no. 3 (Oct 2002): 299–316.

——. "On Beauty and Nearness: A Hermeneutic Reflection." *Annales D'Esthetique* 36 (1998): 115–38.

——. "Educative Passions." *The Welsh Journal of Education* 6, no.1 (1997): 56–68.

——. "On Theoria and Theoros in Aesthetics." *Annales D'Esthetique* 34 (1995): 205–11.

——. "The Hermeneutics of Passion: Nietzsche and Gadamer on the Subjectivity of Interpretation." *International Journal of Philosophy* 2, no. 1 (September 1993): 45–64.

——. "Hermeneutics, Language, and Science: A Critique of Gadamer's Distinction between Propositional and Discursive Language." *Journal of the British Society for Phenomenology* 24, no. 3 (Oct. 1993): 250–65.

——. "A World of Hope and Optimism Despite Present Difficulties; Gadamer's Critique of Perspectvism." *Man and World* 23 (1990): 273–94.

Oliver Davies. *A Theology of Compassion.* London: SCM Press, 2003.

——. *A Theology of Compassion.* London: SCM Press, 2001.

Walter Davis. *Inwardness and Existence, Subjectivity in/and Hegel, Heidegger, Marx and Freud.* Madison: University of Wisconsin Press, 1989.

Jacques Derrida. *Limited Inc.* Evanston: Northwestern University Press, 1997.

Wilhelm Dilthey. *Selected Writings.* Ed. P. Rickman. Cambridge: Cambridge University Press, 1976.

Robert J. Dostal, ed. *The Cambridge Companion to Gadamer.* Cambridge: Cambridge University Press, 2002.

Hans Peter Duerr. *Dreamtime, Concerning the Boundary between Wilderness and Civilization.* London: Blackwell, 1985.

Terry Eagleton. *After Theory.* London: Penguin, Allen Lane, 2003.

——. *The Ideology of the Aesthetic.* Oxford: Blackwell, 1990.

Paul Feyerabend. *Farewell to Reason.* London: Verso, 1987.

Günter Figal. *Begegnungen mit Hans-Georg Gadamer.* Stuttgart: Philipp Reclam, 2000.

Günter Figal, Jean Grondin, und Dennis Schmidt. *Hermeneutische Wege, Hans-Georg Gadamer zum Hundersten.* Tübingen: Mohr Siebeck, 2000.

Gemma Corradi Fiumara. *The Symbolic Function.* London: Blackwells, 1992.

——. *The Metaphoric Function.* London: Routledge, 1995.

——. *The Other Side of Language.* London: Routledge, 1990.

Gavin Flood. *Beyond Phenomenology, Rethinking the Study of Religion.* London: Cassel, 1999.

Andrew Ford. *The Origins of Criticism, Literary Culture and Poetic Theory in Classical Greece.* Princeton: Princeton University Press, 2002.

Henri Frankfort. *Before Philosophy. The Intellectual Adventure of Ancient Man.* Baltimore: Penguin, 1971.

Anthony Giddens. *Modernity and Self-Identity.* London: Polity, 1991.

Jean Grondin. *Sources of Hermeneutics.* Albany: State University of New York Press, 1995.

———. *Introduction to Philosophical Hermeneutics.* New Haven: Yale University Press, 1994.

———. *The Philosophy of Gadamer.* London: Acumen Press, 2003.

Pierre Hadot. *Philosophy as a Way of Life.* Oxford: Blackwells, 1995.

Lewis Edwin Hahn. *The Philosophy of Hans-Georg Gadamer.* Chicago: Open Court, 1993.

Werner Hamacher. *Premises, Essays on Philosophy and Literature from Kant to Celan.* Cambridge: Harvard University Press, 1976.

Daphne Hampson. *After Christianity.* London: SCM Press, 2002.

Vàclav Havel. *Letters to Olga.* London: Faber and Faber, 1988.

Martin Heidegger. *Being and Time.* Oxford: Blackwell, 1960.

———. *Poetry, Language, and Thought.* Trans. A. Hofstadter. New York: Harper, 1971.

———. *On the Way to Language.* New York: Harper, 1971.

Susan Hekman. *Hermeneutics and the Sociology of Knowledge.* London: Polity, 1986.

Michael Holquist. *Dialogism.* London: Routledge, 2002.

Edmund Husserl. *The Crisis of the European Sciences and Transcendental Phenomenology.* Evanston: Northwestern University Press, 1970.

———. *Logical Investigations.* New York: Humanities Press, 1970.

Wilhelm von Humboldt. *The Limits of State Action.* Ed. J. W. Burrow. Cambridge: Cambridge University Press, 1969.

Wolfgang Iser. *The Range of Interpretation.* New York: Columbia University Press, 2000.

Hans Jauss. *Question and Answer, Forms of Dialogic Understanding.* Minneapolis: University of Minnesota Press, 1989.

Immanuel Kant. *The Critique of Pure Reason*. Trans. N. K. Smith. London: Macmillan, 1970.

Theodore Kisiel and John Van Buren. *Reading Heidegger from the Start: Essays in His Earliest Thought*. Albany: State University of New York Press, 1994.

Hans Herbert Kögler. *The Power of Dialogue, Critical Hermeneutics after Gadamer and Foucault*. Cambridge: MIT Press, 1994.

Bruce Krajewski, ed. *Gadamer's Repercussions, Reconsidering Philosophical Hermeneutics*. Berkeley: University of California Press, 2004.

Cristina Lafont. *The Linguistic Turn in Hermeneutic Philosophy*. Cambridge: MIT Press, 1999.

Gordon Leff. *History and Social Theory*. London: Merlin, 1969.

David Levy. "Europe, Truth and History: Husserl and Vöglin on Philosophy and Identity in Europe." *Man and World* 26 (1996): 170.

Andrew Louth. *Discerning the Mystery, An Essay on the Nature of Theology*. Oxford: Clarendon Press, 1989.

Alistair MacIntyre. *After Virtue, A Study in Moral Theory*. London: Duckworth, 1993.

Jeff Malpas, Ulrich Arnswald, and Jens Kertscher. *Gadamer's Century*. Cambridge: MIT Press, 2002.

Adrian Marino. *The Biography of the "Idea of Literature" from Antiquity to the Baroque*. Albany: State University of New York Press, 1996.

Diane P. Michelfelder and Richard E. Palmer. *Dialogue and Deconstruction, The Gadamer Derrida Encounter*. Albany: State University of New York Press, 1989.

Jürgen Moltman. *On Human Dignity*. London: SCM Press, 1984.

Kurt Mueller-Vollmer. *The Hermeneutics Reader*. Oxford: Blackwell, 1985.

Iris Murdoch, *Metaphysics as a Guide to Morals*. London: Penguin, 1993.

———. *Existentialists and Mystics, Writings on Philosophy and Literature*. London: Chatto and Windus, 1997.

The New Oxford Dictionary of English. Oxford: Oxford University Press, 1999.

Friedrich Nietzsche. *Kritische Studienausgabe*. Berlin: de Gruyter, 1980.

———. *Daybreak*. Cambridge: Cambridge University Press, 1982.

———. *Beyond Good and Evil*. Trans. R. J. Hollingdale. London, Penguin, 1973.

——. *The Twilight of the Idols*. London: Penguin, 1968.

——. *The Will to Power*. Trans. W. Kaufmann and R. J. Hollingdale, London: Weidenfeld and Nicolson, 1968.

——. *On the Genealogy of Morals*. Trans. W. Kaufmann. New York: Vintage, 1969.

——. *The Gay Science*. New York: Vintage, 1974.

——. *Human All Too Human*. Trans. R. J. Hollingdale. London: Cambridge University Press, 1986.

Michael Oakeshott. *On Human Conduct*. Oxford: Clarendon Press, 1991.

Gayle Ormiston. *The Hermeneutic Tradition*. Albany: State University of New York Press, 1990. 2 volumes.

Wolfhart Pannenberg. *Theology and the Philosophy of Science*. London: Darton, Longman, and Todd, 1976.

Catherine Pickstock. *After Writing: On the Liturgical Consummation of Philosophy*. London: Blackwell, 1998.

Karl Popper. *Objective Knowledge: An Evolutionary Approach*. Oxford: Clarendon, 1974.

T. J. Reed. *The Classical Centre, Goethe and Weimar, 1775–1832*. Oxford: Clarendon Press, 1986.

Howard Rheingold. *They Have a Word for It. A Lighthearted Lexicon of Untranslatable Words and Phrases*. Louisville: Sarabande, 2000.

John Richardson. *Existential Epistemology*. Oxford: Clarendon Press, 1986.

Paul Ricouer. *Hermeneutics and the Human Sciences*. Ed. John B. Thompson. London: Cambridge University Press, 1981.

James Risser. *Hermeneutics and the Voice of the Other*. Albany: State University of New York Press, 1997.

J. Roberts. *German Philosophy, An Introduction*. London: Polity, 1988.

Richard Rorty. *Philosophy and the Mirror of Nature*. Oxford, Blackwell, 1980.

Stanley Rosen. *Hermeneutics as Politics*. London: Oxford University Press, 1987.

Edward Said. *Orientalism*. London: Penguin, 2003.

Jean Paul Sartre. *L'Idiot de la famille*. Paris: Gallimard, 1971.

Anthony Savile. *The Test of Time*. Oxford: Clarendon, 1982.

Gisela Schmidt. *Mirror Image and Therapy*. Oxford: Peter Lang, 2001.

Lawrence Schmidt. *The Epistemology of Hans-Georg Gadamer*. Frankfurt: Peter Lang, 1985.

——. *The Specter of Relativism, Truth, Dialogue and Phronesis in Philosophical Hermeneutics*. Evanston, Northwestern University Press, 1995.

Alan Schrift. *Nietzsche and the Question of Interpretation*. London: Routledge, 1990.

Arthur Schopenhauer. *The World as Will and Representation*. New York: Dover, 1969. 2 volumes.

Charles E. Scott and John Sallis. *Interrogating the Tradition, Hermeneutics and the History of Philosophy*. Albany: State University of New York Press, 2000.

Hugh J. Silverman, ed. *Gadamer and Hermeneutics*. London: Routledge, 1991,

——. *Questioning Foundations, Postmodernity, Hermeneutics, Semiotics*. London: Routledge, 1993.

Nicholas H. Smith. *Strong Hermeneutics, Contingency, and Moral Identity*. London: Routledge, 1997.

Henry Staten. *Wittgenstein and Derrida*. London: University of Nebraska Press, 1984.

George Steiner. *Real Presences*. Is There Anything in What We Say? London: Faber and Faber, 1990.

——. *Grammars of Creation*. London: Faber and Faber, 2001.

Max Stirner. *The Ego and his Own*. London: Jonathan Cape, 1971.

Peter Strawson. *Individuals: An Essay in Descriptive Metaphysics*. London: Methuen, 1959.

L. Stryk and T. Ikemoto, ed. *Zen Poetry*. London: Penguin Books, 1981.

Peter Szondi. *Introduction to Literary Hermeneutics*. London: Cambridge University Press, 1995.

Charles Taylor. *Sources of the Self*. Cambridge: Cambridge University Press, 1989.

John B. Thompson. *Critical Hermeneutics: A Study in the Thought of Paul Ricoeur and Jürgen Habermas*. Cambridge: Cambridge University Press, 1981.

Gianni Vattimo. *Nietzsche, An Introduction*. London, Althone, 2002.

——. *The Transparent Society*. London: Polity 1992.

Hans Waldenfells. *Absolute Nothingness, Foundations for a Buddhist-Christian Dialogue*. New York: Paulist Press, 1980.

Georgia Warnke. *Gadamer, Hermeneutics, Tradition and Reason*. London: Polity, 1987.

Joel Weinsheimer. *Gadamer's Hermeneutics, A Reading of Truth and Method*. New Haven: Yale University Press, 1985.

——. *Philosophical Hermeneutics and Literary Theory*. New Haven: Yale University Press, 1991.

Andrez Wiercinski, ed. *Between the Human and the Divine: Philosophical and Theological Hermeneutics*. Toronto: Hermeneutic Press, 2002.

R. Williams. *The Wound of Knowledge*. London: Darton, Longman, and Todd, 2002.

——. *On Christian Theology*. Oxford: Blackwell, 2000.

——. *Lost Icons: Reflections on Cultural Bereavement*. Edinburgh: T. and T. Clark, 2000.

Ludwig Wittgenstein. *Tractatus Logico-Philosophicus*. London, Routledge, 1969.

——. *Zettel*. Oxford: Blackwells, 1967.

Janet Wolff. *Hermeneutic Philosophy and the Sociology of Art*. London: Routledge, 1975.

Julian Young. *Heidegger's Philosophy of Art*. Cambridge: Cambridge University Press, 2001.

Index

INDEX

self-understanding, 16, 141, 230, 232,
    234, 236, 248
Seneca, 47
Shrift, A., 147
sign, 139
Smith, P. C., 190
Sophists, 35
spectorial distance, 169
speculative, the, 162, 212
speculative disclosure, 161
speculative experience, 116–119, 121,
    131, 152
speculative insight, 124–126, 130, 140,
    141, 143, 144
speculative reversal, 123
speculative sensibility, 26
speculative thinking, 87, 102, 103, 111,
    113–115, 139
speculative understanding, xi, xiv, xv, 78,
    109, 110, 112, 126–128, 161, 162
spirit, 57
spontaneity, 44
Sprachlichkeit, 112, 122
Sprachwelt, 47, 65
statement, xii, 73
Steiner, G., 89, 98, 207
Stierle, K., 90
Strawson, P., 150
subject, the, 162
subject matter, xii, 13, 21, 23, 38, 49, 51,
    53, 63, 64, 67, 69, 71–73, 81–84,
    87, 102, 195, 202, 262n
subjective understanding, 176
subjectivity, 18, 19, 34, 41, 58, 80, 103,
    109, 110, 139, 154, 179
    as constellar, 176
subjectivization, 16

tact, 6, 88, 89, 243, 250
theoria, 28, 169
tolerance, 228
tradition, xii, xiv, 3, 40, 41, 50–54, 69,
    75, 93, 94, 107, 148, 155, 156,
    158, 159, 163, 168, 204, 220, 268n
    as transformative, 53
    humanist tradition, 39

transcendence, xi, xiii, xv, 8, 15, 26, 31,
    33, 57, 59, 62, 66, 68, 95, 96, 98,
    103, 106, 132, 133, 135, 137, 141,
    142, 144, 151, 153, 156, 162, 187,
    188, 190, 191, 193, 216, 229, 230,
    234, 236, 237, 242, 243, 246,
    255n, 260n
transformation into structure, 118, 125,
    127, 131, 135–137, 138, 140, 142,
    156, 164, 167, 168, 210, 211
translation, xi, xv, 4, 7, 20, 45, 104, 105,
    137, 144, 149, 153, 192, 232, 244,
    273n
    difficulty of, 178
transmission, 50
truth, 67, 159, 165
truth-content, 116

understanding, xi, xiii, 2, 5, 10, 13–17,
    33, 34, 36, 38, 41, 43, 45, 85,
    100, 105, 111, 137, 140, 141,
    143, 155, 161–164, 166, 167,
    172, 183, 186, 188, 202, 211,
    223, 236
    as a passion, 211, 218
    as dialogical, 243
    as differentiation, 175
    as difficult, 2, 51, 52, 270n
    as longing, 175
    as reason, 185
    as social achievement, 10
    as transformative, 199
    as unfinished, 20
    effects of, 173
    finitude of, 196
    hermeneutic, 100, 231
    historicity of, 77
    impossibility of, 172
    incompleteness of, 188
    instability of, 184
    limits of, xiii, 14
    movement of, 184, 188, 218, 223
    negativity of, 12
    sadness of, 136
    transformative capacity of, 214
    wantonness of, 171